Beyond Death Anxiety

Robert W. Firestone, PhD, is a clinical psychologist, author, and artist, who has established a comprehensive body of work that explains how defenses formed by children early in life in relation to interpersonal pain are strongly reinforced as they become aware of death. These defenses impair people's ability to sustain intimate adult relationships and have a damaging effect on their children. Dr. Firestone was engaged in the private practice of psychotherapy from 1957 to 1979, working with a wide range of patients, expanding his original ideas on schizophrenia, and applying these concepts to a theory of neurosis. In 1979 he joined the Glendon Association as its consulting theorist. Dr. Firestone's major publications include *The Fantasy Bond, Compassionate Child-Rearing, Fear of Intimacy,* and *The Ethics of Interpersonal Relationships.* His studies of negative thought processes—or internalized "voices"— led to the development of an innovative therapeutic methodology described in *Voice Therapy, Suicide and the Inner Voice, Combating Destructive Thought Processes, Conquer Your Critical Inner Voice, Creating a Life of Meaning and Compassion: The Wisdom of Psychotherapy,* and *Sex and Love in Intimate Relationships.* In collaboration with his daughter, Dr. Lisa Firestone, he developed three assessment instruments based on the concept of the voice process: *The Firestone Assessment of Self-Destructive Thoughts* (2007), *The Firestone Assessment of Suicide Intent* (2007), and the *Firestone Assessment of Violent Thoughts* (2008).

Joyce Catlett, MA, author and lecturer, is the coauthor of *Fear of Intimacy* (1999), *Psychological Defenses in Everyday Life* (2000), *Conquer Your Critical Inner Voice* (2002), *Creating a Life of Meaning & Compassion: The Wisdom of Psychotherapy* (2003), *Sex and Love in Intimate Relationships* (2006), and *The Ethics of Interpersonal Relationships* (2009). She has collaborated with Dr. Robert Firestone in writing peer-reviewed articles and several other books, such as *The Fantasy Bond* (1985), *Compassionate Child-Rearing* (1990), and *Voice Therapy* (1988). Ms. Catlett is a lecturer and workshop facilitator in the areas of child-abuse prevention and couple relations. She has coproduced 40 video productions for the Glendon Association in the areas of parent-child relations, suicide, couple relations, and voice therapy. A child mental health specialist, Ms. Catlett has developed and trained instructors in the *Compassionate Child-Rearing Parent Education Program* throughout the United States, Canada, and Costa Rica.

Beyond Death Anxiety

Achieving Life-Affirming Death Awareness

ROBERT W. FIRESTONE, PhD
JOYCE CATLETT, MA

SPRINGER PUBLISHING COMPANY

New York

Springer Publishing Company, LLC
11 West 42nd Street
New York, NY 10036
www.springerpub.com

Acquisitions Editor: Jennifer Perillo
Project Manager: Mary Zemaitis
Cover design: Mimi Flow
Art: Robert W. Firestone
Composition: Publication Services, Inc.

Ebook ISBN: 978-0-8261-0552-3
09 10 11/5 4 3 2 1

Library of Congress Cataloging-in-Publication Data

Firestone, Robert.
Beyond death anxiety : achieving life-affirming death awareness / Robert
  W. Firestone, Joyce Catlett.
     p. cm.
  Includes bibliographical references and index.
  ISBN 978-0-8261-0551-6
  1. Death. 2. Fear of death. I. Catlett, Joyce. II. Title.
  BF789.D4.F57 2009
  155.9'37—dc22   2009015802

Printed in the United States of America by Hamilton Printing

To Fred Branfman, with affection and appreciation for his support in writing this book.

Contents

Foreword

This book represents a towering synthesis of personal and clinical wisdom about death. Particularly for the first author, Robert Firestone, this book could be viewed as a capstone for his illustrious career as both existential-analytic practitioner and theorist. However, *Beyond Death Anxiety* is much more than a book about death: at its heart, it is a meditation on life and how to live it really well.

Beginning with a superb overview of the psychology of death and death anxiety, the volume gradually and methodically wends its way through Dr. Firestone's development of both Separation Theory and Voice Therapy. In his formulation of these theories, Dr. Firestone draws on the best of the existential-humanistic as well as the psychoanalytic thinkers to address a flourishing path toward self-realization. I am especially moved by the authors' embrace of spirituality and awe—within their worldview, and by the personal and practical nature of their findings. If one is to address a topic as nebulous and intricate as death anxiety, it is essential to ground one's observations in both practical and living case illustrations; and this, the authors accomplish with aplomb.

Although the authors focus ostensibly on the negative voices (or *voice attacks*, as they call them), their aim ironically is to help clients find their authentic voice or true self. To this extent they affirm the transformative power of the voice dimension, which is much subtler than is generally recognized. Indeed, as R. D. Laing, one of Dr. Firestone's most ardent supporters, well knew, the voice is an instrument of one's whole bodily being—one's whole sensibility about life—and not merely the movements of some isolable vocal chords. To find one's voice, as the early Gestalt, analytic, and existential-humanistic pioneers also tacitly (as well as on occasion explicitly) recognized, is to find one's way, comparatively unencumbered, toward what really matters; and what really matters is the centerpiece around which this volume revolves.

To sum, this book shows how the finding of one's authentic voice is integral to death awareness and to the absorption of the anxiety related to that awareness. In this light it is both akin to and a practical application of the writings of Ernest Becker, whose insights into the vicissitudes of death, as well as its denial, are unsurpassed.

If we are to achieve a sane existence, much more of this terrain needs to be plumbed in the coming years; and much more will be, I'm convinced, in the wake of this volume.

—Kirk J. Schneider, PhD
Part-time faculty, Saybrook Graduate School
Author, *Existential-Integrative Psychotherapy* and *Awakening to Awe*

In essence, we attempt to escape from death concerns by avoiding life. The unique purpose of this work is to suggest that the acceptance of death and dying as a reality and an awareness of the typical defenses that people develop to counter the dread can be life-affirming rather than leading to cynicism or depression. Challenging psychological defenses formed in childhood and reinforced by death anxiety can lead to more personal satisfaction in living and expand the opportunity for self-realization. Facing one's mortality and feeling the appropriate emotions of sadness, anger, and fear can give greater meaning to life and make it all the more precious. This awareness also places one's experience in perspective and helps to avoid trivializing one's existence.

This book is *not* about dying and death; rather, it is about facing death in the prime of life instead of limiting life through the process of denial. The book, with its numerous personal stories, illustrates an important truth: that defensive denial of death has profoundly negative consequences for each person's life.

Most people spend their lifetime without a great deal of self-awareness, living lives of emptiness and drudgery based on their early programming. They rarely reflect on their circumstances but rather are addicted to a lifestyle of form and routine. Few develop a life plan or project that gives value and substance to their daily lives. The search for transcendent goals, supported by death awareness, makes life more meaningful. Humans are a meaning-seeking species. When this experience is limited or entirely excluded, one is deprived of one's human heritage.

However, when one breaks through one's defensive barriers, there is always tension and anxiety and a marked tendency for the issue of death to manifest itself. Uniquely positive events make one aware of the value of life, but are also a reminder that life is temporal. The more we invest in life and love, the more we achieve, the more we are valued, and the more we are aware of our existence, the more we are reminded of our eventual non-existence. When we love life and the people closest to us, we must mourn the ultimate loss of loved ones and ourselves. This explains why most people limit their experiences, forsake a purposeful life, and hold on to illusions that help them escape from painful realities.

Death denial has other destructive complications. Religious faiths that offer the promise of an afterlife provide comfort but tend to polarize people of different beliefs against one another. People are threatened when their defensive resolutions of the death issue are challenged by nonbelievers. They become hostile and aggressive when their defenses are disrupted by people with different attitudes and customs. Much of the destruction caused by warfare and ethnic cleansing is due to these defensive machinations.

In some sense, all people maintain a belief that they will not die despite conscious awareness to the contrary. In their magical thinking, free from logical constraints, they are able to maintain the fantasy or dream of immortality in their unconscious minds. Certain attitudes and belief systems support the illusion whereas other events and circumstances challenge it. For example, moving along the life cycle from childhood to maturity, separation experiences that make us aware of our aloneness and signs of aging and ill health dispel the illusion, whereas religious beliefs, an imagined fused identity in personal relationships, vanity, and fantasies of omnipotence help to maintain it. When this internal fantasy process is disrupted, the original suppressed fear reaction is activated and there is considerable hostility directed toward the source.

Lastly, the authors feel that the subject of death must be brought out of the closet. People need to be free to think, feel, and talk about the subject. Addressing the issues surrounding death has a therapeutic effect. However uncomfortable or painful this may be, it is preferable to the emptiness of the unexamined life.

This book is divided into three sections. The first section explains the impact of death anxiety, particularly unconscious death anxiety, on the life experience. Most people do not think much about death on a daily basis, and many feel that they have come to terms with the fact of death. But the majority are still driven by unconscious death fears and resort to a variety of defenses that exert a negative influence on their lives. This section also describes the dawning awareness of death in children, the psychological defenses that characterize everyday life, the literal and symbolic defenses against death anxiety, and the dynamics of microsuicide that arise as an attempt to achieve mastery over death concerns.

The second section presents the first author's (Robert Firestone) theoretical position. It describes the *fantasy bond* as the core defense against separation and death anxiety. The fantasy bond refers to a fantasy of connection or fusion with other individuals, starting with the mother or primary caretaker. The illusion offers a false sense of continuity and security at the expense of honesty and a genuine attachment. Eventually it is applied to one's relatives, one's couple relationships, and one's children. The sense of merged identification is extended to one's neighborhood, city, country, etc., and is encompassed in one's religion and nationality. One feels a sense of superiority toward other people with different beliefs and they are seen as outsiders.

Separation Theory combines psychoanalytic concepts and the concepts of existential psychology. It explains how defenses formed in childhood in relation to interpersonal stress are intensified and rigidified as the child becomes aware of his or her mortality. The combined effect of the defended posture acts as a core resistance in psychotherapy and is a harmful, maladaptive barrier to personal growth and the evolution of the self. The *voice,* a critical and destructive thought process, supports a mode of defended living. This process, which is sometimes conscious but often unconscious, can be accessed in Voice Therapy. Action can then be taken to release the associated feelings, identify and challenge defenses, and alter self-limiting and self-destructive behaviors, thereby helping the individual move toward a more positive, fulfilling life.

The third section examines several subjects that enhance life in the face of death. Chapter 9 deals with challenging the defenses that interfere with living a full life, including breaking destructive addictions and routines, disrupting the fantasy bond, and maintaining independence and respect in couple and family relationships. This chapter also discusses the importance of being aware of microsuicidal tendencies and of breaking with religious dogma and cultural worldviews that are limiting and damaging to self and others.

Chapter 10 addresses the value of psychotherapy for the so-called *normal* individual, the personal qualities of an effective therapist, the death of depth therapy and psychoanalysis, the practice of Voice Therapy, and the effectiveness of corrective suggestions.

Chapter 11 discusses facing death and dying with appropriate emotion. It describes the merits of sharing one's death anxieties in an open forum.

Chapter 12 elucidates the concept of love. It defines the dimensions of a truly loving relationship and distinguishes love from emotional hunger. It describes how the ability to love can be learned like any other skill, and how a person can develop in relation to both giving and receiving love. It speaks of the importance of sexuality and of respect for each other's goals, personal boundaries, and personal freedom.

Chapter 13 delineates the various aspects of a meaningful life. It emphasizes the importance of love, generosity, the therapeutic value of friendship, the development of empathy, and a love and respect for all people. It also includes accepting one's feelings uncritically, developing self-knowledge, formulating one's unique value system, pursuing a personal project or search for meaning in life, transcendent goals, and spirituality. In concluding, the authors outline many of the significant insights that were learned within a unique reference population.

The first author begins Chapter 14 with a brief autobiography. He then describes the evolution of his perspective on life and of his personal system of values. He discusses his relationship to the reference population and the development of his ideas in the field of psychology. He concludes the book with a reflection upon his life. In conveying his professional legacy, he briefly summarizes the scope of his fifty-year investigation of resistance in psychotherapy and people's resistance to a better life in general. The chapter closes with his personal legacy in relation to his loved ones.

Acknowledgments

We wish to express our appreciation to Tamsen Firestone, Jo Barrington, and Susan Short for their exceptional skill in editing the manuscript. We are also grateful to Anne Baker, who worked closely with us to reference and complete the final draft of this work. Our thanks go to Jennifer Perillo, Acquisitions Editor at Springer Publishing Company, for recognizing the book's potential value.

We want to acknowledge Neil Elgee, Director of the Ernest Becker Foundation, who sponsored lectures on "Life-Affirming Death Awareness" at which documentary films about people's defenses against death anxiety were shown. We want to thank Sheldon Solomon, Terror Management theorist and researcher, for his support and encouragement. Lastly, we are grateful to Fred Branfman, who convinced the first author that this book needed to be written.

We express our gratitude to the men and women whose personal stories are recounted throughout this work. We thank them for their courage and honesty in describing their feelings and thoughts about a topic that is difficult still for many people to openly discuss. They were strongly motivated to share the insights they gained so that others might benefit from their experiences.

The names, places, and other identifying facts in the personal stories contained in this book have been fictionalized, and no similarity to any persons, living or dead, is intended, with the exception of Robert Firestone, Tamsen Firestone, and Fred Branfman.

Beyond Death Anxiety

The Subjective Impact of Death Awareness and Its Denial

PART
I

1   Overview

When I was a teenager I realized that most people were living as though death did not exist. I saw men and women trivializing their relationships and lives with petty arguments and melodramatic reactions to insignificant events, while failing to notice basic issues of personal identity and ignoring existential realities. Their passivity, conformity, and inward lifestyles indicated their lack of regard for themselves as unique, feeling entities.

As a boy I shared a room with my grandfather, who as he got older was afflicted with various physical ailments. He would cough and moan in his sleep and sometimes he would sound like he couldn't catch his breath. At those times I would wait with mounting suspense until his breathing would return to normal. Sometimes there would be a loud gasp, like a death rattle, and I would be sure that he was gone. He had trouble with his eyesight and I would imagine what it would be like to lose my vision. It tortured me to picture a life of blindness. The thought of being deprived of all images was akin to death, a kind of living death. I realized that at some future date, the clock would advance and it would be my turn to sit on the edge of life, close to the ominous event.

My grandfather had lived with my family since I was born and so I knew him well. He had spent his life in a kind of half-dazed, yet somehow contented, state of mind, and now he was nearing the end.

It seemed like he had no real sense of his impending death. I dreaded the possibility that he might suddenly wake up one day as from a sleep and realize that he was at the end, that only yesterday he had been a boy like me, and that he had spent the intervening years not really living. I was terrified that he would recognize then that he had wasted his life in meaningless grievances, family disputes, and long, tedious hours at a job he hated. He would be struck by the realization that it was too late—that there was no time left to live.

To my mind this would be the most horrifying thing that could happen to my grandfather. I hoped that he would not wake up but just die peacefully without this unbearable realization. The years passed and he died, leaving me with a lasting impression of a man who had missed his own life.

From this experience came a strong motivation on my part to try to live differently than my grandfather. I never wanted to be faced with the kind of final realization that I had dreaded for him. I wanted to experience all the facets of my life, the bad and the good—all of the painful and joyful events (Note 1).

This book is not about death as such, nor is it about the process of grieving—subjects usually addressed by books of this genre. It is about the impact of defenses that deny mortality and death anxiety and their effect not only in limiting but also in damaging people in their everyday lives. It outlines an approach to nondefensive living that exposes and challenges psychological defenses formed in childhood. It teaches people the importance of facing death awareness, how to cope with existential angst, and then goes on to describe significant dimensions of the *good life*. In addition it explains how once these defenses against death anxiety are developed, protecting them is at the core of resistance in psychotherapy and indeed at the core of resistance to a richer, more fulfilling life. Ironically, the awareness and acceptance of one's mortality combined with learning to express one's sadness, anger, and death fears can lead to a potential for deeper satisfaction, more personal freedom, and a greater appreciation for the gift of life.

For the past four decades the coauthors and their associates were involved in studying a group of 150 or more individuals, families, and friends who had a strong interest in philosophy and psychology. They also shared many other aspects of living, including business ventures, travel, and child-rearing functions. During this time they maintained an open forum for honest communication, in which they revealed their deepest thoughts and emotions and where no subject was taboo. In discussion groups and seminars, they spoke of concerns in their personal and family lives, relationships, and sexuality, as well as issues of aging and death.

In both observing and participating in this unique psychological milieu, we accumulated considerable data indicating that death anxiety and death awareness play an instrumental part in people's lives. In their discussions, these individuals repeatedly reported incidents where unusual successes, positive experiences, a close, loving relationship, or other new, significant developments in their personal lives led to the surfacing of previously suppressed thoughts of death and feelings of fear and apprehension in relation to that awareness. In addition, many people said that they had more dreams or nightmares following positive experiences that were especially meaningful to them.

It became increasingly apparent that the converse was also true that in order to avoid death salience and stirring up unconscious fear and anxiety, people tend to give up significant parts of their lives. The participants in the discussion groups spoke honestly and straightforwardly about the negative behaviors and habit patterns they utilized to avoid psychological pain. They revealed personal defenses and behaviors that restricted their lives and attempted to work past these destructive patterns. Breaking with defenses invariably led to anxiety and increased thoughts about death. Nevertheless, talking and expressing their emotions about death concerns in the group experience strengthened these individuals, helped them to expand their lives, and gave the majority a sense of community and purpose.

In recent years, we have observed the evolution of a more philosophical point of view about death among many of these people. For example, in a discussion that took place last year, Tamsen, who once recoiled from even thinking about death because it was *too unbearable,* talked about a fundamental change that had taken place in her attitude and feelings about the subject.

> Today I feel that life is an incredible gift. I'm aware of death as a reality, so there's always a certain sadness in everything that I experience. All my happiness has a poignancy to it that actually makes it deeper and richer than when it was just 'happy.'

Tamsen's statement reflects one of the major themes in this book: the fact that facing death openly and with feeling challenges defenses, and therefore enlarges life experiences and enhances the meaning of existence. In a sense people are split between having an alliance with death and an alliance with life. In aligning oneself with death, one chooses destructive inward patterns of defense that preclude love and compassion and shrink one's life space. One conserves life to avoid death. By contrast, aligning oneself with life enables one to experience the full range of feelings, both positive and negative. The less defended individual feels more alive, has the opportunity to experience more freedom and independence, and has a greater chance to evolve and fulfill his or her human potential. Making this choice is what the authors refer to as *life-affirming death awareness.*

The authors' purpose in writing this book is to stress the implications—psychological, social, and political—of the subject of death in contemporary life and to advance our knowledge regarding belief systems and maladaptive behaviors that represent defensive solutions to this existential reality. Our second, equally important objective is to explore methods for ameliorating the destructive consequences of these defensive solutions and to suggest ways for people to use the fact of their mortality to live more fully, with compassion for themselves and for others as they all share the same fate.

The human experience is such that people are both blessed and cursed with the capacity to make use of abstract symbols, enabling them to have an awareness of their own existence. Their remarkable propensity to experience life on a feeling level combined with their ability to utilize symbolic logic adds a multitude of dimensions to the life process. These unique characteristics of Homo sapiens allow for creativity and magnificent accomplishments in music, art, literature, and science. Like the God they worship, people have created a vast and wondrous world on earth. They fly through the air, sail on the sea, bridge the raging rivers, and harness the forces of nature. They have enormous power to shape their environment and the intellectual resources to forge their own personal destiny. Along with these endowments, human beings have the exquisite sensitivity to feel deep emotion. They can feel for themselves and their own lives, and they have the capacity for empathy toward their fellows as well. Without these rare and distinctive qualities they would be less than human. Tragically, this singular energy source or force has not only been utilized for extraordinary achievement and constructive purpose but also for extraordinary destructiveness; not only for expressions of kindness and sensitivity but also for manifestations of cruelty and evil that surpass other creatures in all dimensions.

FORMATIVE INFLUENCES

Human beings are very frightened animals because they are privy to the conscious awareness of their own mortality. This "curse of consciousness ... gives rise to a fear reaction of serious proportions. Indeed, the manner in which an individual handles death anxiety as an evolving being, faced with growing knowledge of existential issues, acts as one of the primary determinants of the course of his or her psychological life" (R. Firestone, L. Firestone, & Catlett, 2003, p. 185).

All children go through a series of developmental stages as they learn about the finite span of life: first an awareness that their parents will die, then that they cannot sustain their own lives, and finally that humankind and the earth itself most probably will perish. Faced with this tragic awareness, the child must choose between a life of denial and regress to an infantile state of nonawareness or accept the painful reality and embrace life in spite of death. A person could choose to cherish every moment of his or her life all the more because of its temporal quality. Rather than denying death and employing defenses to avoid painful existential realities, a person could face the fact of death and use it to give life more meaning.

However, this is not a philosophical decision where the advantages are meticulously weighed as pros or cons by a judicious mind-set. The resolution of this conflict is born of turmoil and emotional upheaval that is torturous for the vulnerable little person. And it is a real problem for real children as early as three or four years of age.

What factors determine whether this dilemma is resolved in a negative or a positive fashion? This is a proper question of extreme relevance. To answer it, one must look at the psychological dimensions of each child's earlier life experience—before he or she developed an awareness of death—and thereby come to understand how the defenseless infant learns to cope with life in a relationship constellation.

A certain amount of defense formation is a necessity even when the parental atmosphere is ideal because there is inevitable frustration in the developmental process. However, when the child is the victim of immature, inadequate, or hostile parenting, the traumatic impact of extensive frustration on the all-encompassing reactivity of the infant causes incredible psychological pain and the only escape is an excessively defended posture. The hurting child defends him or herself by adopting a fantasy process, and a marked tendency to suppress or repress primal pain takes over in an attempt to ease the suffering. The child ceases to identify with him or herself as the helpless victim of abuse by identifying with the overpowering aggressor. Thus the child joins with the powerful mother, parent, or caretaker, and this imaginary fusion reduces anxiety and provides partial relief of the tension associated with the frustration of basic needs. The illusion of connection to the powerful parent, together with self-nurturing patterns, such as thumb-sucking, nail-biting, and masturbation, act to alleviate the distressing feelings of hurt and frustration. This defense, which is called the fantasy bond, creates an illusion of pseudoindependence in an effort to avoid ego disintegration (R. Firestone, 1984, 1985).

The greater the rejection, the stronger the imaginary attachment in fantasy and the greater the loss of reality testing. The rejected child clings desperately to the family, idealizes his or her parents at his or her own expense, internalizes a negative self-concept, and projects the destructive characteristics of his or her parents onto the environment at large, fostering a paranoid view of the world.

Somewhere between the ages of three and six, the child becomes aware of death; and no child is spared. Even the child who is provided with the necessary emotional sustenance by loving parents and is then able to live in the real world, with less need to depersonalize or develop defenses to avoid psychological pain and frustration, still faces death. The defenses that children have developed to deal with their early separation experiences bear directly on how they deal with this ultimate separation experience. The child is now faced with the core conflict—when confronted with an awareness of death, whether to feel his or her emotions or to disconnect from emotional investment in life; whether to develop compassion for him or herself and others or to resort to an inward, self-protective lifestyle where relationships with people play a less significant role. The greater the pain and frustration before the child's full realization of death, the more likely it is that the child will choose the defensive alternative (R. Firestone et al., 2003) (Note 2).

OPEN vs. DEFENDED LIFESTYLE

Therefore, the critical issue pertinent to pursuing an undefended rather than a defended lifestyle is the emotional climate that the child is born into. In that sense a damaging psychological environment condemns the child to a substandard existence and a situation that is difficult to reverse.

This is not to deny that people can change. However, "All the king's horses and all the king's men couldn't put Humpty together again."

To the degree that people succumb to a defensive posture (e.g., by distorting, projecting, or forming addictive attachments and habit patterns), their adjustment will suffer and it is unlikely that they will approach their potential. Although these self-protective mechanisms may succeed in temporarily minimizing psychological and existential pain, as with any other addiction, there are unhealthy side effects. The suppression of feelings and the distortion of reality brought about by fantasy processes are inextricably connected to pathological symptom formation. There is no way to cut off emotions without elevating anxiety and bodily tension. The symptoms manifested may be psychological or psychosomatic, but in either case they are detrimental to the person's well-being. Worse yet, people cannot be innocently defended; their defenses have a damaging effect on their loved ones and are particularly destructive to their children (R. Firestone & Catlett, 2009).

If one chooses to embrace life and lead an honest undefended life-style, one will experience both the joy and the pain of one's existence; whereas, the defended person's attempt to block out pain neutralizes the life experience and deprives the individual of life's enrichment. Understanding people in relation to both interpersonal pain and death anxiety helps to explain many strange and puzzling phenomena about human behavior, not the least of which are human beings' propensities for self-destructive thoughts and behaviors.

The concept of the fantasy bond helps to explain why people are prone to make self-defeating, self-limiting choices that condemn them to repeat the unfortunate circumstances of their early lives. This defense is erroneously considered to be a matter of life and death, and must therefore be protected. A person utilizing this defense can only tolerate gratification in fantasy; therefore, real gratification and goal-directed behavior threaten the equilibrium of the defensive solution. Subsequently, real achievement and accomplishment in life are avoided to protect the fantasy bond.

People very often do not want what they say they want. They relinquish their freedom, give up their point of view, choose conformity over personal expression, and find innumerable ways to sacrifice their autonomy and humanness. Indeed, to varying degrees people choose suicidal alternatives and even actual suicide in place of a full-blown life experience. Many avoid personal gratification and prefer not to be loved and valued by others because it makes them more cognizant of their own death. They choose to merge with others and lose their distinctive characteristics rather than invest in a life they must certainly lose. "Why care, when your destiny is so futile? Why want anything? Who gives a damn? Who needs people anyway? So what if you do find someone to love; relationships don't last forever. If you don't want anything, you won't be disappointed" (R. Firestone et al., 2003).

THE EFFECT ON SOCIETY

Individual lifestyles based on psychological defenses combine to affect social phenomena. Social pressure then acts back on the individual, creating a perpetual cycle. Most people choose reliving over living, bondage over freedom, the old over the new, the past over the now (R. Firestone, 1984). They try to recreate a parent or parents in other persons or institutions and search for a personal savior on earth or in the heavens. Their solution is the abrogation of real power in exchange for a form of childish dependency. They are willing to relinquish genuine friendship, free choice, and love in favor of familiarity and false safety.

People have a stake in their mode of defense and are threatened by those with different outlooks and customs. They are afraid of alternative philosophies and ideologies because they perceive them as threats to their own defensive solution. Faced with differences in race, color, religious beliefs, lifestyles, and habit patterns, they experience anxiety, aggression, and hostility. One must either convert those who are "misguided and mistaken" or take the necessary action to eradicate them, for they disturb one's frame of mind. They are the enemy.

On a societal level, such thinking is at the core of nationalism, patriotism, and other *isms*. This accounts for the pervasiveness of ethnic strife in the world today. People around the globe continue to fight about age-old religious differences without the slightest conception of why they hate and why they must destroy each other. Yet these ethnic and cultural differences threaten to annihilate life on the planet (R. Firestone, 1996).

RELIGION AND SPIRITUALITY

Religious ideology and secular belief systems represent serious efforts to cope with and allay death anxiety. They offer a good deal of comfort and security but they fail to completely reassure us about the subject of our own death. Besides, there is a marked tendency for believers to sacrifice important elements of their present day lives for their imagined afterlife.

In addition, few people are completely satisfied by the idea that living a pious life will lead to the hard-won victory of an afterlife in heaven. It is difficult to conceptualize the form this eternal life will take; the concept of an infinite life is in itself disquieting. Nor does the postulation of one's salvation through reincarnation or becoming at one with the universe offer total relief.

Human beings are terrified about any change in the present shape or form of their existence. The anticipation of an altered state of consciousness is horrifying; any transition is frightening, and death clearly represents a transition of major proportions. Both Western and Eastern religious doctrine sacrifice the body, the ego, or the self-system for the higher good, but neither salve the break in continuity.

Whether a person believes in religion, an afterlife, a spiritual oneness with the universe, or some other form of enlightenment, or if one chooses to suspend belief or even to disbelieve, the true realization of death, the cessation of all consciousness and feeling for oneself as well as the loss of loved ones, remains an experience of agonizing proportions. The only appropriate response is despair. According to Kierkegaard (1849/1954), despair is endemic to the human condition and the inability to experience despair is an even greater torture.

An effort can be made to transcend or obscure this pain by relinquishing every aspect of ego or self and by disconnecting from love objects in an attempt to achieve spiritual enlightenment. In the authors' shared opinion, this cannot be attained without a significant loss of feeling and a deadening restriction of human potential for love and experience. Distance and detachment are too great a price for peace of mind. Irvin Yalom (2008) has stated: "Death anxiety is the mother of all religions, which, in one way or another, attempt to temper the anguish of our finitude. God, as formulated transculturally, not only softens the pain of mortality through some vision of everlasting life but also palliates fearful isolation by offering an eternal presence" (p. 5).

People cannot tolerate direct confrontation with the concept of death or the interminable cessation of conscious awareness, and the majority retreat from these realizations. Nonetheless, most people are confronted with the essential ambiguity of life and with fears of the unknown that exist in their unconscious. As Piven (2004b) rightly observed: "Immersion in personal or social fantasies quells the conscious fear of death.... These fantasies do subdue conscious fear, but conscious feelings of security do not dispel unconscious tremors. Underneath these fantasies, dread and terror impel rigid adherence to whatever fantasy system provides subjective feelings of safety and salvation" (p. 245).

Faced with this inescapable dilemma, how can an individual live a constructive life? The answer is to appreciate the mystery of life and death without false resolution by transcending vanity and illusions of omniscience and accepting vulnerability without shame. The truth is that we can give value to our lives and that of our fellows in spite of acknowledging our finite existence in the world. We can live without sacrificing our integrity and without resorting to deadening painkillers, dishonest manipulations, and a myriad of other psychological defenses. To achieve this goal, we must face the fact of our own mortality, accept our destiny, and live with existential despair. In a sense we must mourn the eventual death of our loved ones and ourselves and thus feel the true sadness of life. Paradoxically, only by facing this essential despair can we enjoy life to its fullest for self and others, and only turn to battle in self-defense (R. Firestone, 1996).

CONCLUSION

One cannot face one's mortality directly without protecting oneself; therefore, some defenses against the painful realization of death and dying are essential. Defenses against death anxiety are manifested by all people to varying degrees. The problem is that when children are damaged in their upbringing, they rely excessively on defense formation and these defenses are compounded by death anxiety. Even when the parental environment is more or less ideal, the issue of personal mortality is so painful that it must be blocked out to varying degrees from conscious awareness. The authors describe the many defenses against death anxiety that are adverse to personal fulfillment in life. They suggest a methodology for challenging these defenses and coping directly with existential feelings of sadness, aloneness, and death fears. Lastly they describe a positive approach to death concerns that enhances life and gives meaning to one's existence.

In concluding, not enough interest and research in the field of psychotherapy have been devoted to the subject of death anxiety as it affects human behavior. However, Becker, Yalom, Langs, and Piven, among others, have approached this topic and have made significant contributions.

Our work is based primarily on clinical evidence from patients in an extensive psychotherapy practice and from an observational study of individuals and families over a 36-year period.

In addition, our concepts and conclusions are supported by empirical data accumulated over the past 25 years by researchers in Terror Management Theory (TMT). For example, numerous studies by Sheldon Solomon, Tom Pyszczynski, and Jeff Greenberg have repeatedly shown people's increased reliance on defense mechanisms as a result of experimentally manipulating their death salience and have described the effect these defenses have on human behavior and choices (Solomon, Greenberg, & Pyszczynski, 2004). Their systematic research has added a great deal to our understanding of the rich source of material provided by Ernest Becker (1973/1997), specifically his theory that an awareness of death impels people to first construct and then immerse themselves in cultural worldviews and institutions that deny death. The authors are indebted to these researchers for their persistence in investigating Becker's original thesis and emphasizing the important impact of death anxiety on the life process.

NOTES

1. Throughout the book, the first author's personal statements appear in italics.
2. Attachment theorists have found that an insecure attachment pattern between parent and child is often correlated with early separation experiences, deprivation, trauma, or loss. Whether a child develops a secure or an insecure attachment appears to partly determine his or her subsequent reactions to his or her evolving knowledge of death. For example, findings from two studies (Mikulincer & Florian, 2000; Mikulincer, Florian, & Tolmacz, 1990) that investigated differences in attachment styles as related to the fear of personal death indicated that, in general, secure persons reported less fear of death than insecure persons as assessed on Hazan & Shaver's (1987) questionnaire on attachment history. Interpreting these results, Mikulincer and Florian (1998) concluded that: "Adult attachment style [which has been shown to be correlated with childhood attachment patterns] shapes the way people cope with the terror of their own mortality" (p. 149).

2 The Uncharted Terrain of Death

The irony of man's condition is that the deepest need is to be free of the anxiety of death and annihilation; but it is life itself which awakens it, and so we must shrink from being fully alive.

—Ernest Becker, The Denial of Death *(1973/1997, p. 66)*

I often feel that death is not the enemy of life, but its friend, for it is the knowledge that our years are limited which makes them so precious.

—Rabbi Joshua L. Liebman (1961)

We live in a suppressive culture of denial in relation to the subject of death and dying, and this defensive attitude has a profound negative effect on people's lives. Like other painkilling drugs and habit patterns that insulate us from feeling the anguish of the core existential issues that confront humankind, there is a price to pay for this indulgence. In a somewhat futile attempt to cut off negative emotions, we are inhibited in our capacity for joyful living and lose our human initiative.

Society represents a pooling of individual defenses, and eventually the social mores of the culture at large reflect on the individual in a feedback loop that intensifies defensive modes of living. Over the millennia people have created increasingly complex institutions, social mores, and belief systems in their attempt to adapt to death anxiety. Each succeeding generation has added its own building blocks to the system of denial, which is imparted through the socialization processes within the family to the next generation (R. Firestone, 1990b). It is now possible to imagine all that is human disappearing, with people progressively losing contact with feeling, embracing self-deception, exiting from reality, and accepting substitute gratifications that destroy the real self in favor of provisional roles that are designed to make people *feel better.* Throughout history, in spite of our scientific achievement and greater understanding, there is a tragic progression toward defensive denial and depersonalization. As our advancing technologies outrun our rationality and our humanity, this evolution constitutes a threat to our very existence on the planet.

DEFINITION OF DEATH ANXIETY

The authors have described death anxiety as a complex phenomenon that represents the blend of many different thought processes and emotions: the dread of death, the horror of physical and mental deterioration, the essential feeling of aloneness, the ultimate experience of separation anxiety, sadness about the eventual loss of self, and extremes of anger and despair about a situation over which we have no control. In some ways death anxiety reflects a basic paranoid attitude because from the beginning of life human beings are at the mercy of physical and social forces beyond their power to control—forces that threaten their very existence. But it is tragic when this core paranoia frames the perception of their interpersonal world. Although death anxiety includes a broader spectrum of painful emotions as noted above, the first author's essential definition refers to both the unconscious anxiety about and the conscious realization of the fact that our lives are terminal, that we face separation from loved ones, and find ourselves conjuring up painful imaginings of infinite nothingness or nonexperience, a mental state that when faced directly is truly intolerable (R. Firestone, 1994b, 1997a) (Note 1).

In describing his experience of death anxiety, one client wrote that, "The concept that my life is terminable is too awful. How could it be that life ends when it feels so permanent? I know it can't really end; there must be a way out. How can death stalk on such a sunny day? Death should be reserved for the nighttime or at the very least for a cloudy or rainy day. Is there no respite? I thought of Orpheus and Eurydice and their desperate struggle to escape the dark shadow that followed her. He fought valiantly for her, but he could not save her, or himself.

"I tried to imagine the possibility of eternal life. I pictured my wife and myself walking through life together hand in hand. This gave me a modicum of comfort at times, but the concept generally eluded me. I could not stand the ghastly alternative of facing death all alone, forever. With all these thoughts, my emotions ran the full gamut: sheer terror, blind fury at my destiny, a monstrous outrage."

One woman conceived of death as a punishment: "What have I done to deserve this predicament? Is it some sort of punishment? I have searched my memory for clues to unimaginable crimes I might have committed and then banned from my consciousness. When I couldn't make that connection, I sought other explanations. Maybe my crime was related to intention rather than action. I imagined that I was being punished for my thoughts rather than my deeds. What good is it to protest my innocence? The verdict is already in; my crime will remain unspecified forever. It might provide some solace if I could fathom the charges. Then perhaps there would be the possibility of atonement."

Death anxiety can be distinguished from the poignant feelings of sadness that emerge when we contemplate the inescapable end of our existence. We can never overcome the sadness associated with the obliteration of the self as we know and experience it in our everyday lives. In a sense we must mourn this anticipated loss to retain our capacity for genuine feeling. Sadness is therefore an inescapable part of a feelingful existence (R. Firestone, 1994b).

To a fully alive, feeling person who has invested meaning and affect in his or her life experience, no death is acceptable—instantaneous death in a car accident or plane crash, an extended and painful illness, senility, or a quiet death in one's sleep. As Simone de Beauvoir (1966/1976) wrote concerning her mother's death:

> The knowledge that because of her age my mother's life must soon come to an end did not lessen the horrible surprise. . . . There is no such thing as a natural death: nothing that happens to a man is ever natural, since his presence calls the world into question. All men must die: but for every man his death is an accident and, even if he knows it and consents to it, an unjustifiable violation. (p. 526)

INDIVIDUAL REACTIONS TO DEATH ANXIETY

In reacting to death anxiety, most people regress and become emotionally cut off. To varying degrees they choose to depersonalize. Their defensive posture tends to limit their capacity to relate to others, restricts their ability to make choices, and narrows their life experience. Rigid belief systems offer some respite from death fears but often inspire distrust and hatred. Many religious wars involving mass destruction have been fought over sectarian systems of thought.

Nevertheless, there are people who show unusual courage and are able to turn the issue of death's inevitability to an advantage, giving greater meaning to their lives and more consideration and respect for the lives of others. In *Creating a Life of Meaning and Compassion* (R. Firestone et al., 2003), we wrote of a conversation with a 54-year-old political analyst/journalist and the encounter with death that had a powerful impact on his life:

In August 1989, I had an experience which was to change my life forever. I was ... spending time with my mother who had recently suffered a stroke. The experience had shaken the foundations of my psyche, loosening rigid structures that only those who have participated in the slow deterioration of a parent can fully understand. Also, I was doing a lot of meditating during this period, focusing on observing my thoughts, feelings, and body sensations as they arose. It was thus perhaps no coincidence that I had this particular experience at this particular time.

It was early in the morning, 3 or 4 A.M., and I awakened from a deep sleep.... As I lay there, half asleep, half awake, I noticed a fear of death beginning to arise. For the first time in my life, I noticed the fear as it emerged and noticed myself automatically start to push it away as well. And, suddenly, I found myself saying, 'No! I won't push it away this time. Let it come!' And I did. I let it come.

The next minutes were the most excruciating I had ever experienced. My whole body went into shock. I felt paralyzed, as if I could not move. I had difficulty breathing; at times I felt as if I were suffocating. At other times, I felt like I was burning alive.... I was out of my head, in some kind of an unexpected hell.... What I remember most was screaming at the top of my lungs. Only I was so in shock, so paralyzed, that no sound would come out.... I felt as if I would not, I could not, survive what was happening to me.

Finally, after what seemed like a lifetime, it was suddenly over. At first I felt just sort of numb, shaken, still halfway between two worlds. And then, all of a sudden, out of nowhere ... I suddenly began feeling more alive than I had ever felt before. I began experiencing both an aliveness and a sense of deep peace that I had never before dreamed existed. I do not mean that I suddenly found myself feeling, 'Oh boy, I'm still alive! I didn't die after all.' There was no verbal content.... It was about having a very different experience of life, a state of being. (p. 188)

In a later conversation, this man provided additional details of what he referred to as his *transformation:*

> On the simplest level, I saw things as I had never seen them. If I were to try to verbalize it, I would use words like 'aliveness,' 'quiet joy,' 'deep peace,' 'happier than I'd ever been.' And words were not important. I was transported into another realm, another dimension, very different from the one in which I had lived my entire previous life. It was a dimension in which prior concerns seemed unimportant indeed.
>
> This feeling persisted. I remained far more alive than I had ever been. The morning light was precious, as was an orange, the smile of an old person, almost any feeling at all. I felt the deepest possible love for my mother. And within, I felt a loosening of fears never before understood.
>
> Until this experience, I had intellectually known, of course, that I would one day die. But it had been an 'idea' not an 'experience.' Actually experiencing my feelings about my death had changed everything.
>
> First, until that moment, my reaction to death was similar to that of most people I know: I thought that I would only worry about it when I had to, that it was not relevant to my present life. This experience proved beyond any doubt, however, that I was harboring enormous *unconscious* death anxiety; otherwise I could not have had such a powerful experience. I realized that my attitudes toward death were having an enormous impact on my life, but that I had no real idea of what that impact was.
>
> Second, I decided overnight to abandon my relatively successful political career, including my present position leading a think tank advised by many of the nation's leading economists. My experience of aliveness after my encounter with my unconscious feelings about death had been so powerful that it made my present work-life seem dull and boring by comparison. I wanted not only to understand what had happened to me, but also to reexperience both the painful and joyful feelings that I had touched for the first time as a result of facing my death.

Because death anxiety exists on an unconscious as well as on a conscious level, most people would say they do not consciously think about death. However, on an unconscious level, the fear of death influences significant aspects of their lives and motivates many of their actions. People avoid death anxiety in a variety of ways. Although this defended approach does help to avoid anxiety states, it has numerous costs in terms of the damage inflicted on the individual, the family, and the children. Unlike the example above, most people respond negatively to being confronted with death awareness.

Rachel, 18, moved home to California after her freshman year in college. She had not been happy in school—she did not like living in the small college town, she had few friends, but worst of all, she was involved in an abusive relationship. After she moved to California, her boyfriend called her often, but she made it clear to him that their relationship was over. Rachel was glad to be back in her hometown among her old friends, and she began making plans to continue her schooling at the nearby university. She said that she was beginning to feel like her free-spirited old self again.

Soon after coming home Rachel visited Helen, 65, a woman who had offered Rachel valuable counsel and support during her teenage years. Rachel had come to regard Helen as a personal friend and a mentor. Since Rachel had been away Helen had been diagnosed with cancer and was given less than a year to live. Over the next six months, Rachel visited her often. Rachel felt deeply sad as Helen's health deteriorated, and when Helen died Rachel wanted to commemorate the life of this woman who had been so important to her. Rachel decided to make a documentary about Helen, and over the next months she interviewed people, gathered photographs, shot film, and edited a documentary. When the film was complete, Rachel held a screening for Helen's family and friends, and everyone was moved by Rachel's tribute.

Over the next weeks, Rachel seemed somewhat distant to her friends, and one day Rachel's roommate came home to find that Rachel had moved out of their apartment. No one knew where Rachel had gone. They called and e-mailed her, but received no answer. One month later her roommate received an e-mail from Rachel. She had driven across the country to be with her old boyfriend. Her roommate was shocked. She responded by expressing her concern that Rachel had returned to an abusive relationship, but she never heard back from Rachel. A year later she heard that Rachel had married her boyfriend. Rachel's friends and family were mystified by her behavior; what had happened to their friend?

Even though there are some people who, like the man in the first example, have a life-affirming response in relation to a confrontation with death, our experience is that most people respond more like Rachel. When their death anxiety is aroused, they tend to become increasingly defensive in ways that are harmful to themselves and often to others as well. Even when they respond positively at first and embrace life more fully, more often than not, people gradually return to their defended posture. They protect themselves and live as though they will never die and can afford to squander their most valuable experiences.

This regression to a state of denial tends to be demoralizing and takes on many forms: some people increase their drinking or turn to drugs;

others adopt compulsive work habits or routines that are distractions and give an illusion of permanence. Many people embrace a religious dogma that offers them the hope or promise of an afterlife. Others preoccupy themselves with trivial matters and obsess over pseudo-problems that act as diversions from realistic concerns about life and death. Some people over-intellectualize about death, taking a kind of philosophical position that keeps them one step removed from experiencing any feeling about their own mortality. Others repress their thoughts about death altogether, denying they ever think about it.

On a deeper, more unconscious level, some people imagine that death happens only to other people, never to them; their sense of specialness makes them feel immune to the fate that awaits the masses. Others find a different solution; they believe that someone will ultimately save them—a relationship partner, a charismatic leader, or a celebrity—or at the very least they believe that they will live on through their children. Tragically, many individuals seem to lose their spirit altogether. They become rigid and controlling, diminishing their range of experiences to such a degree that it could be said they are no longer invested in living. They become cynical and self-hating, give up interests that once excited them, engage in behaviors that are harmful to their physical and mental health, and become increasingly depressed and futile about life.

Some people become overly dependent on a mate, while others give up meaningful relationships, avoid commitments, or never become involved in a relationship at all. They retreat from intimacy and closeness because they are afraid of losing their loved one through rejection or death. The fear of object loss is akin to the fear of losing oneself and can also trigger a pattern of withholding that limits loving responses and personal involvement. In distancing themselves to protect against the fear of loss, men and women gradually relinquish the real substance of their life together and retain only the form, a fantasy bond or imaginary connection (R. Firestone, 1984, 1985). This illusion of fused identity imbues them with a sense of immortality.

THE CORE CONFLICT

Acceptance of the inevitability of death, which when faced can give dignity to life ... ennobles the whole face rather than furrowing the forehead with the little anxious wrinkles of worry. Worry in an empty context means that men die daily little deaths. (Mead, 1956/1960, p. 177)

How can one establish a nondefensive lifestyle that incorporates an awareness of death while maintaining a rich and meaningful investment in self and others? In other words, how can one embrace life in the face of death? Why should a person invest in loving relationships, search for truth and meaning, and devote oneself to humane pursuits and transcendent goals of creativity, spirituality, and service to others when all will be lost in the end? Is it really better to love and lose than never to love at all? How can human beings live with existential pain and anxiety? Wouldn't it be more expedient to be concerned only with pleasure and the pursuit of happiness? Wouldn't it make more sense to put these disturbing matters out of mind, deaden oneself to the obvious facts of sickness, aging, and death, the awesome reality of the unknown, and the ongoing holocaust of human brutality? Why not take the drug, cut off these unpleasantries, and submit to the predicament? Why not surrender to the obvious defense mechanisms of denial, fantasy, and addiction and lead an inward, self-protective existence?

The question of commitment to one's feelings, one's freedom, and the valuing of one's life implies a concomitant intensification of death awareness. Kathy illustrates this concept when, in the course of her free associations, she realizes why she refuses to commit to a loving, sexual, and romantic relationship.

I was thinking about my anger toward my husband, just saying anything I thought as it came up and it got pretty ugly. The more I thought about my relationship, the angrier I got. I had this interesting feeling come up in me about why I'm not committed to my feelings. If I'm committed to my feelings toward someone, that means there's an end, because if I'm committed, I know what I feel, I know where I stand, and there's an end in sight, whereas if I'm not committed, I'm safe.

I don't know what I want, I don't know where I want to live, I might not even choose to live with my husband. I might not be with him in 10 or 20 years, who knows? I might want to meet somebody else. I might want to be with somebody else. Who knows? I realized that if I did know what I wanted, if I knew what my feelings were, then I would know what my life was. There would be an end in sight. The other way it's all over the place. I don't even have an end in sight. My life seems way longer. Death seems not even an issue, really. I've got a long life to live. I can just meander around for the rest of my life and for eternity. Whereas if I don't just wander around, I have things to face, meaningful things that could happen in my life, painful things that will happen to me in my own existence. What I'm really avoiding is committing to living my life in the face of all of these painful issues.

This has been an important realization, because it made me feel something. Now that I am aware of this, I can hang in there and go through the anxiety. I'm sick of not knowing what I feel because of the fear of facing painful issues.

Dr. Firestone: To you, commitment means that you actually will die. That's what makes you so angry at your husband at the time. If you are not committed to your life, you are not committed to your death, that's a very important defense.

Kathy: In that situation when anger comes up, if I fight through it, I feel really sad. The feelings that come up are just really, really sad feelings.

Dr. Firestone [later in the conversation]: What you said about sex was interesting, too. Sex doesn't scare you if it's with a stranger.

Kathy: If I'm attracted to someone that I know casually, I can picture being in a sexual situation with that person, and I picture that it would be very nice, actually, like it would be a physical enjoyment. But when it comes to a close intimate sexual situation, that same anger comes up of not wanting to deal with whatever those feelings would be. I feel like something is wanted from me, and then I'm going to have to be committed to that situation again and again. In the other situation, there's no strings attached. I'm just cut off from feelings. I feel like I've had this defense forever. When I was a teenager I was drunk a lot and doing a lot of strange things and the thing I was proudest of was not being afraid to die. Now I tell myself, 'Remember how it was when you weren't afraid to die? You could always go back to that lifestyle because you wouldn't be afraid anymore.' I always felt that I had that 'out' if I got too afraid. I really appreciate talking about this with you a lot. It gives me real insight. I really do want to struggle with my life.

The core conflict within each individual centers on the choice between contending with emotional pain, both interpersonal and existential, or avoiding these painful realities. The universal dilemma is whether to live with the pain of awareness or to disengage from the self (R. Firestone et al., 2003). The majority chooses some degree of denial and escape and suffers the consequences in a loss of personal identity, freedom, and autonomy. Unfortunately, one cannot circumvent emotional pain and suffering, repress the existential dilemma, and lead a *happy* life without losing real feeling and individuality. Thus, the defensive choice dehumanizes the individual.

We do not consciously decide to defend ourselves; we do not weigh the issue of whether or not to adopt psychological defenses on a rational scale. Children utilize defenses as a survival mechanism when faced with overwhelming emotional pain and the threat of ego-disintegration. Psychological defenses are a reaction to the stress induced by insecurity and faulty parenting practices in early life. These defenses congeal when children become aware of their mortality, and these patterns come to constitute a lifestyle. In the case of the neuroses and the psychoses, abnormal defensive processes evolve into so-called mental illness.

THE DILEMMA OF DEFENSES

For the individual, psychological defenses malfunction in a manner that is analogous to the body's physical reaction in the case of pneumonia. In this situation the body's defensive reaction to a dangerous bacteria or virus is what causes the damage. Similarly, defenses that originally alleviated the pain and frustration children experienced in their first interpersonal relationships are the principle cause of emotional suffering in later life (R. Firestone, 1985).

We are all faced with an essential dilemma, a no-win situation: if we give up our customary defenses and fully invest in our lives, we are struck by the magnitude of the loss we face through death; if, on the other hand, we retreat from life and fail to develop our unique potentialities, we are plagued with regret for a life not truly lived. The process of disengaging leads to a fundamental existential guilt for denying life and forgoing the project of becoming an authentic self. There is a sense of having betrayed oneself in choosing defended ways of living and being (R. Firestone, 1987b; M. Stern, 1968).

The need to rationalize or deny reality fosters a division or split in the psyche that is largely unconscious, but all the same, its crippling effects are felt throughout the whole spectrum of our personal and professional lives. Because defensive patterns spread and eventually become habitual, they ultimately manifest the same properties as an addiction. This generalized defensive reaction leads to progressive debilitation in broad areas of functioning, such as sexuality and other life-affirming activities.

An inward, self-deceptive, protective approach to life predisposes psychological and psychosomatic symptom formation. For example, when anger (the normal response to frustration) is obscured, angry feelings are either internalized or projected. The former leads to self-denigration and self-attack; the latter to a counter-aggressive, paranoid focus toward others. On a physiological level, repression of ideation and affect elevates anxiety and tension, consuming energy that could be directed toward more optimal functioning and positive, goal-directed pursuits. When the truth is obscured, there is a build-up of internal pressure. A person not only loses initiative and develops symptoms of distress but also is unclear as to the reason for the malfunctioning. Since defenses are often activated before there is an awareness of feeling threatened, the person finds it difficult to explain disturbing changes in mood or behavior.

In contrast, an undefended life leads to an increased potential for feeling and experiencing all of our emotions. The less defended individual feels integrated, experiences more fulfillment, retains the capacity to find happiness and joy in life, is better able to tolerate intimacy, and tends to be more humane toward others. Tension is minimized in an honest, open approach to life.

By definition, a defended individual lacks integrity and therefore cannot communicate honestly. For example, if people deny their real wants and priorities, they deceive themselves as well as others about their true intentions. If, on the other hand, they fail to pursue the goals and experiences they claim to want, their behavior directly contradicts their words. This internal discrepancy accounts for the prevalence of mixed messages in personal communication that have a devastating effect on people's sense of reality. These mixed messages become an internal part of the social matrix and add support to the defensive process that mitigates against individuation. When these defenses are acted out on a mass scale, the result is social pathology. As noted, defensive machinations threaten to destroy civilization as people find it impossible to live with others who differ along racial, class, and religious lines. Groups whose mores contrast with our own are perceived as a threat. We are willing to both kill and die for our defenses in order to ward off existential anxiety (R. Firestone, 1996).

It would seem that defenses are essential when faced with our inhumanity to ourselves and to others. Yet cruelty and injustice are an outgrowth of personal deception and reliance on illusions that preclude our living with feeling and compassion for humankind. Because our defenses inevitably hurt others, maintaining emotional integrity and avoiding self-deception become ethical issues as well as sound mental health principles. Considering the alternative between defensive and nondefensive living, there is no real contest. Remaining vulnerable and undefended not only allows us to avoid neuroses and live fuller lives, but also becomes a positive human value.

CONCLUSION

The tragedy of the human condition is the fact that the capacity for reason and logic makes human beings acutely aware of their eventual demise. The ability to conceptualize and imagine has negative as well as positive consequences because it predisposes anxiety states that culminate in a defensive form of denial.

There is no defense or protection against death, but there is a way to live that is life-affirming rather than life-denying. In an essay, "Life Fear and Death Fear," Otto Rank (1936/1972) asserted that not all anxiety could be overcome therapeutically. It was death anxiety that Rank was referring to in his declaration that it is impossible to face the truth of human existence without anxiety (R. Firestone & Catlett, 1989).

Although despair is endemic to the human condition, there are ways to ameliorate the anxiety and dread that emerge when one contemplates one's mortality. People can share their feelings about death and dying with close friends and associates and find essential meaning in existence. Rather than searching outside for the essence or purpose of life, people can shape their lives and give their world form and color according to their own feelings and inclinations. They can maintain a strong sense of self and invest in goals that transcend the narrow focus of their own priorities. It is the nature of Homo sapiens to develop a personal project or transcendent goal and maintain a unique identity. Men and women can approach their fellows with compassion and a feeling of empathy, for people everywhere face the same existential crisis.

> With enlightenment on the subject, people could choose to embrace life and live with an awareness of death, rather than deaden themselves prematurely. Coming to terms with death as a reality appears to be the only viable alternative to a life of tedium, conformity, and alienation from oneself and others. In choosing to live full and honest lives with a minimum of defense, people can move away from the morbid contemplation of death or its denial toward a life of adventure characterized by freedom of choice, enthusiasm, and optimism. (R. Firestone et al., 2003, p. 208)

NOTES

1. Tomer and Eliason (1996) provided a *working definition* of the concept of death anxiety in their paper "Toward a Comprehensive Model of Death Anxiety." They wrote: "The concept of death anxiety, as used here, is that of a negative emotional reaction provoked by the anticipation of a state in which the self does not exist" (p. 345).

Although a number of theorists (Becker, Rank, Choron, and Zilboorg) contend that the fear of death and the cessation of consciousness affect human beings more than any other existential "given," others cite different conditions that they claim give rise to an even more profound terror. For example, David Loy (1992) in "Avoiding the Void: The Lack of Self in Psychotherapy and Buddhism" argued that the most powerful defenses are those formed against a perception of our groundlessness or the void.

3

The Dawning Awareness of Death and Its Impact on the Developing Child

What we call the child's character is a *modus vivendi* achieved after the most unequal struggle any animal has to go through; a struggle that the child can never really understand because he doesn't know what is happening to him, why he is responding as he does, or what is really at stake in the battle.... To grow up at all is to conceal the mass of internal scar tissue that throbs in our dreams.   *—Ernest Becker,* **The Denial of Death** *(1973/1997, p. 29)*

The human infant is born into the world in a state of complete and utter helplessness and dependency. Left on its own, without care and sustenance, it most surely would die. When frustrated and hungry, the baby wails until milk is provided or the diaper is changed and then follows the satisfied sounds of relief and contentment. When the mother, parent, or caretaker provides adequate, timely, and sensitive care, the child develops a secure pattern of attachment. However, when there are misattunements, insensitive treatment, or otherwise destructive machinations on the part of caretakers, as well as a consistent failure to repair such misattunements, the baby will suffer from emotional pain and frustration with negative consequences for its future. Even in the most ideal situations it appears virtually inevitable that some of the foregoing will occur. These patterns become hardwired in the still-developing brain of the infant during the early years and thereafter bear strongly on the future development of the individual.

Imagine the harrowing experience of the infant who screams to be fed but no one comes. The rage and despair are all consuming, the tiny infant shakes and quivers, there is a full-bodied agonizing primal scream and a seemingly endless period of torment before the baby actually dies. Although obviously less extreme than this example, faulty parental responses and separation experiences also have a traumatic effect on the developing infant. As described in Chapter 1, the child compensates for emotional deprivation by developing fantasies of fusion as well as self-nurturing patterns of behavior in order to partially allay the anxiety. Thus, the infant develops defenses early in life to ward off emotional and physical pain. These primitive defenses are intensified, confirmed, and become rigidified when the child first becomes aware of death.

Imagine the terror of a helpless child who realizes that his or her parents will die. There are two distinct aspects inherent in how this dawning awareness of death impacts young children. First, the anticipated loss of the dependency source on a survival level fills them with terror and, on a deep, often unconscious level, the anticipation that they will die the agonizing death described above. Second, the prospect of losing the love object (the mother, the father, or the caregiver), the source of warmth, affection, and love, evokes deep sadness and pain. Although the anticipated death of the parents is traumatic, the child is able to maintain an illusion that he or she can take care of him or herself. This illusion is possible because in the fantasy bond with his or her parents, the child has to varying degrees incorporated the internalized parent into his or her unconscious mind (R. Firestone, 1985, 1988).

Later when children apply the concept of death to themselves and discover that there is no recourse, the reality completely shatters their world of permanence and safety. The stable life that they once knew is forever altered. Even though powerful defenses are instituted to block its awareness from consciousness, children's terror is preserved whole in the unconscious, much as it was originally experienced. This terror is partially relieved by the fact that on some level they maintain a magical belief in a fantasy that they will never die.

Thereafter, the suppressed fear of death continues to exert an influence on the life of the developing child and later on the adult. The torturous screams of the frustrated infant have long since been subdued and repressed by myriad defenses that prevent death anxiety from surfacing. Nevertheless, when there is death salience or when there are indirect reminders of death, the primitive fear reaction tends to surface and one must cope with the pain, either by feeling it and *sweating through it* or by resorting to defenses that either deny it or offer a pacifying solution to the dilemma.

Death anxiety is a powerful force in shaping human experience. Ernest Becker, Irvin Yalom, R. D. Laing, Robert Langs, Jerry Piven, Terror Management theorists, and the authors have all attempted to delineate the manner in which people are affected by the different aspects of the death anxiety issue. In *The Primal Scream*, Arthur Janov (1970) recognized that the suppressed scream plays a significant role in psychological suffering. Indeed in relation to the impossibly harrowing direct confrontation with death's finality, the primal scream is the appropriate emotional response.

SEPARATION THEORY

The first author's approach, known as Separation Theory, elucidates the relationship between separation anxiety and the dread and anxiety surrounding death—the final separation from self and others. There are several elements common to separation anxiety and the fear of death, as well as certain differences between the two. One emotion inherent in both instances is the fear of being cut off from others, alone and isolated from fellow humans.

> This fear of object loss recapitulates the infant's anxiety at being separated from the mother. An individual's profound terror, however, is caused by contemplation of the obliteration of the ego. This dread goes beyond separation anxiety. The cessation of the ego's existence in any knowable or recognizable form is horrifying. (R. Firestone, 1997a, p. 264)

Life is a series of progressive separation experiences—birth, weaning from the breast, separation from the mother or primary caregiver, from parents, from other family members, the first day at school, leaving for college, moving away from home, the first sexual experience, moving in with a romantic partner, getting married, buying a home and furniture, pregnancy, becoming a parent, becoming a grandparent. As people individuate they are forced to recognize that they are moving away emotionally from the initial security in the family. Each event involves new situations that are potentially traumatic because they signify a loss of parental support and arouse separation anxiety.

The First Separation—Birth

Separation is a vital part of the human life process. Every human being suffers to varying degrees from the anxiety of being separate and alone. This suffering begins at birth with the severing of the umbilical cord, a dramatic event that leads to a realistic subjective awareness of being unattached. This first real separation experience is referred to as *birth trauma*. Describing how he visualized this *traumatic* event from the infant's perspective, Rank (1936/1972), quoting from the Talmud, wrote:

> Suppose a child in its mother's womb to know that after a lapse of time it will leave the place it occupies. That would seem to it the most grievous thing that could happen. It is so comfortable in the element that surrounds it and protects it against outside influences. However, the time of separation approaches, with terror it sees the protecting envelopes torn asunder and it believes the hour of death has arrived. (p. 184)

Early Infancy

The newborn is highly reactive to his or her surroundings. Neuropsychiatrist Dan Siegel (1999) contends that the development of the baby's mind is almost completely dependent on stimuli from people in its immediate environment. The prolonged dependency and the desperate need of the baby for its parents make the formation of defenses imperative. It is absolutely necessary for the infant to protect itself from overwhelming stress and painful intrusions from the outside world (R. Firestone, 1985).

Developmental psychologists Margaret Mahler (Mahler, Pine, & Bergman, 1975) and Louise Kaplan (1978) have described the overriding need of the infant to avoid being overcome by anxiety states even at the earliest stages:

> [At first,] from the infant's point of view there are no boundaries between himself and mother. They are one. This is how we first discovered merging bliss and inner harmony. This is how our psychological birth began.... Yet all was not harmony in these early months. Disturbing tensions, feelings of loss of balance, extremes of heat or cold, digestive upsets, made us stiffen away from mother—away from bliss and body-molding oneness. (Kaplan, 1978, p. 28)

There is a primitive anxiety that an infant experiences during the inevitable separations that occur in every childhood—as when its mother leaves the room for a few minutes to warm a bottle. Winnicott (1958) has referred to this intense anxiety as *annihilation anxiety*. Lacking any sense of time, the baby feels abandoned forever; it is alone, hungry, and desperate.

Stages in the Child's Developing Knowledge of Death

> The child is overwhelmed by experiences of the dualism of the self and the body from both areas, since he can be master of neither. He is not a confident social self, adept manipulator of symbolic categories of words, thoughts, names, or places—or especially time.... Nor is he a functioning adult animal who can work and procreate.... He is a prodigy in limbo. (Becker, 1973/1997, p. 28)

In general the concept of death and the realization of a finite existence evolve gradually as the young child matures. For many children, their first encounter with death occurs when a pet dies or when they accidentally come across a dead bird or other animal. On a fishing trip, three-year-old Tim watched in fascination as his father hooked and then hauled a large mahi-mahi onto the deck. As the large fish expired, its bright turquoise color fading to a deep grey, Tim was horrified and cried out, "It's dead, it's dead. I don't want it to be dead! Make it come back!"

In the days that followed, Tim was angry at his father and clingy with his mother. Each night he tearfully insisted that she read to him as he fell asleep, a routine that required increasing amounts of time. If she tried to leave the room before he fell asleep, he cried mournfully until she gave in and returned to his bedside.

The authors have noted several stages through which children progress in their understanding of death. These stages appear to be associated with the successive steps taken by children to differentiate themselves from their parent or parents, and to separate from the original symbiotic relationships with them. Stages in this process include:

1. From birth to six months, a child's denial of separateness from the mother or primary caregiver is achieved through the subjective feeling of being at one with the mother. This is the primary fantasy bond, an *illusion* of connection, originally an imaginary fusion or joining with the mother's body, most particularly the breast.

2. From six months to two years, the child gradually accommodates to the awareness of being separate from the mother or

primary caregiver. At this stage of development, the infant or toddler experiences intense episodes of separation anxiety and a terror of annihilation or loss of self, although there is as yet no structured concept of death. At these times children tend to regress to the earlier phase where they imagine that they and their mother are one.

3. From three to six years, there is a significant point at which children become aware that their parents will someday die. Again, they tend to regress to an earlier fantasy of fused oneness and consequently believe that they can control a parent's life or death by their wishes (infantile narcissism). In this phase, the fantasy bond becomes strengthened as children incorporate traits and attitudes of both parents and develop secondary defenses. Children are now connected to an internalized image of the parent and develop a pseudo-independent posture, a belief that they can survive on their own. Negation also plays a significant part in the thinking of many children about their own death. They are aware that their parents will eventually die, yet they somehow feel exempt from this fate. This form of thinking typifies this stage in the child's development.

4. Finally children come to realize that they themselves will die. Some researchers believe that this awareness develops between the ages of 5 and 9 years (Nagy, 1948/1959). Others place it at an earlier age, between ages 3 and 7, or even earlier (Hoffman & Strauss, 1985; Rochlin, 1967; Speece & Brent, 1984). In one example, Robert Kastenbaum (2000) reported a case in which this more complete understanding seemed to occur at the age of 16 months. Yalom (1980) noted that:

> Other workers ... have arrived at the conclusion that the young child, regardless of whether theoretically he or she is intellectually equipped to understand death, grasps the essence of the matter. Anna Freud, working with young children in the London blitz, wrote: "It can be safely said that all the children who were over two years at the time of the London blitz realized the house will fall down when bombed and that people are often killed or get hurt in falling houses." (p. 88)

Regardless of when this discovery occurs, it effectively destroys children's illusions of self-sufficiency. The world that they believed to be permanent is literally turned upside down by their dawning awareness that people, parents, and even they must die. On an unconscious level they deny the reality of their personal death by regressing to a previous stage of development and to the fantasy bond with the parental image. At the same time, they accept the *idea of death* on a conscious level. In their desperation to escape a situation that they know is hopeless, they cling tenaciously to this familiar solution. As a result, the self-parenting process or fantasy bond is strengthened, and becomes more deeply entrenched as a core defense after the child becomes acquainted with the concept of death. (See Chapter 15 in R. Firestone, 1985.)

CHILDREN'S REACTIONS TO THE KNOWLEDGE OF DEATH

> From this moment [when the child becomes aware of the difference between life and death], the idea of death sets the child's curiosity in action, precisely because, if every cause is coupled with a motive, then death calls for a special explanation. (Piaget, 1959, p. 178) If the child is at this stage puzzled by the problem of death, it is precisely because in his conception of things death is inexplicable. (pp. 180–181)

Denial and Repression

Clinical studies have shown that denial of the knowledge of death may be immediate—or it may be slow to develop (Anthony, 1971/1973; Kastenbaum & Aisenberg, 1972). According to Kastenbaum (2000) and Solomon et al. (2004), "The paralyzing terror produced by the awareness of one's mortality leads to the denial of death awareness and the repression of death-related thoughts" (Florian & Mikulincer, 2004, p. 61).

There are several defense mechanisms that children employ in denying the reality of death and repressing thoughts of their mortality, including a belief in their invulnerability, the idea of a *uniquely personal ultimate rescuer*, the belief that children do not die, and personification of death (Yalom 1980). As Yalom has noted:

> Though the child searches for reassurance, he or she must deal with death: he or she may panic in the face of it, deny it, personify it, scoff at it, repress it, displace it, but deal with it the child must. (p. 91) The beliefs in specialness and the ultimate rescuer serve the developing child well: they are the absolute foundation of the defense structure that the individual erects against death terror. (p. 96)

In discussing denial through a personification of death, Kastenbaum and Aisenberg (1972) observed that children often conceptualize death as a creature or person. They claimed that this image enables the child to imagine death in a more idiosyncratic way that helps him or her cope with thoughts of death. In a chapter titled "The Concept of Death in Children," Yalom (1980) proposed:

> Most children between the ages of five and nine go through a period in which they anthropomorphize death. Death is given form and will: it is the bogeyman, the grim reaper, a skeleton, a ghost, a shadow. . . . The process of death personification is an anxiety emollient. . . . As long as a child believes that death is brought about by some outside force or figure, the child is safe from the really terrible truth that death is *not* external—that, from the beginning of life, one carries within the spores of one's own death. (pp. 98–99)

Other primitive forms of thinking assist the child in denying his or her personal mortality. Anthony (1971/1973) asserted that younger children often use deductive or primitive forms of thinking, other than those of classical logic, to deal with the knowledge of death, as, for example, the belief expressed by one child that "If God doesn't die, all men won't die" (Katz & Katz, 1936). Another example involving recapitulation of primitive thinking has been observed in children who appeared to believe in some form of reincarnation:

> Francis [age 5] . . . saw a coffin being carried into a house [and said], 'Of course the person who went away (i.e.[,] in the coffin) will become a baby, won't he? . . . When John (F's baby brother) was born, someone must have died.' All this was said in a tone of conviction, as though there were no doubt about it. (Anthony, p. 21)

It is interesting to note Bowlby's (1980) remarks regarding the effects on children of beliefs that deny the inevitability and irreversibility of death. Florian and Mikulincer (2004) cited Bowlby as asserting: "Cultures that emphasize ideas of divine purpose and reincarnation can inhibit the development of the view of death as an irreversible outcome of natural processes" (pp. 64–65).

Many children use primitive forms of thinking to personalize their fears of death and imagine that other people are trying to harm or kill them. Anthony (1971/1973) called attention to this fact, noting that very young children tend to conceptualize death in a manner similar to that of ancient, or modern pre-industrial, man in the face of death:

> Some young children in our sample, and some older children of low intelligence, were found to think in this way. When given a series of English words ... and asked to say what each word meant, these children said that *dead* meant *killed* or *murdered*. The condition, for them, involved *who*, an animate agent, essentially. (pp. 19–20)

The Desire to Remain a Child

The desire to remain a child rather than grow up quickly because of the belief mentioned above that *only old people die* was also found in a large number of children who were interviewed by Anthony (1971/1973). This wish was associated with the belief that one dies only when one is older, which was assessed during story-completion tests administered to a group of young children. "In responses to story-opening #10 [Note 1] it was found that thirty-one out of eighty-eight children gave a preference for staying a child a long time rather than growing up quickly" (p. 155). As Yalom (1980) noted when commenting on this study, "Contrary to common belief that the child is impatient to grow up and become strong and effective, over 35 percent of the children expressed in their story completions a preference for staying young, since they linked growing old to death" (p. 78). In equating maturity and old age with dying, it follows that children would continue to manifest immature, even infantile, behaviors as a defense against death anxiety.

The authors have observed children who expressed anxieties about death and old age throughout childhood and adolescence. Their responses upon discovering death typically include a denial through regression to childish behaviors, as suggested above. Children often withdraw from close personal contact with their parents when they begin to think in terms of their own death or when they comprehend that their parents are vulnerable to death. They intensify the imaginary connection with them through regressive, dependent behaviors that elicit caretaking responses, while relinquishing real closeness and affection.

In one case, a five-year-old boy initiated a conversation with his father in which he questioned his father regarding his age (the father was 57). Later that day the youngster expressed anger toward his father and said he didn't like talking with him. For several days the boy was sullen, ignored both parents, and appeared to have lost his characteristic vitality and spirit.

He also reverted to childish behaviors, including whining and thumb-sucking. It was clear from his general mood and actions that he had pulled away from the close, affectionate contact that he usually enjoyed with his family. His parents were aware that he might be upset by the subject of his father's age, so they treated him with sensitivity and patience. The regressive episode eventually passed; however, the boy is likely to manifest similar withdrawal patterns and immature behavior in the future whenever he feels particularly frightened of separation or death.

As in the example, some children become distrustful, hostile, and aggressive toward their parents when they become aware of the reality of death. They experience considerable guilt for these angry attitudes and death wishes that sometimes leads to an obsessive concern about dying. Becker (1973/1997) explained that from the perspective of the very young child:

> When the child experiences inevitable and real frustrations from his parents, he directs hate and destructive feelings toward them; and he has no way of knowing that malevolent feelings cannot be fulfilled by the same magic as were his other wishes. Psychoanalysts believe that this confusion is a main cause of guilt and helplessness in the child. (p. 18)

Nightmares

Many children have nightmares filled with themes about death and feelings of vulnerability about their bodies. These terrifying nightmares seem to occur more frequently in children who have not yet successfully repressed their emotional reactions to the knowledge of death. Common themes of children's nightmares include being threatened, pursued, defeated, or killed by monsters, ghosts, witches, criminals, and so forth. The subjects that seem to recur in these nightmares are similar to the topics of many fairy tales, stories that are both frightening and fascinating to young children (Bettelheim, 1985).

In general the frequency of nightmares about death decreases during later childhood and early adolescence, a fact that may indicate preadolescents' (8- to 12-year-olds) increased ability to repress thoughts about death and dying (R. Firestone, 1985). This notion is supported by several empirical studies. As Becker (1973/1997) observed: "The nightmares become more and more widely spaced" (p. 20) as the child grows older. Becker went on to pose the following question: But how do "the vast majority—seem to survive the flurry of childhood nightmares and go on to live a healthy, more-or-less optimistic life, untroubled by death? ... Repression takes care of the complex symbol of death for most people" (p. 20). However, Feldman and Hersen (1967) and Lester (1968) reported findings from interviews with adult individuals in which: "A subject who has suffered (especially when under the age of ten) the death of close friends and relatives is more likely to have death nightmares. ... Those individuals who have very high *or* very low conscious death anxiety tend to dream of death" (Yalom, 1980, pp. 53–54).

Suppression During the Latency Phase

Many children of latency age (9–12 years) attempt to relieve the fear of death by taunting death. Yalom (1980) pointed out that boys, in particular, of this age "engage in feats of reckless daredeviltry. (Quite possibly some male adolescent delinquent behavior may reflect a persistence of this defense against death anxiety)" (p. 100). Anthony (1971/1973) also described the latency phase as the *dare phase*, in which "children devise a mixture of reality and fantasy in facing their fears" (p. 165). Meyer (1975) has drawn attention to the fact that life and death are central themes in adolescence, "as is clearly shown by the frequency with which young people attempt to commit suicide" and suggested that the loss of a love relationship "may easily cause the adolescent to step across the boundary of the will to survive" (p. 27).

Alexander and Adlerstein (1958/1965) used a word association test combined with psychogalvanic skin reflex to test children's reactions to death-related words. They found that "two subgroups, 5 through 8 and 13 through 16, show significant decrease in skin resistance. No reliable differences on this measure are found in the 9 through 12 group" (p. 122). In other words, latency age children seem to show less responsiveness to death-related words. In support of these findings, Meyer (1975) noted that "between the eighth year and puberty [the fact of death] becomes step by step subject to a process of repression that in many respects runs parallel to the development of sexual taboos" (p. 82). The apparent tranquility of the *latency period* may be related more to the repression of death anxiety than to the repression of sexual impulses.

Fantasized Reunion With a Loved One After Death

In her study of children's understanding of death, Anthony (1971/1973) noted "the tendency to defend against the knowledge of death by imagining a union with the loved one after death" (R. Firestone, 1985, p. 247). Anthony's research indicated underlying fantasies on the part of many children that a reunion with the mother, in a deep sense, insures immortality: "In all these instances, anxiety is clearly about death as separation from the love-object, and the defence has taken the form of a belief or hope of union in death; indeed, unconsciously of a closer union in death than was possible in life" (Anthony, p. 151).

Anthony's findings tend to coincide with our observations and the hypothesis that the unconscious, fantasized connection with the mother is associated with a general sense of immortality in children. As the child advances through the stages of intellectual development, he or she does not necessarily abandon the primitive thinking characteristic of earlier stages, especially with respect to ideas about death.

Other Reactions

At approximately the same age they begin to form a concept of death, many children manifest a strong curiosity about sex. Otto Rank (1968) believed that children feel guilty about their bodies because they are aware that their bodies are mortal and therefore vulnerable. Their guilt leads to anxious questions about sex and reproduction that may really be questions about the meaning of the body, the terror of living in a body that grows old and dies.

> Children's revulsion at the thought of their parents having sexual intercourse, that is, the trauma of the *primal scene,* may be due simply to their rejection of the undeniable physicalness of an act performed by people who they believe to be immortal and invulnerable and therefore *above* things of the body. (R. Firestone, 1985, p. 248)

Failure in Repression

With some children, a failure in repression of the awareness of death can lead to a morbid preoccupation with dying. Directly confronting death or the end of the self is analogous to looking straight into the sun without shielding one's eyes, and so it serves no purpose to dwell on the subject. The majority of healthy children gradually learn to repress the direct realization of death. However, in some cases, there is a failure in repression, and children, especially those who may have suffered unusual trauma and early losses, tend to find it difficult to successfully rid themselves of morbid thoughts. These children often develop symptomatic or maladaptive behavior patterns, including generalized anxiety, panic disorders, phobias, obsessive compulsive disorder (OCD), asthma, or other psychosomatic complaints (Furer & Walker, 2008; Kosloff et al., 2006; Monsour, 1960; Noyes, Stuart, Longley, Langbehn, & Happel, 2002; Randall, 2001; Strachan et al., 2007; B. Wolfe, 2008). According to Becker (1973/1997), the successful repression of death-related thoughts in children and adults functions as "normal self-protection and creative self-restriction" (p. 178). However, Becker also observed, "Some people have more trouble with their lies than others. The world is too much with them" (p. 178) (Note 2).

In one case, a young, precocious girl became preoccupied with thoughts of illness and death as she approached puberty. During her early years, she experienced a subtle form of maternal rejection. (Her mother frequently left her in the care of a relative.) When she was four, following the death of a family friend, she regressed in many areas of functioning. At age eight, the little girl, who was advanced intellectually and had a rich fantasy life, composed a lengthy fictional biography (over one hundred pages) depicting the life of a young girl, also age eight, who lived in London.

In the story, the girl's mother suddenly becomes ill and dies. The mother's death is followed by the illness and death of the girl's father, and the child is sent to live with relatives. Once again she faces a traumatic loss when she discovers her aunt is seriously ill and her uncle, whom she loves and trusts, becomes deeply depressed. After the death of her aunt, the small girl becomes obsessively worried about her uncle's health. At school she finds it impossible to make friends because of an overwhelming dread of potential loss and abandonment. The girl avoids friendships by telling herself, "Why make new friends, they'll just get sick and die, so what's the use?"

As an adolescent, the author of this story developed an obsessive/compulsive disorder requiring long-term treatment with behavioral therapy. The onset of puberty, with its bodily changes and emerging sexual feelings, reawakened her original fears of abandonment and death. Unable to repress thoughts of illness and death and the associated affect, she attempted to relieve her anxiety by severely restricting her activities and engaging in ritualistic behaviors. For several months she suffered from obsessive thoughts about health issues and cleanliness reminiscent of those that had tormented the heroine in her story.

CLINICAL MATERIAL FROM A STUDY OF CHILDREN'S REACTIONS TO THE KNOWLEDGE OF DEATH

In a small pilot study, L. Firestone (1987) observed two groups of preschool children and recorded the children's responses to the Play U situation created by Wass et al. (1983). In this situation the child is presented with three neutral puppets and told that one of them is dying (to be selected by the child). The child is then encouraged to play with the puppets and talk about what the puppets are doing and feeling. In addition, each child is asked questions modified from Koocher's (1973) death concept interview. The questions are asked in relation to the puppet rather than the child: "Why is he dying?" "How do the other puppets feel about his dying?" The sessions with the children were videotaped in order to be coded for content and affective expression.

Results showed that most of the children expressed negative affect when talking about death even though they were only ages two to five. Children with a higher developmental level were found to have spent a significant amount of time with a serious expression. Some sad or serious expressions were found even in children who clearly displayed an immature concept of death. These preliminary results support the hypothesis that children have feelings about death long before they fully understand all of its implications. Two brief excerpts from the videotaped responses are reported here.

Subject #1, female, age 4:
Dr. Lisa Firestone: How did he [the puppet] die?
Hilary: He flew up in the air (from a swing) without asking.
LF: What happens when people die?
Hilary: They stay dead forever, and they can't walk.
LF: How do people feel when somebody dies?
Hilary: They feel bad.
LF: What are they doing now?
Hilary: The momma and the girl got dead again because they walked across the street without looking. The really mean one died and that's the end of the story.

Subject #4, male, age 4 (initially very quiet and noncommittal):
LF: Is it hard to talk about the game?
Sam: Yeah.
LF: What makes people die?

Sam: They're sick and they can't find anybody. When my mommy died, she was sick. [Later]
LF: How do they feel [the two puppets] about that one dying?
Sam: When this one is dying there aren't any more, and it's too late. She's the only one left.
LF: She's the only one left. How do the other ones feel?
Sam: If it's dying, it's sick. [sad, sniffing]
LF: Can they come back to life?
Sam: Uh-uh. [shakes head no]

Approximately seven years following the study described above, several children who had participated in the original study were videotaped in a discussion with their younger siblings.

Heather (age 6): It makes me sad when it's my birthday.
Dr. Robert Firestone: It does? Why? What do you feel?
Heather: I feel so glad that I'm getting older, but I get scared.
RF: What are you scared of?
Heather: That I'm going to die sooner and sooner.
Colin (age 11, in original study): One thing that doesn't really scare me is dying. I'm scared of my friends dying more than I'm scared of me dying.
RF: What Colin said was interesting. He said he himself isn't afraid of dying, but it scares him that anything would happen to people he loves.
Edward (age 10): I'm not really scared of me dying, it's just when I hear of someone else dying, I feel scared or bad when I think about dying.
RF: Do you have these thoughts a lot of the time?
Kevin (age 11, in original study): Yeah, sometimes if I see a movie where somebody dies, then I think of what would it feel like when my friends die.
Lynn (age 13): I think more about other people than about myself. I mean, I dream of my parents or Heather, Marsha, or Wendy [sisters] dying; those are the people I dream of dying. And it's always my job to save them in the dreams, but I can't save them. It's sad. It's like I'm really close to saving them [tearful] but then if it's a burning building, all of them fall back in the burning building, but I'll get out. I'll be trying to save them, but they all somehow end up back in the building, but I end up out of it, to torture myself that I didn't save them. But I always miss them.
RF: Does anybody else have thoughts like that?

Heather: I feel bad when I think about my parents dying sometimes. I try not to think about it, but sometimes I see a movie or something that tells about it; so it makes me scared and it makes me think about it again. And I think about when I would die [sad] and how all my friends would feel if I died.

Marsha (age 9): One time I had a dream that Wendy and Lynn both died. They weren't dead yet but that they were going to die, and I knew and I was telling all the girls and I was crying because I didn't want them to die.

Wendy (age 11, in original study): I always feel that after all the people I know die, I just want to die too. Right now I don't want to die, but if everyone I love died then I don't think there's really any reason to live.

Colin: I had a dream that I was driving with my family and some of my friends in our station wagon, and we drove off the cliff and all of a sudden it got really hot and the car was about to blow up. So I was trying to push everybody out of the car. But I started pulling my grandfather's hand out and his hand got stuck in the door and then the car blew up. [pause] Then I woke up.

RF: That's a painful dream. So a lot of people have fears, like almost every day. Is that really right? And what about thinking about dying, is that something that happens a lot?

Many children: Yes.

RF: It does?

Gene (age 6): I think about it a lot, but it usually never happens! [laughter]

RF: I'm glad it doesn't. I'm surprised you think about these things so much.

FEAR OF INFANTICIDE AND PARENTAL DEATH WISHES

In some children, death anxiety is accentuated and compounded by a fear of infanticide and parents' death wishes toward the child. A number of researchers investigating parental attitudes and their effects on young children have reported findings related to this phenomenon. For example, Joseph Rheingold (1964, 1967) interviewed over 2,500 pregnant women and new mothers in the course of a twelve-year study. The data from these interviews indicated ambivalence on the part of these mothers regarding their pregnancy and their infants. Rheingold emphasized that whatever nurturing tendencies a mother may have, she still has a certain hostile or aggressive component in her personality that exerts a harmful influence on her baby. In commenting on the infant's vulnerability to the mother's hostility and the long-term effects on the child's functioning, he wrote:

> The infant is maximally vulnerable to the noxious influence because of its preternatural perception of the mother's mood and wishes and its almost total lack of defensive devices. It experiences basic anxiety and acquires a basic ambivalence toward life, which together with the innate dispositions and the vicissitudes of being, determine its character organization, modes of adaptation, patterns of behavior, and liability to disorder. (Rheingold, 1964, p. 132)

The child psychoanalyst Dorothy Bloch (1978) has written extensively about children's fears of infanticide and their defenses against such fears: "Once I began to probe the function of children's fantasies, it became apparent that they were a means of survival and defended the children against their fear of infanticide" (p. 13). Fears of potential danger from parents' aggression, which is often perceived by children as life-threatening, exacerbate early separation anxiety and can predispose serious emotional disturbance in older children and adolescents.

These dynamics were clearly operant in the family of one young woman who developed a serious anxiety disorder. In the process of tracing her fears of death to early childhood experiences, she was able to gain a measure of control over her anxiety and learn better methods of coping with stress. In a discussion group she described destructive thoughts and fears that she identified as originating in her mother's hatred toward her. She also recalled other incidents that she felt had contributed to her preoccupation with catastrophic, life-threatening events.

Jane: For some reason, during the last five years, I've found myself thinking about death all the time. It's different than thinking of growing old and dying, I think about dying in an accident or some terrible thing happening suddenly. I know that I scare myself a lot.

There are key times throughout my life that have had an effect on me. I know that when I was little two things happened. Once was when I was three years old, I almost drowned. My parents got really scared because they realized how fragile I was, and from then on they were bizarrely overprotective and treated me like I was going to die.

The second thing is more psychological. My mother was very ambivalent toward me and I was aware that she had hateful and angry feelings toward me. At times, she really did partly want me to die. So I think that this confused me and left me feeling like death is somehow a punishment.

When a parent has strong death wishes toward the child, the child tends to identify with the aggressor and internalize the parent's death wishes. In turning against the self, the child is constantly on guard and aware of death in pathological terms of wanting to harm or destroy him or herself. In a sense children who are treated in this manner make an alliance with death. To protect themselves against the emergence of incorporated death wishes (in the form of injunctions to harm oneself), they retreat from living and may even become somewhat addicted to their ruminations about illness and death. We have found, however, that people who are preoccupied with thoughts of dying can identify the underlying self-attacks and subsequently control their obsessive thoughts regarding torturous themes.

To the extent that children have incorporated a parent's negative feelings toward them, they also incorporate the parent's compensatory maneuvers in relation to those feelings. Parents with unconscious death wishes toward a child are often overly vigilant about dangers to their child's physical life. For example, they excessively caution their offspring to be careful not to hurt themselves while playing, not to run into the street, to be wary of strangers. As adults these children obsessively caution themselves through the use of internalized parental warnings that guard and protect them from every anticipated contingency. They are blocked in their spontaneity and restricted in their actions. Their denied fear of death is displaced from its source and becomes transformed into specific phobias or compulsive, ritualistic behavior.

THE EFFECTS OF EARLY LOSS THROUGH DEATH OF A PARENT

In general, there are many negative consequences of the early loss of a parent. In *Losing a Parent to Death in the Early Years,* Lieberman, Compton, Van Horn, and Ippen (2003) concluded: "There is abundant observational and clinical evidence that the death of a parent represents a cataclysmic event in the psychological landscape of a young child" (p. 128). There is an increased reliance on defenses and an intensification of the fantasy bond in particular. In many cases, the death of a parent is an important causative factor in many forms of emotional disturbance or maladjustment. For example, Mack (2001) found that adults who suffered the loss of a parent through death or through divorce during childhood had more problems and were not as well-adjusted as those who came from intact families. Mack found that children who had experienced the loss of a parent were significantly more depressed and had less self-confidence than children who had not experienced such a loss.

Other studies (Raveis, Siegel, & Karus, 1999; Saler & Skolnick, 1992; Thompson, Kaslow, Price, Williams, & Kingree, 1998) examined contextual variables that either ameliorated or intensified maladaptive behavior and/or depression in individuals who had suffered early parental loss. Thompson found that the mode of death, the suddenness, and the extent to which the death could "be attributed to human intent" were important factors in predicting the degree of later maladjustment. "One interesting study finding to emerge was that youths who lost a parent to homicide, but not youths who lost a parent to natural death, were more likely to manifest externalizing distress than were nonbereaved youths" (p. 363).

A number of psychologists, among them Yalom (1980), Searles (1961), and Karon and VandenBos (1981), have suggested that early loss of a parent, difficulty in mourning the loss, and an inability to manage death anxiety may be related to schizophrenia. Yalom has observed, for example, that:

> First, the anxiety of facing death is infinitely greater in those who do not have the strengthening knowledge of personal wholeness and of whole participation in living.... A second reason that the schizophrenic is overwhelmed by death anxiety is that the patient has suffered enormous losses so early in development that he or she has not been able to integrate them.... A third source of intense death anxiety emanates from the nature of the schizophrenic patient's early relationship to mother—a symbiotic union from which the patient has never emerged but in which he or she continues to oscillate between a position of psychological merger and a state of total unrelatedness.... Furthermore, the schizophrenic patient perceives that the symbiotic relationship is absolutely necessary to survival. (pp. 151–152) (Note 3)

Research related specifically to *enormous losses* cited by Yalom above has demonstrated a greater incidence of deaths of mothers of schizophrenic patients (Hilgard, Newman, & Fisk, 1960) and depressives (A. Beck, Sethi, & Tuthill, 1963) than in matched samples from the normal population. It was hypothesized that these early losses aroused emotions of mourning and melancholy that the children could not successfully handle through the normal processes of grief. It is likely that the blow to these children's narcissistic sense of omnipotence was so profound that their subsequent regression into fantasy was more severe and longer lasting than those experienced by children who had no early experience with death. However, even when children have no familiarity with death in the early years, there is a gradual loss of spontaneity and joy with progressive, habitual denying of the pleasures of life after they learn about death and begin to apply the concept personally to their own lives.

Kate, a woman in her 50s, had great difficulty in sleeping, was plagued by anxieties, and compelled to get up in the middle of the night, hoard food, and binge. She had been in group therapy for three years when the group went for a four-day retreat in the country. Kate had come to trust her fellow participants and looked forward to sharing a deeper emotional experience with them. One of the practicalities of the weekend was that meals would be provided but only on schedule. Kate was surprised by her reaction when she heard this; for some reason she felt noticeably relieved.

On the first evening, Kate spoke of her reaction, "The first thought I had was, 'Oh, good! There won't be any food in the middle of the night.' For as long as I can remember, I get up in the night and eat. I always know where the food is, and I wake up in a daze and go for the food. I'm not really myself; I am like a crazed animal. When I realized there would be no snack food, I felt relaxed; like this crazy pattern would be interrupted."

Later that night, one of the participants spoke movingly of his feelings about a friend dying and about getting older himself. As others discussed their feelings about death, Kate began to think about when she was 10 and her mother died. She was surprised that when she started to talk she began to cry uncontrollably. Previously, she had only mentioned her mother's death in passing, she never really thought much about it. But on this night, she described how lost and lonely she felt when her mother died. Suddenly she had the insight that her quest for food was related to her mother's death and originated at the same time period. She was surprised that she had never made that connection before. That night Kate did not wake up; she slept through the night until daylight woke her. The next day, Kate explored her feelings further. She recounted the situation in which she heard that her mother had actually died:

"My mother was sick in the hospital and I was at my uncle's house. My uncle came in and said, 'I'm sorry to tell you that your mother has died.' And I remember I said the strangest thing. I said, 'No, she's not dead. She's just asleep.' I felt like it wasn't even my voice talking; it was like listening to a voice from a movie. And I felt nothing." Kate then said, "After I lost her, food was all I had."

The following nights, Kate slept through the night. During the retreat she had insights into why she had been so tortured in her sleep. She realized that she had equated sleep with death. At those times, she felt like she was going to die. She had to get food; she had to get out of this state. Sometimes she would go out in the middle of the night to get food. "Even if it was cold and raining, I would go out. I realized that I was in such a state of desperation that I would do anything to get food. It was like I would have done anything to have that connection with her and to deny her death."

After the weekend retreat, Kate's progress continued and she was able to sleep uninterruptedly without seeking food. After 46 years, her powerful intellectual and emotional insights altered a life-long pattern of misery.

PARENTS' RESPONSES TO CHILDREN'S QUESTIONS ABOUT DEATH

When children come to realize that they are mortal, they lose their illusions of being all-powerful and manifest a wide range of reactions to the loss. Many cut off their feelings, become inward and distant from parents, siblings, and peers, and express anger and hostility as they go through the process of realization. Their questions to parents indicate a significant increase in anxiety and concern about death.

Most parents, feeling protective and wishing to spare their child anxiety, avoid the subject of death in conversations with family members, especially their younger children. Often mothers and fathers try to reassure their children with platitudes or cliches that deny the fact of death and block out the painful feelings associated with the child's growing awareness of his or her personal mortality. They offer counsel and beliefs such as: "You don't have to think about that at your age." "Only old people die." "Your father and I would never let anything happen to you." "People don't really die, they go to heaven."

Anthony (1971/1973) presented numerous examples of children who failed to cope with death anxiety and were assisted in their denial of death by parents who were too threatened to listen to their child's questions or to take them seriously. For example, a mother comforted and reassured her distraught 3-year-old daughter who had just asked, "Does everyone die?" by telling her that people died "when they were old and tired and therefore glad to do so" (p. 138). In another case a mother felt compelled to deny to her anxious child the fact of his personal mortality:

Theodore [age 5] . . .: Do animals come to an end, too?
Mother: Yes, animals come to an end, too. Everything comes to an end.
T: I don't want to come to an end. I should like to live longer than anybody on earth.
M: You need never die; you can live forever. (p. 158)

Other studies conducted by Kastenbaum (1974) and Wass et al. (1983) have contributed empirical findings regarding children's reactions to death as well as parents' reactions to children who are in the midst of this developmental phase. Kastenbaum reported that more than three-fourths of the respondents to a questionnaire expressed the opinion that children "are better off not thinking of death, and should be protected from death-relevant situations by their parents" (p. 12). In more recent research, including interviews with mothers of schoolchildren, Kastenbaum (2004) found that:

It is clear that experiences, attitudes, and ways of coping with death are part of the intimate flow of life between children and their parents.... Many of us, though, must first overcome our own reluctance to accept the fact that death does touch children and children are very much attuned to loss and separation experiences. (pp. 342–343)

Anthony (1971/1973) cited cases where parents' denial or a *modified negation* of death played a part in the subsequent development of neuroses in the children. She and other researchers have noted that many parents believe that children think of death only infrequently. Parents may use this belief as a rationalization to support the taboo against discussing the subject with their offspring. However, Anthony reported findings from "research carried out in Geneva to discover the emotional problems of disturbed children [in which] the investigators reported their surprise at the frequency of references to death in children's completions of story openings in which no such reference was made" (p. 78). "It was found that forty-five of the ninety-eight children referred in their 'completions' to death, funerals, killing[s,] or ghosts" (p. 80). Further analysis of these cases revealed that *allowing* children to go through the stage in their development where they become progressively more knowledgeable about death arouses considerable anxiety and feelings of anticipatory grief in *parents* (Dugan, 1977).

In a seminar about existential issues conducted by the authors, a number of participants recalled childhood fears of death and parents' answers to their inquiries about death and dying:

Joan: I remember when I thought about my own death as a small child. First, I had been worried about my parents dying and they kind of hushed me up about that. Then I realized that I could die and I was really afraid. I was talking to my mother about this one night before I went to bed. I was crying and she said, "Don't worry. Your body is just like an overcoat. You'll just take off this one and put a new one on." (She believed in reincarnation.) But I kept trying to tell her that I was afraid that didn't fix it. I still didn't know what happened, what everything was made of, what the ending was like, but that's the only answer she would give me. So I knew not to ask anymore.

Kurt: When I was about 5 or 6, there was this prayer that we were supposed to say before we went to bed. "Now I lay me down to sleep. I pray the Lord my soul to keep. If I should die before I wake. . . ." But I didn't want to die! So that really bothered me. I started thinking, what does death feel like? Just the thought of nothingness really disturbed me, of not waking up and seeing anything ever again. I remember having all kinds of nightmares during that period of time. I don't know how I resolved it, but I quit thinking about it after a while.

Sharon: Nobody ever talked about death in my house. My parents were so protective of me, they made up ridiculous stories. Just as an example, an absurd thing, if I heard an ambulance siren, I would ask what was that noise and they'd say, "Oh, somebody's going to the hospital to have a baby," and so that's what I thought ambulances were for.

TALKING WITH CHILDREN ABOUT DEATH

It is ... evident that children hone their minds on death-related phenomena as part of their general grasp of the world: curiosity and concern are engaged when they observe disappearances, decay, nonresponsiveness, and so forth. As adults we will not succeed in protecting them from all such experiences—and, as adults, we will be modeling attitudes toward death that are either open or closed, consistent or inconsistent, anxious or comforting. (Kastenbaum, 2000, p. 60)

As noted, many parents try to avoid the subject because they feel protective, wishing to spare their child what they consider to be unnecessary anxiety. According to Grollman (1990), "Most parents today are convinced that they should be honest in discussing the biological processes of birth, but when it comes to life's end they may fall strangely silent" (p. ix). In his book, *Talking about Death,* Grollman tells parents: "Death is a universal and inevitable process that must be faced by people of all ages.... Your children are human beings, worthy of respect and openness, not pretense and equivocation. Two of their greatest needs are for *trust* and *truth*" (p. 40).

A father in the research group related a personal experience he had with his 6-year-old son in a talk:

> Last night I had a really painful talk with little Chris to the point where both of us were crying. He came into my room crying because he had seen something on TV that scared him. He was watching "Imitation of Life" with some of the older kids and in the movie, the mother dies, so I guess that's what upset him. He was trying to tell me the story of the movie, but he was crying so hard I couldn't understand what he was saying at first. All I knew was that something serious was on his mind.
>
> At the time, I didn't know if death was on his mind or if that's why he came and found me, but he was crying and in a very scared mood and I could understand some of what he was trying to say.
>
> He said: "I'm going to die, you know. And I could die now or I could die later." He was panicked. He reminded me of my wife when she gets into a panicky state, so I felt a lot for him. He was terrified, "I'm going to die, and nobody can do anything! We're all going to die. We're all going to die, and I don't know what to do."
>
> At that moment there was no way that I was going to say "Don't worry about it," because he had already figured it out. And there was no way I was going to say, "It probably won't happen now or soon" because he had already said "I could die now or something could happen to me now." In the past, he had felt fearful about something happening to me or my wife or his grandfather but this time, he was saying it about himself and he was really panicked.
>
> He kept crying and crying, really loud, really hard, like a moan. All I could do was just hug him. [sad] I wished I could have reassured him, but I just told him it was really painful and I had the same pain. I said "It's really hard to see people who are older because I know they're going to die," and he said, "What are we going to do when grandpa dies, because I know he's going to die. What am I going to do then—cry forever?" Then he just started moaning, so I just held him and let him feel what he was feeling. Eventually his sadness passed. I felt so much.

At this point Chris came into the room where this discussion was in progress. He looked calm, comfortable, and self-possessed and seemed to be in good spirits.

> "I'm glad that you're here, Chris, and I'm glad that you came to me last night when you were feeling bad. And I hope that you won't torture yourself with this, although it's really painful. And I feel guilty, too. The way I feel guilty is that you didn't do anything to make this happen. But it also made me feel good, too, because the experience gave me a new perspective somehow on everything."

The key concept in talking with children about death and dying is to allow the child to fully express his or her ideas and feelings on the subject. First, it is important that parents take their children's inquiries about death seriously and not attempt to change the subject or brush it aside with platitudes. The time that a child first becomes aware of the temporal nature of life constitutes a true crisis in that child's life. Sometimes a sudden change in behavior is the only clue parents have that the child is beginning to be aware of his or her predicament. The child who begins to act *out of character* (e.g., a quiet, reserved child becoming loud and rebellious, or a child provoking punishing responses from parents) may be experiencing anxiety related to this unsolvable dilemma. At this juncture understanding parents would sense that the child's defensive actions are probably motivated by deeper feelings of insecurity, fear, terror, and/ or confusion. Rather than punishing or ignoring the child, they could ask, "Is anything bothering you? You don't seem to be feeling very good." Parents who are genuinely concerned about their children's well-being could then listen respectfully to any feelings the child is willing to express, without offering false protection. When children use this opportunity, as they usually do, to ask direct questions about death, parents could honestly share their own feelings on the subject while answering their inquiries.

> Justin, aged 9, returned home after having a particularly bad day at school. He had deliberately tripped a younger child, started a fight with another boy on the playground, stubbornly refused to finish his lesson, and turned down an invitation to go for ice cream with a friend after school, which in Justin's case was unheard of. When Justin's father heard about his son's behavior from his teacher, instead of being angry or punitive, he indicated his disapproval of the misbehavior, but also asked Justin if something might have happened earlier to make him feel bad. Justin could think of nothing.

Later, the father learned that the previous evening, Justin had found his mother reading *The Last Lecture* by Randy Pausch (2008), which describes his thoughts on life and death after learning that he had only three months to live. When he asked his mother what the book was about, she explained the story to him, perhaps in greater detail than was sensitive to a child of his age. It was clear to Justin's father (and later to Justin) what had happened. The conversation with his mother about illness and death had triggered intense anxiety in Justin, which he had coped with by reverting to a number of negative, childish behaviors he had previously given up.

Parents' answers to their children's questions about death should be individual to each child and appropriate to his or her respective age and emotional maturity. Children of any age, and especially young children, need not be given long, elaborate explanations or more information than what they asked for at the time. Sensitive parents refrain from over-explaining or using the occasion to deliver a lecture. They recognize that the child will continue to ask questions as he or she matures—often the same questions. As Grollman (1990) has noted, "For every child, the meaning of death is reexamined as life changes" (p. 35).

Nagy (1948/1959) found that young children have three recurring questions about death: What is death? What makes people die? What happens to people when they die; where do they go? Ideally, in answering such questions, parents would talk with their children openly, honestly, and with feeling. If their child asks, for example, "What happened to Mr. Smith?" parents could answer honestly and directly: "Mr. Smith died. He's no longer here." In being comfortable with and respectful of their child's feelings, parents do not try to ease a child's pain and sadness by offering false explanations about death, for example, that only sick people, old people, or careless people die (R. Firestone, 1990b). By not interrupting the feeling process with false reassurances, parents teach children that even the most painful emotions can be tolerated.

In contrast to many conventional views that children should be protected from the knowledge of death, we believe that parents must refrain from attempting to soothe them by covering over the truth. Parents can honestly communicate the fact that the process of dying and death is a mystery, and that they do not know all the answers, without making the child feel insecure or fearful. For example, if the child asks if everybody dies, a parent could say, "Yes, we're all going to die, but I don't really know when or how it will happen or what death actually is. Some people believe there is an afterlife, but no one really knows" (R. Firestone, 1990b, p. 215).

Being honest and straightforward with children about this subject tends to arouse painful feelings of sadness in parents about their own mortality. The purity and intensity of children's dismay, pain, and sadness also stir their parents' feelings about death, emotions that they may have been suppressing for years. Parents who are less defended against these feelings are better able to respond appropriately to their child's feelings, that is, to not cut them off, but to encourage the child to go through the feelings. They are aware that even emotions as intensely painful as those about death are better felt and not avoided. These parents accompany the child through this process by offering empathy, compassion, and understanding as the child expresses his or her distressing thoughts and emotions.

"If parents are willing to endure the sadness and pain of acknowledging their child's mortality as well as their own limitation in time, they can develop a true sense of empathy with their children rather than becoming alienated" (R. Firestone, 1990b, p. 215). Thus, when children are facing the issues of death, parents would be providing them with the greatest security by facing these existential issues themselves, telling the truth to their children, and allowing their children to experience their own feelings about these deeply disturbing subjects.

CONCLUSION

Infants and young children defend themselves from feelings of annihilation and separation in their initial struggles for survival; later, this same protection becomes debilitating as they extend these defenses to include increasingly broad areas of psychological functioning. Seeking gratification in fantasy and self-nurturing behaviors limits the possibility of finding actual satisfaction in interpersonal relationships and is a denial of the natural human need for affiliation with other people. Inhibiting feeling responses in close relationships tends to negate all that is alive, pleasurable, or spontaneous in one's life experience.

In attempting to elude death, people eventually give up their lives to varying degrees, rationing their aliveness and spontaneity, carefully doling out or restricting pleasant or enriching experiences. They gradually become indifferent to important or relevant events and numb themselves by attending to life's trivialities. Indeed, living a full life, with meaningful activity, compassion for oneself, and a poignant awareness that all people share the same fate, appears to be too agonizing for many to endure. The majority are not strong enough to live fully in the face of dying, and so tend to retreat to a self-protective, inward lifestyle. Identifying and learning to challenge defenses move life in the opposite direction.

The first author wishes to conclude this section with a personal note:

I initially thought that my fear of death began during my adolescence, but then I remembered that it was much earlier. In thinking about it, I recollected that when I was something like four or five, I learned about death and thought of my parents dying. I remember that I couldn't stand thinking about it because the pain was too great. The thought of losing my mother or father was unbearable.

I was an intelligent child. It was only a matter of time until I stumbled on the obvious inference that I faced the same fate myself. It would happen to me and it was unavoidable. As I propelled this notion into the far future, I thought, thank God. It will happen later when I am old, and by then it won't matter.

Now in my later life I do not find my age to be of any consolation. I still appreciate my life as I did previously. I hope to live as long as possible and place as much value on my life as ever.

NOTES

1. Story-opening #10 reads as follows: "Then the fairy said, 'You are growing into a big boy; do you want to be big and growing, or would you like to stay a child for a long time, perhaps for always?' The boy said. . . . What did he say?" (Anthony, 1973, p. 79)
2. See S. Freud's (1896/1962) use of the term *failure of repression* in "Notes on a Case of Obsessional Neurosis," wherein the inability to repress impulses that were in conflict with or not satisfied during childhood return in modified form in a panic attack or a phobia.
3. Yalom's (1980) discussion regarding the schizophrenic patient's maintenance of *psychological merger* with the mother is similar in some respects to the first author's description of the fantasy bond, an illusion of being merged with the mother or primary caretaker. He also emphasized that neurotic as well as normal individuals strive to preserve the imagined connection with the parent or parents as a protection against death anxiety. (See Chapter 15 in R. Firestone, 1985.)

4

The Effects of Death Anxiety in Everyday Life

Death. The fact that we are mortal constantly whirs beneath the membrane of life and influences our experiences, our actions, and our coping abilities. Our unavoidable mortality is a primordial source of anxiety and, as such, is the primary fount of psychopathology.

—Israel Orbach, "Existentialism and Suicide" (2008, p. 285)

Reactions to death anxiety take many diverse forms and predispose an altogether different lifestyle than does fully investing in life despite the awareness of a finite existence. Although all psychological defenses do not necessarily relate to death anxiety and often develop in a relationship context, they are strengthened by death fears. If we are personally hurt in a close relationship and thereby learn to distrust others, our cynicism becomes more inclusive and is generalized to a number of life and death issues. Death salience combines with reactions to personal trauma to increase defensive behavior. This leads to a general decline in feeling, problems in relating, the use of the defense mechanisms of projection, distortion, and other maladaptive responses. The result is that most people live in a state of psychological equilibrium that they established early in life. They find a neurotic, compromised solution to the core problem in life and sacrifice opportunities to live in order to avoid death anxiety.

When people exist within this defensive equilibrium or homeostasis, they rarely feel consciously anxious about death. However, if their equilibrium is disturbed by a negative event (e.g., a rejection experience, important loss, reminder of death) or an unusually positive event (e.g., an especially close, satisfying sexual or love relationship or powerful career success), they tend to experience varying degrees of death anxiety. Unfortunately, the anxiety that surfaces and the subsequent regression are difficult to assess or analyze because people usually act out defensive behaviors before death anxiety reaches a fully conscious level of awareness (R. Firestone, Firestone, & Catlett, 2006).

People's defensive reactions to personal trauma, separation issues, and especially death anxiety impact their lives at three distinct levels: (1) on an individual level, their reactions predispose withdrawal into a more inward, self-nurturing, and self-protective lifestyle (R. Firestone, 1997a); (2) on the level of interpersonal relationships, their responses can trigger a retreat from love or loving relationships and/or a generalized rejection or avoidance of intimacy and sexuality (R. Firestone & Catlett, 1999); and (3) at the societal level, their fear reactions intensify the need to subordinate themselves to a leader or authority figure and reinforce the need to conform to the conventions, beliefs, and mores of a particular group, institution, or nation (R. Firestone, 1994b). The in-group identification polarizes the insiders against people who look, believe, or act differently, leading to ethnic strife, religious persecution, religious wars, or warfare in general (R. Firestone, 1996).

WITHDRAWAL TO AN INWARD, SELF-PROTECTIVE LIFESTYLE

To avoid the associated anxiety and dread that come with the full realization that their lives are temporary, people usually retreat to an inward, self-protective state of mind. In this defensive attempt to maintain the fantasy bond and cope with death's painful reality, they narrow their life experience by cutting off feeling for themselves and others. They imagine, on an unconscious level, that they can evade the experience of death. As Paul Tillich (1952) asserted: "One avoids being so as to avoid nonbeing."

In *The Politics of the Family*, R. D. Laing (1969/1972) described the inward process as follows: "I consider many adults (including myself) are or have been, more or less, in a hypnotic trance, induced in early infancy: we remain in this state until—when we dead awaken, as Ibsen makes one of his characters say—we shall find that we have never lived" (p. 82). A large majority of people in modern society appear to exist in the dazed, trancelike state depicted by Laing; removed from feeling and unable to grasp the fact that they are deeply involved in a way of living that significantly diminishes their human qualities. As people become inward, they neutralize their experiences and lose feeling for themselves and others.

When people are in this self-protective state, their gaze is focused inward on themselves, rather than outward toward others. They feel self-conscious rather than conscious of self or centered in themselves. They care more about how they appear than how they actually think or feel, more about their image and façade than their true identity. Their capacity for giving and accepting love is impaired, and they tend to limit personal transactions of both giving and receiving.

This process begins with the child's renunciation of the true self, and his or her withdrawal into an emotionally deadened existence is the best adaptation that he or she can make in the struggle to preserve some rudimentary sense of self in the midst of his or her emotional turmoil and fear. However, these patterns of defense tend to persist and become habitual, leading to progressive problems in broad areas of functioning.

Essentially, inwardness involves an insidious process of regarding oneself more as an object than as a person. To varying degrees people block out feelings and emotions in a way that causes them to deviate from the true course of their lives. Each individual develops specific ways of dulling, deadening, and disconnecting from emotions and from life experience.

Inwardness needs to be distinguished from self-reflection, introspection, time spent alone for creative work, meditation, or other spiritual and intellectual pursuits (R. Firestone, 1997b). It is also important to distinguish the real feelings being blocked out from the melodramatic reactions that many people have in relation to personal slights or imagined rejections (R. Firestone, 1997a). What we are describing are genuine feelings rather than role-determined or inappropriately intense emotional reactions to events in one's life. To better understand the narrow focus inherent in living an inward lifestyle, the loss of experience, and the propensity for self-destruction, it is necessary to take an incisive look at the characteristics of the inward person.

CHARACTERISTICS OF AN INWARD PERSON

The first author's concept of *inwardness* describes a syndrome of specific personality traits and behavior patterns that play a central role in all forms of psychopathology. The major characteristics of the inward person are: (a) a loss of feeling and sense of depersonalization, (b) a reliance on addictive, self-nourishing behaviors, (c) isolation and a preference for fantasy gratification over satisfactions derived from real achievements or in an intimate relationship, (d) cynical, suspicious attitudes toward others and self-critical, self-hating attitudes toward oneself, and (e) a lack of a direction in life that leads to a sense of despair and futility, depression, microsuicidal ideation and behavior, and in some extreme cases actual suicide (R. Firestone, 1997b). The overall effect of inwardness contributes to a self-limiting, self-denying, and self-destructive lifestyle.

Personality traits and behaviors can be represented on a continuum ranging from an outward lifestyle of pursuing goals in the real world to an inward lifestyle (R. Firestone, 1997a; R. Firestone & Catlett, 2009; R. Firestone et al., 2003). (See Table 4.1.)

Loss of Feeling and Depersonalization

In accommodating to painful existential realities, most people progressively lose feeling for themselves and for others. This state of nonfeeling is characterized by varying degrees of withdrawal of interest and affect

Table 4.1

OUTWARD VS. INWARD LIFESTYLE

Outward Lifestyle	Inward Lifestyle
Social involvement	Isolation
Active; assertive	Passivity; victimized orientation
Maintaining a separate identity	Seeking a merged identity and fusion
Feeling state	Cutting off or withdrawal of affect; impersonal relating
Goal-directed behavior; self-fulfillment; self-affirmation	Seeking gratification in fantasy; self-denial; self-destructiveness
Lack of self-consciousness; realistic self-appraisal	Hypercritical attitudes toward self
Adaptability	Nonadaptability
Facing up to pain and anxiety with appropriate affect and response	Using substances and routines as painkillers to avoid feeling
Self-fulfillment	Self-denial
Personal sexuality	Impersonal, masturbatory, or addictive sexuality
Searching for meaning and transcending goals	Narrow focus

from others in their interpersonal world. Most people move in and out of an inward posture and present two distinct and separate personalities from one state to the other. When self-protective and withdrawn, they feel estranged from their real selves. In describing this they may say, "I just don't feel like myself" or "I feel so removed." Many people live their lives suspended in this emotionally cut-off, depersonalized condition, feeling little compassion or genuine emotion for long periods. The times that they are in touch with themselves and close to their feelings are more the exception than the rule.

Clinicians and researchers have written extensively about depersonalization when describing some of the more subtle manifestations of the inward, self-protective state. In *Death and Neurosis,* Meyer (1975) differentiated depersonalization from other, more obvious reactions to death anxiety: "In contrast to those forms of defense against fear of death that become manifest as phobias, hypochondriases, obsessional neuroses, and anxiety neuroses, the states of depersonalization signify a flight from reality into the seclusion of no longer being touched—that is, of isolation from affect" (p. 60).

Symptoms of depersonalization may be long-lasting or of brief duration. In an early study, Trueman (1984) found that 34 percent of the normal or nonclinical subjects he interviewed reported depersonalization. According to Trueman: "'Depersonalization' is a state in which an individual experiences ...his feelings, thoughts, memories, or bodily sensations as not belonging to himself. Often there is a feeling of 'strangeness' about oneself, a feeling of this 'not being me,' or a sense of unreality of oneself" (p. 107). Reactions of depersonalization can occur in normal individuals under conditions of stress.

Frey (2003) cited an example of several rescue personnel from the September 11, 2001, terrorist attacks on the World Trade Center and the Pentagon who experienced episodes of depersonalization after a day and a half without sleep.

In narrowing life experience and becoming cut off from genuine feelings and sexual sensations, one gradually eliminates oneself as a feeling person. Within the imagined safety of this restricted existence one is able to maintain a sense of invulnerability, as if retaining some control over death (R. Firestone & Seiden, 1987).

Reliance on Addictive, Self-Nourishing Behaviors

The addictive power of self-nurturing behaviors and routines lies in their ability to reduce tension and block out the highs and lows of the life experience (R. Firestone, 1985). Methods of self-parenting, both nurturing and punishing, are psychologically debilitating and dull one to the realities of existence. They diminish one's awareness of a limitation in time by giving the illusion of being suspended at a certain age or stage of development. Whenever positive events or significant achievements make a person aware of how much there is to lose through death, he or she often becomes anxious and withdraws into a more isolated, inward state and increases the use of addictive substances (R. Firestone, 1985, 1994b).

Negative events or tragedies that are reminders of mortality also trigger the need to soothe and comfort oneself through self-feeding habit patterns. For example, one survey found that there was a significant increase in alcohol consumption in 42 percent of Manhattan residents one week after the 9/11 attacks and also after 6 months (Hasin, Keyes, Hatzenbuehler, Aharonovich, & Alderson, 2007; Vlahov, Galea, Ahern, Resnick, & Kilpatrick, 2004). In another study conducted in Israel where rates of alcohol disorders are low, Schiff, Zweig, Benbenishty, and Hasin (2007) found that physical proximity to a terrorist attack predicted binge drinking in a large sample of adolescents.

In general, addiction to substances, eating disorders, and habitual routines and rituals function to suppress both positive and negative feelings. They help modulate and regulate "intense and painful depressive affects such as feelings of inadequacy, guilt, worthlessness, and hopelessness" (Blatt, McDonald, Sugarman, & Wilber, 1984, p. 163). Meyer (1975) has observed that, unlike obsessive or phobic individuals who are concerned about the future, the addicted person's defense is "aimed at a present lack and not at all concerned with the future or the consequences for the future" (p. 61). The addict believes wholeheartedly in his or her invulnerability to death, which is an extreme manifestation of the pseudo-independent stance expressed as "I can take care of myself. Nothing can happen to me."

At the point where addictive behaviors become associated with a more generalized retreat from the world, they are no longer as acceptable to the person as they were initially, and these behaviors then arouse considerable guilt. Most people become extremely defensive about indulging their addictive habit patterns, their lack of feeling, depersonalization, and inwardness. When they retreat from their external goals and instead seek gratification in substances, objects, or routines, they also suffer from feelings of existential or ontological guilt (R. Firestone, 1987b).

Addiction to Physical Substances: Food, Alcohol, Drugs

For many people food becomes their primary focus and takes on an added meaning other than simple enjoyment and gratification of a physical need. When food is consistently used as a drug or painkiller to minimize painful emotions or existential anxiety, it becomes part of an addictive pattern. Eating disorders, such as repetitive cycles of overeating and dieting, bingeing and purging, or starving oneself, are inward, self-centered, and functionally maladaptive (R. Firestone, 1993). The dynamics involved in eating disorders revolve around the central issues of control, self-parenting, and a pseudo-independent posture toward life, as described in the previous chapter. The same issues are central in drug abuse and alcoholism. It is difficult to break these patterns, because the anxiety allayed by the use of these substances surfaces during withdrawal. The recovering addict is left in a state of disorientation and helplessness and is again faced with the painful realities of his or her life. This includes the awareness of his or her mortality, which had been deadened through the abuse of food, narcotics, or other pain-killing substances.

Addiction to Routines, Rituals, and Repetitive Activities

Repetitive behaviors, routines, and rituals can come to have addictive properties; they tend to dull our sensitivity to painful feelings and lend an air of certainty and permanence to a real life of uncertainty and impermanence. Obsessive thinking and compulsive rituals that temporarily reduce fear and anxiety become habitual and later foster more anxiety. People with OCD imagine that they can control death by guarding and protecting themselves and anticipating all contingencies. In these cases, the denied fear of death, displaced from its source, can become transformed into specific phobias or compulsive, ritualistic behavior. For example, Terror Management researchers Pyszczynski, Solomon, and Greenberg (2003), in describing two studies that involved the raising of death salience in normal individuals and those with phobias and OCD, noted that:

> These findings are consistent with the notion that phobic and obsessive-compulsive individuals transform overwhelming anxiety about death into specific and, hence, controllable fears and obsessive-compulsive activities, respectively. In so doing, they "manage" terror somewhat, but this defensive death-denying shrinking of life to an avoidance of spiders or washing of hands is ultimately limiting and unsatisfying. That is why Yalom [1980] describes mental illness as clumsy death denial. (p. 120)

On a less severe level, and within the normal range of functioning, many people become addicted to routines and personal habits, such as TV watching, video games, Internet browsing, compulsive work patterns, shopping, and exercising. These routines are often perceived as acceptable or even desirable. For example, people use what might otherwise be considered constructive activities to isolate themselves, cut off feelings, and soothe their pain. Many workaholics effectively retreat from their personal lives and intimate relationships, while utilizing rationalizations that justify hard work (R. Firestone, 1993).

Even certain types of sexuality, such as excessive masturbation and impersonal modes of sexual relating, can be used in an addictive manner. Sexual relationships can function as a means of partially gratifying primitive longings for reassurance and security as well as reducing the anxiety about one's finite existence. Over time many couples fall into a routine, automatic style of lovemaking, devoid of affectionate contact or a full sexual response. There is an emphasis on fantasy to increase excitement when the self-gratifying, withholding modes of sexual relating that accompany addictive sexuality come into play. Whenever sex is being used primarily for purposes other than its natural functions of pleasure and procreation, the quality of the sexual relationship generally deteriorates and the participants are left feeling empty (R. Firestone, 1987a, 1990e; R. Firestone et al., 2006).

Isolation and a Preference for Fantasy Gratification Over Satisfaction in Real Life

People who are in a defended, inward state seek isolation and solitude; at the same time, they tend to depend on fantasies to gratify their wants and needs and to escape painful existential realities. It appears that they require seclusion and extended periods of time alone, not for creative or productive work, but as protection against any intrusion into their world of fantasy.

As noted in the previous chapter, fantasy arises early in life in response to a lack of affection, love, and concern in the child's environment (R. Firestone, 1984, 1985). Human beings possess a remarkable capacity for imagination which research has shown can provide partial satisfaction of emotional needs and reduce emotional pain and frustration (R. Firestone & Catlett, 1999; R. Firestone, et al., 2006). People deprived of the ingredients necessary for emotional growth and sustenance during childhood come to rely increasingly on fantasy to relieve interpersonal distress and to escape existential angst. Excessive reliance on fantasy processes, however, tends to be progressively debilitating because it interferes with goal-directed activity in the real world. Many people plan and fantasize yet hesitate in taking action to make their fantasies become a reality. For example, they may postpone taking their dream vacation by procrastinating endlessly, trying to decide where to go and when they can get away, all the while deriving some degree of satisfaction from imagining their future adventure.

To a certain extent, most people avoid pursuing their dreams in actuality because real achievement interferes with the fantasy process, which leaves the individual with a heightened sense of loss of control and feelings of increased vulnerability. This is why most people don't really want what they say they want; they can tolerate gratifications in fantasy or imagination which they are actually intolerant of in real life (R. Firestone, 1985).

Paradoxically, important successes, approval, love, and acknowledgment in actuality can disrupt fantasies and illusions that people have been relying on for a sense of security, safety, and gratification since childhood. On a deeper level the achievement of a meaningful goal makes one acutely aware that nothing lasts forever—except in one's imagination. This explains the person who responds adversely to a significant accomplishment. He or she may react angrily because valued successes arouse anxiety that had previously been effectively repressed (R. Firestone, 1990a). As Eric Hoffer (1955/2006) perceptively said: "We do not really feel grateful to those who make our dreams come true, they ruin our dreams" (p. 97).

People who are inward feel compelled to restrict social interactions and friendships and to avoid potentially meaningful relationships because the real happiness and satisfaction that they might experience would disturb the emotionally deadened, solitary state in which they exist. Some individuals are able to obtain gratification from fantasies alone, while others use selected elements of reality (e.g., an occasional chance meeting with an old friend) to reinforce the illusion of having friendship in their lives (R. Firestone, 1993). In the meantime they continually retreat, disengage, and give up friendships and relationships that were once meaningful to them.

Personal development and the dismantling of neurotic defenses lead people to experience more of the happiness and the pain inherent in living an open life (R. Firestone, 1988, 1994b). As Becker (1973/1997) remarked "Not everyone is as honest as Freud was when he said that he cured the miseries of the neurotic only to open him up to the normal misery of life" (p. 271). When patients expand their life space and begin to pursue more meaningful goals, death anxiety is heightened.

Case Study

Michelle, a 28-year-old social worker, sought professional help because of depression and intense anxiety attacks. At the time, she was overweight and essentially living as a recluse in a large house with her father and younger brother. Michelle took pride in her strength, her invulnerability, and the fact that she could take care of herself without asking anybody for help. She also assumed the full-time care of her brother, which left no time for social activities with her peers or for dating. She spent any spare time in fantasy, dreaming of her future career as an actress. She longed to move to Los Angeles where she could fulfill her dream.

During three years of therapy, Michelle lost 40 pounds and developed into an attractive, sexual woman. In one session she revealed that she had always thought it was food that was crucial for her survival, but now realized that isolation was far more meaningful to her. She felt as though her small bedroom was a safe place where she could be alone and feel warm and secure. "It felt almost like being held by someone." This insight was accompanied by deep sadness.

After therapy, Michelle developed numerous friendships, enjoyed an active social life, and eventually married. Several years later, however, after she and her husband talked about having a baby, she began to suffer from anxiety and depression, feelings she believed she had put behind her. She allowed her looks to deteriorate and regained most of the weight she had lost. Her desire to have a child aroused renewed fears of abandonment, separation, and death.

Michelle's anxiety focused on doubts she had about her ability to be a mother. She projected her self-critical thoughts onto close friends, imagining that *they* thought she would be terrible as a mother. She then began to avoid them and spent more and more time alone, watching TV in her apartment. She began to pull away from her husband and their sexual relationship became nonexistent. Eventually the couple separated and divorced. Over the years she withdrew more and more from her friends and the lively, social life she had once enjoyed.

Now she lives alone, allowing herself only brief interactions with one or two old friends. She is able to fool herself that she still has close friendships and is seemingly unaware of the emotional distance between herself and others. Her sole interest is in attending film festivals, where she vicariously gratifies the dream she has had since childhood—that of being an actress.

This woman's story underscores the compelling nature of an inward defensive lifestyle where isolation is a predominant feature. In spite of significant therapeutic progress, these character defenses tend to persist and worsen over time. Often the so-called cured patient in psychotherapy is not so cured, because when character defenses are not sufficiently worked through, they will continue to influence the personality development of the individual and become increasingly more limiting and destructive.

Cynical Attitudes Toward Others and Critical Thoughts Toward Oneself

People who are inward and self-protective hold on to negative thoughts and attitudes toward themselves and cynical, distrustful attitudes toward others that they developed early in life; both forms of destructive thinking predispose alienation (R. Firestone, 1988). As adults they tend to distort other people and events, responding to them with negative or fearful expectations. Self-depreciating thoughts and cynical attitudes toward other people strongly reinforce the tendency to isolate oneself and to gratify oneself in fantasy. The propensity for being self-critical and/or cynical and distrusting of others originally develops in relation to emotional pain experienced early within the family; however, this tendency is later exacerbated by death anxiety. The following example illustrates how critical attitudes toward oneself act as a defensive barrier in life:

> Craig, 30, lives an isolated existence even though he is a warm, likeable person. He continues to receive numerous invitations from friends to social events although he has consistently declined them in the past. He becomes irritated and even angry when they persist in their overtures. Craig has self-hating thoughts which center around his mistaken belief that he has a strong offensive body odor. He has utilized this delusion to rationalize his self-denial, a pattern he learned early in life. He systematically rejects pleasurable activities and friendships, in effect, saying "no" to himself in much the same way that his father and mother responded to his requests when he was a child. Craig's thoughts of self-degradation and his unfounded beliefs about his physical nature prevent him from having romance in his life and from enjoying close friendships.
>
> As a teenager, Jim, Craig's father, had been an active, adventurous person. However, after marrying and starting a family, he settled down into a comfortable life. He became increasingly cynical and pessimistic and began to eliminate sports and other favorite activities from his life. By the time

he was 40, he had stopped making love with his wife because he believed that he was inadequate as a man and lover. Jim progressively gave up life as he got older, a relatively common defensive reaction to death concerns as people age.

Jim's cynicism manifested itself by his consistent refusal to grant any of his children's requests. He humiliated and shamed them for asking, implying that they were selfish, inconsiderate, and foolish for having needs or desires. In effect, Jim projected his cynical feelings onto his children, and in this way passed on his inward style of living and his cynical attitudes to the next generation.

Defended, inward people usually criticize and attack themselves. However, when they are intolerant of experiencing their self-attacks and self-hatred, they are prone to project these negative attitudes onto others, in particular onto their mates and authority figures. As a result they distort other people and experience them as more angry and critical than they are. They then react with anger and defensiveness, which in turn provokes the other to actually feel angry toward them. Thus, their projections lead to a self-fulfilling prophecy that negatively impacts their relationships, yet maintaining these attitudes provides a distraction in relation to painful realities of life and death.

For example, at the time Walter entered psychotherapy, he was a graduate student living alone on campus. He soon fell in love and became engaged, but this new development disturbed him and caused him intense anxiety. Walter's problem revolved around a deep-seated, almost delusional, form of paranoia, which seemed rooted in the negative thoughts he had about himself. He ruminated over imagined imperfections and attacked himself viciously for his appearance, his work, and his sexual performance. He externalized these self-attacks and projected them onto others, which gave him some relief. However, as a result of these projections, Walter perceived other people as highly critical of him, and even dangerous, and was afraid of physical attack from imagined enemies.

In his therapy sessions, Walter became freer in expressing the anger and negativity that fueled his paranoia. The following excerpt was taken from a session during that period. In free-associating about his doubts and fears, Walter revealed some of the components of his paranoid thinking:

Walter: Hi, Doc, you look cheery this morning. I envy you. I started picking at myself last night, listening to the people upstairs creaking the furniture—like they wanted to bother me, the smug bastards. I really hated them and wanted to kill them. What the fuck are they trying to do to me?

And driving home yesterday, those bastards on the freeway, crawling along—and, you know something, I hate those cars that come up from behind you. You can't trust them—watch your exhaust pipe—maybe those cars are going to ram right into my rear end. Yeah, I know, Doc, that sounds real homosexual and paranoid.

Dr. Firestone: You know, you really sound like you're giving yourself the business this time.

Walter: I really kick myself around, don't I? I sure do. I remember when I was really afraid for you to mention the subject of marriage, and I couldn't even think of it without terror. Hell, now I'm engaged, and I feel great.

In the early stages of therapy, when Walter was deeply troubled, he projected his self-critical thoughts on to other people and feared attacks from them; he rarely talked about death anxiety. However, as he recovered and began to value his life, he not only worried more about his physical health, but also expressed concerns about aging, dying, and death.

A Lack of Direction in Life

Studies have shown that people who suffer loss or trauma early in life often find it difficult, if not impossible, to formulate goals for their personal lives or careers. Even those adults who seemingly had normal childhoods can become disconnected from themselves under stressful circumstances and lose touch with their basic wants and desires. One of the most damaging elements in parent-child relations occurs when parents are so rejecting that they discourage their offspring from wanting anything, as was clear in the story of Jim and his son, Craig. People's goals and their priorities are a basic part of their identity; in retreating from one's wants, one truly does not know who one is. The resulting lack of direction in life is analogous to voyaging on a ship that has no compass or rudder.

The process of progressively relinquishing one's interests and desires over an extended period of time can lead to a state of emptiness and futility, feelings that Orbach (2008) believes contribute to a sense of meaninglessness. This lack of purpose predisposes depressed states, microsuicidal behaviors, and, at the extreme, suicide. Of even more significance, the characteristics and behaviors of individuals who lead inward lives correspond directly to the precursors of suicide as delineated by suicidologists Edwin Shneidman and David Shaffer (R. Firestone, 1997b). Isolation, substance abuse, withdrawal from favored activities and pleasures, strong self-attacking thoughts, a sense of unhappiness and despair, and suicidal thoughts are powerful warning signs of a potential suicide.

On the other hand, when people embrace life and give it value and meaning, they are prone to conscious recurrences of death anxiety (R. Firestone, 1994b). The painful realization of their personal mortality tends to drive them into a more defensive posture in which they relinquish their wants and desires, distance themselves from loved ones, and embark on a general retreat from a purposeful life.

Understanding the effects of death anxiety and realizing the negative consequences of living an inward, defensive lifestyle can help people to avoid some of the pitfalls of this mode of adaptation. It is crucial that people come to identify these dynamics as a first step toward becoming less defended and more alive to their life experience. Admittedly, as people emerge from a self-protective state, they will necessarily be faced with painful truths about their lives. However, despite the fact that inwardness provides some comfort, it is far more effective to deal more openly with life and death concerns. This is because the damage caused by living defensively, whether clinical or subclinical, is far more extensive than many people would like to believe.

THE EFFECTS OF DEFENSIVE REACTIONS TO DEATH ANXIETY ON RELATIONSHIPS

The heightened awareness of death affects the quality of relationships in two principal ways: (1) unconscious death anxiety and subsequent defensive reactions induce a fear of intimacy, which leads to the avoidance of close, feeling, and personal contact; and (2) conscious death awareness is often aroused when there is loving and intimate relating which again leads to distancing behavior. In both cases, death salience has a powerful effect on relationships. Although, as described above, the effect of death awareness is most often reacted to negatively, some individuals are able to use the experience to strengthen their emotional ties and become increasingly loving and respectful in their relationships (R. Firestone, et al., 2003).

People's fear reactions to the awareness of death create a need to control all aspects of their interpersonal world. They try to maintain control by placing limits on what they are willing to give and accept in their intimate relationships. To varying degrees, they ration the amount of affection, tenderness, and sexuality they will accept as well as how much they will give. Many people push away their loved ones by withholding their positive responses and the unique, personal qualities that their partner especially appreciated: often they stop doing a special thing that their partner particularly liked and enjoyed. In general, inward, defensive behavior patterns function to keep loved ones at a distance and also under control (R. Firestone & Catlett, 1999).

When people are the most open and vulnerable to their partners, they often experience feelings of sadness and anxiety about his or her inevitable loss or the loss of themselves. The experience of falling in love, commitment to a relationship, an ongoing, moving, personal dialogue between friends, mates, and one's children make people cognizant that life is precious but must eventually be surrendered (R. Firestone, 1984, 1985). This awareness often surfaces when people are feeling the most tender and loving. They tend to withdraw before the anxiety associated with this newly awakened awareness reaches consciousness.

For example, a couple made plans for a romantic tropical vacation. Both looked forward to a relaxing week and to having long hours for talking and for making love. The first half of the vacation, they lived out their expectations. However, on Friday morning the woman woke depressed and listless and seemed somewhat cool and remote to her partner. Although she attempted to recapture her feelings of excitement, she was clearly uninterested in being sexual or even feeling close and affectionate. Puzzled by her behavior, her partner asked what was going on, but she was unable to think of a reason for her change in mood. After returning home she realized that she had unconsciously pulled away from being close to her lover in anticipation of their going their separate ways at the end of the week. Putting some distance between them had the effect of decreasing this woman's anxiety, yet it ruined the last part of their trip. For many people even the anticipation of a separation following times of special closeness is intolerable because separation symbolizes endings and may even induce feelings of dread concerning the ultimate separation from self and others (R. Firestone, 1984).

Often couples withdraw to a seemingly safer, more comfortable distance as their relationship becomes more meaningful, or after they have made an important commitment to living together, marrying, or starting a family. These relationships often deteriorate, becoming emotionally deadened by habitual contact, fewer personal communications, a decline in sexual activity, or an increase in routine, unfeeling sexual relating. In other cases, where people are less defended and allow peak experiences of love, sex, and personal intimacy to occur, they often react negatively and become more distant causing a good deal of pain in relationships. When fears are awakened, withholding defenses may come into play and men and women stop being playful or having fun; they may allow their looks to deteriorate, shy away from activities they once enjoyed together, are increasingly distant, and sometimes become intimate enemies (R. Firestone & Catlett, 1999).

Reactions like those described above are not restricted to intimate relationships but occur between friends as well.

> One night, Peter, 50, suffered a painful nightmare as he was falling asleep. As he dozed off, he felt like he was actually dying and that everything was over. He woke suddenly, confused about whether it was a dream or reality. He recognized it as the same recurring dream that had haunted him as a boy. When he became an adult this negative experience of death anxiety basically diminished.
>
> In a therapy session, Peter spoke of his nightmare and identified an event that triggered it. Peter had been a successful attorney; however, for the last five years, he had been involved in a business with a close friend. Originally, the two men had enjoyed working together; however, gradually their relationship became more and more strained. In business meetings, Peter became defensive and contentious when he and his friend discussed their ideas and plans. He became so antagonistic that the previous week his partner had initiated a personal conversation to discuss what had happened to their friendship.
>
> When Peter was confronted about his defensiveness, he realized that he had been distorting his friend's comments and had irrationally felt attacked. He recognized that he had been projecting his own self-attacks and criticisms onto his good friend. After their conversation, Peter once again felt close to his friend and more relaxed in his business and personal life. He felt happier than he had for a long time.
>
> However, every night since the conversation with his friend, Peter had his nightmare. Afterward he would lie awake for the rest of the night, plagued by feelings of death anxiety and unable to fall back to sleep. He recognized the connection between the positive developments in his life and the recurrence of his death anxiety.

This man's insight was clear and unusual, yet most people are unaware of the causal relationship between positive experiences in their lives and recurring death thoughts and dreams. They unconsciously maintain a negative psychological equilibrium, precluding important gratifications to avoid experiencing death anxiety.

When personal relationships and friendships are going well and people are investing more of themselves in them, they often experience apprehension regarding inevitable future losses. This was true in another example.

The first author is acquainted with two men whose friendship and camaraderie were based on their mutual interest in business and their spirit of adventure and love of travel. When they first met, one of the men, Bill, was experiencing serious problems in his marriage and the new friendship with Stuart provided him with an objective, empathic listener, for which he was grateful. Several months later Stuart left on a business trip to the Orient, and Bill experienced considerable anxiety. He had an irrational fear that Stuart's plane would crash, or that his friend would encounter some other unforeseen catastrophe. Bill soon recognized that his heightened sense of dread and foreboding was due to the fact that he had invested so much emotionally in the friendship and that his friend meant more to him than he had realized. This story illustrates the link between increased emotional investment and death fears. In this case Bill recognized that his new feelings of friendship had brought about concern for his friend's well-being.

Fearing the loss of a close friend or loved one unconsciously reinforces one's own death anxiety. It is one step removed from primary concerns about one's own life. Some people can tolerate the painful feelings of dread that are aroused by the awareness that a person close to them will eventually die, but they repress the dread about their own death. Most retain unconscious illusions that they will never die despite intellectual awareness to the contrary. They tend to live out their lives accordingly without much feeling, meaning, or purpose.

Similarly, positive experiences that lead to individuation and the sense of being valued and especially chosen have a powerful impact on people's lives in terms of the death anxiety that is aroused. For this reason individuals attempt to modify those experiences rather than go through painful feelings of existential awareness. They accomplish this by withholding positive responses and reacting coldly or with hostility to admiring or loving feelings being directed toward them. Most people are even refractory to simple compliments and brush them aside or react negatively. One of the most paradoxical truths about human beings is that very often the beloved is compelled to reject or even punish the lover who offers affection, tenderness, and sexual gratification. People usually will not permit the reality of being loved and admired to disrupt their psychological equilibrium of their defensive solution to the existential dilemma (R. Firestone & Catlett, 1999).

> Geraldine, 24, an attractive, vivacious young woman, revealed that recently she has been disturbed by thoughts and dreams about death and children dying. She commented that as a child, teenager, and young adult, she felt proud of the fact that she wasn't afraid of death; in fact, she had rarely thought about it at all.
>
> Recently, developments in Geraldine's personal life and career have brought her much gratification. She has a loving relationship with her husband that has made her happier than at any other time in her life. She derives much satisfaction in her career as a child care specialist, where she offers the ideal combination of psychological expertise, knowledge, and compassion in the treatment program she helped establish for troubled children.
>
> She recently realized that more choices were opening up to her in her professional life. Her husband encouraged her to seriously consider the new position being offered her, where her work would have an even broader impact on children and families. Geraldine was excited to accept this higher level position. She revealed that she felt freer in her life than she ever imagined was possible.
>
> The night before Geraldine was to assume the new position, she had a horrifying nightmare and woke up to the sound of her own crying. She lay awake for hours but could remember only fragments of the dream's content. She did recall that two of the children under her care were in danger of drowning. She desperately wanted to save them and was tortured when she could not. In the dream she could only stand by, watching helplessly as the children sank beneath the surface of the water. The next night, she was tormented by a similar nightmare. During the day, she was obsessed with morbid thoughts about death. Sometimes she found herself preoccupied with thoughts about her husband dying of a terminal illness. What would she do then? Or she had thoughts about herself. In her mind she saw herself trying to leap from a train that was speeding toward certain disaster, bringing death to everyone aboard, including her.
>
> Geraldine grew distant from her husband and her relationship with him suffered until she talked about these dreams and thoughts with her therapist. She noticed that after having an especially close sexual experience with her husband, she would pull away sharply and preoccupy herself with household chores and practicalities of her job. She also recognized that almost immediately after making love she would have fleeting thoughts: "What does it matter how good you feel right now? You're going to lose him in the end anyway. Just protect yourself."

Counseling helped Geraldine to connect her nightmares to her career success, promotion, and good feelings about her life. In relation to her husband, she realized that the preciousness of the relationship reminded her of her potential loss of him through death. She saw that she was altering her life in a negative way to avoid these death concerns.

In response to their fears about death, people unconsciously seek ways to avoid love and sexuality in an intimate relationship. Their philosophy of life includes cynical attitudes toward loved ones, such as the types of thoughts that Geraldine experienced: "Don't be vulnerable! You're just going to get hurt!"

As described earlier, the first author's clinical experience has shown that people not only react to unusual positive events with defensive reactions to death awareness, but obviously they also react to negative events. Whereas the latter is more acceptable, the former is more counter-intuitive and therefore usually denied as the trigger mechanism (R. Firestone, 1990a).

For example, one evening Todd and his wife were particularly romantic and loving. At the end of the evening, before going to sleep, they watched the docudrama *Shadowlands* on television. The film tells the compelling story of C. S. Lewis's romance and marriage during his later years to a young, attractive poet from America. As the film ends, Lewis is devastated by his grief and mourning over his wife's unexpected death.

Todd, an outgoing, affectionate man who was very much in love with his wife, a younger woman, identified closely with Lewis. At the point in the film where Lewis's beloved wife dies, Todd felt a surge of deep sadness, imagining the emptiness of his life should his wife die; he had never pictured her dying before him. The next morning Todd was uncharacteristically cool and aloof and pulled away from his wife's embrace and tended to be remote during the next week. Later, in a therapy session, Todd recognized he had reacted adversely to the reminder of death illustrated in the film. Unlike Todd, most people have no conscious awareness of this process; they tend to act out these patterns and provoke distance in their relationships without meaning to. Typically there is then a corresponding reaction from their mate, which leads to a downward spiral in the relationship.

Todd's response is not gender-specific. As we have seen, both women and men tend to react in a similar manner when unconscious fears of death are aroused in the course of everyday life. Although less common than these negative reactions, some people respond positively to a heightened sense of death awareness, aroused either by positive or negative events, and use it to deepen a sense of meaning in their lives and enhance their investment in living.

One man in particular comes to mind in this regard. After having a nightmare where he is suddenly face-to-face with a terrifyingly vivid image of his impending death (a nightmare that he has experienced at different times since adolescence), he becomes even more committed to the core projects in his life that are meaningful to him and give purpose to his life. He finds himself feeling even more deeply the love and tenderness he has toward his wife and cherishes each moment spent with his children. Whether he is reminded of his mortality by his recurring nightmare or when he feels a poignant sadness about the future loss of his loved ones and himself, he feels more loving in general and feels more appreciation for his life.

In another case, Diane, a woman who usually reacted to close, romantic sexual experiences with her husband by becoming critical and remote from him, sought professional help in an effort to improve the relationship and become more tolerant and accepting of his love. She recognized that her reactions were related in some way to fears and superstitions she had about something happening to him and their children. In one session Diane free-associated about the subject and was encouraged to say anything that came to her mind. She spoke about her outrage and feelings about the death issue—the hopelessness of the situation, the inevitability of losing her husband, the concerns about her children's lives being lost, and the despair about her own death. The therapist encouraged her to let out her feelings. Diane responded to the suggestion and at times her expression of emotion reached a primal level. She screamed out loudly in frustration, rage, and sadness about the fate that awaited her and her loved ones. When her emotion was exhausted, she reported feeling immediately relieved and in an entirely different, more positive frame of mind.

The following week Diane spoke about her reactions to the session and described how she felt since she unleashed her powerful feelings:

> Diane: I've felt so relaxed, probably more relaxed than I have in a long time. I still have some anxiety; my awareness of death is definitely still there but I feel different. This week, I've felt so much closer to my husband, which is actually a real improvement for me. Usually it scares me to have any feelings for him when I think about this subject, but now I feel stronger, more adult. I felt so much love for him this week.

Before, when I had feelings about death, I would focus on a lot of different scenarios of how it could happen. I'd think to myself, "Oh, my God, this could happen in a car accident or something terrible could happen to the kids." Now it's more a sad, deep feeling about existence, and of knowing that my children are going to go through the pain that I'm going through—the knowledge that they're going to die. It's just a very deep feeling that's different from being morbid. I feel like I've been much more vulnerable to my husband, and really letting him love me and really loving him back. In just feeling the love and the tenderness, the companionship, then a very deep, sad feeling comes over me. But it passes and I feel happier than ever.

We have found that people who openly face the issues of death and dying and feel the anxiety and sadness about their finite existence, as Diane did in the weeks and months following her session, tend to experience richer, fuller lives.

THE EFFECTS OF DEFENSIVE REACTIONS TO DEATH ANXIETY AT THE SOCIETAL LEVEL

Defensive reactions to death anxiety on the part of the individual are combined with others to form a significant aspect of culture (R. Firestone, 1996, 1997a). These socially validated mores, rituals, and institutions in turn continually reinforce the defenses each person employs to protect against the fear of death. Ernest Becker (1973/1997) called attention to this interaction between the individual and society:

> Everything that man does in his symbolic world is an attempt to deny and overcome his grotesque fate. He literally drives himself into a blind obliviousness with social games, psychological tricks, personal preoccupations so far removed from the reality of his situations that they are forms of madness—agreed madness, shared madness, disguised and dignified madness, but madness all the same. (p. 27)

Neil Elgee (2004) also emphasized how society functions to support each individual's illusions and myths about personal immortality: "All viable cultures, whether religious or secular, are 'sacred' at their root because they provide meaningful answers to the otherwise threatening questions of existence" (p. 292).

It is important to explore how society reinforces the defensive, inward lifestyle, conformity, and conventionality of its members, an unconscious conspiracy that effectively destroys the democratic process. Democracy depends on an intelligent, informed, free-thinking independent populace. Fused identity and blind submission to group identification, over-dependence, and hero worship of leaders, together with susceptibility to psychologically based manipulations that offer respite from fear, combine to make true democracy an impossibility.

The acute awareness of the inevitability of death has the potential to create two opposing desires in human beings. It can motivate people to become more fully engaged with life, to continue to challenge and develop themselves as unique individuals, and to attempt to contribute something of significance to family and/or community. More often the accompanying anxiety they experience about death and dying generates powerful needs in people to become securely embedded in a collective social order (McCoy, Pyszczynski, Solomon, & Greenberg, 2000). The sense of being alone, on one's own, and standing out from the crowd evokes existential fears. In his writings on self-actualization and individuation, Maslow (1971) emphasized this truth: "We fear our highest possibilities (as well as our lowest ones). We are generally afraid to become that which we can glimpse in our most perfect moments" (p. 34).

McCoy et al. (2000) have also called attention to the link between the fear of individuation and the fear of death in explaining why most people find it impossible to sustain a genuinely creative, individualistic way of being and living: "Independence from social consensus, creation of a truly individualized worldview, and a broad concern for all humankind are difficult to achieve" (p. 58).

Many children grow up in families where the parents exert excessive control through rules and prohibitions that demand blind obedience and conformity. In these families the satisfaction of children's needs for survival, security, affection, and love is contingent upon their unquestioning loyalty to their parents, whether it is deserved or not. Thus throughout their lives, they are easily influenced and manipulated by other people. They have been successfully programmed to be selfless, that is, to accommodate to the wishes, demands, and opinions of others at their own expense (R. Firestone & Catlett, 1999). Becker (1973/1997) cited Fritz Perls in arguing that the resultant conformity is part of a neurotic process that destroys critical thinking, yet people are mostly unaware of their conformity and submission. Fritz Perls's ideas support this view. Perls:

> Conceived the neurotic structure as a thick edifice built up of four layers. The first two layers are the everyday layers, the tactics that the child learns to get along in society by the facile use of words to win approval and to placate others and move them along with him: these are the glib, empty talk, "cliché[,]" and role-playing layers. Many people live out their lives never getting underneath them. (p. 57)

Individuality and nonconformity require unusual courage and dedication because there is always guilt and fear from breaking with tradition. It increases one's sense of aloneness, loneliness, and sense of isolation; and, in addition, there are significant prejudices, repercussions, and retaliation directed toward an outsider with different views. The uniqueness and free expression of the nonconformist threaten the conventional person because they raise existential anxiety.

Becker (1973/1997) and Fromm (1941) pointed out that most individuals seek an *ultimate rescuer* or idolized hero, whether within a personal relationship, in the entertainment, sports, or music world, or in the business or political sphere. People who are more submissive or conforming in their orientation transfer the desperate feelings and dependency needs that originally characterized their relationship with their parents onto new figures and ideologies and thus feel relief from existential fears. They are especially susceptible to the influence of charismatic, authoritarian leaders who promise them certainty and safety.

The authors contend that the fear of death drives individuals to support destructive, toxic leaders and embrace patriotic, nationalistic movements in a search for security and immortality. Dependence on a particular group, idolization of a leader, and mindless allegiance to a cause function as defenses against death anxiety (R. Firestone & Catlett, 2009). In her book *The Allure of Toxic Leaders,* Lipman-Blumen (2005) emphasized the fact that many destructive and ineffective leaders remain in power because they fulfill basic needs of their constituents or followers:

> The real tragedy of the human condition is not that we must die, but that we choose to live by illusions.... Illusions are the umbilical cord linking

leaders and followers. Leaders understand their followers' need for illusions.... In a terrifyingly uncertain world, the illusions that leaders spin
offer us a lifeline. They free the other side of our natures—the creative,
thoughtful, spiritual side—permitting even us small, short-lived creatures
to become significant figures in the grand universe. (pp. 50–51)

By subordinating their views to those propagated by an idolized
leader and by conforming to the group consensus, frightened individuals
merge their identities with that of the group. This imagined fusion imbues
them with a feeling of immortality and invulnerability. They imagine that
although they may not survive as separate individual entities, they will
live on as part of something larger that *will* continue to exist after they are
gone (R. Firestone, 1996; R. Firestone & Catlett, 2009).

Ultimately people living within a functional democracy are account-
able for their government's policies, for the goals that their leaders pursue, for the actions taken on their behalf, and most importantly, for the
means their leaders use to achieve these ends. Unfortunately, there will
always be a large number of individuals who seek out irresponsible, toxic
leaders in an attempt to compensate for their own failings and dependency needs and to protect them from facing their aloneness and personal mortality (Lipman-Blumen, 2005; J. Post, 2004).

Terror Management researchers, in their vigorous study of the effect
of death salience on human attitudes and behavior, have empirically ver-
ified aspects of Ernest Becker's theoretical formulation. Their experimental design involves the comparison of two control groups; one that is
exposed to words that are designed to subtly arouse death salience, and
one that is not. The researchers then observe how each group responds
to various issues. (See meta-review in Solomon et al., 2004.)

Their findings indicate that after subjects were presented with the
word *death* subliminally in an experimental setting, they more strongly
endorsed the worldview of their own ethnic group or nation; at the same
time they denigrated members of other groups whose worldviews dif-
fered from their own. Other studies showed that people tend to be more
moralistic toward people whose behavior conflicts with society's social
or moral codes. For example, judges whose death awareness was raised
set higher bails on prostitutes than judges in the control group. These
reactions were also evident at the behavioral level: subjects whose death
salience was elevated administered larger amounts of an aversive substance to people of a religious denomination and ethnic background different than their own.

These reactions to unconscious stimuli may also affect political choices. For example, two recent studies, post-9/11, found that subjects in the high death awareness group favored a candidate whom they perceived as charismatic and who insisted on an aggressive agenda toward their enemies over one who urged a more diplomatic path (F. Cohen, Ogilvie, Solomon, Greenberg, & Pyszczynski, 2005; F. Cohen, Solomon, Maxfield, Pyszczynski, & Greenberg, 2004).

If the single word *death* introduced subliminally in an experiment can produce significant changes in subjects' attitudes and actions, one can only imagine the powerful effect of countless events in the real world that remind people of their mortality (R. Firestone, 1988). Witnessing a horrible accident on the freeway, or watching the fatalities of war on the evening news, or hearing about the death of a friend or famous person are reminders that seriously impact the nature of the sensitive human being. Even though we have become habituated and desensitized to the visual images of tragedy that we are exposed to everyday, these images still have a profound influence on our unconscious minds and significantly alter our motivations and behaviors.

CONCLUSION

The ideal defense against death anxiety is to relinquish desire and wanting in favor of a self-protective stance that cuts off feeling for one's self and denies the need for affiliation with others. Instead the person relies primarily on fantasy gratification. We imagine that if we deny our wants we can no longer be hurt or rejected. This inward posture of relinquishing our priorities is particularly applicable when dealing with the issue of death and dying. In a magical way eliminating life precludes death.

An inward, isolated orientation to life leads to a severe restriction of give-and-take interactions. This posture feels safe but is actually far more dangerous and uncomfortable in the long run. This form of defensive adaptation is perilous because in seeking isolation and self-nurturance, we are maximally exposed to destructive voices and self-attacks. In parenting ourselves, we relive a pattern of rejection that was internalized in childhood. The person essentially reexperiences his or her past instead of living in the present, and the process of looking inward leaves him or her maladapted in coping with the exigencies of life.

In relation to death anxiety, giving up life prematurely acts as a powerful defense that negatively affects relationships and career and increasingly restricts one's comfort zone. In retreating from life, a person cannot maintain integrity, and he or she will be duplicitous in his or her communications. This form of defensiveness becomes a moral issue when our defenses lead to the hurt and rejection of others (R. Firestone & Catlett, 2009).

Most people progressively give up the only life that they have to make death more tolerable. By the time they reach old age or even middle age, many people have effectively reduced their life to a repetitive, petty, humdrum, role-playing existence.

Altering the defensive barriers to the evolution of self offers a far more positive eventuality. In the examined life there is the possibility of powerful changes that involve a movement toward a meaningful existence. The human experience can involve genuine love and compassion, empathy, kindness, and joyfulness in being, as well as sad and painful issues of aging, disillusionment, deterioration, and mortality.

5 Literal and Symbolic Defenses Against Death Anxiety

The knowledge of death is reflective and conceptual, and animals are spared it. They live and they disappear with the same thoughtlessness: a few minutes of fear, a few seconds of anguish, and it is over. But to live a whole lifetime with the fate of death haunting one's dreams and even the most sun-filled days—that's something else. . . . I believe that those who speculate that a full apprehension of man's condition would drive him insane are right, quite literally right.

—Ernest Becker, The Denial of Death *(1973/1997, p. 27)*

LITERAL IMMORTALITY

Denial is the major defense against death anxiety, and there are two basic forms of death denial: literal and symbolic. Literal denial manifests itself in religion or religiosity and is the key defense that negates the obvious scientific conclusion that human beings die like other species and that there is no scientific proof of an afterlife. Monotheistic religious beliefs as well as some pantheistic or monistic spiritual traditions offer the believer various forms of literal immortality (Clark, 2002) (Note 1). Symbolic defenses relate to living on through one's creative productions, investment in causes, and one's children. One imagines leaving a legacy or imprint that lives on after one dies.

The authors have emphasized that death anxiety impacts the child at a relatively young age, that the awareness has considerable consequences, and that the unbearable pain is repressed and relegated to the unconscious (R. Firestone, 1994b). Thereafter, it takes many defensive forms. In the unconscious, associations are not bound by the usual logic and there is a kind of magical thinking in relation to psychological pain and death anxiety, which is part denial and part wish fulfillment. The fantasy processes of connection to our all-powerful parents that once assured us of survival and immortality have been expanded to monotheistic belief systems. These have led to a socially shared magical conclusion that there is a God in the sky or heavens that acts much like a parental figure. According to scripture, *He* rewards and punishes us for following or not following his lead, and in this regard fits the psychological profile of an immature, authoritarian father figure. If followers are obedient and behave, that is, if they adhere to a particular belief structure, then they will somehow be saved; but if they misbehave they will be brutally punished. In the Christian creation myth, God punished Adam and Eve for ignoring his command to not eat from the Tree of Knowledge by evicting them from the Garden of Eden and depriving them of everlasting life (Pagels, 1988, 2003).

The Old Testament story of Job provides another example of God's parental, punitive nature meted out even to his believers. In this story God makes a wager with Satan that no matter how much adversity, devastation, and death God inflicts on Job, he (Job) will still hold fast to his beliefs and will remain God's faithful servant. What follows is an endless succession of tragedies imposed on Job by God. First, Job learns that all of his oxen, sheep, and camels have been stolen and his servants murdered. Next, a messenger tells him that all his children have been killed by a great wind. Lastly, Job develops boils "from the sole of his foot to his crown," yet he refuses to speak out against God despite his sorrow, despair, and misery. The story of Job's maintaining his faith is a testament to one man's conviction, but it is not a credit to the deity that put him to the test (Job 1:13–22, 2:7–10; King James Version).

Faced with death anxiety, human beings have projected an all-powerful parent on to God and imbued Him with very human qualities, even negative attributes, in a defensive effort to achieve a modicum of comfort. As such, organized religion has been a major social defense against the fear of death and dying. Religious dogma and ritual continually function to reduce death anxiety. When there is an increase in fear, there is a concomitant increase in ritual and other defensive behaviors as well as in aggression toward those with different beliefs or rituals (Arndt, Greenberg, Pyszczynski, & Solomon, 1997; Greenberg, Pyszczynski, Solomon, Simon, & Breus, 1994; Pyszczynski, Greenberg, & Solomon, 1999; Simon et al., 1997).

Yet such is the power of magical thinking that even if one is not religious or is a nonbeliever, and consciously knows that he or she will ultimately die, this individual may still unconsciously harbor a sense of immortality. This is manifested through elaborate fantasies of connection to persons, places, groups, organizations, institutions, and ideologies. In relation to fantasies of fusion with other persons, Hart and Goldenberg (2008) observed that "As Becker suggested, the modern era seems to have ushered in a spirituality of romantic love, an explicitly human-attachment-related solution to merge with others.... Modern psychodynamic research shows that people use romantic relations to protect themselves from the fear of death" (pp. 107–108). Furthermore, self-nurturing routines and habit patterns act as rituals to facilitate death denial and preserve the magical belief that one will never die. Indeed orthodox nonbelievers, even died-in-the-wool atheists, hold on to many of these unconscious illusions. These illusions are evidenced during those times that nonbelievers suffer irrational levels of pain and aggression, whenever their self-soothing routines and fantasies of survival are disrupted or challenged.

Reincarnation is another widespread belief system that relates to a literal negation of ending and death. This belief system takes many forms, but all systems fall short of offering the full comfort we desire. For, even if we believe that we will be reborn, how can we take full comfort at the thought of losing all we love in this life, including loved ones, treasured experiences, and the wisdom we have spent a lifetime developing?

Over many millennia, conventional religious ideologies from both Western and Eastern societies have contributed to the denial or negation of death (R. Firestone, 1994b). While they relieve death anxiety or assure an afterlife, they also reinforce the tendencies to denigrate and move away from bodily concerns and pleasures or to obliterate all desire and ego. Typically, Western religious belief systems offer the hope of a life after death, but immortality is achieved at the cost of forsaking a real life in the present, a trade-off of the body that must die for the surviving soul. "Alive sensual fulfillment and the capacity for genuine feeling may become a willing sacrifice in exchange for a disconnected life of the mind that has no flesh or physical component and therefore cannot be lost. In that sense the disembodied life offers the promise of immortality" (R. Firestone et al., 2003, p. 379).

In a discussion of the historical development of Western and Eastern religious ideologies, Moore and Williamson (2003) wrote:

> Christians of the Middle Ages gave themselves over to the reality of death by associating the death of the body with the freeing of the spirit to spend eternal life with God. Religious systems of the Eastern world evolved ideas of continual rebirth and the attainment of freedom from the cycle of rebirth through enlightenment or nirvana. (p. 4)

In recent years, there has been a renewal of nondenominational spirituality, a *new-age* movement in which approximately 20 percent of Americans are involved (Armstong, 2006; Barnia, 1996; Kyle, 1993) (Note 2). In describing this movement Armstrong observed: "Since the late 1970s there has been a spiritual revival in many parts of the world, and the militant piety that we often call 'fundamentalism' is only one manifestation of our postmodern search for enlightenment" (p. xvi). According to Neimeyer (2008), many of the more recent spirituality movements emphasize "the prospects for transcendence of existential isolation in the face of death through cultivation of relatedness to others (as in the work of Buber or Levinas) or to a sense of oneness with the natural world (as in the work of Brown or Wilber)" (p. 2).

Often having no holy text or dogma, many of the adherents of the new spirituality, seeking a more personal faith, have incorporated certain aspects of new-age thinking into their traditional religious belief systems. Most commonly they adhere to the teachings of a particular guru or spiritual leader. They believe, for example, in the idea that God exists everywhere including within oneself. According to Hart and Goldenberg (2008) many of these modern spiritual traditions, as well as some Eastern belief systems, offer the individual the promise or hope of "the merging of the spiritual self with the ultimate pantheistic reality" (p. 104). Others, in an outgrowth of the human potential movement of the 1970s, use alternative methods to help them attain an advanced level of spirituality or self-transcendence. These include channeling, astrology, and contemplative practices, such as meditation, holistic medicine, and metaphysical or post-metaphysical spirituality, based on nondualistic thinking. (See discussion of spiritual teachings of Martin Buber, Emmanuel Levinas, Ken Wilber, and Paul Tillich in "Existentialism and Death Attitudes," Tomer & Eliason, 2008, pp. 17–22.)

Observing early attempts of psychotherapists to combine religion and therapy into a new-age spirituality, Becker (1973/1997) emphasized the illusory, defensive nature of the movement:

> The psychotherapeutic religionists are claiming…that the life force can miraculously emerge from nature, can transcend the body it uses as a vehicle, and can break the bounds of human character.… Many of the leading figures in modern thought slip into some such mystique, some eschatology of immanence in which the insides of nature will erupt into a new being. (p. 276)
>
> It can all be summed up in the simplest and sharpest terms: how can an ego-controlled animal change his structure; how can a self-conscious creature change the dilemma of his existence? There is simply no way to transcend the limits of the human condition or to change the psychological structural conditions that make humanity possible. (pp. 276–277)

Religious teachings, originally intended to enhance the spiritual aspects of life, have instead supported self-sacrificing orientations that encourage the denial of the body and the ego. For example, when St. Augustine postulated that death was the punishment for Adam's act of disobedience in the Garden of Eden, he proposed that if one denied sexual desire and bodily pleasures, one's soul could triumph over the body and survive death (Pagels, 1988) (Note 3). Similarly, many people have adopted the teachings of Taoism and Buddhism and have assumed that all desire, striving, ego must be given up if one is to attain enlightenment (Suzuki, Fromm, & DeMartino, 1960; Watts, 1961) (Note 4).

Nevertheless, the question remains, why do millions of people automatically follow religious dogma and new-age visionaries? As noted, transcendence over the body which must die, the postulation of a soul or spirit, and the union with a powerful being are primary motivations. "To use a spiritual teaching (whether of a god or a Buddha) to procure an absolute, unqualified security in the face of a realistically uncertain future often destroys the inherent value and meaning of that teaching" (R. Firestone, 1994b, p. 233).

Paradoxically, religious dogmatism supports self-limitation and self-abrogation, leading to the restriction or suppression of people's natural desires and feelings, which in turn contributes to an increase in violence and immorality (Prescott, 1975; Vergote, 1978/1988). Moreover, religious philosophies that equate thought with action are in essence a form of thought control. These judgmental values lead to guilt and suppression that play a significant part in psychological maladies (R. Firestone & Catlett, 2009).

Although the church and religious dogma are associated with morality, in reality, these beliefs have often led to immorality. Indeed, many people believe that without the moral rules of a sacred text to guide them, human beings would naturally revert to living unethical, immoral lives. However, many modern philosophers, notably Peter Singer (1993), argue that morality exists separate from religion: "Ethics is not something intelligible only in the context of religion" (p. 3). E. O. Wilson (1998) agrees, asserting his belief that "moral values come from human beings alone, whether or not God exists" (para. 4).

In terms of immoral acts, the warlike tendencies of religious groups vary. Some groups (e.g., certain fundamentalist factions of Christian, Jewish, and Islamic religions) have an aggressive approach to upholding their beliefs, whereas others (e.g., Buddhism, Taoism, and Hinduism) generate far less animosity and are more peace-loving and tolerant toward people of different persuasions. Religious dogma that is rigid, restrictive, and inflexible instills strong hatred and malice in believers toward nonbelievers (R. Firestone, 1996). Some religious factions endorse individual sacrifice in war as a tenet of their doctrine: a heroic death in a religious war offers guaranteed entry into the afterlife (Brooks, 2002; Bukay, 2006).

The first author's view regarding the issue of morality and religion is that the average religious person benefits morally from his or her religious convictions and does not constitute a threat to other individuals and their beliefs. However, when collectively mobilized and manipulated by misguided or, worse yet, corrupt leaders of the church or community at large, they have been responsible for acts of cruelty, prejudice, ethnic cleansing, and warfare that throughout history have constituted a major threat to civilized life. Nevertheless, even when the practice of religion has not manifested an aggressive component, there is a price to pay for fantasies and illusions that avoid death anxiety. There is a tendency to retreat from or postpone gratifications in this life in favor of an afterlife and a tendency to renounce the body and sexuality. The condemnation of our natural animal nature and the shame and guilt about nudity and sexuality have led to increased aggression, sexual problems, and varied forms of sexual dysfunction (R. Firestone et al., 2006). In our clinical research, most people have sustained some degree of sexual guilt and sexual problems in their development; these include critical attitudes toward their bodies, self-consciousness and doubts about sexual performance, gender concerns, and a generalized retreat from sexuality.

The authors believe that true morality would be an inherent characteristic of human beings were they not damaged in their formative years (R. Firestone & Catlett, 2009; Hauser, 2006). Unethical behavior, human rights violations, both personal and organizational, and power plays are consequences of destructive child-rearing practices and the resulting psychopathology. Morality need not be paired with religious belief systems and can be established in a humanistic context. Facing and accepting death squarely and maintaining a sad, poignant feeling about one's life and death foster a feeling of compassion and humanity toward others.

SYMBOLIC IMMORTALITY

The first author has described symbolic immortality as a way of imagining extending one's life and meaning through defenses such as: living on through one's works, living on through one's children, vanity (imagining one's life being spared because of one's specialness), and the accumulation of power and wealth.

Living On Through One's Works

A number of theorists, including Robert Lifton, conceptualize creativity as a mode of symbolic immortality. In his writing, Lifton (1979) has emphasized the continuity of artistic creation through time and quotes Jacques Choron's assertion that artistic creation is the means by which "not the individual, but man, human continuity, reveals itself.... More than any other activity, art escapes death" (p. 21) (Note 5). Lifton goes on to say: "Similarly, each scientific investigator becomes part of an enterprise larger than himself, limitless in its past and future continuity. Whatever his additional motivations—the need to know and the quest for personal glory and reward—he operates within a framework of larger connectedness" (p. 21).

Creative contributions, as a mode of symbolic immortality, may also be manifested in dedication to a life of service and helping others. Physicians, psychotherapists, and social workers can derive satisfaction in knowing that they are having a healing or a positive effect on people.

According to Lifton (1979), caregivers often feel that their therapeutic efforts exert beneficial influences which "carry forward indefinitely in the lives of patients and clients and *their* children or posterity. Consequently, any sense on the part of care-givers that those efforts are ineffective can set off in them deep anxieties about ultimate personal questions" (p. 22).

Other theorists, including Becker, Rank, and Yalom, acknowledge the obvious limitations to this mode of symbolic immortality, as when people are driven by the desperate need to utilize their talents, their work, and their dedication to others as a way of ensuring their eternal life. The illusion that one can truly live on through one's creative works, whether in art, literature, or science, is doomed to failure.

The authors agree with Lifton in one sense: there *is* a thread or an interconnectedness in people's life stories and contributions, which survives after they are gone. The vision of an unending chain of beautiful statues, sculptures, art works, and literature from the past that still exist to inspire people the world over does offer a certain degree of satisfaction. However, the notion of symbolically living on through a tangible or material piece of work fails to allay people's core anxieties when contemplating the finality of death, the separation from their imaginative powers, and the cessation of their conscious awareness as they know it. In reality there is no living on through our creative endeavors or service to humanity. In fact the work that is the closest to us during our lives is separated from us in death.

On a personal level, my idea of living on through my own works, art, and books, was shattered at the death of R. D. Laing. Ronnie and I had known each other through our writings and personal communications but became very close friends shortly before his death. Although we had grown up and spent our lives on opposite sides of the Atlantic Ocean, we were on the same wavelength. In St. Tropez, less than two months after our first meeting in Austria and subsequent sailing together in the Mediterranean, this brilliant, extraordinary, and lovable man collapsed and died in my arms. There he lay, the empty shell of the man who had made an outstanding contribution to the world. In spite of all his accomplishments, now he was just a piece of meat. At that moment, any notion that I might live on through my works was completely demolished. One minute he was clever, alive, funny, competing on the tennis court, and the next minute, the unique person that he had been only a moment before had completely disappeared forever. In the days that followed, I wrestled with the irony of the horrific event that deprived me of the camaraderie I had known. Certainly, his life and work will be remembered and valued, but this fact, in his present state, is of little or no consequence; it bears only an illusory relationship to his mortality.

Nevertheless, simply using creative works as a defense against death anxiety does not exclude the possibility that the desire to make such a contribution can also be an integral part of the search for meaning in life. The sense of purpose and transcendent goals has considerable value. Because human beings are capable of deep feeling, logic, and symbolism, they need to seek authentic personal meaning in their lives through their relationships, children, work, and creativity (R. Firestone et al., 2003). There are many diverse paths that lead to finding an endeavor that lends significance and purpose to one's life: artists, writers, poets, and musicians find meaning in self-expression; others through serving people; and still others by contributing to a humanitarian cause or to policies that will improve the lives of future generations. These causes are usually personally gratifying and represent a contribution to others. Their function as a defense against death anxiety is limited, but their true value to humankind is limitless.

Living On Through One's Children

According to Lifton (1979), gene survival, the "biological mode of immortality, is epitomized by family continuity, living on through—psychologically speaking, *in*—one's sons and daughters and their sons and daughters, with imagery of an endless chain of biological attachment. This has been the most fundamental and universal of all modes" (p. 18). In our experience with the longitudinal study, the authors observed that the birth of a child affects parents in conflicting ways. In one sense children represent a symbolic victory over death by perpetuating one's identity into the future, a concept referred to as *gene survival*. By transmitting their beliefs, attitudes, vocational skills, and other types of cultural knowledge to their offspring, people establish a sense of connection to the future. Support for this position can be found in Terror Management research where reminders of death led to increased scores on a measure of the importance of the biological mode of symbolic immortality (Mikulincer & Florian, 2000).

At the same time, however, children are a source of existential threat to parents because genuine experiences of emotional closeness to children reawaken feelings of separateness and evoke annihilation anxiety. In becoming a parent, especially a first-time parent, one senses that this step into adulthood represents another turn of the wheel of time, so to speak, a turn that brings one even closer to old age and death (R. Firestone & Catlett, 2009).

Parents' proprietary attitudes (i.e., the notion that children belong to their biological parents) are driven by the need to shape the child into the right kind of legacy. These attitudes are further supported when parents adopt conventional parenting roles that protect them against the death anxiety evoked by experiencing authentic interactions with their children. Both parents and children imagine that this *belonging* or merger somehow imbues them with immortality. Rank (1936/1972) intuitively sensed that this belief existed in children and that it led to guilt in separating from their parents and developing their unique personalities.

> The problem of the neurosis itself is a separation problem and as such a blocking of the human life principle, the conscious ability to endure release and separation, first from the biological power represented by parents, and finally from the lived out parts of the self which this power represents, and which obstruct the development of the individual personality. It is at this point that the neurotic comes to grief, where, instead of living, of overcoming the past through the present, he becomes conscious that he dare not, cannot, loose himself because he is bound by guilt.... In these guilt reactions, the problem of separation shows itself as related to the problem of difference. (pp. 73–74)
>
> The biological power represented by parents referred to by Rank is the special transcendental quality that parents hold out to their children—that is, the possibility of triumphing over death by merging with them. This illusion of fusion is costly, however, because, as Rank emphasized, the child...feels too guilty to individuate and live his or her own life. (R. Firestone et al., 2003, p. 195)

Society strongly supports parents' assumption that they have proprietary rights over their children.

This particular defense against death anxiety has further costs. Children are able to relieve or buffer parents' death anxiety only if the children adopt the cultural worldview or religious beliefs of their parents. Children who are too dissimilar from their parents may actually be an added source of existential concern. The child who chooses not to carry on the family business or who embraces a different religious, political, or sexual orientation not only negates the possibility of the biological mode of symbolic immortality but also poses a threat to the validity of the parents' cultural worldview, which also serves as a buffer against death anxiety (Note 6).

Movement toward self-differentiation often arouses survivor guilt in adolescents and adults who manifest these differences from their parents. "Indeed, a common response to 'survivor guilt' and death anxiety is to renounce the very activities and relationships that give one's life the most value" (R. Firestone, 1987b, p. 226). In a lecture on "Modern Psychology and Social Change," Rank (1938, quoted in Kramer, 1996) pointed out the impact that survivor guilt and the fear of separation have on individuals: "Now, because of his awareness of the guilt and inferiority feelings arising from the perception of his *unlikeness* to other individuals [including parents], the neurotic is unable to separate or detach himself from emotional ties and live independently" (pp. 269–270).

> For example, Janet, 28, had progressed in therapy, overcome her depression, and was becoming increasingly more self-assured and independent. She was in the process of studying for her master's degree in psychology and also had taken several steps to emancipate herself from her family-of-origin. Specifically, she had chosen a career different from the one her mother had planned for her, dropped her membership in the fundamentalist church of which her mother was a member, and was romantically involved with a man who loved her and with whom she was sharing a writing project. All was going well and Janet was very happy until she received a call from her sister urging her to come back East to help care for their mother as she recovered from a serious operation.
>
> Returning after spending two weeks with her mother, Janet seemed distracted and was unable to concentrate on her studies. She soon broke off the relationship with the man she loved and refused to continue working on their book project even though it was nearly completed. She became increasingly depressed and retreated from her closest friends. Her regression lasted for several months until in a therapy session she had insight into the *survivor guilt* she was experiencing.
>
> Janet told her therapist that she felt she had betrayed her mother by no longer serving as her [the mother's] symbolic link to immortality. In the session she revealed that "At first my mother was furious, but then she fell apart after I told her I was no longer attending church. She broke down and cried, and told me that I was killing her by giving up her religion. She begged me to rethink my decision, saying, 'I just can't live with the knowledge that you won't be in heaven with me.' I guess that's a pretty direct statement about her fantasy of everlasting life and her imagined union with me."

Vanity—Specialness and Magical Thinking

The child meets the terror of life and aloneness first by asserting his own omnipotence and then by using the cultural morality as the vehicle for his immortality. By the time we grow up, this confident, delegated immortality becomes a major defense in the service of the equanimity of our organism in the face of danger. One of the main reasons that it is so easy to march men off to war is that deep down each of them feels sorry for the man next to him who will die. Each protects himself in his fantasy until the shock that he is bleeding. (Becker 1973/1997, p. 120)

The authors have defined vanity as a fantasized positive image of the self that an individual uses to compensate for feelings of inadequacy and inferiority. It represents remnants of the child's imagined invincibility, magical thinking, and omnipotence that live on in the psyche, always available as a survival mechanism in times of stress or when the person becomes too conscious of the fallibility of his or her physical nature and the impermanence of life. It expresses itself in the universal sentiment that death happens to someone else, never to oneself. The psychoanalyst Sandor Rado (1942) has described this sentiment or fantasy as follows: "[The soldier is able] to ignore the dangers surrounding him as though disregarding his own life.... He is able to take this remarkable attitude because the situation touches off in the depths of his mind the eternal human illusion of one's own invulnerability and immorality" (p. 364). Similarly, Shaw (2005) contended: "I have noted the importance of this dynamic when soldiers go into combat. These soldiers cherish the conviction that they are mysteriously impervious to spattering bullets and exploding shells; the little spot on which they stand is rendered secure by their standing on it" (p. 5).

The consequences of having one's illusions of invulnerability destroyed were described by McNally (1993) in a chapter about post traumatic stress disorder: "Indeed, most people live under the illusion that trauma can happen to others but not to themselves.... But a sudden, terrifying encounter with death can destroy their illusion and alter the representation of the self as secure and invulnerable" (p. 73).

Many people consider themselves to be exceptional, special, and capable of performing at unreasonably high levels; however, when their performance falls short of perfection, severe self-castigation and demoralization result. Yet they are willing to accept the tension associated with vanity in a desperate attempt to avoid feeling *ordinary* and subject to death as ordinary people are (R. Firestone & Catlett, 2009).

The sense of unlimited power, omnipotence, and immunity to death that is experienced by individuals who have inflated self-images can be traced to early childhood and to primary narcissism, which originally offered an illusion of complete self-sufficiency and invulnerability that functioned to protect the child from a sense of helplessness and fears of annihilation. As noted in Chapter 3, when children first learn about death, they tend to regress to earlier stages in the developmental sequence and to ways of thinking and feeling that characterized these phases. This is also true of the adult. Piven (2004a) has noted that:

> Another defense utilized to avoid death anxiety is regression, as individuals may return to a more infantile way of thinking. . . . Regression also means the restoration of magical thinking, and thus through regression people can hallucinate the belief in divine parents and an afterlife, deny their helplessness, and withdraw from reality or retard their capacity for perceiving it. (p.112)
>
> It is precisely the impact of this powerlessness which motivates repression, identification, and even engenders fantasies of omnipotence and domination. . . . Thus, the child attempts to free oneself from one's weakness and dependence with narcissistic fantasies of grandeur. (p. 52)

In the face of death, adults experience the same sense of powerlessness and helplessness that they felt as children when they first learned of their ultimate fate. As S. Freud (1917/1957a) emphasized in "Mourning and Melancholia," the ego panics at the threat of death and reacts self-protectively. "In addition to a heightening of 'flight' or 'fight' responses, there can be self-deceptive maneuvers to minimize or deny this threat involving narcissistic fantasies, either of invincibility or of participation in the protective powers of an outside agency" (Piven, 2004a, pp. 97–98).

In his novel, *The Razor's Edge,* W. Somerset Maugham (1944/1963) depicted the downside of vanity in one of his characters, Elliot Templeton, who was an absolute snob and whose superiority and sense of specialness depended upon his claiming royalty, celebrities, and statesmen as intimate friends. Later when Maugham describes the narrator's reaction to Elliot's death, he underscores the fact that Elliot's image of inflated self-importance served only to trivialize his life:

> He was dead. . . . His eyes were open and. . . I stared into them for a minute. I was moved and I think a few tears trickled down my cheeks. . . . It made me sad to think how silly, useless, and trivial his life had been. It mattered very little now that he had gone to so many parties and had hobnobbed with all those princes, dukes, and counts. They had forgotten him already. (p. 241)

Magical thinking is an integral part of a belief in one's specialness and immunity to death. To varying degrees, people retain elements of primary narcissism which involve "the creation of fantasies which hallucinate a sense of self-importance, grandiosity, security, invincibility, or love" (Piven, 2004a, p 98). This self-deceptive thinking helps people to deny their mortality through the construction of various fictions that negate the fact of death. For example, in *The Year of Magical Thinking,* Joan Didion (2005) is unusually candid in admitting the specific kinds of infantile thinking she experienced following the death of her husband: "I recognized [in retrospect] that through the winter and spring there had been occasions on which I was incapable of thinking rationally. I was thinking as small children think, as if my thoughts or wishes had the power to reverse the narrative, change the outcome" (p. 35). Preparing to give her husband's clothes away, she decides to start with his shoes:

> I stopped at the door to the room.
> I could not give away the rest of his shoes.
> I stood there for a moment, then realized why: he would need shoes if he was to return.
> The recognition of this thought by no means eradicated the thought. I have still not tried to determine (say, by giving away the shoes) if the thought has lost its power. (p. 37)

The Accumulation of Power and Wealth

> Kierkegaard, Scheler, and Tillich...saw that man could strut and boast all he wanted, but that he really drew his "courage to be" from a god, a string of sexual conquests, a Big Brother, a flag, the proletariat, and the fetish of money and the size of a bank balance. (Becker, 1973/1997, p. 56)

Power

In business, politics, and organizational life in general, the drive to accumulate power is often motivated by a misguided attempt to maintain a sense of specialness and invulnerability. Conscious fears of death are temporarily alleviated by symbols of power and influence. However, these same fears still exist on an unconscious level and often increase in intensity as an individual amasses greater power. For this reason the accumulation of power has addictive properties; leaders must increase their power base in order to compensate for feelings of inferiority, insignificance, and vulnerability. When in power they tend to be suspicious and overly sensitized to potential threats to their position from competitors and enemies, whether real or imagined. Many leaders, especially dictators, start off with humanistic values and ideologies but become increasingly more paranoid over time.

Power is like a narcotic in another sense: it offers a feeling of exhilaration unlike any other defense. The power-struck individual becomes progressively more addicted to the high of being powerful—as Henry Kissinger once quipped: "Power is the greatest aphrodisiac." When one's power is threatened, either internally or externally, one requires greater power to quell the ensuing anxiety and dread. As Yalom (1980) rightly observed:

> This mode of adaptation often decompensates into a runaway defense. Absolute power, as we have always known, corrupts absolutely; it corrupts because it does not do the trick for the individual. Reality always creeps in—the reality of our helplessness and our mortality; the reality that, despite our reach for the stars, a creaturely fate awaits us. (p. 127)

History has shown that in numerous cases pathological leaders who assumed positions of power early in life became increasingly paranoid and punitive as they grew older (J. Post, 2004). For example, as Stalin aged, his feelings of insecurity and paranoia appeared to intensify, and he embarked on a program to purge the party of suspected political heretics. According to Radzinsky (1996): "As soon as the war was over he [Stalin] had begun harping on his age" (p. 527). In 1946 Stalin "began his purge of the country by striking first at his lieutenants" (p. 527). In 1949 "two thousand Party officials had been arrested in Leningrad" (p. 535) in what came to be known as the Leningrad Affair.

Similarly, Lipman-Blumen (2005) described Chairman Mao as "a vivid example of an initially positive leader who eventually turned toxic.... In his later years, Mao declined into paranoia, which frequently drove him to order the elimination of his closest associates" (p.146).

Destructive or toxic leaders tend to have elements of authoritarianism, paranoia, and sociopathy in their personality structure, as well as "fear of the unknown, fear of failure, mistrust of people, feelings of inadequacy, lack of confidence, or extreme overconfidence" (Wilson-Starks, 2003, "What causes a person to become a toxic leader" section, para. 1). They exercise power and authority as a means of bolstering an inflated self-image and as a defense against feelings of insecurity, inferiority, and vulnerability to death. Their charismatic, narcissistic leadership styles both resonate with and exacerbate feelings of fear, inferiority, and insecurity in their followers, especially during times of crisis and uncertainty (R. Firestone & Catlett, 2009). In an analysis of this type of leader-follower relationship, J. Post (2004) proposed that there are crucial aspects of the psychology of the leader such as narcissism and the "ability to convey a sense of grandeur, omnipotence, and strength" (p. 191) that, like a lock-and-key relationship, attract followers. "When these ideal-hungry followers find a mirror-hungry [vain, narcissistic] leader, we have the elements of a charismatic leader-follower relationship" (p. 199).

In describing the dynamics of the collusion that exists between charismatic leaders and their followers, Lipman-Blumen (2005) stated:

> Illusions are the umbilical cord linking leaders and followers. Leaders understand their followers' need for illusions. So do their entourages, who promote illusions about the leader's omnipotence and omniscience. (p. 51) Many of us look to leaders who project an aura of certainty—real or imagined—that we lack within ourselves. And if they are not *actually* knowledgeable and in control, we convince ourselves that they truly are, to satisfy our own desperate need. (p. 53)

According to Liechty (2004):

> Given the choice between accepting this reality [that one is mortal] or giving oneself over to illusions of greatness and importance that the leader imparts to followers, the mass of human beings will choose illusion over reality, lies over truth, fiction over fact and will strike out in holy rage against anyone or anything that threatens to shatter the illusion to which they have committed themselves. (p. 166)

In many instances, as followers become increasingly disillusioned, they become more fanatic in their beliefs or in their adherence to dogma or rules. On the other hand they can turn viciously against the leader who fails to deliver on his or her promises. If a leader who offered safety and life-everlasting shows signs of weakness, his or her followers feel justified in rebelling and in punishing or even destroying the same person they once loved and idolized. As Liechty (2004) emphasized:

> The leader offers the group opportunity to maintain the illusion of power in the face of ontological finitude.... [However] the group, therefore, holds the leader hostage to the expectations of the group, and, as the history of exiled and beheaded potentates demonstrates, the group will not hesitate to

move against a leader who ceases to exhibit this ability to lead, the ability to reflect back to them a resolution of the problem of finitude. (pp. 166–167)

Wealth

There are some people who use wealth to strengthen their imagination of being invulnerable to death. As is true of any defense that is used to allay death anxiety, there are negative consequences to the unrelenting drive to uphold the defense, in this case, to acquire money, position, and prestige. Paradoxically it appears that the more wealth that these individuals accrue during their lifetime, the greater their sense of insecurity and their fear about the future. As they grow older they realize that "You can't take it with you." At this point they become disillusioned and realize that the fact of being rich and famous cannot save them from a fate that faces all people, rich and poor alike.

This is the situation that the character "Big Daddy" (in Tennessee Williams's [1954] play *Cat on a Hot Tin Roof*) is forced to confront after being told by his doctor that he has very little time left. In a painful conversation with his son, the dying man initially brags about the immense wealth he has accumulated and the material things he has acquired in his travels throughout his life. Then he ruefully and philosophically admits:

> But a man can't buy his life with it, he can't buy back his life with it when his life has been spent, that's one thing not offered in the Europe fire-sale or in the American markets or any markets on earth, a man can't buy his life with it, he can't buy back his life when his life is finished. (p. 66) The human animal is a beast that dies and if he's got money, he buys and buys and buys and I think the reason he buys everything he can buy is that in the back of his mind he has the crazy hope that one of his purchases will be life everlasting!—Which it never can be. (p. 68)

Preoccupation With Pseudo-Problems and Other Distractions

Although not related directly to the imagined continuity of life, trivial concerns are effective in shielding oneself against death fears. Most people seem intolerant of a simple, satisfying life and prefer to occupy their minds with melodrama and pseudo-problems. They often are diverted by everyday events to which they overreact with intense primal feelings or inappropriate emotions of rage, fear, and panic. When preoccupied in this way, they shut off feeling for real issues and are unnecessarily tortured by innocuous situations, leaving them less vulnerable to death anxiety (R. Firestone, 1994b).

Many distractions in everyday life can serve a defensive function in alleviating death anxiety. The fast pace with which most people live, along with the seemingly unlimited array of entertaining distractions available to them, often keeps them from a more serious contemplation of the meaningful issues of life. Furthermore, in contemporary life, remaining cool and unemotional is admired, whereas appropriate responses to emotional situations are disparaged. The result is often a life lived on a superficial level, devoid of deep feeling. Kierkegaard referred to this mode of existence as philistinism. As Becker (1973/1997) put it:

> For Kierkegaard, "philistinism" was triviality, man lulled by the daily routines of his society, content with the satisfactions that it offers him: in today's world the car, the shopping center, the two-week summer vacation. Man is protected by the secure and limited alternatives his society offers him, and if he does not look up from his path he can live out his life with a certain dull security. (p. 74)
>
> The Philistine trusts that by keeping himself at a low level of personal intensity he can avoid being pulled off balance by experience; philistinism works, as Kierkegaard said, by 'tranquilizing itself with the trivial.' (p. 81)

EVALUATING DEFENSES AGAINST DEATH ANXIETY

> The modes of symbolic immortality described by Lifton are often defensive means of not coping with death. Each mode of symbolic immortality spans a continuum from healthy to deeply pathological investment and derangement. (Piven, 2004a, p. 229)

Defenses against death anxiety can be evaluated according to their constructive or destructive effects (Langner, 2002) (Note 7). An analogy can be made with Becker's attack on cultural relativity, which states that cultural traditions not only vary but also are more or less beneficial to humankind. This is also true of defenses against death anxiety. Becker (1973/1997), in appraising the value or destructiveness of illusion and denial, said:

> The question of human life is: on what level of illusion does one live? This question poses an absolutely new question for the science of mental health, namely: What is the "best" illusion under which to live. . . . You will have

to define "best" in terms that are directly meaningful to man, related to his basic condition and his needs. I think the whole question would be answered in terms of how much freedom, dignity, and hope a given illusion provides. These three things absorb the problem of natural neurosis and turn it to creative living. (p. 202) A creative myth is not simply a relapse into comfortable illusion; it has to be as bold as possible in order to be truly generative. (p. 279)

Obviously some defenses against death anxiety have a beneficial effect; for example, the belief in symbolic immortality fostered by living on through creative works in art, literature, and science. Finding lasting meaning in devotion to family, friends, and people at large and attempting to leave a positive imprint has a positive valence.

Other defenses such as living on through one's children have a generally negative effect. Many children have suffered in their development as their parents tried to make them into carbon copies of themselves. This defense leads to a great deal of insensitivity to the child's true nature. Children have their own unique genetic structure that is different from either parent, and this uniqueness deserves loving and sensitive nurturance.

Another defense that has a particularly negative effect is vanity, which is destructive to both oneself and others. The arrogance, defensiveness, and sometimes aggressive response of the vain individual are provoking to others. However, the pressure to maintain illusions of grandeur has an equally destructive effect on the individual. Maintaining any sense of omnipotence leads to painful states of tension and anxiety that can only be relieved by relinquishing the defense. Similarly the accumulation of power and wealth as a way of avoiding death fears has obviously contributed to the perpetuation of societal destructiveness throughout history.

In relation to religion as a defense, religious dogma, whether inspired by literal translation of the Bible, direct communication from God, or other pious teachings, is considered sacred and the person who so believes is admired and valued as a true person of faith. The nonbeliever is castigated. This type of polarity on a small scale is characteristic of a broader menace to society and nations, whereby people of different customs and religious beliefs must challenge the outsider because his or her belief system is perceived as a threat to their own. In that regard, religiosity, particularly extreme religious beliefs, has led to pain and bloodshed throughout history. Thus, the positive value and comfort of religion has been tempered by its negative impact.

Many social theorists have thought of religious beliefs and rituals as analogous to the use of drugs, emphasizing that religion has been utilized to control and manage people in a social system. They agree with Karl Marx that "religion is the opiate of the people." Contrary to S. Freud (1927/1961b), who argued that all religious belief was a defense, in that the effects of religious consolations may be likened to that of a narcotic, other theorists have suggested that there are some religious motivations that are nondefensive in nature. For example, R. Beck (2004) contrasted *defensive religious belief* (fundamentalism, the belief that sacred texts are literally true) with *existential religion* ("faith stances that fully recognize our existential situation but which actively refuse to believe as a means to repress existential terror") (p. 210). Prominent among thinkers who have described this position are Soren Kierkegaard, William James, and Ernest Becker.

In empirical research, Beck found that *defensive believers* displayed the tendency to see in-group targets more favorably than out-group targets; conversely, existential participants tended to see in-group and out-group targets as equally attractive or capable (Note 8). Recent studies have also contrasted two types of religious orientations. Friedman and Rholes (2007) found that when subjects had to contemplate contradictions in Bible passages, describing details of the resurrection, Christian fundamentalists experienced an increase in thoughts about death, whereas nonfundamentalist Christians did not.

In summary, the defense of literal immortality, constituted by a variety of religious beliefs, has mixed effects. Yet there is a general tendency to deny the body and renounce gratifications in this life for a hypothetical afterlife that may or may not exist. There is a marked tendency to deny our animal nature and pleasures of the flesh as a trade off for a hypothetical soul that survives.

CONCLUSION

Spiritual thoughts and feelings, as Terror Management Theory (TMT) theorists Hart and Goldenberg (2008) have noted, are among the most effective of defenses in helping reduce death anxiety. Nevertheless, in the end all defenses against death awareness, whether literal or symbolic, fail on some level to completely reassure us about our immortality. There is still a generalized anxiety and dread that shapes our lives. The authors suggest that dealing with death directly by bringing the subject into the foreground, feeling the painful affects, and using the emotional release to affirm life is the most positive approach.

The first author would like to conclude this chapter on a personal note: *When I was a young child, my parents told me that as an infant I had been very sick and it was their prayers to God that saved my life. The result was that at an early age I became aware that I was mortal and indebted to both my parents and God for my survival. I believed them and I attempted to perfect myself according to their beliefs. I felt that if I were a good person, I would be rewarded and that I would be safe.*

In Sunday school these ideas were reinforced, but as I developed in life I gradually came to see things differently. First, I realized that most people were living as though there were no such thing as death; there was a general denial. Second, I soon learned that to talk about death, to be inquisitive or questioning about it, evoked annoyance and anger in my parents and others. When I thought about the Bible, and then looked at the world around me, I realized that the way God was portrayed didn't make sense to me. Why was there so much cruelty and horror in the world? I felt sure that if there were a God, it was not anything like the God in the Bible. In that same Sunday school where I learned about God, I also learned about the Holocaust and it terrified me. I couldn't buy the traditional religious answers to these dilemmas. Furthermore I was disillusioned about the idea that goodness was rewarded and badness punished when I experienced the contrary over and over in everyday living. I no longer felt the safety and immunity I previously believed in.

As an adolescent I tried out new and different solutions, a kind of mystical connecting with the universal unconscious, the concept of a parallel universe where my life would continue in some way, and I tried to figure out a concept of time that would allow for a birth-rebirth cycle that would make death itself an illusion. All of these attempts failed to comfort me, but I still hoped for some form of future life and maintained an element of belief in prayer. When I wanted something really badly, something important, I would tend to pray for it, not formally but sort of wishing or hoping. When sick, I prayed that I would get better, and I prayed for my mother and father's well being as though some outside force would help.

As an adult, I became progressively more disenchanted, sad, and demoralized about death and dying. Learning about evolution effectively demolished the creation myth and any security that surrounded it. I came to realize that I was an animal like any other and that my life was finite. I learned that there was no essential rhyme or reason to life or being and that I must find my own meaning and purpose. I devoted myself to a life of absolute honesty and integrity, which made my life very difficult at times. I maintained my belief in kindness, goodness, and compassion from my childhood days, but without hope of external reward. The reward was in my own personal satisfaction and good feeling. Though I have no special belief in a deity, at crucial times I find myself praying that I, myself, or my wife, children, and friends will be safe. Prayer as I have indulged in it could be considered a form of organized wish fulfillment rather than a religious practice, although I'm sure it contains unconscious elements of magical thinking from childhood. I have been fortunate so far.

I believe there is still mystery in the world, because our Aristotelian minds cannot fathom the simple fact of existence. We know that something cannot come from nothing, yet I believe we exist. Even if we imagine that it's all God's creation, where did that essence come from? This riddle troubles me but offers a kind of hope of other unknown possibilities. Still in relation to death, I have come to believe that it is the end of life, the end of me. The thought of losing those close to me, the pleasures of life, and ultimately my consciousness makes me very sad. At the same time, I love my life and my loved ones, lead a full life, feel free, and cherish every moment of my existence.

NOTES

1. See Thomas W. Clark's (2002) "Spirituality without Faith," an essay on the benefits and limitations of naturalism. Clark noted that:

   Many, if not most[,] of these traditions, as well as some New Age beliefs, involve the idea of a distinct spiritual realm, something set apart or above the everyday physical world (some types of Buddhism being notable exceptions). The varieties of spirituality are thus to a great extent varieties of dualism, at least in their cognitive contexts (belief systems). This dualism is explained partly by our instinctual fear of death, which many religions allay by positing an immortal soul or spiritual essence which survives bodily dissolution. ("Traditional Spirituality" section, para. 1–2)

   It is primarily this factor (i.e., a dualist orientation of body separate from spirit) that differentiates literal immortality from symbolic immortality.
2. "New Age teachings became popular during the 1970s as a reaction against what some perceived as the failure of Christianity and the failure of Secular Humanism to provide spiritual and ethical guidance" (ReligiousTolerance.org, 2008, para. 5). In an essay "Psychoanalysis and Postmodern Spirituality," Raul Moncayo (1998) made an important distinction between religion and spirituality. He proposed that spirituality was an outgrowth of immediate, direct experience, whereas religion typically refers to

traditional religiosity or religious institutions that function as a means of control and authority and that also serves to satisfy human beings' needs for social affiliation. He goes on to discuss the essence of *nontheism* and *nonduality* as defining nonexistence as *something* that can exist beyond or outside of rational thinking or perceiving.

3. Re: the long-term political and religious implications of St. Augustine's interpretation of the creation myth, see Elaine Pagels's (1988) "The Politics of Paradise" in *Adam, Eve, and the Serpent:*

> Yet with Augustine, in the late fourth and early fifth centuries, this message [the moral freedom to rule oneself] changed.... Instead of the freedom of the will and humanity's original royal dignity, Augustine emphasizes humanity's enslavement to sin. Humanity is sick, suffering, and helpless, irreparably damaged by the fall, for that "original sin," Augustine insists, involved nothing else than Adam's prideful attempt to establish his own autonomous self-government. Astonishingly, Augustine's radical views prevailed, eclipsing for future generations of western Christians the consensus of more than three centuries of Christian tradition. (p. 99) Augustine believes that by defining spontaneous sexual desire as the proof and penalty of original sin he has succeeded in implicating the whole human race, except, of course, for Christ. (p. 112)

In a more recent work, *Beyond Belief*, Pagels (2003) cited another source of the creation myth, which is interpreted as follows: "Another book discovered at Nag Hammadi, *On the Origin of the World*, says that when the first man and woman recognized their nakedness, 'they saw that they were naked of spiritual understanding (*gnosis*).' But then the luminous *epinoia* 'appeared to them shining with light, and awakened their consciousness'" (p. 164).

4. However, the Dalai Lama (1999) challenged the more traditional meaning of Buddhist notion of literal renunciation of the self, emphasizing that what is needed today is a spiritual revolution: "a radical reorientation away from our habitual preoccupation with self [not a renunciation of self]...toward the wider community of beings with whom we are connected, and for conduct which recognized others' interests alongside our own" (p. 23–24).

Andre Comte-Sponville (2006) expressed similar sentiments regarding the relative importance of the ego in his book, *The Little Book of Atheist Spirituality:*

> To me, at least when I manage to feel rather than think, it is more like an ocean of peace.... We are in the universe, part of the All or of nature. And the contemplation of the immensity that contains us makes us all the more aware of how puny we are. This may be wounding to our ego, but it also enlarges our soul, because the ego has been put in its place at long last. It has stopped taking up all the room. (p. 147)

5. Lifton (1979) identified religion as a mode of symbolic immortality; however, he differentiated beliefs in an actual immortal soul, an afterlife, or reincarnation as literal rather than symbolic. He cited theologian Paul Tillich as contrasting "The 'vulgar theology' of afterlife imagery, usually for the 'common people,' with more symbolized and sensitive 'higher theologies' around spiritual attainment."

6. Re: living on through one's progeny as a defense against death anxiety, Bassett (2007) proposed two interesting experimentally testable predictions of TMT that could be

hypothesized: (a) reminders of death should increase attempts to force children to conform to parents' worldview and increase the negative reactions to children who do not conform to parents' worldview, and (b) thinking about a child's failure to conform to a parent's worldview should increase proneness to death anxiety as evidenced by greater accessibility of death-related thoughts.

7. In *Choices for Living: Coping with Fear of Dying*, Langner (2002) delineates a hierarchy of methods of coping with death anxiety (pp. 8–12).

8. Richard Beck (2004) delineated a number of characteristics of a defensive religious orientation and those of existential or nondefensive orientations. See Table 1, p. 213, in "The Function of Religious Belief: Defensive versus Existential Religion." Also see definitions of intrinsic and extrinsic religiosity by A. Cohen, Pierce, Chambers, Meade, Gorvine, & Koenig (2005). These researchers noted that: "The core concept of intrinsic religiosity (IR), as originally proposed, is living one's religion with sincerity and intentionality. In contrast, the core idea of extrinsic religiosity (ER), as originally proposed, is using religion for instrumental purposes including for the cultivation of social relationships" (p. 310).

6 Microsuicide: Death of the Spirit

Character armor garrisons the ego but impedes motility. We repress ourselves from fear of death; we deny reality[,] and cocoon ourselves in a womblike, fragile web of illusions. We cannot individuate if we remain tied to illusions. If we are too deluded and cocooned to embrace reality, then we are in fact killing ourselves.

—Jerry Piven, "Transference as Religious Solution to the Terror of Death"
(2002, pp. 239–240)

In the end each man kills himself in his own selected way, fast or slow, soon or late.

—Karl Menninger, Man against Himself (1938, p. vii)

Statistics (Lester & Tartaro, 2002) show that suicide intent is high in prisoners awaiting execution on death row, necessitating suicide watches and other strict preventive measures (Note 1). This paradox illustrates the relationship between human self-destructiveness and the fear of death. The situation faced by the prisoner is analogous to the circumstances faced by all human beings (R. Firestone, 2000; R. Firestone & Seiden, 1987). Like the convict, people are aware of an inescapable sentence of death as a function of life itself (R. Firestone, 1997b).

The prisoner attempts to take life and death into his or her own hands in an effort to have some measure of control over death rather than live with the agony of waiting and knowing that soon he or she will be dead. Similarly most people commit small suicides on a daily basis in an effort to accommodate to the anxiety and dread surrounding the awareness of death. As individuals give up their lives through progressive self-denial and other self-defeating behaviors, they are able to maintain a sense of invulnerability, as if they can retain some power over life and death. In withdrawing feeling or affect from personal pursuits and goal-directed activity, they reduce their vulnerability to hurt, rejection, and potential loss (R. Firestone, 1997b).

Suicidal behavior does not always involve overt attempts on one's life. Indeed it includes a wide spectrum of behaviors not always thought of as suicidal (Shneidman 1973/1999). *Microsuicide* encompasses actions, communications, attitudes, or lifestyles that are self-induced and threatening, limiting, or antithetical to an individual's physical health, emotional well-being, or personal goals. These behavior patterns are pervasive in the normal population, yet they are severely restrictive of the experience of the individual and of the life process.

THE INTERRELATEDNESS OF SELF-DESTRUCTIVE BEHAVIORS

There is an essential continuity of self-destructive behaviors; they differ only in quantity, nature, and degree. Emil Durkheim (1897/1951) asserted: "Suicides do not form, as might be thought, a wholly distinct group, an isolated class of monstrous phenomena, unrelated to other forms of conduct, but rather are related to them by a continuous series of intermediate cases. They are merely the exaggerated form of common practices" (p. 45).

Suicidologist Edwin Shneidman (1966), in his description of inimical (unfriendly) patterns of living, wrote about the "multitudinous ways in which an individual can reduce, truncate, demean, narrow, shorten, or destroy his own life" (p. 199). And in *The Many Faces of Suicide,* Farberow (1980) delineated specific self-destructive behaviors which "by their very familiarity and frequency of occurrence . . . must merge into the normal, acceptable end of the continuum of behavior. On the other hand, if they can be so self-destructive or self-injurious, they must merge into the pathological end of the continuum represented by overt suicidal activity" (p. 2).

In *Man against Himself,* Menninger (1938) delineated the numerous, often perversely ingenious, ways that people manage to accomplish their self-defeating objectives, such as ascetic denial, repetitive accidents, alcohol addiction, unwise financial speculation, and failure to follow medical advice.

In this chapter we will focus on those acts against the self that, while not necessarily leading directly to actual death, are nevertheless so widespread in the general population that we have referred to them as the *microsuicides of everyday life*. Mental health professionals have long recognized that people engage in self-damaging lifestyles and behaviors without having conscious awareness that their aim is self-destruction. Such behaviors have been referred to by a variety of names, including: indirect suicide or sub-intentioned death (Shneidman, 1996), partial death, installment-plan suicide, slow suicide, inimical patterns of behavior, masked suicide, hidden suicide (Meerloo, 1968), parasuicide (Linehan, 1993), as well as focal and chronic suicides described by Menninger (1938). Although there are minor distinctions between these terms, they all describe lifestyles of gradual self-destruction. As Shneidman (1996) noted in his description of indirect suicide or sub-intentioned death: "There are two obvious deleterious things we can do to ourselves: We can shorten life's length, and we can narrow life's breadth. Make it shorter than need be, or make it less than it ought to be—a narrow, pinched, and unhappy life" (p. 63).

THE DYNAMICS OF MICROSUICIDE

Self-limiting and self-destructive behaviors are based on powerful feelings of self-hatred and negative attitudes toward the self that were incorporated by the child during the formative years (R. Firestone, 1994a). Clinical data obtained from our investigations indicate that the majority of these destructive thoughts originate in negative family interactions. In many situations, only fragments of this destructive thought process reach consciousness, and these are but the tip of the iceberg: isolated elements of a well-integrated system of destructive thoughts toward the self. Under certain conditions these thoughts can become progressively ascendant and take precedence over thoughts of rational self-interest, as in a suicidal crisis.

Our research has shown that these negative thought patterns vary along a continuum of intensity from mild self-criticisms to malicious self-accusations and suicidal thoughts. Similarly, microsuicidal behavior exists on a continuum ranging from asceticism or self-denial to

Exhibit 6.1

CONTINUUM OF SELF-DESTRUCTIVE THOUGHTS AND BEHAVIORS

Any combination of the voice attacks listed below can lead to serious suicidal intent. Thoughts leading to isolation, ideation about removing oneself from people's lives, beliefs that one is a bad influence or has a destructive effect on others, voices urging one to give up special activities, vicious self-abusive thoughts accompanied by strong anger, voices urging self-injury, and a suicide attempt are all indications of high suicide potential or risk. Copyright © 1996 by The Glendon Association.

Levels of Increasing Suicidal Intention	Content of Voice Statements
Thoughts that Lead to Low Self-Esteem or Inwardness (Self-Defeating Thoughts)	
1. Self-depreciating thoughts of everyday life	*You're incompetent, stupid. You're not very attractive.*
2. Thoughts rationalizing self-denial; thoughts discouraging the person from engaging in pleasurable activities	*You're too young (old) and inexperienced to apply for this job. You're too shy to make any new friends. Why go on this trip? It'll be such a hassle.*
3. Cynical attitudes toward others, leading to alienation and distancing	*Why go out with her (him)? She's cold, unreliable; she'll reject you. You can't trust men (women).*
4. Thoughts influencing isolation; rationalizations for time alone, but using time to become more negative toward oneself	*Just be by yourself. You're miserable company anyway; who'd want to be with you? Just stay in the background, out of view.*
5. Self-contempt; vicious self-abusive thoughts and accusations (accompanied by intense angry affect)	*You idiot! You bitch! You creep! You stupid shit! You don't deserve anything; you're worthless!*
Thoughts that Lead to the Cycle of Addiction	
6. Thoughts urging use of substances or food	*It's okay to do drugs, you'll be more relaxed. Go ahead and have a drink,*

Exhibit 6.1

followed by self-criticisms (weakens inhibitions against self-destructive actions, while increasing guilt and self-recrimination following acting out)

you deserve it. (Later) You weak-willed jerk! You're nothing but a drugged-out drunken freak.

Self-Annihilating Thoughts

7. Thoughts contributing to a sense of hopelessness, urging withdrawal or removal of oneself completely from the lives of people closest

    See how bad you make your family (friends) feel. They'd be better off without you. It's the only decent thing to do. Just stay away and stop bothering them.

8. Thoughts influencing a person to give up priorities and favored activities

    What's the use? Your work doesn't matter any more. Why bother trying? Nothing matters anyway.

9. Injunctions to inflict self-harm at an action level; intense rage against self

    Why don't you just drive across the center divider? Just shove your hand under that power saw!

10. Thoughts planning details of suicide (calm, rational, often obsessive, indicating complete loss of feeling for the self)

    You have to get hold of some pills, then go to a hotel.

11. Injunctions to carry out suicide plans; thoughts baiting the person to commit suicide (extreme thought constriction)

    You've thought about this long enough. Just get it over with. It's the only way out!

accident-proneness, withdrawal from activities and close relationships, culminating in self-mutilating acts or actual suicide (R. Firestone, 1997a, 1997b). (See Exhibit 6.1, Continuum of Self-Destructive Thoughts and Behaviors.)

The core of one's critical thoughts about oneself, which we refer to as the critical inner voice, is directed toward self-denial and ultimately toward the destruction of the individual. Thus, the voice is the mechanism that regulates, dictates, and rationalizes an individual's self-denying, microsuicidal behavior. The voice process will be discussed at length in Chapter 8.

MICROSUICIDE AS AN ACCOMMODATION TO DEATH ANXIETY

> The common denominator of all negative ways of dealing with anxiety is a shrinking of the area of awareness and of activity.... We are afraid to die, and therefore we are afraid to live.... The avoidance of anxiety then means a kind of death in life. (Rheingold, 1967, pp. 204–205)

The idea that suicidal and self-destructive behavior can alleviate fears of death and dying may at first seem paradoxical, yet the phenomenon has been a topic in literature, philosophy, and psychology for centuries. According to Minois (1995/1999), in both *Faust* (philosophical suicide) and *The Sorrows of Young Werther* (1774, romantic suicide), Goethe portrayed suicide as a method for taking destiny into one's own hands, thereby overcoming torturous feelings of insignificance in the face of one's inevitable fate. When Faust's illusions of being all-powerful were completely destroyed, he asked: "But what is 'being' if one is not everything, does not know everything, cannot do everything? 'Nothing.' Faust knows now that man cannot master universal knowledge or truth, so he makes his choice: not to be...he chooses self-destruction" (p. 271).

In *Six Tales of the Jazz Age*, F. Scott Fitzgerald (1920/1960) succinctly wrote about self-limiting, self-denying behaviors that serve the function of helping us adapt to existential inevitabilities:

> The years between thirty-five and sixty-five revolve before the passive mind as one unexplained, confusing merry-go-round.... For most men and women these thirty years are taken up with a gradual withdrawal from life, a retreat first from a front with many shelters, those myriad amusements and curiosities of youth, to a life with less, when we peel down our ambitions to one ambition, our recreations to one recreation, our friends to a few to whom we are anaesthetic; ending up at last in a solitary, desolate strong point that is not strong where...by turns frightened and tired, we sit waiting for death. (p. 110)

In *Veronika Decides to Die,* novelist/philosopher Paul Coelho (1998) set forth his views about mental illness through his protagonist, the psychiatrist "Dr. Igor," who believes it is caused by bitterness:

> In the case of bitterness, the right conditions for the disease occur when the person becomes afraid of so-called reality. Certain people, in their eagerness to construct a world no external threat can penetrate, build exaggeratedly high defenses against the outside world, against new people, new places, different experiences, and leave their inner world stripped bare....
>
> The great problem with poisoning by bitterness was that the passions—hatred, love, despair, enthusiasm, curiosity—also ceased to manifest themselves. After a while the embittered person felt no desire at all. He or she lacked the will either to live or to die, that was the problem.... From the social point of view, the only advantage of the disease was that it had become the norm. (pp. 90–91)

In the professional literature, several writers have proposed that the process of restricting one's life and withdrawing from relationships provides a measure of relief from the fear of death. For example, Jacques Choron (1964) cited Tillich's perspective on how the neurotic person responds to the awareness of dying, death, and nonbeing.

> Tillich explains this...as "a state of existential anxiety under special conditions. The neurotic is more sensitive to the threat of nonbeing than the average man."... The neurotic, who is aware of nonbeing, wants to banish it and is ready to pay a very high price for this. He eschews self-affirmation; he lives on a cautious and reduced scale. (pp. 153–154)

According to David Bakan (1968), people who engage in self-limiting, self-destructive behavior or who ultimately kill themselves maintain certain illusions about death and immortality. He noted that an individual's "act of self-injury...puts death under the control of the will, giving the illusion that otherwise there is immortality" (p. 127).

In considering microsuicide or *death of the spirit,* the authors propose that psychopathology or mental illness can be conceptualized as a limitation in living that is manifested in self-limiting and/or self-destructive lifestyles. In this sense varieties of so-called mental illness could be categorized as subclasses of suicide rather than the reverse (R. Firestone & Firestone, 1998). Indeed all aspects of giving up oneself, one's sense of reality, and goal-directed activity represent a defensive, self-destructive orientation toward life, which when it becomes severe leads to neurotic or psychotic symptom formation. Neurotic and psychotic symptoms are reflected, in turn, in repetitive, self-sabotaging ways of living in which people act out microsuicidal behavior in an effort to alleviate existential dread and terror.

Other theorists have written about the relationship between mental illness and the fear of death. For example: "R. Skoog reports that over 70 percent of patients with a severe obsessional neurosis had, at the onset of illness, a security-disturbing death experience. As the syndrome develops, patients are increasingly concerned about controlling their world and preventing the unexpected or accidental" (Yalom, 1980, p. 48). Lazarus and Kostan (1969), on the basis of an extensive study of patients who suffered from hyperventilation syndrome, suggested that the underlying death anxiety is probably "transformed into a series of other phobias. An inability to bind death anxiety sufficiently results in the hyperventilation panic" (Yalom, p. 49).

Laing (1960/1969), Searles (1979), and Karon and VandenBos (1981) have hypothesized that the terror of death or of being killed is at the core of severe mental illness, particularly schizoid disorders and schizophrenia. According to Laing, "For the schizoid individual direct participation 'in' life is felt as being at the constant risk of being destroyed by life" (p. 95). "In the last resort, he sets about murdering his 'self,' and this is not as easy as cutting one's throat. He descends into a vortex of nonbeing in order to avoid being" (p. 99). Karon and VandenBos observed: "In several schizophrenic patients whom we have treated, both acute and chronic, it was clear that an overwhelming conscious fear of death immediately preceded the psychotic break... It is certainly clear that every schizophrenic patient believes that he could not live without his symptoms" (p. 143).

Similarly, Searles (1961) has pointed out that "the fact of death's inevitability has a more than merely tangential relation to schizophrenia" (p. 633). He went on to note that:

> In working with schizophrenic patients, one soon comes to realize that many, if not all, of them are unable to experience themselves, consistently, as being *alive*. (p. 639) The anxiety concerning life's finitude is too great to face unless one has the strengthening knowledge that one is a whole person.... A person cannot bear to face the prospect of inevitable death unless he has had the experience of fully living, and the schizophrenic has not yet fully lived. (p. 640) (Note 2)

Although the earliest roots of schizophrenia may antedate the time in the individual's life when death's inevitability tends to confront him, it is the writer's impression that this particular deeply anxiety-provoking aspect of reality is one of the major threats which the schizophrenic process is serving to deny. (pp. 663–664)

Suicidal ideation and fantasies about suicide often have the effect of diminishing thoughts and fears about death in normal or neurotic individuals. According to Shneidman (1973/1999):

The fantasies of one's own suicide can represent the greatest possible combination of omnipotence and potential realization of effectiveness—greater even than one's fantasies of the assassination of another, group revenge, mass murder, or even genocide. Any "average" individual can say: "From my point of view suicide destroys all"—and it can be done. (p. 185)

In a study investigating the relationship between suicidal thoughts and anxiety states in bipolar patients, Simon, et al. (2007) found that: "Individuals with current anxiety disorders had more severe suicidal ideation, a greater belief suicide would provide relief, and a higher expectancy of future suicidal behaviors" (p. 255). Indeed, as Nietzsche (1886/1966) put it: "The thought of suicide is a powerful comfort: it helps one through many a dreadful night" (p. 91).

At times relatively well-adjusted people experience brief thoughts of suicide that surprise and/or upset them. These unexpected thoughts or impulses are often indicative of an underlying dread of death and dying. For example, the psychiatrist/psychoanalyst Harold Searles (1979) reported the following personal experience and resultant insight in *Countertransference and Related Subjects:*

For several years, I have spent a long day each month working as a consultant at the New York Psychiatric Institute in New York City. One evening a year or so ago, as I was returning by cab on the Triboro Bridge, on the way to LaGuardia to catch the shuttle plane back to Washington, I was seized by an urge to leap from the cab and hurl myself off the bridge. Such urges are no stranger to me, a sufferer since childhood from a phobia of heights. But the urge this time was particularly powerful, and the determinant I was able to glimpse, this time, of this tenacious, multirooted symptom was particularly memorable, humbling, and useful to me. (p. 236)

Searles went on to explain why this especially strong suicidal urge forced its way into his conscious mind at this juncture in his life:

> I felt I had to destroy myself because I simply could not face returning to my usual life in Washington, and the reason I found it intolerable to face was that I felt so shamefully and desperately unable "simply" to face the living out of my life, the growing old and dying, the commonest, most everyday thing, so my panicky thoughts went, that nearly all people do—all, that is, with the exception of those who commit suicide or take refuge in chronic psychosis.
>
> However unique to my own individual life history must be the pattern of determinants that give rise to my particular omnipotent urge to destroy my life rather than surrender to the eventual losing of it through living and aging and dying, I insist that my urge is not entirely irrelevant to what transpires in my fellow human beings in general: I am convinced that each of us in his or her own particular way must cope with some such irrationally omnipotent reaction to inevitable loss. (p. 236)

The authors propose that microsuicidal behavior constitutes this kind of irrationally omnipotent reaction to the inevitable loss of self and loved ones through death. In this sense, all people are suicidal; it is only the individual style and strength of the movement toward self-destruction that varies from one person to the next. It also follows that this universal tendency for self-destruction is *not* due to a death instinct, but represents instead a powerful defense against death anxiety.

Microsuicidal responses of criticizing and attacking oneself are often utilized in an attempt to minimize the threat of death. The following example helps to illustrate the point.

> A young woman came into her session complaining that she had been utterly miserable, depressed, and filled with self-attacks. When I asked her about her life and her relationship with her boyfriend, she said that everything was going fine and she added, "That's why I'm so puzzled by my negative mood." I then asked her to take a deep breath and relax in her chair. Then I told her to think about her depressed mood and to say the first word that came to her mind. To my surprise she immediately said "death." Then she went into a long painful expression of her fears about death and of the rage she felt about being trapped in life with no way to avoid death's inevitability. "I hate it, I hate it, I can't stand it!" she proclaimed, and she wept. The release of feeling continued with "I can't believe that I'm going to die and so are the people I love. It's too terrible." Afterward, she reflected on the emotions she had expressed and came to realize that she had turned her

anger about death and dying against herself. This was the essence of her criticality toward herself. She also realized that being happy in her life had probably aroused her death anxiety; she felt that now, more than ever, she had a lot to lose. Experiencing these insights, she immediately felt much better in the session and there was considerable relief. This progress was sustained in future contact.

People do not want to die, yet they do want to protect themselves when faced with the specter of death. Individuals become suicidal or self-destructive because they are aware that they must die. Most people accommodate to this reality by committing microsuicides in their everyday lives and, in doing so, they convert the fear of death into a fear of life; that is, a fear of becoming too involved in or attached to life. Engaging in a wide range of microsuicidal behaviors enables people to deny death on an unconscious, personal level; it allows them to gradually adapt to the fear of death by giving up or seriously restricting their lives (R. Firestone, 1994b, 1997a; R. Firestone & Seiden, 1987).

PATTERNS OF MICROSUICIDAL BEHAVIOR AND LIFESTYLES

> The certainty of death and the uncertainty of the hour of death is a source of grief throughout our life. (E. Morin, French philosopher)

Microsuicidal behaviors and lifestyles can be divided into several basic categories. Although the behaviors are not discrete and occur in combination in the lives of many people, they can be delineated as follows for the purposes of clarity and elucidation: (1) addiction and other actions antithetical to one's self-interest; (2) merged identity in couple and family relationships; (3) progressive self-denial; (4) withholding or a renunciation of personal and vocational goals; (5) isolation and withdrawal from relationships into an inward lifestyle; and (6) other maladaptive, self-defeating behaviors.

Commenting on the diversity of microsuicidal behaviors, Morrant and Catlett (2008) have noted:

> These often pass as normal enough, but at best resemble a litany of gloomy virtues: progressive self-sacrifice, self-denial, self-criticism, overwork, the choice of parasitic or abusive companions, or minor forms of enslavement to exercise, television, and the computer. More obvious microsuicidal

behavior includes self-neglect, ignoring medical advice, running away, and...conjuring up situations that damage one's best interests. (p. 364)

Addictions and Other Actions Antithetical to One's Self-Interest

There are a myriad of behaviors, including smoking, drinking to excess, drug abuse, obesity, and eating disorders, that represent direct assaults against the individual's physical health and that, in many cases, result in an increased probability of an early death (Felitti et al., 1998). In addition, addictive behaviors seriously impact people's mental health and emotional well-being, leading to gradual deterioration. "These self-feeding patterns are...self-centered and functionally maladaptive as they interfere with other areas of a person's existence" (R. Firestone, 1997a, p. 229).

As noted in Chapter 4, addictions, compulsive behaviors, and an overreliance on routine and ritual can serve the function of numbing people to anxious, painful feelings about their own mortality as well as to the eventual loss of loved ones. Working compulsively to the point of exhaustion, accident proneness, psychosomatic illnesses, and noncompliance with prescribed medical regimens also jeopardize people's physical health and safety and are obvious manifestations of self-destructive tendencies (Nelson & Farberow, 1982).

The destructive thought process that supports addictive tendencies also functions to support other forms of self-defeating behavior. In relation to addiction, a seemingly friendly voice initially influences or seduces people into indulging the habitual behavior, then punishes them for succumbing to the temptation. For example, the man with high cholesterol who tells himself: "Go ahead and eat that fried food"; the heavy drinker who thinks: "Just one more drink, what's the harm?" the executive with a heart condition who tells herself: "Skip exercising today, you can use the time to get ahead with your work"; the drug abuser who rationalizes: "You had a hard day, you need to relax"; or the driver, in a hurry, who rationalizes: "You don't have to put on your seatbelt, you're only driving a short distance." These destructive behaviors are typically followed by self-accusations and self-recriminations such as: "You have no will power"; "You're a hopeless drunk"; "You're going to kill yourself"; and other self-abusive thoughts. These voices lead to painful feelings of shame and self-hatred that in turn increase the need for relief in the form of more painkillers.

Merged Identity in Couples and Families

The illusion of being connected to another person and the resultant merged identity existing in many couples and families operate as powerful defenses against the anxiety of being separate, basically alone, and susceptible to death (R. Firestone, 1994b, 1997a; R. Firestone & Catlett, 1999). Often as a relationship deteriorates in actuality, the partners and family members become more involved in a fantasy of being fused. The process is circular in that the pretense of love leads to a neurotic lifestyle that is antithetical to the survival of an ongoing relationship characterized by genuine affection, intimacy, and companionship. Indeed, forming a fantasized union with another person leads to a steady decline in personal relating. Both partners tend to give up broad areas of independent functioning in order to cling to an *illusion* that offers them a false sense of security and immortality. A progressive loss of identity and individuality is symptomatic of the mutual self-destructiveness inherent in an addictive attachment or fantasy bond. In some cases there is observable physical deterioration or emotional disturbance directly attributable to the dysfunctional style of interacting that characterizes bonds formed within the couple.

The problem inherent in relationships in which the partners have attempted to merge their identities is that each individual essentially gives up his or her real self for an illusion of connection and finds life increasingly empty and meaningless. Thus, the sense of being fused or of *belonging* to another person is a form of microsuicide. Furthermore, society's conventions support the myth of enduring love in couples and families. Conventional responses based on routine relating and role-playing act to cover up the truth and prevent people from becoming aware of or understanding the basic source of the personal problems in their relationships. The dynamics of this type of merged identity that characterizes many relationships are discussed in Chapter 7, "The Basic Defense Against Death Anxiety: The Fantasy Bond."

Progressive Self-Denial: Giving Up Interest in Life-Affirming Activities

The tendency to give up interest in and excitement about life is built into an individual's defensive posture and may manifest itself as early as in childhood (R. Firestone, 1990b). Examples of how people constrict their lives or put limits on their experiences can be observed in every area of human endeavor: a premature giving up of participation in sports and physical activities, a diminished interest in sex and reduction in sexual activity, a loss of contact with old friends, and a decline in social life. At the same time, there may be an increase in sedentary or self-nurturing occupations, and people frequently become plagued with a sense of boredom and stagnation. This process of gradual self-denial is supported by consensually validated attitudes in society at large about age-appropriate roles and behavior.

Furthermore, many people deny themselves pleasure and enjoyment because on an unconscious level, they feel guilty for surpassing other family members who may not be as fortunate (R. Firestone, 1987b). Guilt in relation to individuation, nonconformity, or standing out from the crowd can also contribute to the development of a self-denying lifestyle. According to Rank (Kramer, 1996), although a necessary part of growth, separation and individuation have an emotional price. "The more we individualize ourselves...the stronger is the formation of guilt-feeling that originates from this individualization and that again in turn unites us emotionally with others" (p. 236).

An analysis of the destructive thought patterns that influence the process of self-denial indicates that the majority of these injunctions and rationalizations are attempts to limit life by persuading the individual to gradually eliminate exciting and spontaneous pursuits (R. Firestone, 2000; R. Firestone & Seiden, 1987). For example, when planning a vacation, some people may question themselves: "Why go on this trip? It'll be such a hassle." Or when trying to advance their career and apply for a new position, they might think to themselves: "You're too inexperienced for this position, so why even bother sending them your resume?" A recently married man may tell himself: "It's time to settle down. You have responsibilities now. You're not a teenager anymore, you can't always do everything you want!" In this way, people's physical lives are maintained, yet every day they are committing emotional suicide as they gradually narrow their world and trivialize their experiences.

Withholding: A Renunciation of Personal and Vocational Goals

> Of all animals...[man] is the best equipped for action in the external world. But his supreme uniqueness lies not only in this. Of all animals, paradoxically, he is at the same time, alone in being able to stop external action completely, and to keep activity going in controlled inner thought processes

alone. Thus the same mechanism that enables him to find an external world more rich than any other animal, permits him to lose the capacity to act in it. (Becker, 1964, p. 73)

Withholding refers to a pattern of holding back positive responses, talents, and capabilities as a form of distancing behavior and self-denial (R. Firestone, 1985; R. Firestone et al., 2003). As such, it plays a significant role in microsuicide. Whenever an individual withholds behaviors or qualities that were once an important expression of his or her personal motivation, he or she is no longer goal-directed and becomes more oriented toward failure. Withholding, passive aggression, or negativistic behavior can become habitual with a subsequent reduction in one's ability to function adequately in the real world (Cavaiola & Lavender, 2000). Furthermore, acting in opposition to one's basic wants has serious consequences; it implies a withdrawal of affect and psychic energy from previously enjoyed activities, which is indicative of a movement toward stillness and psychological death.

In a broader sense, withholding is not restricted to the holding back of positive qualities and behaviors from others, but relates also to limiting one's own capabilities and denying to oneself the enjoyment and happiness in activities that enhance one's self-esteem and bring one happiness and satisfaction.

There are three brief examples to illustrate withholding behaviors. The first involves withholding from oneself and the next two involve withholding from others.

Evan, 45, worked hard and was successful in his career, but his greatest joy was driving his fast powerboat on the weekends. He loved to speed out to the islands, and enjoyed the motion of flying across the waves even when the ocean was rough. However, as time progressed he spent more and more time at work and found himself spending fewer and fewer weekends at the marina. Even though he realized that he was neglecting the boat and denying himself the pleasure of driving it, he never seemed to be able to reinvolve himself in his favorite pastime. Eventually, he sold the boat.

Charles, 27, had a lifelong pattern of being passive-aggressive and his withholding behavior continually aggravated his wife. Despite her constant nagging, he reluctantly completed his PhD at age 35. For quite a while he had difficulty finding work in his field. His wife suspected correctly that in his passivity he was not anxious to find employment. When Charles eventually got a decent job, he was lethargic about advancing and making more money. As their relationship progressed, Charles became even more passive and inept, to the point of being unable to light his own cigarette without fumbling.

One day Charles dropped a lit cigarette in his bed, started a fire, and was severely burned. In the burn ward, his wife begged him to do his physical therapy, but he refused to take the necessary steps prescribed by the doctor. Sadly his passive-aggressive pattern continued to manifest itself and currently his wife is still pushing him to take action.

In the third example, a man and woman had been working closely together on a scientific project when the man expressed his admiration for her brilliance. His acknowledgment initially made the woman feel good, but soon afterward she became confused and somewhat addled in performing the same high-level functions that her coworker had come to appreciate. On an unconscious level, the man's appreciation and respect for her contribution to their equally shared project made her anxious and aroused deep-seated insecurities in her. She reacted by regressing to a lower level of functioning and her performance deteriorated. Ultimately, she provoked a negative response from her associate, invalidating his original impression of her.

For the most part, people adopt a withholding posture and inhibit their positive responses with little or no awareness of the underlying reason. They resort to defensive behavior to allay their unconscious anxiety, and in doing so cause damage to their personal relationships. Unless they develop insight or explore the phenomenon of withholding, preferably in a therapy situation, they may never understand what has gone wrong between them.

Withholding responses are *crazy making* for the victims. Often people profess love but unconsciously act out the opposite, provoking aggression in their partners. Bach and Deutsch (1979) applied Bateson's (1972) *double-bind* concept to analyze how people use positive verbal communications to rationalize passive-aggressive, withholding behaviors as simple mistakes, errors of judgment, carelessness, or innocent forgetfulness. They stressed the fact that "people are not usually aware that they are sending two conflicting messages" (Bach & Deutsch, p. 17), nonetheless, these double messages confuse, mystify, and drive the recipient crazy (R. Firestone & Catlett, 2009).

Within a personal relationship, the withholding individual retreats from an adult posture and an equal relationship with his or her partner, thereby recreating the situation of his or her childhood in present-day interactions. By regressing to more childish modes of relating and by withholding adult responses, he or she is able to manipulate another person into taking care of or criticizing him or her. In this way the person preserves the imagined security of the original illusion of connection with his or her parents. Thus, behaviors that elicit or provoke negative parental reactions—worry, fear, anger, or even punishment—act to cement the fantasy of being connected to another person and relieve the anxiety of being separate, alone, and vulnerable to death (R. Firestone & Catlett, 1999).

Often achievement, unusual success, or personal fulfillment in a relationship leads to anxiety states that precipitate withholding responses. In these cases an individual holds back the adult, competent behavior that led to success or accomplishments (R. Firestone, 1990a). In one instance, a man was promoted to president of a large manufacturing firm. At the end of the quarter, he received a substantial bonus and stock options because he had succeeded in halting the company's slide into bankruptcy and had actually turned a profit. In addition the chairman of the board personally expressed his appreciation and admiration for his outstanding performance. Over the next several months the man appeared to lose the passion and energy that had brought him such success. He began to delegate many of his responsibilities and to defer vital decision-making to his subordinates. Two years later, he was fired by the Board of Directors for incompetency.

This example tends to corroborate previous research indicating that positive life events can trigger stressful reactions and regression (Paykel, 1974). Although positive events have been accorded some recognition as causative factors of self-destructive behavior, many therapists still characteristically tend toward conventional explanations; that is, they stress negative circumstances as being the more logical antecedents while failing to note the real causes (R. Firestone, 1990a).

Withholding, as an ongoing defensive posture, is symptomatic of a pervasive tendency to renounce life that, unless interrupted, results in a shutting down, a paralysis, of that part of the individual that strives for emotional health and growth. Essentially, the process of withholding involves a progressive elimination of oneself as a feeling human being (R. Firestone, 1997a).

Isolation and Withdrawal From Relationships Into an Inward Lifestyle

Many people tend to retreat from close relationships and distance themselves from loved ones in an unconscious effort to avoid feelings of vulnerability in relation to potential loss or rejection. Therefore, the breakup of a previously satisfying relationship for no appropriate reason can be thought of as a self-destructive act, especially when one is not moving on to something better. People who suddenly leave relationships often do so in order to isolate themselves, to maintain an inward posture, and to more freely act out other microsuicidal habit patterns. The self-destructive component involved is frequently more alarming than the loss itself. There is a sense that the *runaway* is acting on self-destructive impulses, which arouses considerable fear and concern in others.

Incidents of adolescents running away as well as mysterious disappearances of adults can be symptomatic of this form of pathology (Robbins, 1998; Utech, 1994). The U.S. Department of Justice (2007), citing Centers for Disease Control data, noted that talk of running away or attempts to do so were warning signs of adolescent suicide. According to Robbins, studies have shown that among adolescents "suicide ideation is associated with a very clear cut form of escape behavior, 'running away'" (p. 57). Utech reported that: "Running away, although potentially dangerous, is an alternative [to suicide] selected by many adolescents" (p. 200), in particular those who have been sexually abused or experienced incest. Richard Heckler (1994) has provided an analogy explaining how running away and withdrawal from one's friends and family are definite steps in this kind of dangerous progression toward suicide:

> One pulls further away from genuine interpersonal exchange and, over time, loses a sense of who or what could be helpful. It is as if a person has become lost in the forest and finds a cave in which to sleep for the night. . . . Every rustle of leaves or crack of a twig is interpreted as a sign that something alive and dangerous is drawing nearer, and one pulls back into the cave, withdrawing deeper and deeper. The further the person retreats from the cave's mouth, the less the possibility of his or her distinguishing face from fear, help from danger. (p. 56)

Continually changing relationships, jobs, or careers, as well as frequent moves to new physical surroundings, are often indicative of a self-destructive lifestyle. Men and women who repeatedly make unfortunate choices of romantic or marriage partners and who invariably end up recreating the unpleasant circumstances of their family can also be considered "microsuicidal."

A gradual withdrawal into isolation and fantasy, loss of feeling for the self, obsessive ruminations, unusual shyness and quietness, withdrawal of affect from loved ones and friends, and a shirking of responsibilities are other signs of regression to an inward posture. Studies have shown that isolation is related to self-destructive behavior. Gove and Hughes (1980) demonstrated that alcoholism and suicide are two forms of social pathology that are related to social isolation, operationally defined as living alone. These self-destructive behaviors were found to be much more prevalent in those living alone than in those who lived with others. Joseph Richman (1993), in his book *Preventing Elderly Suicide,* listed social isolation (e.g., living alone, living in the inner city or a socially disorganized area, few or no friends, and social withdrawal of a couple) as factors significantly correlated with suicide in this age group (Note 3). Research has also shown a positive correlation between high suicide rates and areas of low population density with its resultant physical and social isolation (Seiden, 1984).

By promoting a state of passivity and feelings of self-hatred, destructive thoughts or voices contribute significantly to an individual's defensiveness and withdrawal. To complicate matters, an inward person frequently projects angry, self-critical thoughts onto other people and perceives *them* as critical or hostile.

Destructive thoughts, or voice attacks, that predict rejection are common in people who become isolated, inward, and secretive. For example, they tell themselves: *"They* won't want you as a friend once they really get to know you"; or "Don't get too involved—*she or he* will reject you sooner or later." In effect, the voice persuades men and women to avoid the risks of close attachments, which in turn contributes to their tendencies toward isolation and a defended posture (R. Firestone, 1988; R. Firestone & Catlett, 1999).

Many people experience thoughts advising them that privacy and isolation are necessary (R. Firestone, 1986). These seemingly friendly thoughts are difficult to counter because they appear reasonable. Obviously one does need some degree of isolation for creative or concentrated work and for time away from the stresses of daily living. However, as noted in the studies cited above, extended periods of isolation from social contacts can be detrimental to mental health. In one case a woman who came close to dying from a serious suicide attempt reported that prior to her self-destructive act, her voice told her: "You never have any time for yourself, to do what you want to do. You need some time alone so you can think." Once she was alone she began planning the details of her suicide. In retrospect, she realized that suicidal thoughts had not occurred to her when she was among friends, yet she had felt compelled by her voice to seek isolation, where she was at the mercy of vicious self-attacks and suicidal urges (R. Firestone, 1986; Parr, 1985) (Note 4).

People who are isolated and who resist logic or reason that would improve their situation are exhibiting a microsuicidal lifestyle. Being impervious to suggestions to socialize or to make friends, or being reluctant to seek therapeutic help that could provide solutions to one's problems are indications of the strength of one's resistance.

Other Maladaptive Behaviors

Mismanagement of Finances, Vocational Failure, and Compulsive Gambling

There are a number of other behaviors that have a deadening and demoralizing effect on an individual's life. For example, many people fail to handle practical matters in a manner that is effective and functional, yet this indulgent style causes them a great deal of misery. Often people who mismanage money rationalize that their overspending is due to inadequate funds or insufficient earnings, but when they earn more money they get even more into debt. This is a form of microsuicide that leads to chronic worry, self-demeaning thoughts, and self-attacks and serves the function of distracting a person from the more significant realities of life.

Before his father's death, Patrick managed to live well on his earnings as a prominent lawyer. He saved money, bought a condo, and enjoyed a feeling of financial success. He made other real estate investments and they prospered. After the sad event, there was a complete turn-about in Patrick's practical affairs. At first it was gradual, his spending increased out of proportion to his earnings, and he made some minor bad investments. Later this pattern expanded and eventually grew to the point where financial problems consumed his entire interest in life. Within five years he was a million dollars in debt, had little to show for it, and was constantly harassed by bill collectors.

There are many people like Patrick who create a similar situation and fail to recognize it as a self-destructive process. In Patrick's case the cause was apparent: his father's death had caused him to identify more closely with a man who spent his life as a chronic failure financially. In essence, Patrick repeated his father's pattern and spent many years tormented by his plight. In therapy he was able to develop insight and reverse the situation.

The young student who consistently flunks his or her college courses despite a high IQ is engaging in a self-defeating pattern with negative consequences for the future. Still others manage to fail at work despite having the necessary intelligence and skills. Negative attitudes toward work, provoking behaviors, problems with authority, and other self-defeating machinations lead to chronic problems and unhappiness in life. People rarely have insight into the true cause of their microsuicidal lifestyles. They tend to blame their lack of success on outside circumstances and rationalize their failures.

Compulsive gambling is an extreme form of microsuicide that has ruined many lives. When gambling becomes an addiction, it completely dominates the person's thoughts and feelings and may rage out of control. This addiction is not restricted to the casino, race track, or other forms of gaming but can involve speculation on the stock market and other precarious, high-risk business investments that are considered to be more legitimate.

In all of the matters considered above, participants are involved in self-destructive behavior that is aimed at a partial annihilation of the self. The pain that these problems cause can lead to actual suicide. In addition, individuals who increase their acting out of degrading microsuicidal behaviors over an extended period of time become demoralized, which in turn gives rise to feelings of self-condemnation and self-hatred. Guilt about behavior that goes against a person's self-interest contributes to a feeling of inwardness, withdrawal, and paranoia toward others.

Neglect of Personal Hygiene and One's Surroundings

Lack of concern with one's personal appearance and hygiene as well as neglect of one's living circumstances are symptomatic of underlying self-destructive tendencies. When individuals allow their home or work environment to become cluttered, dirty, or unattractive, there is an indication of pathology. The way people keep and attend to their surroundings reveals hidden attitudes and feelings about themselves. For example, Greg (28) habitually kept his personal belongings and workspace in a complete shambles: it was difficult for him to locate his clothes each morning; he consistently misplaced important items or lost his car keys in the mess that surrounded him. In an early session he revealed that as a young teenager he had felt especially futile and helpless whenever he ruminated about death, which was quite frequent.

> The thing I hated most about death was that it wasn't in my control. I knew for certain that it was going to happen. All of us have a common fate even though we act as though it's not true. But it's going to happen. Just the idea

of having it in my control took that pain away. I could go ahead and do it any time I wanted to. I could take the control out of fate. I could take the control out of the eventuality simply by completing it right then.

In describing his early family life, Greg went on to say:

From the time when I was seven, I didn't let anything matter to me. Nothing mattered to me. I'd let nothing have any value in my life at all. I didn't care about school. I wouldn't try to get good grades. I would not take care of anything. I refused, stubbornly refused, to let anything into my life that had any value.

Greg progressed well in therapy and made significant personal changes. A follow-up session some years later revealed that Greg had continued to develop and had adopted a different perspective on life. In his vernacular, he cleaned up his act. Greg had systematically organized his room and office and had begun to enjoy not only the cleaning up process but also took delight in the results.

For so many years, I lived my life not being invested in my life at all. Only over the last ten years, I've slowly let things begin to matter to me. It may seem like a small thing, but it's not really. It means a lot to me. Now I take pride in keeping things neat and orderly. Things in my life are extremely valuable to me; especially my friends. But now I have fear since I have so much to lose. It feels almost good to have fear; I like being concerned about my life. I like trying to take care of myself and to preserve my body. It does matter to me. And that level of awareness of my life increases as a direct result of my investing more and more in it. (Parr, 1991a, 1991b)

MICROSUICIDAL BEHAVIOR IN OLDER PEOPLE

Patterns of withholding and other defensive, microsuicidal behaviors are increasingly relied upon as individuals grow older (R. Firestone, 2000). Indeed the methods that people habitually use to defend themselves against the dread of death tend to intensify and over time become a basic part of their character structure. Established patterns of giving up favorite activities, special interests, and gratifications eventually reach the point where individuals feel increasingly demoralized.

By the time most people reach their middle or later years, the specific self-destructive behaviors that they have engaged in for decades become more pronounced and increasingly interfere with the pursuit of personal and career goals. Their positive strivings are diminished, their hopes dimmed, and, in a society characterized by attitudes of ageism which tend to dismiss older people as expendable, they may find themselves feeling isolated and abandoned. They become depressed as they notice that their opinions and feelings are largely ignored. Psychological suicide, the obliteration of the personality, can be the outcome as older people come to face their physical deterioration, other adversities, and the fact of their impending death.

In the United States in the year 2000, the suicide rate for people aged 75 to 84 was 17.7 per 100,000, nearly double the overall United States rate. White men over the age of 85 are at the greatest risk of all age, gender, and race groups. The suicide rate for these men was 59.6 per 100,000, nearly six times the overall rate (FirstLink, 2008). As Diekstra (1996) pointed out, "Those prone to suicide are more likely to be older men, more often unmarried, divorced[,] or widowed, living alone and unemployed or retired" (p. 18). Furthermore, according to McIntosh and Hubbard (1988), many elderly people use methods that are not as obviously or instantaneously suicidal, but result in premature avoidable death. They stop engaging in behaviors that "would sustain life and health, including neglecting routine medical examinations and prescribed medical treatment, ignoring or delaying needed medical aid, and refusing medications and/or nourishment" (p. 37).

In studying people's potential for microsuicide and suicide at various stages of life, particularly in the later stages, one must take into consideration idiosyncratic moods associated with each person's sense of meaninglessness, purposelessness, or emptiness in life. These are among the attitudes that suicidologists Fournier, Motto, Osgood, and Fitzpatrick (1991) have described as contributing to older people experiencing their lives as essentially spiritless or without satisfaction. According to Maris (1995), "Every [elderly] suicide is chronic in the sense that the etiologies develop over about 40 to 50 years" (pp. 173–174). In an earlier work (R. Firestone, 1997b), the first author contended that: "The degree of vulnerability in terms of the amount of psychological pain that an older person can tolerate is closely related to the extent to which he or she has used self-destructive defense mechanisms to cope with pain and stress throughout the life cycle" (p. 107).

It is equally important to recognize that although all people utilize psychological defenses that cut into their experiences to a certain extent, they cope differentially with problems of aging. Some rise to the challenge posed by existential threats (e.g., being diagnosed with a terminal illness) and continue to strive and to love life, while others tend to progressively give up. People essentially give meaning and purpose to their lives through investing themselves emotionally in personal relationships, activities, interests, and causes that express their true identity. Sustained investment leads to a zest for life. The philosophy that "it is better to have loved and lost than never to have loved at all" offers a resolution to the dilemma faced not only by older people but also by every human being.

CONCLUSION

Microsuicide involves many forms of self-destructive responses to life that act to shield one from the unpleasant realization of aging, the wretchedness of imagining being on one's deathbed, and the fact of death as an ending. Perversely, holding back from investing in one's life can function as a kind of adaptation to these painful issues. It represents a method of taking over power and control in a situation where one is, in reality, totally powerless. The renunciation of events and experiences that are meaningful in life is akin to a death of the spirit, a partial death on earth. Yet giving up on life, denying one's wants, and retreating from love and closeness can provide a partial relief from death anxiety.

Many children have learned early in their lives that withholding their desires is adaptive in contending with negative circumstances in the family constellation. The anticipation of hurt or rejection leads them to abandon goals and objectives that they imagine will be unfulfilled. In addition, there may be no direct outlet for their anger and frustration, so they learn to find passive means to express their aggression. They either become passively aggressive or turn their anger against themselves in a manner that negatively impacts their whole lives. Later in adulthood the same withholding patterns that were once functional, adaptive, and protective serve as serious limitations (R. Firestone, 1997a).

Many people adopt addictive, self-negating lifestyles and become shackled in destructive relationships that involve dishing out and accepting human rights violations on a daily basis. (See Chapter 3 in *Fear of Intimacy*, R. Firestone & Catlett, 1999.) In seeking a merged identity, safety, and security, many accept abuses that they would otherwise consider intolerable. Regarding addictions in general, and their destructive effect on the personality, substances and routines that were once effective in reducing pain and tension and originally considered to be ego-syntonic later have the opposite effect (R. Firestone, 1993). It is important to emphasize that addictions to substances play a significant role in microsuicide, violence, and actual suicide. According to Roizen (1997), for example, about 86 percent of homicide offenders were drinking at the time of their offense. Similarly, a report by *The Injury Prevention Network Newsletter* (Violence Prevention Coalition of Greater Los Angeles, 1991) showed that 50 percent of adolescent suicides are under the influence of alcohol at the time of their death. Ironically, the destructive behaviors that are so averse to living are those that effectively deny death awareness.

In conclusion, defensive machinations that were once adopted by the frustrated child in the family situation are applied to the terrifying issue of death and dying, causing one to live indifferently, carelessly, or self-destructively. If one is basically critical or mean toward oneself, self-denying, cynical toward others, and miserable enough, life may cease to be worth living. For those who have erected impenetrable defensive barriers, isolated themselves from the warmth of emotional contact, and spent a lifetime in psychological pain and distress, death may be considered a friend instead of an enemy. Indeed if one is overly self-restrictive, alienated, and severely limiting of one's choices and movements in life, it can make one's anticipated demise a nonevent.

NOTES

1. According to Lester and Tartaro (2002), the suicide rate of death row inmates was 113 per 100,000 from 1976 to 1999, approximately five times the suicide rate for males in the United States.
2. Searles (1961) further elucidated the microsuicidal aspect of schizophrenia of not being really *alive* as well as the function served by omnipotent fantasies that are held by many schizophrenic patients:

> The author has long thought that this [lack of aliveness] has to do mainly with their widespread repression of the gamut of their feelings—feelings of all sorts. But he has come to wonder whether this repression *in toto* may serve an additional defensive function: One need not fear death so long as one feels dead anyway; one has, subjectively, nothing to lose through death.
>
> And it certainly seems to the writer that a second great aspect of schizophrenic symptomatology, the fantasy of personal omnipotence, ties in closely with the subject of this paper. It is often mentioned that the schizophrenic patient views himself, and other persons, as being omnipotent; but we need to remind ourselves that the companion of omnipotence is immortality. These two subjective qualities are in fact

two sides of the same coin; whenever the gods are thought of they are assumed to be *immortal* gods. (pp. 639–640)

3. Richman (1993) emphasized that social isolation as a couple can be as deadly as isolation for an individual. In discussing the dangers of symbiotic partnerships, he asserted: "The problem in suicide is not only separation, but the wish to merge, to become one with the person who is lost or unavailable" (p. 106).
4. The references to Parr indicate a series of film documentaries produced for the Glendon Association by Geoff Parr: *The Inner Voice in Suicide* (1985), *Life, Death, and Denial* (1991b), and *Defenses against Death Anxiety* (1991a).

Core Defenses Against Death Anxiety

7 The Basic Defense Against Death Anxiety: The Fantasy Bond

Only humans can hallucinate their way out of danger.... The ego regresses to a more primitive state of magical thinking in the attempt to restore the safety and security of symbiotic bliss.

—J. S. Piven, Death and Delusion (2004a, p. 128)

The wish for fusion and merger denies the reality of separation and, thus, the reality of death.

—James B. McCarthy, Death Anxiety (1980, p. 201)

One significant aspect of the defensive apparatus involves the formation of the fantasy bond, which sanctifies the family, enveloping it and other forms of group identification in an illusion of connection that assures immortality. The fantasy bond, an imagined fusion with another person, a group, or a cause, offers security at the expense of self-realization, autonomy, and individuation. The fantasy solution originally arises to cope with interpersonal pain and separation anxiety in infancy or early childhood and is significantly strengthened when the child learns about death (R. Firestone, 1985). Thereafter this imagined merger becomes the most powerful and effective denial of death, providing relief from the pain and anguish associated with the awareness of existential realities (R. Firestone, 1994b).

Once the fantasy bond is formed, there is a strong resistance to any incursions from reality. Resistance is inevitable because if the core defense were to break down, the person would be faced once again with the pain of his or her original trauma. When the fantasy bond is threatened, it gives rise to an intense fear reaction, disturbing the defended person's psychological equilibrium. The fantasy bond is not only a form of self-deception with various consequences to one's adjustment, but also includes attitudes and behaviors of aggression, hostility, and malice toward those who challenge its function (R. Firestone, 1996).

DEFINITION OF THE FANTASY BOND

Many personality theorists are accustomed to thinking of bonds as constructive attachments typified by long-lasting love and devotion or in terms of the positive bonding that occurs between an infant and its caregiver in the context of a secure attachment. "It is important to differentiate . . . [our] specific use of the word 'bond' from its other uses in psychological and popular literature. . . . Our concept of the fantasy bond uses *bond* rather in the sense of bondage or limitation of freedom" (R. Firestone, 1985, pp. 36–37). In his Foreword to *The Fantasy Bond*, R. D. Laing (1985) stated:

> [The fantasy bond is] a sort of bondage shared by millions of men and women throughout the western world. After living together and being in love for awhile, they begin to feel tied to each other, bound to each other, connected to each other. They are not, except in fantasy. . . . The fantasy bond is an illusion, a fantasy; even more, it is virtually and literally, a *mirage*. There are oases. They are to be found, sometimes, by some of us. But we shall *never* find an oasis in the spell of the mirage. (p. 17)

The primary fantasy bond can be defined as an illusion of connection, originally an imaginary fusion with the mother or primary caregiver. It is a core defense and is protected by secondary defenses, which are patterns of thoughts and behaviors that are antithetical toward the self and others. The term *fantasy bond* describes both the original imaginary connection formed during childhood and the transference and intensification of this internal image of oneness to significant others in the adult's intimate associations. The process of forming a fantasy bond leads to a subsequent deterioration in the adult's personal relationships (R. Firestone, 1985).

This chapter focuses on the formation of the original fantasy bond during childhood and on people's imagined connections with significant others. Although these connections provide a sense of security and immortality, they cause serious damage to individuals, their marriages and family lives, and ultimately to society at large.

BRIEF HISTORY OF THE DEVELOPMENT OF THE CONCEPT OF THE FANTASY BOND

Developing an awareness of the detrimental effects of maintaining fantasy bonds has been an ongoing concern for the group of friends in the longitudinal study described in Chapter 1. A great deal of time and energy has been spent exploring and trying to understand every aspect of relationships to the benefit of all concerned. In the group process the authors, along with the participants, devoted considerable effort to exposing dishonesty and duplicity in personal relationships. We learned that recognition of the inherent problem of maintaining and protecting fantasies of fusion was the first step in coping with the destructive process.

In the course of our explorations, we found that many people confuse an internal fantasy or feeling of love with external indications or physical expressions of love. They erroneously expect their loved ones to feel that they are loved and cared for even when there is a lack of any outward manifestation.

Edgar and Sean had been involved for three years and were planning to move in together when Edgar began to have doubts about the relationship. He realized that over the past several weeks, Sean had seemed distant and had made no effort to contact him. On the one occasion that they had gone out, Edgar noticed that Sean showed no affection toward him and was uncommunicative and irritable. He began to worry that Sean was thinking about breaking up with him.

Because he placed significant value on the relationship, Edgar finally got up the courage to tell Sean his concerns. Sean was shocked and puzzled by Edgar's complaints and his doubts about their relationship. He almost couldn't believe what he had heard because he had a very different picture. He told Edgar that he loved him more than ever and indeed he had fantasized about making love with him often over the past weeks. To Sean, this was ample proof of his deep love for Edgar.

In this case, the discrepancy between Sean's imagined love for his partner and the lack of real affection and communication served the purpose of supporting Sean's fantasy bond with Edgar and offered him a sense of security and safety; at the same time it had led to real trouble in the relationship.

Many people mistake a fantasy of love for the real thing and act out destructively while maintaining the illusion. How often have romantic partners claimed that they loved each other while treating each other disrespectfully or consciously deceiving each other about monetary issues or outside sexual relationships? In talking openly our associates and friends have exposed and scrutinized these contradictions as part of a concerted attempt to understand the causes of dishonesty in both couple and family interactions. In addition, human rights issues in personal relations were a primary consideration, and people developed a standard that emphasized the personal integrity of each individual (R. Firestone, et al., 2003). In understanding the detrimental effect of mixed messages on child development and mental health in general, we have emphasized the importance of people's actions corresponding to their spoken words. In this atmosphere, people have challenged illusions in their relationships, and a great deal has been learned about the fantasy bond.

We have also investigated the function of the fantasy bond in relation to death anxiety. In couples' discussion groups, people have talked about how their defensive behaviors were motivated by fears that went beyond a concern with being rejected or hurt in their relationships. They seemed to engage in these aversive behaviors after feeling exceptionally close to their partner. They began to recognize that interactions in which they were overly critical of their partners or had acted out angry, provoking behaviors served as distractions from underlying concerns about potential loss, separation, and death. In exploring their deeper motivations, they found that there was a positive correlation between increased death concerns and denying themselves satisfying sexual experiences, cutting off feelings, and retreating from emotional intimacy. Feeling especially close, loving, or compassionate, they could not bear the thought of losing their partner, or themselves. The more they felt alive and vital the less they could tolerate the painful imagining of their eventual demise (R. Firestone & Catlett, 1999).

Findings from this ongoing study have been disseminated through numerous books, films, and articles. As a result, over the past two decades the concept of the fantasy bond has become integrated into the mainstream of psychological thought. The founder of family systems theory, Murray Bowen (personal communication, 1987), noted that the concept of the fantasy bond provides an in-depth analysis of how the defenses of each individual family member operate to maintain the *emotional ego mass* that characterizes much of traditional family life and that in turn restricts each person's movement toward individuation and self-differentiation (R. Firestone, 1997a). Other theorists, beginning with Hellmuth Kaiser (Fierman, 1965), have also dealt with the subject of this defensive, illusory mode of relating that exists to varying degrees within the majority of couple and family relationships (Karpel, 1976; Wexler & Steidl, 1978; Willi, 1975/1982).

THE FORMATION OF THE PRIMARY FANTASY BOND

As noted in Chapter 3, the point in the developmental sequence when the child first discovers death is the critical juncture where his or her defense system crystallizes and shapes his or her future. Thereafter, a person's most profound terror centers on contemplating the obliteration of the ego, the total loss of the self (Meyer, 1975; M. Stern, 1968; Zilboorg, 1943). As described earlier, most people adjust to the fear of death by withdrawing energy and emotional investment in close, personal relationships, sexuality, and other lively pursuits. To whatever extent they renounce real satisfactions in the interpersonal environment, they rely increasingly on internal gratification, fantasies of fusion, and addictive painkillers. No child has an ideal upbringing; therefore, all people depend to varying degrees on internal gratification from the primary fantasy bond which develops in the context of the child's earliest attachment relationships (R. Firestone, 1985).

Every child needs warmth, affection, direction, and guidance from adults who ideally would possess both the desire and ability to provide satisfaction of these basic needs (R. Firestone, 1957, 1984). However, many parents lack the ability to offer the nurturance or guidance that children need for their emotional development. At times, the parents' inadequacies lead to insensitive treatment that intensifies the child's feelings of frustration, emotional pain, and fears of abandonment. Morrant and Catlett (2008) explained how an infant copes with these conditions:

> When "love-food" [Note 1] is scanty, or the mother is mostly emotionally absent, the infant experiences "separation anxiety," a euphemism for being overcome by rage and the terror of annihilation. Then imagination, as Healer, steps into the breach. To cope with this anxiety, the infant imagines

a make-believe mother, a *fantasy*, to comfort loneliness and dread. He or she incorporates all the experiences of the mother, transforming the woman of flesh and blood into a cognitive image. The infant develops a relationship with this inner fantasy of the mother.... [This fantasy bond] is the primary and greatest defense against separation anxiety [and later death anxiety] and gives a counterfeit comfort in the place of insufficient love, sensitivity, tenderness, and control. (pp. 357–358)

The fantasy bond develops as a basic response to inevitable deficiencies in child-rearing practices and becomes the child's core defense (R. Firestone, 1987a). Even before they discover death, children use this imaginary connection with the mother or caregiver, together with primitive self-nourishing behaviors, to avert ego disintegration; that is, to avoid the possibility of being overwhelmed by the intensity of their reactions to separation experiences and other disturbing events. The prolonged dependency of the infant, its desperate need for its parents, and faulty or abusive parenting make the formation of the primary defense imperative. The fantasy bond allows children to conjure up their mother's image whenever she is absent or when they are under stress. In the child's inner world of fantasy, magical thinking rules the day; there are no separations, time has no meaning, and everything is impervious to logic, including existential realities involving one's life and the lives of loved ones.

The Self-Parenting Process

The imagined fusion with the parent is highly effective as a defense because a human being's capacity for imagination provides partial gratification of needs and reduces tension. For example, studies conducted by Keys, Brozek, Henschel, Mickelsen, and Taylor (1950) demonstrated that fantasy can be rewarding under conditions of physical deprivation. Subjects whose food intake was restricted to the minimum sustenance level reported that their physical hunger was partly relieved by fantasizing about food. Even more relevant are Silverman, Lachmann, and Milich's (1982) experimental studies: when these researchers presented subjects with the subliminal message "Mommy and I are One" on the tachistoscope, the words functioned to ameliorate severe symptoms in schizophrenic patients and in other, less disturbed individuals.

The fantasy bond originates from the child's attempt to parent him or herself and involves self-nourishing habit patterns as well as self-punishing attitudes and behaviors. Self-nourishing behaviors begin with thumb-sucking, compulsively fingering or holding onto a blanket, or stroking oneself, and can develop into eating disorders, alcoholism, drug abuse, excessive masturbation, an impersonal style of sexual relating, and other routine or compulsive activities that reduce pain. Self-critical thoughts, guilt reactions, attacks on self, and self-limiting, self-destructive actions are examples of the self-punishing component (R. Firestone, 1997a).

Self-nourishing behaviors support an illusion of pseudo-independence in children, a feeling of being able to gratify themselves and of needing little from the outside world. The child experiences this false sense of self-sufficiency because he or she has introjected an image of the good and powerful parent into the self system. Unfortunately, at the same time, the child necessarily incorporates the parent's covert or overt rejecting attitudes toward him or her. These incorporated parental attitudes form the basis of the child's negative self-concept. In this way children develop an illusion of being at once the good, strong parent and the bad, weak child. This leads to a form of psychological equilibrium, an imaginary self-sufficient system that is generally detrimental to one's later adjustment (R. Firestone, 1984, 1985).

The degree to which these maladaptive defenses and illusions are manifested in one's adult life is proportional to the amount of stress that one suffered early on. Children who have experienced excessive stress, rejection, or deprivation often come to prefer self-gratifying habit patterns and fantasy over deep feeling and associations with others. These self-parenting behaviors eventually become part of an addictive process that persists into adult life, providing protection against the dread and anxiety surrounding death (R. Firestone, 1997a). According to Piven (2004a), "To the extent that people wish for reunion with mother, they face to some degree an existential alienation and impulse driving them toward fantasies of bliss and cessation of pain" (p. 145).

Distortions Inherent in the Self-Parenting Process

The self-parenting process or fantasy bond is intensified and becomes an integral part of the defensive apparatus as children evolve their concept of death. While the process of parenting oneself *does* allay the anxiety of feeling separate and alone, it creates numerous distortions. It is valuable to delineate the various defense mechanisms involved in self-parenting and to describe the many distortions of oneself, other people, and the real world that these defenses predispose.

First, in order to maintain the sense of immortality and imagined safety of family ties, one must idealize one's parents and family. Even people who criticize and blame their parents for their own unhappiness tend to be involved in an idealization process. On some level they refuse to acknowledge the limitations of their parents, who, because of their own defenses, were unable to provide loving care and nurturance. (See Chapter 5, "Idealization of the Family," in R. Firestone, 1985.) For example, a successful business executive, powerful and influential in his own life, refused to answer his home phone because he was afraid the incoming call might be from his mother. Thus, although he was sharply critical of his mother, he gave her power over his life that he granted to no one else. Because this defensive idealization is supported by society's belief in the sanctity of the family, it is rarely challenged as one matures and moves on in life.

Second, the idealization process must be maintained for the fantasy bond to work effectively. To do this, children conceptualize themselves as bad or unlovable to protect against the awareness that their parents are inadequate, rejecting, or destructive (Arieti, 1974; Kempe & Kempe, 1978; Oaklander, 1978, 2006). Rather than accept the painful truth of negative parental characteristics, children internalize a corresponding negative image of themselves.

Furthermore, children are helpless and dependent and so cannot cope with the emotional pain of dysfunctional family life without fragmenting. Instead of identifying with their hurt selves, they depersonalize and identify with their parents' destructive point of view. This identification with the aggressor and internalization of the parent, during moments of punishment and stress when the parent is at his or her worst, effectively turns the child against himself or herself (Ferenczi, 1933/1955; A. Freud, 1966). The child takes on the characteristics of the hurtful or frightening parent in order to relieve anxiety and gain some measure of security. However, in the process the child incorporates not only the parent's animosity and aggression directed toward him or her, but also the parent's guilt, the fear, indeed, the total complex of the parent's defensive adaptation in the form of a self-hating inner voice. (See Chapter 5, "Identification with the Aggressor," in R. Firestone, 1997a.) The incorporated anger is either internalized as self-hatred, leading to self-denial and depression, or it is externalized as angry, paranoid attitudes and aggressive behavior toward others.

Third, the powerful feelings of self-hatred inherent in the child's negative view of him or herself are ultimately displaced onto other people. Later on, particularly in times of emotional stress, people tend to unleash the same anger on themselves and against others that they experienced as children (R. Firestone, 1990b). This concept explains the intergenerational transmission of child abuse.

In the unconscious drive to preserve the imagined connection with one's parents, one also displaces and projects one's negative self-concept onto romantic partners, which leads to a great deal of misery within the couple (R. Firestone & Catlett, 1999). Regarding the negative effects of these defenses on relationships, families, and society as a whole, Piven (2004b) noted: "First of all, children identify with the aggression of their parents, and adults themselves identify with the aggression of their surrogate parents, that is, society.... Second, aggression...becomes displaced onto scapegoats who are targeted for their evil or pernicious qualities" (p. 248).

These dynamics have been demonstrated in situations where prison guards have acted out the internalized anger of the harsh parent toward their child-selves through their sadistic treatment of inmates (Bettelheim, 1952/1979b ; A. Miller, 1980/1984). In the German concentration camps, for example, the guards, who themselves had been abused and mistreated as children under the guise of order and discipline, had come to consider themselves as inferior, unworthy, and unclean. In an attempt to absolve themselves of painful feelings of self-hatred, they then projected these characteristics onto anyone they saw as different and at their mercy, such as the Jews and gypsies (Fromm, 1941; A. Miller). They were unconsciously compelled to mistreat these minority groups in a manner similar to the way they had been mistreated as children.

This phenomenon was also observed in the torture of prisoners at the hands of seemingly normal individuals, both in wartime (Abu-Ghraib) and in experimental settings. The classic Stanford Prison experiment, in which normal students played the roles of guards and prisoners, had to be called off after only six days because of the aggressive, dehumanizing behavior of *guards* who became progressively more parental, authoritarian, and sadistic toward the *prisoners* (Haney & Zimbardo, 1998; Zimbardo & White, 1972). Similarly, Milgram's (1974) experiment demonstrated that subjects were willing to deliver increasingly strong electric shocks to fellow subjects under direction of the experimenter (authority figure).

To preserve the idealized image of their parents, children must dispose of their parents' actual negative qualities. They deny or block from awareness those parental characteristics that are especially harmful to them and project them instead onto the world at large. (See Chapter 7 in R. Firestone, 1985.) For example, if their parents were hypercritical they come to experience the world as an unpleasant, critical place. By judging their parents as right or superior to others and other people as wrong or inferior, children (and later, adults) preserve their illusions about the family. Stereotypes, prejudice, and racist views represent extensions of these distortions into a cultural framework (Berke, 1988; Lasch, 1984).

On a societal level, negative parental qualities are projected onto those individuals or groups who are different culturally, racially, or ethnically or who have different customs, religious beliefs, and worldviews (R. Firestone, 1996). Because these projections are based on a core psychological defense, they stubbornly persist in the face of logic and contrary evidence. In idealizing his or her family, an individual also adopts the parents' biases and idiosyncratic beliefs and imitates their negative responses toward other people. More fundamentally, they imitate their parents' ways of coping with stress and these psychological defenses become a part of their own defensive apparatus (R. Firestone, 1990b).

All of the tendencies noted above are significant aspects of the fantasy bond and its effect on interpersonal relationships. Just as the imagined merger with one's family provides family members with an illusion of immortality, group identification offers individuals immunity from death through an imagined fusion with the membership (R. Firestone, 1984) (Note 2). In merging one's identity with that of a group, each person imagines that although he or she may not survive as an individual entity, he or she will live on as part of something larger which *will* continue to exist after he or she is gone (R. Firestone, 1994b, 1996).

THE DEVELOPMENT OF THE FANTASY BOND IN COUPLE RELATIONSHIPS

> When two people begin to move toward one another with the expectation of closeness, the emotionality or intensity that accompanies this process may result in fusion followed by a desperate need for space or distance. (Betchen, 2005, p. xv)

The decline in the quality of intimate relating and sexual passion observed in so many long-term relationships and marriages is usually attributed to familiarity, gender differences, economic difficulties, or other stresses of modern life. In truth, this decline is more appropriately attributable to the development of a fantasy bond in the couple or family. In the first stages of a relationship people often step outside of customary ways of defending themselves and to a certain extent become more open and vulnerable. As time passes, there is frequently a shift in the internal dynamics of a relationship; fears of potential loss or rejection emerge, painful feelings from childhood surface, and partners retreat to a more defended stance.

By the time they reach adulthood, most people have solidified their defenses and exist in a psychological equilibrium that they do not wish to disturb. Although the state of being in love is exciting, it can also be frightening. As people come to feel truly loved and experience loving feelings in return, it is inevitable that at times they would experience anxiety relating to the possibility of losing the prized relationship. There is also the dawning realization of the inevitable loss of the relationship through death. At the point where they begin to feel this anxiety, many people retreat from feeling close and form an imaginary connection with each other, gradually giving up the most valued aspects of their relationships. (See Chapter 3, "Couple and Family Bonds," in R. Firestone, 1985.)

Manifestations of the Fantasy Bond in Couple Relationships

In observing couples in the context of the longitudinal study, we noticed that in their friendships people generally seemed to get along harmoniously, maintain respect for each other, and treat each other kindly and decently. Disrespectful behavior, criticality, or abusive trends were manifested more within couples and families. Although at first this seems to be incongruous because our mates are the people we have chosen for special intimacy, it does make sense from another vantage point. Those closest to us challenge our deepest defenses and represent the greatest threat or intrusion into our self-protective posture toward life.

Even when couples get along relatively well, maintaining elements of a fantasy bond hurts their relationships and limits the individuals involved in their personal development. In committing themselves to a relationship partner, many people relinquish their autonomy and try to control one another in a somewhat futile effort to assure themselves that they are safe and secure. Often, each partner begins acting out of a sense of obligation rather than from a genuine desire to be with the other. In forming an addictive attachment with a romantic partner, they gradually give up special interests, reject meaningful friendships, and isolate themselves in an exclusive relationship. In this process they substitute habit for choice, lose their vitality and feeling, and there is generally a decline in the quality of their sexual relating. Often they stop making eye contact and limit or restrain their communications. All the while, they desperately attempt to retain an illusion of closeness and demand that their mates respond in kind. When one partner fails to offer the expected assurances, the other generally becomes harsh and punitive.

Couples in a fantasy bond often engage in habitual routines, family rituals, and superficial conversation to preserve the fantasy of being in love. These everyday practices, schedules, anniversary celebrations, family reunions, and the expected Saturday night dinner out, among many other traditions, become symbols of togetherness and romance, which are used to reinforce the couple's mutual fantasy of closeness and love. Gradually these form responses, and role-determined behaviors replace the substance of love, sensitivity, affection, and mutual respect that the partners initially expressed toward each other (R. Firestone & Catlett, 1999).

As a clinician, the first author has been impressed by the extent to which people reject genuine closeness with their loved ones and appear to prefer debilitating, conventional forms of safety, security, and togetherness.

> They fail to realize that to use a relationship to obtain security—that is, to secure a lie about life from another person—is tantamount to losing that relationship. The same is true of sexuality. To use sex...for any function other than its natural purposes of pleasure and reproduction bends the individual out of shape psychologically and sexually. One of the major reasons people are afraid of intimacy is that having a deeply satisfying sexual experience combined with close emotional contact and friendship paradoxically makes people more aware of their separateness. (R. Firestone, 1994b, p. 229)

Most people are uncomfortable with combining love and sexuality in an intimate relationship because it arouses anxiety about their vulnerability and death concerns. Experiencing the unique blend of love and sex often reminds them of the fragility of the physical body and of life itself. As a result, some people become sexually withholding to escape an awareness of being connected to their body, which is vulnerable to illness, aging, and death. An unusually close sexual encounter can be experienced as a powerful intrusion into their sense of safety and security. It actually shatters the false security of the fantasy bond (R. Firestone, 1984; R. Firestone & Catlett, 1999).

As Becker (1973/1997) put it, "Sex is of the body, and the body is of death" (p. 162). "The sexual conflict is thus a universal one because the body is a universal problem to a creature who must die. One feels guilty toward the body because the body is a bind, it overshadows our freedom" (p. 164). Terror Management researchers Goldenberg, Pyszczynski, McCoy, Greenberg, and Solomon (1999) have conjectured "that high-neuroticism individuals are conflicted by sex and that the conflict is rooted in mortality concerns" (p. 1184). In an experiment, Goldenberg, Cox, Pyszczynski, Greenberg, and Solomon (2002) found that anxious individuals "who are especially likely to find sex threatening, rated the physical aspects of sex [on a scale] as less appealing when reminded of their mortality" (p. 310).

The fear of losing a loved one through death is akin to the fear of losing oneself and can lead to a withdrawal of loving responses. We have found that when people experience emotional and sexual intimacy or when they experience reminders of death, they retreat from genuine closeness and intensify elements of the fantasy bond.

> In general, the more individuals become reconnected to the body and the more they become emotionally invested in a sexual partner or mate, the more anxiety and sadness they experience.... People often respond to the resulting rise in anxiety and emotional pain on a preconscious or unconscious level by reverting to a defended posture with little or no awareness of any alteration in their behavior. (R. Firestone, et al., 2006, p. 166)

Jenna and Don had been involved for six months when they decided to go away for a romantic weekend together. They made plans to meet in a nearby city, where Don would be completing a business conference on Friday evening. Jenna left work early on Friday; the ride up the coast was perfect: the weather was beautiful, her favorite CD was playing, and she looked forward with excitement to being with Don. Suddenly traffic slowed, and Jenna saw a gruesome car accident ahead. As she slowly drove by the scene, she was horrified to see paramedics covering a body with a sheet. Attempting to shake off her disturbing feelings, she told herself that the accident had nothing to do with her or her life. She turned up the music and sped off toward the city to meet Don.

During the weekend, the weather was warm and sunny, and on Saturday Jenna suggested a walk along the beach. That evening they went out to dinner and saw a movie. On Sunday morning, Don mentioned to Jenna that even though they were having fun together, he felt empty, as though something were missing. He realized that even though things had been friendly between them, Jenna hadn't been as affectionate as usual. They had been joking around, but they hadn't really talked personally. And it hadn't really felt intimate to him when they were sexual. At first, Jenna was puzzled; she had thought that everything was fine. But as they continued to talk, she remembered passing the accident on Friday. As she related the experience to Don, she became tearful. Seeing the dead body had brought up painful thoughts about how she would feel if that had been Don. She experienced the sad feelings that she had tried so hard to avoid after witnessing the accident; she and Don cried together. They felt deeply about how much they had come to mean to each other. For the remainder of the weekend, they felt tender toward each other and were close to their loving feelings.

In talking openly, this couple was able to explore their feelings and become closer as a result. Unfortunately, reminders of death usually have a negative effect without people becoming aware of the cause.

Implicit, Unconscious Contracts in a Fantasy Bond

Collusions become pathological when they commit the partners to restricting their interactive effectiveness to a particular form. This leads them to infringe upon each other's personal integrity and autonomy. The partners become unacknowledged accomplices in maintaining the collusion by accepting the destructive demands of the other without resistance, and by accepting behavior which hinders their personal development. (Willi, 1999, p. 94)

People's capacity for self-deception makes it possible for partners to collude in an illusion of closeness and connection while acting out aversive behaviors that contradict any recognizable operational definition of love. As R. D. Laing (1961) noted: "Collusion... is a 'game' played by two or more people whereby they deceive themselves, [and] settle for counterfeit acts of confirmation on the basis of pretence" (pp. 108–109).

Laing's analysis of the development of collusion is similar to the authors' conceptualization of the process of forming a fantasy bond in the couple. As part of this collusion, couples construct layer upon layer of defensive maneuvers to obscure the truth of what has happened to their love. As Piven (2004a) emphasized: "Not only is the reality of death disavowed, but the fact that one is lying and dissimulating a fiction is also denied awareness" (p. 24). Piven (2004b) posed the question: "Can there be criteria for determining fantasy when we are all to some degree self-deceptive?... Fantasy describes the intense investment in an idea or belief, attachment and immersion in an idea such that the belief is not subject to alteration or disconfirming instances" (p. 260).

The reality is that we are all essentially alone, and there is no way to effectively become one half of a whole with another person. When we attempt to connect to another and give up our individuality, we are of little or no value to ourselves or our partners. In immersing or losing ourselves in relating to the other, we gradually disappear and have little to offer in the way of emotional sustenance (R. Firestone & Catlett, 2009).

Sensing potential threats to the illusion of connection, partners negotiate agreements about certain rules and in essence commit to implicit contracts to reassure themselves that they are still in love (Hellinger, 1998; Sager et al., 1971). There are numerous unspoken rules governing conventional and obligatory behaviors that replace spontaneous acts of affection and kindness which characterized the initial phases of a relationship.

Frequently, these contracts reflect gender role expectations and erroneous stereotypes—views of women as weak, dependent, and helpless and of men as strong, masterful, and dominant. In a couples' seminar, a man who complained of his wife's dependency, inability to hold a job, social awkwardness, and deference to him for all decisions became aware of the unspoken contract between them. "I realize that my deal with my wife is that I'll take care of her, financially, emotionally, in every way. And her deal is that she'll continue to need to be taken care of. I realize that feeling needed by her and being essential to her well-being makes me feel like a man, strong, masculine. Otherwise I feel like a nobody."

Kipnis (2003), in a chapter aptly titled "Domestic Gulags," delineated more than 100 such unspoken rules of *coupledom* that regulate each partner's behaviors in relation to the other. These prohibitions, based on each partner's expectations about love and marriage, are accepted because they provide protection against perceived threats to a couple's illusion of love and closeness.

> From bathroom to bedroom, car to kitchen, no aspect of coupled life is not subject to scrutiny, negotiation, and rule formation…and love means voluntary adherence to them. (p. 82) What follows is a brief sample of answers to the simple question: "What can't you do because you're in a couple?" (p. 84).
>
> You can't leave the house without saying where you're going. You can't not say what time you'll return…. You can't go to parties alone. (p. 84) You can't sleep apart, you can't go to bed at different times, you can't fall asleep on the couch without getting woken up to go to bed…. You can't get out of bed right away after sex. (p. 86)
>
> You can't have friends who like one of you more than the other, or friends one of you likes more than the other…. You can't be too charming

in public, especially to persons of the opposite sex (or same sex, where applicable). You can't spend more than X amount of time talking to such persons, with X measured in nanoseconds. (p. 90)

Thus is love obtained.... What matters is the form. (p. 92) Exchanging obedience for love comes naturally—we were all once children after all, whose survival depended on the caprices of love. And thus you have the template for future intimacies: if you love me, you'll do what I want or need or demand to make me feel secure and complete and I'll love you back. (pp. 93–94)

Sexual fidelity can be symbolic of an imagined connection between partners. Although it can be based on a genuine desire or mutual agreement, pledges of faithfulness can be damaging if they are based on the false premise that people have proprietary rights over each other, particularly over each other's bodies and sexuality. At the beginning of a couples' therapy group, a new participant gave his name, his wife's name, and then proclaimed, "We may not be in love, but we're faithful." His remark was obviously provocative and led to much discussion. The man had unknowingly given a powerful and accurate definition of a destructive fantasy bond. His explicit, self-conscious declaration seemed to imply that he and his wife's monogamous relationship was based more on the imposition of external mores and conventional standards than on love, freedom of choice, and genuine personal commitment (R. Firestone, 1985).

The more intense the fantasy bond, the more anxiety and pain are aroused whenever either person indicates any form of sexual interest in someone else. The exaggerated need for reassurance that one's mate is always the first and only choice is necessary for the continuation of the illusion of connection. Therefore, implicit, unspoken contracts are entered into to quell the anxiety associated with potential threats to this exclusiveness. This guarantee that one is *special* to another person unconsciously ensures everlasting security, and an illusion of immortality (Note 3).

Recreating the Past Through Selection, Distortion, and Provocation

In their adult relationships, people unconsciously attempt to recapture the more familiar conditions within the family, the conditions under which they formed their defenses. They do this in three ways: through selection, distortion, and provocation. All three maneuvers function to help people maintain their psychological equilibrium against the positive intrusion of being loved and appreciated. All three methods help preserve one's negative identity. In other words, individuals externalize the fantasy bond initially formed within the family of origin and repeat the negative circumstances of their developmental years in their intimate relationships (R. Firestone & Catlett, 1999).

Selection

People unconsciously tend to select partners who are similar in appearance, behavior, and defenses to one of their parents. They are attracted to a person whose style of relating feels comfortable and familiar, someone whose defenses mesh with their own. In other cases people may choose a partner with complementary personal qualities and behaviors in an attempt to compensate for perceived deficits in themselves. Initially there is a good deal of sexual chemistry in these relationships. Both people tend to experience a sense of wholeness from their union, yet in reality both are weakened as they come to depend on each other for these complementary functions and traits. They may come to resent or even hate the traits that they originally sought out in the partner (R. Firestone et al., 2006).

Ken, a clinical psychologist, married Martha, a woman who displayed characteristics similar to those of his mother, particularly her domineering personality and childish, victimized ways of overreacting to disappointment whenever things did not go her way. Ken, passive and disorganized, was immediately attracted by Martha's aggressiveness and seemingly competent handling of practical matters. After the couple were married, Ken became disenchanted with Martha's bossy, abusive manner of relating to him. However, for years he tried to disregard their differences of opinion and interests and strove to smooth over every conflict. He avoided upsetting Martha by consistently giving in to her way of doing things. In spite of his intellectual understanding of the fantasy bond, and his recognition of the fact that he had in effect *married his mother*, Ken was unable to extract himself from the relationship. Ultimately the couple went bankrupt due to his wife's mishandling of their finances, and Ken finally separated from Martha. After consolidating and paying off his debts, he began to feel free and relaxed for the first time in years. But when Martha served Ken with divorce papers, he was devastated and suffered repeated panic attacks.

Ken: In the middle of one particularly intense anxiety attack, I really felt like I was going to die. I believed that I was having a heart attack. I even thought of suicide, momentarily. At first, I couldn't understand why I was having such an extreme reaction; after all, I was the one who initiated the separation. Finally I figured out that the divorce papers must have symbolized the final break in the fantasy bond that I still had with Martha, despite the fact that we had been separated for nearly two years.

Ken's selection of Martha as a romantic partner and their subsequent marriage and separation are reminiscent of the dynamics exemplified in a particular kind of troubled relationship, the enmeshed type described by couple therapists Bader and Pearson (1988): "[This type] is characterized by merger, avoidance of conflict, and the minimization of differences" (p. 10).

Evidence that elements of a fantasy bond are present in a relationship can be found in the intense reactions, such as Ken's, that people have when symbols of togetherness are broken. If either partner moves away from this type of symbiotic or enmeshed relationship toward independence or autonomy, symptoms similar to those manifested in withdrawal from chemical dependency are aroused. These symptoms include feelings of desperation, emotional hunger, disorientation, and debilitating anxiety states. The intensity of these emotional reactions indicates the powerful nature of the fantasy bond existing between the partners (Battegay, 1991).

Distortion

People distort their mates to fit in with their psychological defenses. When partners react to them differently than did their parents or other members of their families, the identity that they formed within the original family constellation is threatened, and they frequently become self-conscious or anxious. In particular, there is increased tension at times when the loving responses of the partner challenge their basic self-image. To relieve their anxiety they attempt to alter the image of their partner to recreate conditions that are more familiar to them. They may distort the other person by exaggerating either their positive or negative qualities to make the person more closely approximate a parent or other significant person from the past. This process is hurtful and maladaptive in a manner that eventually damages the relationship. Each partner may distort the other, especially in a negative direction. Through the process of projective identification, the person who is being distorted is essentially *bent out of shape;* that is, he or she may eventually come to accept the partner's negative evaluation of him or her as true.

Provocation

This defense mechanism is used by the defended person to manipulate others to respond to him or her as the parent did (R. Firestone, 1985). People often act in ways that provoke angry, critical, or harsh reactions from their mate. They may begin to hold back the behaviors, personal communication, affection, kindness, and sexuality that their partners especially valued. These withholding behaviors are for the most part unconscious. Partners may "incite anger in each other with forgetfulness, intrusiveness, silence, and other insensitive behaviors that indicate an underlying hostility" (R. Firestone et al., 2006, pp. 150–151).

Behaviors that provoke parental reactions—worry, fear, anger—act to externalize the self-parenting process within the new relationship. Parental role-playing is the counterpart. Often one partner will revert to childish manipulations that elicit parental or caretaking responses in the other or vice versa. Both types of relating are based on a sense of inadequacy and insecurity and lead to varying degrees of dysfunction within a relationship. According to Willi (1975/1982), *"In the disturbed partner relationship we often observe that one partner has a need for overcompensatory progression while the other seeks satisfaction in regression. They reinforce this one-sided behavior in each other because they need each other as complements"* (p. 24).

The authors propose that the process of reverting to a childish manner of relating can also function as a defense against an awareness of death. Otto Rank (1941) wrote of this human propensity to seek immortality on an unconscious level from a partner who is serving the role of parent or *ultimate rescuer:* "As a rule, we find . . . in modern relationships . . . one person is made the god-like judge over good and bad in the other person. In the long run, such a symbiotic relationship becomes demoralizing to both parties, for it is just as unbearable to be a God as it is to remain an utter slave" (p. 196).

Most people seem to expect far more security from their relationship or marriage than it is possible to extract. There is an expectation that all of one's needs will be met in the relationship and that in some sense one's partner is the source of all happiness. The burden that these anticipations put on the relationship is tremendous: obviously no one person can fulfill such unrealistic expectations or live up to this idealized image. However, people's actions indicate that they believe on some level that by relinquishing their individuality to a more powerful person, as in a fantasy bond, and by giving up their independence and points of view, they are somehow achieving safety and immortality (R. Firestone, 1997a).

Individuals who form a fantasy bond cannot be innocently defended. In attempting to protect themselves from interpersonal pain, sadness, and fears of loss—emotions inherent in all intimate relationships—they unconsciously push away or punish the people who care for them the most. Indeed utilizing one's partner to preserve a negative fantasy of who one is represents a basic dynamic in personal relationships that is more common than most people would like to believe (R. Firestone & Catlett, 1999).

DESTRUCTIVE EFFECTS OF THE FANTASY BOND ON THE FAMILY

> Kierkegaard understood that the lie of character is built up because the child needs to adjust to the world, to the parents, and to his own existential dilemmas. It is built up before the child has a chance to learn about himself in an open or free way, and thus character defenses are automatic and unconscious. The problem is that the child becomes dependent on them and comes to be encased in his own character armor, unable to see freely beyond his own prison or into himself, into the defenses he is using, the things that are determining his unfreedom. (Becker, 1973/1997, p. 73)

The emotional and interpersonal environment into which a child is born is largely determined by the nature of the parents' relationship and the individual defenses in each partner. To varying degrees, in their addictive style of coupling, most people systematically reduce or even eliminate their most desirable characteristics and loving responses, divesting themselves of the special qualities that were valued and loved by the other person, and by themselves (R. Firestone & Catlett, 2009). The entire process takes place primarily on an unconscious level, and the individuals involved remain largely unaware of the underlying causes of the deterioration in their relationship and in themselves. At the same time both parties to a fantasy bond experience feelings of existential guilt and self-hatred, because on some level they sense they have gone against themselves and their basic wants and priorities in their efforts to find security and safety in the relationship.

By the time their first child is born, the addictive attachment within many couples is already well-established. To maintain these unreal emotional ties, these parents necessarily dull or otherwise negate their most intimate experiences including the relationships with their offspring. The psychological equilibrium of the defended couple must not be disturbed by the intrusion of a spontaneous, loving, and affectionate child. Parents' efforts to defend themselves against a possible disruption in their fantasy bond begin early in their child's life. In fact, the unwillingness of defended parents to allow the repressed sadness, fear of loss and death, or other feelings of vulnerability to emerge is the major reason they find it difficult to sustain loving, affectionate relationships with their children (R. Firestone, 1994b).

The infant, vulnerable and completely dependent on the parents, is born into their realm of influence and into the illusion and pretense of their fantasy bond. Despite their concern with protecting and preserving the physical life of their children, most parents inadvertently and unintentionally begin to stifle their child's spontaneity and crush his or her spirit. The infant shows initial signs of pain and struggle but eventually, unable to remain intact in the hands of people who have effectively defended against intrusion into their fantasy bond, gives up the struggle and fits into the family system (R. Firestone, 1990b).

In families where a strong fantasy bond exists, the pretense of love and the idealization of parents and other family members are maintained through dishonest, duplicitous interactions and communications. One of the most detrimental effects of the fantasy bond on children and families can be observed in the proliferation of *double messages*—a mode of dysfunctional communication that supports the *form* while negating the *substance* of a relationship and family. The double message consists of a spoken (positive) message that contradicts a person's (negative) nonverbal cues, bodily posture, mannerisms, and sometimes actions. Parents and family members within a fantasy bond consistently give each other mixed messages to cover up their genuine sentiments and motivations, which may be negative, rejecting, or even hostile (R. Firestone, 1985). Because of the child's dependence on the parents, he or she needs to believe their words and so must sacrifice his or her own sense of reality. Double messages fracture the child's sense of reality, which can lead to serious pathological disturbance, especially when rejection of the child is persistently denied by parents' protestations of love. If family members were to honestly state what they really thought or deeply felt, they would be breaking an implicit pact to maintain a pretense of love and the form of their relationship.

Less defended parents are better able to provide their child with the sensitive care and sustenance required for emotional growth as well as a "safe haven" that would facilitate the formation of a secure attachment. As noted earlier, a number of Terror Management studies have shown that securely attached children and adults reported less fear of death than avoidant and anxious-ambivalent attached persons. For example, Mikulincer and Florian (2000) found that "secure persons reported a higher sense of continuity and lastingness, as assessed by means of Lifton's (1979) concept of symbolic immortality" (p. 261), and secure individuals experienced increased desire for intimacy in romantic relations after being reminded of death in an experimental setting. And Yaacovi (2003) found that securely attached individuals reported "heightened positive representations of parenting following a mortality salience induction" (Mikulincer, Florian, & Hirschberger, 2004, p. 300), whereas insecure individuals did not (Note 4).

In order to place the question of parental love in an appropriate context, the authors would define parental love operationally as a complex of behaviors that enhance the well-being and development of children. From this perspective, parents whose relationship is characterized by elements of a fantasy bond would be unlikely to offer real security or be capable of feeling genuine love for their children. They are often self-nurturing and self-protective, insulated from deeper feeling, and have incorporated a generally negative image of themselves. If they do not love themselves, they cannot pass on love and tenderness to their children. In fact they are more likely to project their negative feelings and undesirable traits onto their children and react accordingly (R. Firestone, 1990b).

The illusion of love that exists to a certain extent in most couples and families is supported by societal institutions, social mores, and beliefs. For example, the precept of unconditional parental love, a fundamental part of society's tenets, leads to considerable guilt feelings in parents. They tend to deny ambivalent feelings, imagine that love is one dimensional, and remain unaware that the feeling of love varies from moment to moment. As an alternative to facing what they perceive to be the lack of unwavering love for their child, they act as though they are loving when they are not. They do not understand that love is a phenomenon that is based on myriad variables.

Parents can come to realize that real love must be matched by corresponding behaviors of affection, kindness, and respect for individual boundaries. Parents who were damaged in their own upbringing are necessarily limited in their ability to give and receive love. This admission, when accompanied by insight into the reasons for one's limitations as a parent and tempered by feelings of compassion for how one was mistreated and misunderstood as a child, is crucial for positive change within family life. As long as the fantasy of love is maintained, there can be no real change.

There are a number of other factors operating in the family bond that can trigger parents' anxiety in relation to their children. As noted earlier, the birth of a first child represents an existential crisis for parents because it indicates another turn in the developmental time-clock that brings one closer to old age and death. This significant step into adulthood arouses considerable anxiety in many parents, unconsciously motivating them to avoid forming a genuine emotional attachment with their newborn (R. Firestone & Catlett, 2009).

Many parents tend to cut off feelings for their infant or young child when he or she becomes seriously ill. They try desperately to shield themselves from caring and feeling about the potential loss (R. Firestone, 1994b). Alex and Marjorie's first-born daughter, Cindy, was hospitalized soon after birth with respiratory difficulties:

Marjorie: I remember taking her to the hospital and her being in an incubator and being really tiny and fragile, I felt a torment that I had never felt before. I was alone in the room with her and watching her laboring to breathe and struggling. And I would pray that she would be okay, just hoping that she would come through it. I remember asking the doctor what's the next step and he said it would be to put her on a respirator. I was really terrified. Then she started getting better and we knew that she was going to be okay.

I just felt so torn apart, and I got really numb after that and really self-destructive. [to Alex] I remember provoking a lot of bad situations between us. Even after Cindy recovered completely, something happened where I wasn't able to maintain feelings toward her. I got very cut off and very distant from her and from my friends and from you. After the crisis was over, it's like I ran from the scene. I was really removed from her and I was afraid to feed her, too.

Alex: I remember looking at her, and later, when Nick was born, looking at him. There's something about looking at my kids, who look like me a lot. There's a strong identification. They're vulnerable like I am, and I can't stand to feel that about myself. I look at them and I feel protective or I feel loving toward them, and it's much harder for me to feel that toward myself, to feel that my life is precious and time is going by or that each moment stands on its own, and I can't recapture it. It goes by and it's gone. I know that after what happened with Cindy, I wanted to be as far from that idea as possible because I couldn't stand to cherish my life in that way.

Sadly, the more self-protective a parent is, the more he or she will act on his or her defenses with the child, become progressively misattuned, and fail to understand and encourage healthy development. In other words when parents are strongly defended, particularly in relation to death anxiety, the child is always more expendable than the parents' defense system (R. Firestone, 1985).

Parental attitudes and fears are passed on through the generations. Parents warn their children of dangers in the same manner as their parents warned them. The result is that many adults tend to exert exaggerated control and watchfulness over themselves, as a part of a self-nurturing process that is restrictive and disadvantageous to their prospects in life. Then they go on to offer the same solutions to their offspring (R. Firestone, 1990b). They imagine that they can control death by guarding and protecting themselves and their children and by anticipating all possible negative contingencies. Their denied and displaced fear of death is transformed into specific prohibitions that adversely affect their children's lives by stifling their spontaneity and making them unnecessarily fearful.

CONCLUSION

The pain of the ending is part of the happiness now. That's the deal. (Joy Gresham, to her husband, C.S. Lewis, regarding her impending death.)

We must learn both to acknowledge the centrality of romantic love to our lives and to maintain other relationships, other avenues to meaning. For, perhaps most important of all for the survival of love, we must not ask it to bear the weight of all meaning. (Person, 1988, p. 321)

In forming a fantasy bond with our loved ones, we attempt to eliminate separation anxiety and deny the inevitability of our personal death. The illusion of being connected to another person, other people, or a group, imbues us with a sense of immortality, a feeling of living forever, but robs us of our everyday lives. In contrast, living an undefended, non-fused state, we are brought face to face with our existential aloneness and separateness which arouses sadness, anxiety, and dread. Indeed the addictive and compelling nature of the fantasy bond lies in the fact that it denies death and relieves these disturbing emotions. "The drawback is that it creates a powerful resistance to living a free, independent existence in harmony and genuine closeness with our loved ones" (R. Firestone, 1985, p. 72).

The authors believe that the destructive effects of the fantasy bond can be challenged and overcome as individuals develop more mature forms of love that allow for ambiguity and uncertainty and as they learn to remain open to all of the inevitable vicissitudes of life and love. For example, becoming aware of and challenging any discrepancies between words and actions when communicating with one's partner and children would enable romantic partners and family members to build a genuine sense of trust and security in each other. In Part III of this work, we delineate methods that have proven effective in helping people identify and cope with elements of the fantasy bond, allowing for the rekindling of genuine affection, friendship, and sexual closeness in couples and families. The ultimate goal is not to depreciate marriage or the family as institutions, but to develop more effective and constructive ways of maintaining long-term associations that would meet the needs of individuals while affirming their personal development (R. Firestone et al., 2003).

NOTES

1. The product of a parent's ability and the desire to provide both affection and direction to the child was originally referred to as *love-food* by the first author in *A Concept of the Schizophrenic Process* (R. Firestone, 1957).
2. In his essay, "Individual and Mass Behavior in Extreme Situations," Bettelheim (1943/1979a) described this function of group identification functioning under extreme conditions of stress in a German concentration camp. On one occasion a group of prisoners was forced to stand all night in subfreezing temperatures as punishment for two prisoners who had tried to escape. More than 80 perished until finally the prisoners were permitted to return to the barracks.

   They were completely exhausted, but did not experience the feeling of happiness which some of them had expected. They were relieved that the torture was over, but felt at the same time that they were no longer free from fear.... Each prisoner as an individual was now comparatively safer, but he had lost the safety originating in being a member of a unified group. (p. 66)

3. To illustrate the mystifying dynamics underlying the implicit contracts made between partners in a relationship or marriage, R. D. Laing (1961) composed a series of poems, *Knots* as he referred to them, which he introduced in his book *Self and Others* as follows:

> Some people undoubtedly have a remarkable aptitude for keeping the other tied in knots. There are those who excel in tying knots and those who excel in being tied in knots. Tier and tied are often both unconscious of how it is done, or even that it is being done at all. (p. 158)

In his Foreword to *The Fantasy Bond*, Laing (1985) composed a Knot—a binding unspoken agreement for couples whose relationships are characterized by illusions of connection, double messages, and a pretense of love:

1. Do you love me?
2. Then believe me.
3. Believe me.
4. You don't love me.
5. You don't love anyone.
6. You are incapable of love.
7. No one loves you.
8. No one could love you.
9. Except me.
10. I am the only one who loves you
    You don't love me
    You don't love anyone
    No one loves you
    No one can love you.
11. But don't believe me
    Because I say so
    or because I love you
    Although
    believe me
    it's only because I love you
    that I say so
    Search yourself
    Look into the mirror and see for yourself
    You will see that every word I've said is true
    Look into your heart
    Look into your heart of hearts.
    You don't love me
    Don't believe me
    You know. (pp. 19–20)

4. Mikulincer and Orbach (1995) described the two insecure types of attachments and individuals as follows:

> On the one hand, avoidant people maintain distance from attachment figures, deny their insecurity and related negative affects, and devaluate the importance of events that may cause painful feelings. On the other hand, anxious-ambivalent people

direct attention toward distress in a hypervigilant way and tend to form dependent relationships that exacerbate their anxiety. (p. 917)

Mikulincer and Florian (2000) found that:

Whereas the two insecure groups reacted to death reminders with more severe judgments of transgressions, secure people showed a heightened sense of symbolic immortality and desire for intimacy (p. 271).

Secure people hold a positive sense of the self and adequate coping skills that allow them to manage distress without defensively distorting their cognitions.... In our terms, these characteristics, which reflect an internalized secure base (Bowlby, 1988), may act as a cognitive shield against the terror of death and may abolish the need to validate cultural worldviews and to derogate persons and opinions that threaten these worldviews. (p. 262)

However, Mikulincer and Florian qualified their conclusions as follows:

It is important to note that our findings cannot discern whether a growth-oriented approach prevails over a defensive approach in shaping secure persons' responses. For example, one may suggest that although intimacy may promote growth, it sometimes could be a regressive response that leads people to excessively immerse themselves into another person at the expense of a sense of individuality. Accordingly, our findings cannot discern whether secure persons' responses differ entirely from worldview validation or are another alternative manifestation of worldview defenses. For example, a person's worldview may include beliefs of living on in one's children or being close with others and may lead the individual to invest in family and close relationships. (p. 272)

Mikulincer and Florian went on to stress the importance of continued research to address these questions.

8

Separation Theory, the Voice, and Voice Therapy

Our life is what our thoughts make it.   —*Marcus Aurelius*

The first author's work has centered on the problem of resistance to positive movement in psychotherapy and people's fundamental resistance to living more fulfilling lives. Over the course of this study, I observed that most of my patients unconsciously manipulated their interpersonal environments in order to maintain an identity and defensive psychological equilibrium that was formed in their earliest years (R. Firestone, 1988). Subsequently, research revealed that many of the high-functioning individuals in our longitudinal study tended to shun, sabotage, or retreat from experiences that were potentially more gratifying or constructive than they were accustomed to. My investigations into this seemingly paradoxical phenomenon led me to conclude that people's core resistance is related to a profound fear of disrupting the psychological defenses that functioned to protect them from emotional pain, separation anxiety, and existential dread. On an unconscious level people fear that if they were to dismantle their defenses, they would be overwhelmed by the same anguish and terror they endured in childhood, both at the time their defenses were formed and again when they first discovered death and dying (R. Firestone, 1997a).

Defenses that function to deny death support an ongoing, largely unconscious illusion that one is immortal. Magical thinking allows for this illogical discrepancy to occur spontaneously along with one's conscious awareness of death's inevitability. Thus, elements of this process persist into adulthood despite the fact that people are faced more directly with death as they grow older. As noted in the previous chapter, certain circumstances, events, and behaviors support or reinforce unconscious illusions of immortality while others threaten to shatter them. For example, the fantasy bond offers a feeling of connection and immortality, whereas a genuine, loving relationship within couples or between family members makes one increasingly aware of a finite existence. Self-nurturing habit patterns, addictions, fantasy bonds in interpersonal relationships, religiosity, vanity, and other microsuicidal behaviors serve to deny death, whereas successive separation experiences, rejection, signs of aging, or the loss of a loved one negatively impact the illusion of immortality. Conformity tends to strengthen one's illusion of fusion with the group or the culture and helps dispel the fear of aloneness and death, whereas independence or nonconformity disrupts the imagined connection and generates anxiety.

The methodology derived from Separation Theory helps to identify and challenge defense mechanisms that act as buffers to the recognition of one's aloneness and death. Although these defenses are soothing and comforting to varying degrees, they are limiting, maladaptive, or self-destructive. The process of exposing and understanding these defensive manifestations not only helps to relieve symptoms of emotional distress but also helps people to break through their resistances and expand their lives.

SEPARATION THEORY

The first author's theoretical approach has come to be known as Separation Theory. In attempting to understand psychological pain and dysfunctional or abnormal behavior, the theory represents a comprehensive system of concepts and hypotheses that integrates psychoanalytic principles and existential systems of thought. Nevertheless, the approach should not be considered eclectic. As noted, the conceptual model explains how early interpersonal pain and separation anxiety lead to the formation of defenses, and how these defenses become more elaborate as the developing child becomes aware of his or her personal mortality. Existential concerns and the associated defenses continue to have a profound impact, usually negative, on individuals throughout their lives, especially in relation to generating defensive, maladaptive behavioral responses.

Psychoanalytic and object-relations theorists have explored the effects of interpersonal trauma, while existentialists have focused their attention on issues of being and nonbeing. The original Freudian psychoanalysts theorized about psychological conflict experienced primarily during the Oedipal phase. Later, object-relations theorists focused on problems during the pre-Oedipal phases, particularly the oral phase, including Balint (1952/1985), Fairbairn (1952), and Guntrip (1969), who described the split in ego function as children endure blows to their dignity, personal freedom, and autonomy. On the other hand, existential psychologists have elucidated individuals' attempts to transcend their dualistic nature and the fact of their mortality, including Bugental (1976), Frankl (1946/1959), Laing (1960/1969); Maslow (1968), May (1981), Schneider (2004), and Yalom (1980), among others. Both systems of thought, psychoanalytic and existential, need to be integrated to fully understand the dynamics of the suicidal process within the individual. Neither system deals sufficiently with the important concerns of the other, and to neglect or minimize either approach places certain limitations on our knowledge of psychological functioning and human behavior (R. Firestone, 1997b).

In Chapter 3, we described Rank's conceptualization of life as a series of successive weaning experiences or separations, originally from the mother and then from other significant figures as people move toward individuation and developing an authentic, autonomous self. Each step or milestone toward self-differentiation (Bowen, 1978) and individuation arouses feelings of anxiety in relation to separation and death. From a developmental perspective, Separation Theory is congenial with Rank's (1936/1972) conceptualizations, but adds a specific focus on the fantasy bond as a means of healing the fracture brought about by separation experiences. The theory provides an in-depth analysis of people's responses to separation experiences, whether real or symbolic, and elucidates the impact of the core defense system, the fantasy bond. Ernest Becker and the authors have acknowledged Rank's contribution to the knowledge of how children cope with separation anxiety, their ambivalent feelings toward parents, the core conflict between dependency and individuation, and the existential guilt that people experience after transforming the fear of death into the fear of living.

It is clear that the concept of *separation* or the idea of being a separate autonomous person, as described from this perspective, is different from isolation, retreat, pseudo-independence, or imagined self-sufficiency; rather it involves maintaining a strong identity and definite boundaries in close relationships. When individuals lack a strong personal identity or well-developed self system, they find it necessary to distort, provoke, or withdraw from intimacy in their closest associations (R. Firestone & Catlett, 1999).

The practice of psychotherapy derived from Separation Theory emphasizes the exposure of destructive fantasy bonds as externalized in interpersonal associations and as internalized in the form of negative parental introjects. The methodology focuses on identifying and then challenging these internalized negative prescriptions (destructive thought processes or *voices*) and then helping the client move toward individuation and independence (R. Firestone, 1993, 1994b, 1996, 1997a, 1997b) (also see Bassett, 2007; Morrant & Catlett, 2008; Tomer & Eliason, 1996). The methodology is multi-dimensional; it includes feeling release therapy with a deep emotional catharsis, free association techniques as in psychoanalysis, and the specialized techniques of Voice Therapy, a cognitive-affective-behavioral method that directly accesses the destructive thought processes mediating defensive behaviors. These techniques are applied as appropriate to the various stages in the therapy process and are tailored to the individual needs of the patient.

Separation therapy represents a particularly direct assault on psychological defenses and therefore must be undertaken with a special sensitivity to both the patient's willingness and tolerance. An important aspect of psychotherapeutic practice, based on the tenets of Separation Theory, is the knowledge that considerable anxiety is to be anticipated and must be dealt with effectively as patients take chances and dismantle their defenses. Resistance, in the form of negative therapeutic reactions, may be anticipated as people make significant improvement because with the decrease in repression, unconscious death awareness will surface, together with heightened feelings of death anxiety (See Robert Langs, 2004.) The anxiety and fear of change or improvement is also related to an increased potential for feeling, experiencing more joy and more distress, new and different problems in interpersonal relationships, guilt about surpassing one or another parent, and lastly the fear and sadness about losing through death everything one has gained through expanding one's boundaries (R. Firestone, 1988).

THE VOICE: SECONDARY DEFENSES THAT PROTECT THE FANTASY BOND

> I could not sleep, although tired, and lay feeling my nerves shaved to pain & the groaning inner voice: oh, you can't teach, can't do anything. Can't write, can't think.... I have a good self, that loves skies, hills, ideas, tasty meals, bright colors. My demon would murder this self by demanding that it be a paragon, and saying it should run away if it is anything less.
>
> **—Sylvia Plath,** "Letter to a Demon"
> (Hughes & McCullough, 1982, pp. 176–177)

Secondary defenses, made up of negative views of the self, cynical views of others, and distorted views of the world reinforce and protect the self-parenting process or fantasy bond. These views are maintained by the *voice*—which has been defined as a system of destructive thoughts and attitudes, antithetical to the self and hostile toward others. We use the term voice to describe the process of constantly talking to oneself (not literally as in the case of hallucinations), but rather evaluating one's thoughts and actions in the form of an inner dialogue. This internal dialogue is unfriendly or outright hostile to the self. It is an internal representation, an incorporation into the self, of negative parental attitudes and attacks. In its simplest form, we criticize ourselves saying "you clumsy fool" or curse ourselves for making mistakes: "you stupid idiot." On a deeper level, it attacks us and other people, and prompts micro-suicidal thoughts and behavior. The voice process predisposes alienation and is at the core of all forms of maladaptive behavior.

In this section we explore the dynamics of the voice, which we consider to be an overlay on the personality that is learned or imposed from without. The voice is an incorporated, systematized cognitive process, interwoven with varying degrees of anger and sadness that strongly influences our behavior to the detriment of our physical and mental health. Destructive thoughts or voices first instigate and then rationalize self-denying, self-destructive behaviors and lifestyles, and in so doing, they serve a critical defensive function: that of enabling individuals to accommodate to death through the gradual restriction of their lives. In describing this defensive function of the voice, Morrant (2003) wrote:

> The voice becomes an autonomous but alien governor of the mind, a ghostly and ghastly inner officialdom which runs almost every aspect of our lives. It

gives an illusion of security, but we do not so much live as *are lived by* the voice process. The voice process, like a bonsai master, cuts, binds and warps our mental growth so we do not especially fear the end of the crippled thing we have become: there's nothing that valuable to lose. (Note 1)

Defensive Functions of the Voice

To understand the voice process is to develop an awareness of the source of the self-destructive apparatus in the personality and to recognize its additional function of protecting people against death anxiety. Most people, beginning in early childhood, try to deny death on a conscious, personal level and gradually adapt to the fear of death by unconsciously restricting the scope of their lives. They gradually lose their freedom and excitement about life, and essentially experience a death of the spirit. In their retreat they are tortured by existential guilt (also mediated by the voice) about a life not fully lived and become increasingly demoralized and disillusioned.

Our clinical material has indicated that a process of actual self-denial on a behavioral level parallels the voice attacks and that this self-denial can lead to a cycle of more serious pathology. (See Exhibit 6.1, Continuum of Self-Destructive Thoughts and Behaviors.) As people deny themselves gratification, they become progressively indifferent to experiences that they once found exciting and worthwhile. "Just as they cut off personal relationships to avoid the prospect of potential rejection, most individuals restrict their personal freedom to varying degrees by refusing to commit fully to a life they must certainly lose" (R. Firestone, 1988, p. 174). We have observed this phenomenon operating in most people in their everyday lives. As they adjust their behavior and lives according to the dictates of the voice, they reduce investment in energetic activities and relationships. By deadening themselves emotionally, they progressively withdraw from living fully as they grow older (R. Firestone & Seiden, 1987).

Negative voices have a powerful destructive effect on the personality and impose strong restrictions on each person's life. As described by Richard Heckler (1994) in *Waking Up, Alive*, in the case of suicide, the ultimate outcome of progressive self-denial and self-attack is a suicidal trance: "a state of mind and body that receives only the kind of input that reinforces the pain and corroborates the person's conviction that the only way out is through death" (p. 61). "The inner pull toward suicide dramatically intensifies. Often it comes in the form of a voice.... Often people experience this voice as relentlessly driving them toward self-destruction" (p. 74).

The Self and Antiself Systems

Our clinical experience has shown that human beings possess two diametrically opposed views of themselves, of others, of the external world, and of their goals and priorities. On the one hand, each person has a point of view that reflects his or her natural strivings, aspirations, and desires for affiliation with others, the drive to be sexual, to reproduce him or herself, and to be creative; on the other hand, he or she has another point of view that reflects tendencies for self-limitation, self-destruction, and hostility toward other people. As noted earlier, this alien point of view is made up of the destructive thoughts that we refer to as the voice (R. Firestone, 1988, 1997a, 1997b). These destructive thoughts are internalized during times of emotional stress when children are particularly afraid, hurt, rejected, or otherwise traumatized. Under these aversive circumstances, children incorporate their parents' negative attitudes toward them and identify with their defensive attitudes toward life.

Parents have both positive and negative feelings toward themselves, which they naturally extend to their offspring. Their positive attitudes toward the child are easily assimilated into the child's self system, whereas parents' negative qualities are not integrated, but instead become deeply etched in the individual, creating the antiself system. Because negative experiences tend to carry a higher emotional valence than positive ones, children incorporate their parents' attitudes when parents exhibit their most destructive responses, when parents are at their worst. As Anna Freud (1966) asserted: "By impersonating the aggressor, assuming his attributes or imitating his aggression, the child transforms himself from the person threatened into the person who makes the threat" (p. 113).

In the process of defending themselves under these conditions, children fragment, into the self and antiself systems. Rather than suffer this fracture many individuals side with the enemy within, and as adults they often retreat to the seeming safety and security of their inner world, which represents, in effect, a form of controlled destruction of the self and the progressive ascendancy of the antiself. In a previous work, the first author elucidated how this antagonistic side of the personality develops:

> The antiself is induced by ineffective or malignant styles of parenting and socialization that are fundamentally authoritarian and moralistic. This creates within the child a self-hating inner voice that seeks to destroy the very project of becoming a self that gives human existence its most significant

meaning. The self is divided against itself, in Kierkegaard's sense, both fearing life and desiring death and desiring life and fearing death. Existentially, this form of despair toward becoming a self in the face of death is not a mere mood or a passing emotion; it belongs to the very structure of the self and, as such, is universal. (R. Firestone, 1997a, p. 71)

The first author's concept of the *division of the mind* (see Figure 8.1) into the self and antiself systems was derived from the observation that

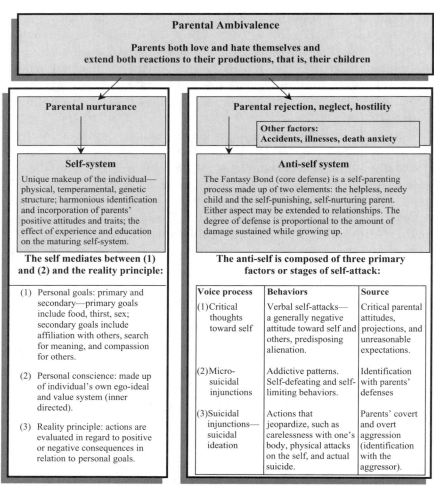

Figure 8.1 Division of the mind.

people are essentially divided between the self and the forces within them that oppose or attempt to obliterate the self. Both the self system and antiself system develop independently within the personality; both are dynamic and are continually evolving. The self system is made up of biological, temperamental, and genetic traits together with a harmonious identification with parents' or primary caregivers' positive traits. An important function of the self is monitoring one's actions in relation to the positive or negative consequences of pursuing one's goals. The antiself system represents the defensive side of the personality and is made up of the two elements of the fantasy bond or self-parenting process—the helpless, needy child and the self-nurturing, self-punishing parent—and is mediated by the voice process (L. Firestone, 2006; R. Firestone, 1997b).

The first author's conceptualization of a divided self is similar in some respects to Eric Berne's (1961) model of transactional analysis (TA). Berne perceived individuals as interacting from either the parent or child mode (which corresponds to either element in the self-parenting process) or from the adult ego state (corresponding to the self system) (L. Firestone, 2006). Most people are noticeably different in their interactions with others, their attitudes, mood, and point of view, depending on which part of their personality is more prominent at a given time, the self (adult) or the antiself (parental/childlike) system (R. Firestone, Firestone, & Catlett, 2002).

This conceptualization of a mind divided against itself can be distinguished from R. D. Laing's (1960/1969) description of a *divided* self (originally conceptualized by Winnicott, 1960/1965). Laing referred to a division between the *false self*—the façade that an individual *uses* in social settings—and the *true self*—an individual's authentic feelings and real intentions, which are honest representations of self.

The concept of the antiself and the voice process is similar in some respects to Fairbairn (1952) and Guntrip's (1969) concept of the antilibidinal ego: "We view the libidinal ego as in bondage to guilt or fear, that is imposed by the antilibidinal ego which in part represents the frightening or accusing parents who have themselves disturbed the child" (Guntrip, p. 202). Emphasizing the dynamics linking the child's negative concept of self to the idealization of parents and family, Fairbairn wrote: "It becomes obvious, therefore, that the child would rather be bad himself than to have bad objects" (p. 65), and that "it is better to be a sinner in a world ruled by God than to live in a world ruled by the Devil" (pp. 66–67). Other theorists and clinicians have long recognized these elements of the antiself system in people's ways of thinking destructively about themselves and others, and have identified *automatic thoughts* (A. Beck, 1976), *irrational beliefs* (Ellis & Harper, 1975) and the *shadow side* of the personality (Jung, 1957) (Note 2).

The voice acts to bind adults emotionally to their parents in the sense that, even though physically distant from the family, they still possess an internal parent that directs, controls, and punishes them. As Fairbairn (1952) emphasized: "No one ever becomes completely emancipated from the state of infantile dependence...and there is no one who has completely escaped the necessity of incorporating his early objects" (p. 56). Thus incorporated voices, although harsh and malevolent, function to maintain the fantasy bond, shielding the individual from experiencing his or her aloneness, sense of separation, and death anxiety. Morrant and Catlett (2008) described the antiself system as follows:

> The fantasy bond and the voice process make up...the antiself system, a project of the mind which helps protect us from death anxiety. If any part is pruned, then death fears awaken, often disguised as emotional numbing, physical suffering, or guilt. Guilt is hatred of the self with a dread of punishment. The voice process is grafted onto the growing personality where it becomes an alien but autonomous governor which dictates our thoughts and feelings about ourselves, other people, and almost every aspect of our lives. (p. 359)

Dimensions of the Voice

The voice represents the language of the defensive process (R. Firestone, 1997a). The first author's definition of the voice excludes creative thinking, fantasy, value judgments, constructive planning, and moral considerations. In order to fit our criteria of the voice, an individual's thoughts must be identified as an incorporated external attack on the self or on others. The voice also must be distinguished from a conscience. Although the critical thoughts of the voice may at times seem to correspond to a person's value system, they often occur as judgmental self-recriminations after the person has engaged in the very behaviors that were instigated by the voice. This punitive voice tends to intensify self-hatred and feelings of demoralization rather than to motivate the person to change or to abstain from engaging in immoral, addictive, or self-destructive behavior. For this reason it must not be mistaken for a moral guide in any sense of the word.

Voice attacks are sometimes experienced consciously as a harsh or belittling internal commentary, but more often these destructive thoughts are only partially conscious or entirely unconscious. For example, most people are aware of calling themselves names or thinking critically about themselves. However, these angry self-attacks are merely isolated fragments of a more complete underlying system (R. Firestone, 1988). For the most part people are unaware of how much their behavior is being regulated by the voice or the extent to which the voice interferes with their pursuit of goals and contributes to a depressed and/or antagonistic mood.

Voices That Promote Narcissism and Vanity

The voice does not always take the form of negative attacks; it also promotes inflated views of the self associated with vanity, which serves as compensation for underlying feelings of inferiority, worthlessness, and self-hatred. On an unconscious level vanity functions as a survival mechanism in that being *special* renders one impervious to death, unlike other, less fortunate, ordinary people who possess no such immunity. In this manner the mechanism acts to deny unpleasant realities, but the defense is costly.

Exaggerated feelings of self-importance, views of oneself as being special, are represented by a flattering, positive voice that sets the person up for subsequent failure and self-recriminations. In essence these voices tell the person: "You're really talented, beautiful, exceptional, etc. You're better than other people." Or "You're great; you can do anything you set your mind to." Subsequently when the person inevitably fails to live up to his or her own aggrandized expectations, the voice viciously rips him or her apart with accusations such as "You can't do anything right! You're a failure at everything you try to do!" (R. Firestone et al., 2002). In the workplace, in social situations, and in relationships vain individuals are generally unappealing, unlikable, and poorly adapted. Yet some people stubbornly cling to their inflated self-esteem as though it were a matter of life and death.

The Dual Focus of the Voice Process

The authors have observed that the voice not only attacks the self but also is directed against others. Both components of the voice predispose alienation from oneself and from others. "Just as individuals have a split view of themselves, they also possess diametrically opposed views of the people in their lives. Both contradictory viewpoints—toward self and toward others—are symptomatic of the deep division existing within all of us" (R. Firestone, 1988, p 47).[1]

When people believe and accept the contents of their voice attacks as statements of fact, they tend to retreat to a defended, pseudo-independent stance where they feel protected by their illusions. They may criticize themselves: "You're so unattractive. Who would want to be involved with you?" or they may attack another person, "He(She) is so rejecting, why would you want to go out with him(her)?" but the outcome is much the same. People are more likely to withdraw their emotional investment in other people and avoid give-and-take exchanges when they are experiencing or *listening to* either component of the voice. They tend to revert to self-parenting defenses and internally gratify themselves through fantasy or addictive behaviors, while pulling back from seeking external gratification in a relationship or in goal-directed behavior (R. Firestone, 1988). Thus the voice functions to support and reinforce the fantasy bond and the corresponding illusion of immortality.

Early Investigations Into the Voice

In the early 1970s, the first author was interested in the emotional pain that patients experienced in group psychotherapy settings when they received certain kinds of feedback. At first we thought the old adage "it's the truth that hurts" was operating in these situations. Later, however, we concluded that even when the negative feedback was not accurate, at times it would produce the same effect of being deeply painful. In these circumstances, the feedback supported the antiself system, confirming the person's own distorted views of him or herself and triggering a self-hating thought process. We thought it would be worthwhile to explore this matter by investigating critical thoughts people held about themselves and the kinds of events that aroused self-attacks. Therefore, we began to study this phenomenon in a discussion group composed of professional associates and selected individuals from the longitudinal study. It was during these early investigations that some individuals began using the term *the voice* to describe their self-critical thoughts and negative views of other people.

Later we developed a method of verbalizing these self-attacks in the context of a group discussion. At first, people expressed their negative thoughts in a rational or analytic style. However, they soon discovered that these thoughts were easily accessible when verbalized in the second person (e.g., *"You're* no good") as though there were another person addressing them. In the first sessions utilizing this form of dialogue, we were surprised by the intensity of the emotions aroused when people expressed their self-attacks and distorted views of self in the second person. The intensity of self-hatred and at times rage toward self that emerged underscored the depth and pervasiveness of the internalized destructive thought process (R. Firestone, 1988, 1997a).

For example, in a group session, Eduardo, 62, who emigrated from Cuba in the late 1950s, verbalized self-doubts about his masculinity in the second person format. As he got into a flow of feelings his self-criticisms took on a snide and sarcastic tone and became more and more contemptuous. His destructive thoughts became increasingly vicious as he expressed the angry diatribe against himself. His Spanish accent, which was barely noticeable when he started, became more pronounced. He began to speak in a louder voice and his self-accusations became more emasculating and degrading the longer he spoke.

> Who do you think you are? You are not a man. You have never grown. You are just a kid. You have heard the story of Peter Pan? Well, that is what you are. You are only a kid. You will never grow. A kid can't have sexuality, he can only play. You are worse than a kid. What kind of disease do you have? The gall bladder! You have the disease of a woman. You are lower than a woman. You are beneath a woman. You are not a man. You will never be a man.

Findings

As various dimensions of the voice process were brought to the foreground in this new group and in work with individual patients, we became aware of the impact of this destructive force in people's lives. As we expanded our study of this phenomenon and systematically examined a variety of methods that could be used to elicit the voice, we found that people's self-attacks could most effectively be evaluated and countered when they were verbalized in the second person format described above.

We were able to delineate three levels of intensity of the voice in terms of affect: at the first level, each person was able to identify an internal running commentary that depreciated and criticized him or her and that contributed to a state of agitation or a depressed mood. At the next level, as people got into a flow of feelings while articulating the voice attacks, they often launched into an angry diatribe against themselves that was shocking in its intensity. These expressions were accompanied by strong emotions (i.e., previously suppressed feelings of anger and sadness). At the third level, there was often a strong rage toward the self, expressed through suicidal urges or injunctions to cause injury to one's self.

In utilizing this technique as a laboratory procedure in group sessions, we discovered that virtually no one is immune from destructive voices that act against one's goals and priorities. Our observations indicated that the degree to which alien elements exist in the personality correlated with the degree of neglect as well as with physical, emotional, or sexual abuse experienced by the individual during his or her formative years. As material of this nature accumulated, it became a logical extension of our work to study this voice process in depressed patients and in those who suffered because of limitations they imposed on themselves in their personal and vocational lives. From these further explorations, the specialized techniques of Voice Therapy, described below, were developed (R. Firestone, 1988, 1997a).

THERAPEUTIC PRACTICES BASED ON SEPARATION THEORY

Psychotherapeutic practices based on Separation Theory represent a multidimensional approach that has proved beneficial in overcoming resistance and encouraging behavioral change. It is a dynamic method involving the analysis of defenses, resistance, and an exploration of neurotic trends in the personality. The therapy integrates a number of theoretical approaches, including psychoanalytical, cognitive-affective-behavioral, abreactive, and existential psychotherapies. However, this approach is not strictly technique-bound and may include any methodology that potentially could help the patient in treatment. The main issue is that the therapy offers clients the maximum opportunity to identify and alter the defenses that are limiting or destroying their lives. They will accept this challenge to varying degrees on their own terms, but the opportunity is there.

The basic steps in the psychotherapy process require incisive therapeutic inroads, not simply symptom reduction or minor alterations in defense mechanisms or addictions. In addition, the therapist must be sensitive to, and capable of, accessing and distinguishing patients' special points of identity (elements of the self system). The therapist helps to challenge the voice and antiself system, and supports the true nature and individual identity of the patient.

Intense Feeling Release

Intense feeling release therapy is primarily affective, and is akin to Arthur Janov's (1970) technique for eliciting and releasing primal feelings. During the 1970s, we worked with more than 200 patients and subjects for a period of four years using this technique. We observed that subjects who progressed through this cathartic experience loosened their controls, became less repressed and defensive, had deep emotional insights, and made significant progress. In addition, people who had experienced primals were more amenable to the specialized techniques of Voice Therapy that were developed at a later date.

Prior to sessions, individuals were asked to avoid addictive substances and other self-nurturing habit patterns that ordinarily would cut them off from their feelings. They spent 24 hours in isolation and self-contemplation, while composing a written history of their life. This prelude to the sessions created considerable anxiety and emotions tended to surface.

During sessions, individuals were encouraged to breathe deeply, to allow sounds to emerge as they exhaled, and to say any thoughts that came to mind. People usually expressed powerful feelings, and then described what they had experienced with clarity. They formed their own insights about what had happened in their developmental years. In the midst of releasing primitive feelings in cries, screams, or angry shouts, they appeared to be genuinely reexperiencing painful events and feelings from early childhood.

The knowledge of self and personal understanding gained through intense feeling release sessions are direct and uncontaminated by interpretations from the therapist or facilitator. Individuals are able to see for themselves the connection between their present-day problems and childhood situations on an emotional level rather than having to figure them out intellectually. Our findings from these sessions tended to confirm the results reported by Janov as well as his thesis that defenses are basically a protection against experiencing primal pain. However, in contrast to Janov, who believed that the pool of primal pain could be drained, leading to a cure, our investigations showed that this pool cannot be emptied. The effects of early interpersonal pain cannot be fully eradicated, and, furthermore, they are not the only factor in patients' suffering. Death anxiety compounds early childhood trauma and reinforces the defenses formed early in life. It becomes an issue of major proportion in its own right and continues to exert an influence throughout the life process. Otherwise Janov's hypothesis and his hopes of a cure might have been realized (R. Firestone, 1997a).

Voice Therapy

Our recognition of the limitations of intense feeling release therapy and our understanding of the core existential realities led to further developments in our search for an effective technique. Voice Therapy is a cognitive-affective-behavioral methodology that can be used to access, identify, and challenge the destructive thought process or voice: it is cognitive in that it is used to identify the contents of destructive thought processes; it is affective in that it encourages the release of emotions associated with these thoughts; and it is behavioral in the sense that patient and therapist collaborate in planning suggestions for instituting behaviors that go against the negative prescriptions of the voice (R. Firestone et al., 2003). As noted, we found that expressing the contents of the voice in the second person, *you*, instead of *I*, facilitated the process of separating an individual's own point of view from the alien point of view promulgated by the voice. When thoughts were expressed in the second person, considerably more affect was released.

Before verbalizing the voice, people usually accepted their negative thoughts as accurate appraisals of themselves, of others, and of events in the world. They were unable to distinguish, isolate, or challenge this destructive interpretation of life, which played a central role in their misery.

The techniques of Voice Therapy are well suited to a group therapy context because participants closely identify with the feeling and emotion of the individual verbalizing his or her voice at the time. It promotes both feeling and insight in the other observers.

In applying the techniques of Voice Therapy in individual sessions or a group setting, the therapeutic process is usually composed of four steps: In the first step, individuals verbalize their negative thoughts in the second person and express the associated feelings, such as anger and sadness. For example, in a group session, Ellen verbalized thoughts that contributed to a sense of self-consciousness that made her feel awkward, self-doubting, and quiet.

> Ellen: I realize that I'm telling myself things that prevent me from saying what I think, like 'No one wants to hear what you have to say. The things

you talk about are so trivial, so stupid! You're such a bother. Why would anybody want to hear from you?'

As Ellen continued to articulate her voice attacks, she began to speak in a loud voice, and eventually yelled out vicious self-attacks that were just beneath the surface:

> You're always in the way. You drive people crazy with your stupid ideas. Besides, you don't know what you're talking about! You are so screwed up in your head. You're crazy. You don't make any sense. You're so weak-willed and disgusting! [intense anger and rage] You think you know something about me? Well, you'd better be quiet! You'd better keep your mouth shut! Who do you think you are, anyway? You're no better than us! Can't you see that you're crazy? Just shut up! Don't say another word!

In the second step, people discuss their insights and ideas regarding the sources of their destructive thoughts. After her release of emotions, Ellen identified the origins of her self-accusatory voices in her mother's hateful attitudes toward her. She recalled being sent away by her mother when she was very young to live with her father and stepmother, who sadistically punished both her and her younger brother. When she had told her mother about the mistreatment, the mother had done nothing to intervene, although she was well aware of the stepmother's emotional instability.

Ellen also recalled a serious accident with her horse for which she was blamed and punished. The accident had been inevitable and was no one's fault, yet the extreme consequences caused Ellen to doubt her sense of reality. This incident along with other confusing communications on the part of her sadistic stepmother and abusive father left Ellen with serious doubts about the validity of her perceptions; she felt that she could not trust her own thoughts.

In the third step, the therapist encourages the person to answer back to the voice in dialogue form, which often elicits much emotion. Subsequently, the person attempts to realistically evaluate the content of self-attacks and determine an objective appraisal of him or herself. This strengthens the person and adds to his or her self-esteem. This step tends to facilitate further insight into the relationship between the person's voice attacks and his or her self-limiting or self-destructive behaviors. Ellen answered back to her voice attacks:

> Ellen: Fuck you! [loud, angry voice] You just stood there and did nothing, and I felt crazy my whole life! You just let it happen! You did nothing. You

gave us away to somebody who was crazy because it was convenient for you. Fuck you!

I'm not crazy! I'm not going to waste the rest of my life doubting myself and hating myself. It's not my fault! It wasn't me! You bitch! How could you just stand by and let it happen? How could you sit there and let your own kids go crazy? [cries] It wasn't me. There's nothing wrong with me! I'm a lovable person! You didn't want me! There's nothing wrong with *me!* [long pause]

Next, Ellen spoke objectively in a calmer tone of voice: "It felt good to get angry back at those attacks. I know that when I walk around thinking I'm a little bit creepy, or when I'm a little bit awkward, or if I feel like I make people uncomfortable by wanting things from them, that's such a protection of my mother. I do feel like I am lovable, and that it's okay to want things. It's also okay to not get what I want. I feel like that's okay too, that I'm still lovable. I can see that my mother was incapable of loving me."

Resistance may be intensified following sessions where individuals directly challenge the voice by answering back. Expressing feelings of hatred and anger, even at symbolic parental figures, can create enormous guilt. Verbalizing angry feelings toward one's internalized parents tends to disrupt the imagined connection that was once a source of security, and regression may follow. In anticipating these negative therapeutic reactions, therapists need to be sensitive to the strengths and weaknesses of each individual and carefully monitor his or her reactions when answering to the voice.

In the fourth step, the individual and the therapist collaborate in planning behaviors that go against the dictates of the voice. These fall into two categories: (a) those that reduce or eliminate addictions and other destructive behaviors, and (b) those that help the person to take chances and move in a positive direction. These include overcoming fears, working through difficult circumstances, challenging fears of intimacy and personal relating, and otherwise altering the negative identity formed within the family (R. Firestone, 1997a). For example, after expressing her voice attacks and answering back to the voice on her own behalf, Ellen took action in opposition to her fears of speaking out and expressing her opinions. In the next group talk she contributed her ideas to the subjects being discussed. In the days that followed, she experienced some anxiety about being more outspoken, but gradually adjusted to these positive feelings about herself.

It is possible to use Voice Therapy techniques as an adjunct to other therapeutic approaches. Even when Voice Therapy is not the treatment of choice, the theory and methodology derived from Separation Theory are of value in understanding the core of resistance to any form of psychotherapeutic movement or constructive behavioral change (R. Firestone, 1988).

RESEARCH FINDINGS BASED ON THE VOICE

A major advantage of Voice Therapy lies in the patient's rapid achievement of personal awareness and insight, independent of therapists' interpretations. Thus, with fewer therapists' interventions in relation to the original data, our approach has proven to be valuable as a research tool (R. Firestone, 1988). The authors have utilized negative self-statements gathered from subjects and patients to develop several instruments for assessing self-destructive and violent behavior.

The instruments were based on the following hypotheses: (1) voices vary along a continuum of intensity from mild self-criticisms to strong self-attacks and even suicidal thoughts; (2) self-destructive behavior exists on a continuum from self-denial and self-limitation to drug abuse, alcoholism, and other self-defeating behaviors, culminating in actual bodily harm; (3) both processes, behavioral and cognitive, parallel each other, with suicide representing the acting out of the extreme end of the continuum (R. Firestone, 1986). On the basis of this continuum, Lisa Firestone developed *The Firestone Assessment of Self-Destructive Thoughts* (FAST) (R. Firestone & L. Firestone, 2006) to assess the potential for suicide (L. Firestone, 1991).

Part of the motivation for developing the scale originated in a suggestion by Dr. C. Everett Koop, former U.S. Surgeon General. Frank Tobe, a political consultant and close friend, met Surgeon General Koop on a plane travelling to Washington, DC. When Frank told Dr. Koop about our ideas in relation to suicide, Koop was interested, but stressed the importance of scientific research to further elucidate the subject. When Frank told us of his encounter, we decided to pursue a research methodology based on the voice. Soon after, L. Firestone's empirical studies established the reliability and validity of her scale, and it has been proven as an effective tool in preventing suicide.

Items on this scale consisted of self-critical statements drawn from clinical material obtained during investigations into the voice. Results demonstrated that items of FAST and the accompanying brief screening scale, *The Firestone Assessment of Suicide Intent* (FASI) discriminate between individuals with a history of suicide attempts and those with no history of attempts better than other instruments currently used in clinical practice (R. Firestone & L. Firestone, 1998). Instruments for assessing the potential for violent behavior in adults, the *Firestone Assessment of Violent Thoughts* (FAVT) (R. Firestone & L. Firestone, 2008a) and in adolescents (FAVT-A) (R. Firestone & L. Firestone, 2008b) are available from Psychological Assessment Resources.

CLINICAL FINDINGS RELATED TO DEFENSES AGAINST DEATH ANXIETY

> Existentially, death is not simply an event that has not yet occurred or that happens to others. Rather, according to Heidegger, it is a distinctive possibility, into which we have been "thrown," that is constitutive of our kind of Being ("existence"). As such, death always already belongs to our existence as a central constituent of our intelligibility to ourselves in our futurity and finitude. (Stolorow, 2007, p. 35)

In discussion groups where the participants explored existential issues, three types of destructive thought patterns based on defensive reactions to the fear of death were noted: (1) those involving prohibitions and warnings to avoid investment in life; (2) those consisting of rationalizations (i.e., seemingly reasonable motives for retreating from life-affirming activities); and (3) those involving existential guilt (i.e., self-attacking thoughts and recriminations for a life unlived).

(1) Participants identified thoughts warning them about the dangers of investing fully in life or in a close relationship, thoughts that triggered fearful premonitions, which in turn effectively stifled their enthusiasm, energy, and sense of adventure. "If you get involved with him or her, you'll only get hurt in the end." "What good is caring or taking life too seriously? You're going to die sometime." "Why get a pet, you'll just end up burying it someday!" These admonitions have overtones similar to those of a parent who cautions children in a way that appears to be in their best interest, yet blocks positive strivings before they can be translated into action. Other thoughts diminish or destroy people's sense of meaning: "So what does it matter if you're in love now? It won't last.

Nothing lasts forever. Nothing matters." In addressing these inimical inner patterns, Israel Orbach (2008) contended:

> This is not just a reflection of a negative self-view, low self-esteem, self-anger, or lack of self-satisfaction; rather it is a hateful offense by the self against itself. (p. 301) Further, it is mental pain that resides at the heart of suicidal wishes, lack of meaning, existential concerns, and emptiness and not that lack of meaning causes suicidal urges or mental pain. (p. 296)

Some participants revealed a pessimistic, protective posture about life and death, "Good times are always followed by bad times." "Good luck can never last." "Sooner or later the axe is bound to fall." These beliefs, even if not consciously subscribed to, prevent people from giving full rein to their exuberance and happiness. As children, they were often chastised by parents who told them, "Don't get so excited! Just calm down!"

People experience voices anticipating misfortune or predicting future loss, illness, or death, in part, because early in life they learned that close, enjoyable times with parents were typically followed by the withdrawal of love or sometimes punishment. Now, as adults, they restrain their enthusiasm, ultimately losing interest in activities that once filled them with excitement. At times, they may even feel relieved when circumstances force them to relinquish activities that had brought them enjoyment, pleasure, and happiness.

When people are aware of expanding their life experience, they are susceptible to self-critical thoughts and attacks. They often have voices reminding them of death's inevitability when they are most excited and involved in life. Transitions and changes in one's circumstances, as well as separation anxiety, will usually trigger these kinds of destructive voices (R. Firestone, 1988). At these times, people's basic ambivalence in relation to living a full life versus pulling back to safety becomes evident.

Brendan, 55, had enjoyed a two-week vacation with close friends, but when it came time to return home, to work, and to his isolated life he began to feel depressed. For some reason on this particular trip, Brendan, though usually somewhat reserved and inhibited, had allowed himself to fully experience the camaraderie, good times, and sense of adventure that he had loved when he was younger. Thus, going home had a deeper significance for him than usual.

Two days before he was to leave, Brendan identified a seemingly comforting way of thinking that he recognized as familiar. This voice expressed the belief that "all good times come to an end" and, besides, "he had had enough":

> Brendan: I found myself thinking things like, 'You did a lot of things on your vacation, so it's enough already. It's OK. You can go home now.' Then I recognized that this voice sounded so familiar. It reminded me of a voice I have about life in general. It's basically my father's philosophy about life: "Well, this might be it for now; this might be the end. But it's O.K. because you've done this and you've done that. Sure, there are a couple of things you haven't done, but it's OK, it's OK, it's not so terrible. It's OK. It's OK."
>
> But then, yesterday I really felt like I wanted to stay longer on vacation. I immediately had an angry self-attack that made me anxious and depressed. It was almost like my father yelling at me, telling me I'd had enough excitement for one day. The soothing "O.K." mantra turned into sarcastic, angry thoughts.
>
> "What do you want to do, anyway? There are just so many things you can do in life, and if you've done them, for Christ-sake, it's O.K. [snide tone of voice] What do you expect? That you can just keep going and going? Are you crazy? Are you out of your mind? You think that you can be open to more and more good things in your life? Are you nuts? What the hell's the matter with you! What do you think you can have more of, anyway? [angry, loud] This is it, buddy!

Essentially Brendan's voice condemned his desire to have more in his life. After expressing his angry self-attacks, Brendan revealed that, in contrast to his usual feeling of contentment with his somewhat comfortable, yet self-denying life at home, he had started wanting more out of life while on vacation. He was saddened to realize that in over-scheduling and routinizing his daily life and in seeking safety in the relationship with his wife, he had transformed his life into a humdrum existence, much like the lives of the men portrayed by Castaneda (1974) in *Tales of Power:*

> That barking, and the loneliness it creates, speaks of the feelings of men.... Men for whom an entire life was like one Sunday afternoon, an afternoon which was not altogether miserable, but rather hot and dull and uncomfortable. They sweated and fussed a great deal. They didn't know where to go, or what to do. That afternoon left them only with the memory of petty annoyances and tedium, and then suddenly it was over; it was already night. (p. 293)

Brendan's experience reflects a common response to positive circumstances. These adverse responses can be explained by the fact that the anxiety triggered by positive changes in one's circumstances often gives rise to a renewed search for sanctuary within the familiarity of one's defense system. As Rollo May (1958) asserted: "Anxiety occurs at the point where some emerging potentiality or possibility faces the individual, some possibility of fulfilling his existence; but this very possibility involves the destroying of present security, which thereupon gives rise to the tendency to deny the new potentiality" (p. 52).

(2) The second type of voice attack utilizes all of one's intelligence, logic, and reason to provide rationalizations for regressing and withdrawing from life. It supports a retreat from gratifying experiences and fosters an inward, pseudo-independent lifestyle. Seemingly logical reasons for self-denial and asceticism are all regulated by the voice. A majority of these rationalizations are supported by conventional thinking. For example: "Why worry if you're not having sex anymore? You're a mother now. You're not supposed to be sexy." Or, "You're too old to play basketball any more, you could get injured." Or, "Romance is foolish at your age, you look like an idiot." These rationalizations cut into people's freedom and active participation in life. Yet in some way, they help to dull or obscure underlying fears of death and dying.

(3) The third type of voice promotes self-recriminations and guilt about *the life unlived*. These thoughts usually follow a retreat or regression and generate painful feelings about betraying oneself. When one restricts one's life through conformity, self-denial, or self-attack, one has a deep sense of unfulfillment and emptiness, as well as a sense of shame and remorse. People feel that their life lacks meaning and purpose and tend to criticize and attack themselves for it. The resultant self-accusations contribute to feelings of demoralization, which tend to trigger a downward cycle consisting of more self-denying behavior and increasingly vicious self-attacks. "You'll never accomplish what you wanted to." "What a waste your life has been!" Or in relation to hurting other people: "Just look at how you've ruined this relationship." "Your family would be better off without you." "They were right, you never did amount to anything." "What have you ever accomplished?"

When people retreat from facing the pain of life and death, they put their defenses above their consideration of or compassion for others. There is justifiable guilt because real people are hurt, particularly our loved ones and most particularly our children (R. Firestone, 1987b).

Thus, voices operate to prevent people from maintaining loving relationships and having a vital, energetic life; they provide rationalizations for denying the self and then condemn people for hurting their loved ones and themselves in the process. Each type of voice described above can be elicited, identified, and overcome through the utilization of Voice Therapy techniques in individual and group sessions.

Patients who progress in any form of psychotherapy are fearful of separating from and losing the internal parent represented by the voice. In a sense, the voice has kept them company all of their lives; therefore, relinquishing these secondary defenses and the companionship, albeit hostile, that the voice provided triggers feelings of aloneness and separateness. The profound sense of being separate and alone, the anxiety aroused by disrupting the fantasy connection with the family, and the prospect of living without one's illusion of eternal life are at the core of resistance to a better life.

DISCUSSION

In a previous work, *Suicide and the Inner Voice* (R. Firestone, 1997b), the first author used a personal example to illustrate my initial investigations into the voice and to show how Voice Therapy works. In the present discussion, I paraphrase several passages from the earlier work:

> In December 1976, my wife Tamsen and I, along with a group of close friends, were transiting the Panama Canal on the first stage of a round-the-world sail. This notable event was marred by the emotional background of the occasion. Tamsen was feeling bad and was in a confused state psychologically. Her reactions had been fitfull and erratic for the past month or so, ever since we had begun talking about starting a family. Something about procreation terrified her and, although she strongly wanted to have children with me, she was virtually in a state of panic.
>
> In a conversation with friends, Tamsen overreacted when a woman friend suggested that the fear of having a child might be related to Tamsen's dread of turning out to be like her own mother. Tamsen was furious and lashed out at her innocent assailant, a style of defensive behavior that was entirely out of character for her. I was very worried and pondered the circumstances, searching desperately to reach an understanding.
>
> I thought back to a theory I had developed from my own experience. I remembered that once, in a group meeting of colleagues, a woman had censured me for being a dominant figure. I was taken aback by the severe attack and felt misunderstood. When I thought about the evening, I remembered that I had been particularly sensitive and kind to her. But if she was wrong about me or had a distorted impression, why was I so hurt and insulted by her attack? Then it dawned on me that her accusation must

have echoed something negative that I thought about myself. I remembered my father had often accused me of being selfish and demanding. He defined any desire or willfulness on my part as intrusive and bossy. He accused me of being a big shot. These childhood experiences tied in with the woman's assault on my character and explained my overreaction.

In recalling these events, I recognized the similarity between my own experience and Tamsen's defensive anger. I wondered what destructive things she was telling herself about becoming a mother. At that point I had the idea that she could reveal her self-attacks in the form of a dialogue or voice. She could say her thoughts as though she were talking to herself as an outsider.

Tamsen sensed that I was on the right track and was eager to uncover the cause of feeling lost or removed from herself and others. Once she grasped the idea, she was anxious to try out the technique. She began the exercise in a calm voice, reciting her self-attacks about becoming pregnant. "I'm not fit to be a mother. I don't know the first thing about it and will probably mess up. I'm afraid of having a baby, like I'm losing something."

I suggested, "Try to say your self-attacks as though they were coming from an outside person. Try to say them as though you were talking to yourself. Like, 'You don't deserve to have a baby. You would be a lousy mother,' and so on."

Tamsen started off tentatively repeating: "You're not fit to be a mother," then gained momentum. "You don't deserve to have a child. You don't know a damn thing about children. Who do you think you are, anyway? You think you're better than me?"

As Tamsen expressed these self-attacks, her face grimaced, her speech pattern changed, and she sounded exactly like her mother. This transition seemed eerie to her friends. "You were such a pain in the neck." She went on. "From the moment you were born, all you did was cry! You drove me crazy! Every single moment, you wanted something from me! I hated it! I hated you!" By this time, Tamsen's expressive movements revealed a combination of rage and agonizing sorrow as she exploded with the torrent of emotional abuse. "Just wait until you have children. You'll see what it's like! Then maybe you'll understand what I went through. I just wish the same burden on you. Kids just take, take, take! There's nothing left for you!! Just wait until you have kids; your life is going to be over. They'll make you sorry you were ever born!!"

This powerful release of feeling left Tamsen exhausted but relieved. The experience was self-explanatory; there was no need for intellectual interpretation. Because of her courage and initiative, what my friends and I witnessed that day was an unintentional yet incredible Voice Therapy session that would later be duplicated by others many times over. The voice had evinced itself for the first time. All who were present sensed that it was an important occasion, that this new methodology was a discovery of deep significance. A person's destructive propensities toward self could be accessed with this new procedure. The spontaneous flow of emotion triggered by the new format not only illuminated the content of self-attacks and permitted a feeling release of considerable magnitude, it also shed light on the source of negative introjects.

After this experience, Tamsen had a clearer understanding of the destructive elements in her own personality. Before this, she had had absolutely no awareness of why she was reacting negatively to having a child. She was a passive victim of an unconscious self-destructive process. When she finished the exercise, she was alert to vicious negative thoughts that punished her for competing with her mother in the area of motherhood and family. She concluded that her mother's hostility toward her, based on immaturity, self-hatred, and withholding, had obviously left an imprint. She understood that she had internalized the aggression her mother felt toward her as a child and had come to see herself as an unlovable and unworthy burden. She anticipated that having her own baby would be an imposition and unconsciously regarded the child as an unpleasant intruder who would repay her for the trouble she had caused her own mother.

From the experience of externalizing her voices, it was apparent to Tamsen that her mother harbored a good deal of resentment toward her and that she, Tamsen, had incorporated the malice into her own personality. In reflecting on what I had observed and on Tamsen's remarks, I thought, "Where else could the negative thoughts or voices have come from? Why did her enunciation and general bearing resemble her mother's speech patterns and mannerisms when she entered the exercise? Why was there so much anger and rage at herself, and why was she so sad afterward?" Tamsen's conclusions seemed to make sense.

As she came to understand the division in her personality, Tamsen began to feel better. She followed up with two similar sessions that were equally powerful and added support to the original theory that she was plagued by the internalization of her mother's attacks. She became aware that having a child represented a turning point in her life. She would no longer be the child but would become the parent, meaning new responsibilities and someone entirely dependent on her. In the transition she would be one step closer to death. Realizing and working through these issues helped her to develop perspective and understanding of her emotional upset. Her problem related to having a child had begun to be successfully resolved.

It is not only the family of origin that affects the voice process; painful existential realities also impact the antiself system. As previously explained, interpersonal traumas suffered early in life are reinforced by death anxiety as the child discovers that his or her life is finite. Understanding the concepts of Separation Theory elucidates the self-destructive machinations of the personality. Therapeutic success involves identifying self-destructive voices, releasing the associated affect, and restructuring one's life in the direction of individuation and personal fulfillment. It necessitates the courage to break with fantasy bonds or illusions of connection. Voice Therapy helps people to pursue personal goals in the real world as contrasted with a reliance on fantasy gratification. It is a motivating force in developing a creative, adventurous lifestyle in which the self predominates (R. Firestone, 1997b).

In summary, Voice Therapy is a broadly based therapy technique derived from a systematic theory of neurosis, based on the conceptualization of the fantasy bond as the core defense which underlies an individual's fundamental resistance to change or progress. The process of Voice Therapy entails exposing the patient's negative thoughts and the accompanying affect, forming insight into their sources, and gradually modifying behavior in juxtaposition to the dictates of the voice (R. Firestone, 1988). The process of identifying the voice and its associated feelings of self-hatred and rage toward self, combined with corrective strategies of behavioral change, significantly expands the patient's boundaries and brings about a more positive sense of self.

NOTES

1. This quote was excerpted from an unpublished review of *Creating a Life of Meaning and Compassion: The Wisdom of Psychotherapy* (R. Firestone et al., 2003), by Chris Morrant.
2. Re: elements of the antiself system, including the negative self-image and the voice process, see Robert Stolorow's (2007) *Trauma and Human Existence*. Stolorow noted that "from recurring experiences of malattunement, the child acquires the unconscious conviction that unmet developmental yearnings and reactive painful feeling states are manifestations of a loathsome defect or of an inherent inner badness" (p. 4).

Choosing Life With the Full Realization of Death

9 Challenging Defenses That Interfere With Living Fully

It is certain that in adult life gratification through fantasy is no longer harmless. . . .
Fantasy and reality become incompatible: it must be one or the other.
—*Anna Freud,* **The Ego and the Mechanisms of Defense** *(1966, p. 81)*

Death may be the last heavily repressed area of our lives.
—*Thomas Langner,* **Choices for Living** *(2002, p. 7)*

In describing the potential for life-affirming death awareness, the authors have emphasized the importance of challenging defenses that limit each person's opportunity for self-development and fulfillment. We have noted that defenses develop in a relationship constellation but are reinforced by death anxiety. Our approach does not suggest that one should focus attention on the subject of death and dying as a therapy but instead that one should come to terms with the character defenses that deny death's reality. However, as a person comes to understand and cope with his or her psychological defenses, he or she will encounter death anxiety in the natural course of living. When death fears surface, the individual can face the realization of mortality, identify and express the accompanying emotions of fear, sadness, and rage, and find a way to communicate his or her thoughts and feelings with others rather than retreat into a defensive posture.

Giving up well-established defenses and dispelling destructive fantasies and illusions is not only possible but is essential to living a more meaningful, rewarding life. In our opinion, approaching life openly, non-defensively, and with maximum vulnerability is the only viable way to live. Furthermore, human beings have a remarkable ability to change, and almost any psychological malady or problem can be overcome if one has both motivation and courage (R. Firestone & Catlett, 1989). This does not negate the fact that considerable anxiety is aroused during this process.

According to Yalom (1980) and Piven (2004a), adult fears differ from children's fears even though they do contain remnants of childhood "terrors and feelings of helplessness barely escaped" (Piven, pp. 73–74). In his writing, Piven described a form of *autistic-contiguous anxiety* experienced by infants and noted that aspects of this anxiety tend to remain intact in the unconscious minds of adults:

> The precategorical terror and struggle of infancy lurks beneath the organization of adult consciousness .... It is a matrix of experience carried into adulthood, which persists beneath defensive facades.... Autistic-contiguous anxiety is the foundation of the fear of unknowing, of not having containment of the chaotic world, and motivates the construction of fantasies and illusions which make people feel secure. (p. 74)

Understandably, people are fearful and therefore reluctant to alter deep character defenses. The fear of these autistic-contiguous anxieties coming to the surface is at the core of resistance to therapy, to challenging defenses, and to moving forward in life. As people break addictive patterns and separate from elements of the fantasy bond in their relationships, they tend to become apprehensive, anticipating that they will once again experience the sense of helplessness and annihilation anxiety that they endured during the first years of life. Nevertheless, when they realize as adults that they are no longer powerless, vulnerable, and completely dependent as they once were as children, they are better equipped to cope with these internalized fear reactions. They can learn to identify and separate primal emotions from the objective realities of their current life (R. Firestone & Catlett, 2009).

However, people are still faced with the reality of death and the ontological anxiety that it arouses. Citing Heidegger's original description of the ontological anxiety experienced by people who live authentic modes of existence, Stolorow (2007) depicted it as "the sense of uncanniness that accompanies the recognition that inherent to our existence is the ever present possibility of its extinction" (p. 26). Because there is no ultimate solution to this problem, the only appropriate reaction to the fact of death is to feel one's way through the painful emotions. In "Psychoanalytic Reflections on Mortality," Rodin and Zimmerman (2008) called attention to the fact that because human beings cannot fully protect themselves against an awareness of death, they "have developed a fundamental mechanism to defend against it—namely that of denial" (p. 183). Although people can address these concerns within a self-help format, significant movement may necessitate working through these feelings in an analytic form of depth therapy or in a group setting that allows for the development of insight and expression of deep feelings. This format may be essential in order for individuals to develop their full potential. The value of psychotherapy will be discussed in a broader perspective in Chapter 10.

A certain amount of progress can also be achieved in the course of people developing on their own (R. Firestone et al., 2002). Individuals can challenge their defenses and attempt to remain close to their emotions. In Chapter 7, we described the fantasy bond as the core defense and explained how it is made up of both self-nourishing and self-punishing components. In order to challenge self-nurturing aspects of the fantasy bond, one must give up self-soothing addictions and routine habit patterns. In dealing with and overcoming self-punishing aspects of the fantasy bond, people need to identify their voice-attacks and hostile attitudes toward self and others, and to understand the origins of the enemy within. They need to become more sensitive to when they are attacking themselves or are engaging in negative behaviors governed by the voice.

One method that can help people identify the voice process is writing down, in a personal journal or daily log, self-critical thoughts and voices in the second person format as though someone were speaking to them: "You're a terrible person." "You never were any good." They can also take note of what the voices are telling them about other people. "People can never be trusted." "They don't really like you." They can then make an effort to distinguish these destructive thoughts from a more realistic conception of self and others. This process of change can also be enhanced by communicating with a trusted friend, an understanding, intelligent, and empathic person in whom they can confide (R. Firestone et al., 2002).

In addition, people can take part in discussions with others who have a similar goal of personal development in much the same way as individuals in the friendship circle have done. These friends shared a strong interest in understanding themselves and applied basic psychological principles in their daily lives. In the open forum of group discussions and seminars, they talked honestly and identified defensive behaviors they were using to alleviate painful emotions of sadness, anxiety, and frustration. Through these discussions and other methods of self-inquiry, they achieved considerable insight into the origins of their defenses. For the most part, these people have overcome addictive behaviors and deadening routines, disrupted dependent modes of relating to others, altered self-denying, withholding behaviors, and become more energetic, vital, and closer to their feelings (R. Firestone et al., 2003).

Although progress can be made by utilizing these methods, the process of exploring deeper issues and investigating the underlying causative factors in defense formation often requires a more in-depth approach. A more thorough, systematic method for investigating the voice would involve participating in Voice Therapy sessions in which individuals would identify destructive thoughts and voices, reveal their source, and formulate corrective suggestions to challenge these behaviors in everyday situations.

Learning to accept one's feelings and expanding the capacity for feeling are also a fundamental part of the process of change. Disrupting aspects of self-parenting in the context of one's intimate relationships and family as well as dispelling illusions of merged identity as a means to deny the reality of death are essential in moving toward an independent, fulfilling life and finding satisfaction in loving relationships and family life (R. Firestone & Catlett, 2009).

CHALLENGING SELF-PARENTING DEFENSES

Breaking Addictions and Routines

Powerful forces are set into motion when one breaks an addiction. Self-soothing, self-gratifying behaviors involve a focus that makes one's life more restricted, compulsive, and rigid, thereby depleting one's energy. In challenging an addictive behavior, the energy that was previously involved in maintaining it is now available for other more constructive purposes. In addition, people cannot suppress feeling in one area through self-soothing mechanisms without becoming blunted emotionally in other areas as well. Although addictions do reduce tension and partially gratify needs left unsatisfied in childhood, they ultimately reach a stage where they are debilitating and dysfunctional. Studies have shown that the use of addictive substances is strongly correlated with both violence and suicide (R. Firestone & Catlett, 2009).

People need all of their faculties to cope with life effectively and to give up self-nurturing defenses and other self-defeating behaviors dictated by the voice. In doing so they are no longer troubled by guilt and self-recriminations about indulging in the addictive behavior and keeping loved ones at a distance. Breaking an addiction or habitual routine opens one up to more real opportunities in life and puts one in touch with one's real wants, desires, and needs (R. Firestone et al., 2003). The real self—the core of one's personality—emerges and takes precedence over the enemy within.

Identifying Addictive Behaviors and Routines

All addictive habit patterns have two characteristics in common: (1) they help people cut off from or suppress painful feelings; and (2) they are influenced by the destructive thought process or voice. There are steps that people can take to disrupt well-established addictions and self-nourishing routines. The first is to become aware of the behaviors and routines one is using to reduce anxiety states or other distressing emotions. For example, habitually turning to food or alcohol when one is upset or angry indicates that these substances are being used as a defense. An awareness of the connection between the addictive behavior and emotional distress would provide the necessary insight for changing these destructive patterns. Secondly, with this awareness people can look for the specific situations that trigger their indulgence in the addictive behavior. Finally, they can attempt to identify the thoughts that influence them to engage in the destructive behaviors and trace them to their source (L. Firestone & J. Catlett, 2004).

It is valuable to become aware of the seemingly friendly thoughts or voices that effectively seduce one into engaging in an addiction as well as the self-accusatory thoughts that surface after the individual has engaged in the addictive behavior (R. Firestone et al., 2002). When people explore the origins of their addictive patterns, they become cognizant of the role these behaviors are playing in limiting their lives. Going through this process facilitates an understanding of the unconscious motivation underlying addictive patterns, thereby enabling one to better control these destructive behaviors.

Breaking Addictive Behaviors

When food has been consistently used to reduce or numb painful feelings, it can lead to recurring cycles of overeating and dieting, bingeing and purging (Sandbek, 1993). Similarly, drugs and alcohol can be used to generate a downward spiral of self-destruction. In challenging addictive habit patterns, it is important to find more constructive ways of dealing with painful situations, interpersonal hurts, and other stresses that invariably arise in the course of daily life. For example, in our discussion groups, people used corrective suggestions offered by other participants regarding strategies they could adopt to strengthen their sense of self and allow them to move toward pursuing their real interests and goals (R. Firestone & Catlett, 2009).

> Jennifer was a secretive alcoholic; none of her friends or family was aware of her drinking. At home and work she would pour vodka into a glass of ice and pass it off as water. Her job as a journalist required that she travel extensively. During her business trips, while alone in hotel rooms and on airplanes, she drank heavily. Jennifer was living in a private hell and her alcoholism was beginning to interfere with her performance at work. Finally, she turned to a group of trusted friends and asked for help. She felt confident that she could challenge her problem at home and in the office, but she was worried about the long periods of isolation when she would be out of town.
>
> One of her friends who offered to help arranged for Jennifer to phone her frequently when she went on a business trip. She suggested that Jennifer call her whenever her anxiety from not drinking became intense. Jennifer called her friend from the airplane, from the airport, and from her hotel room late at night. Her friend was always available, compassionate, and patient with Jennifer, staying with her as she talked and until her anxiety abated. Jennifer was successful in conquering her addiction and has not had a drink in the five years since she overcame her alcoholism.

This process of enlisting help from others points up the fact that for certain people who are unable to give up dependence on food, drugs, or alcohol on their own, a caring friend or a support group can help accomplish the goal of coping with an addiction. An example of this type of assistance is the 12-step program developed by Alcoholics Anonymous. This program and other similar groups have been particularly effective in coping with a variety of addictive behaviors. The group context involves reinforcement and direct support from others and a structured environment or program for those individuals who cannot adopt this structure for themselves. Ideally these programs would simply offer a supportive atmosphere free from the shame or stigma often associated with these debilitating behaviors.

Addiction and compulsivity do not only relate to the use of substances, but to addictive attachments as well. One offshoot of AA is Codependents Anonymous (CoDA), a program where people deal with the fantasy bonds in their intimate relationships (Irvine, 1999). Codependency groups help individuals become aware of their desperation and emotional hunger toward mates and family members, thereby allowing them to develop more independence and freedom in their overall life situation. They attempt to help people break addictive processes and character defenses that would manifest themselves in future relationships.

Addictive defenses are interrelated. Intrusions into one component of the self-parenting process can impact other defenses, often precipitating a kind of domino effect. Challenging an addiction can affect other aspects of the personality that may be far removed from the habit pattern that one is altering.

> For example, Brad, 55, a businessman who thoroughly enjoyed wine and good food also sponsored tours of the nearby wine country and had created his own label. His drinking pattern and focus on food bothered some of his friends and they challenged him about the habit. They felt it made him dull, unavailable, and sometimes nasty. Because he trusted his friends and their input mattered to him, he questioned himself about his reliance on wine.
>
> One summer, while on vacation, Brad decided to try an experiment—to give up wine—simply to see how it would make him feel. He had put on some weight and had complained of feeling sluggish and somewhat jaded and at times he was grumpy, irritable, and sarcastic, particularly with his wife.
>
> Several weeks later Brad mentioned to a friend that he could detect no effects from abstaining, and in fact was surprised that he had experienced none of the physical symptoms of withdrawal that he had anticipated. Others thought differently. It was obvious to Brad's friends that something important was happening on a deeper level. Brad was perceptibly more social, warm, and congenial in all of his personal interactions. Far more significant, however, was the marked improvement in Brad's way of relating to his wife. His responses to her became more loving, empathic, and tender. His hurtful sarcastic remarks and criticality completely dropped out of his behavioral repertoire. His wife remarked to a friend, "I almost don't recognize Brad as the same person I've been married to all these years."

Disrupting Routines

As noted earlier, routines and rituals lend an air of certainty and stability to a life that is uncertain, unstable, and impermanent. Activities such as playing computer or video games, watching television, compulsive shopping, working, or exercising appear acceptable or even desirable. However, there is the potential for addiction because these activities are generally inward and self-involved and tend to cut a person off from feeling (Suler, 2004; Whang, Lee, & Chang, 2003). There are also those who bury themselves in work until they reach the point of exhaustion, using seemingly plausible rationalizations to justify their long hours and their retreat from friendships, mates, and family. In addition, the type of work a person is involved in can make it difficult for them to return to a feeling state at the end of the day (R. Firestone et al., 2003).

> By the time Janice was 38, she had established a thriving business with over 100 employees. While admiring her success, her family and friends were nevertheless concerned about her compulsive work habits. Janice rarely took time off, even on weekends, and could often be found working at her office until late in the evening preparing for the next day. She had lost sight of her original goal, which was to achieve financial success to ultimately have more personal freedom. Finally her husband confronted her and expressed his worry about her and his anger about their deteriorating marriage.
>
> Initially, Janice was defensive, complaining that it was impossible for her to extricate herself from her work schedule. She complained that she felt trapped in her career. Gradually, she became more open and aware of the rationalizations she had been using to justify her long hours of work. Her husband recommended that she set aside Fridays as *her* time and spend the entire day socializing with friends and the evenings with him. He suggested that she simply try it as an experiment for one month. Janice complied. On the first Friday, she was distracted and worried about work, but her friends reassured her that if there were a problem at work she would be called. After a year, she still enjoys her Fridays off. She has pursued an interest in painting by taking art classes. She no longer feels stressed at work, accomplishes much more, and has become closer to her husband.

Janice's story underscores the fact that breaking routine patterns allows people to become more aware of their unique wants and desires, which constitute a basic part of a person's identity. The process of becoming reconnected to oneself and to one's previously suppressed feelings is an integral part of moving toward a more fulfilling, meaningful life.

Challenging the Voice

As described in Chapter 8, the voice is made up of self-punishing thoughts and attitudes that are incorporated early in life under conditions of stress. At these times parents' critical, rejecting attitudes are internalized by the child and become part of an introjected, parental image, which takes on the significance of a survival mechanism. These parental introjects or voices lead to feelings of inferiority and superiority toward self and toward others. The process of challenging the voice disrupts one's negative self-concept formed in the family and breaks the fantasy bond with one's parents.

Formulating and Implementing Corrective Suggestions for Behavioral Change

Behavioral changes are a necessary part of any effective therapeutic procedure. Franz Alexander (1946) originated the concept of the corrective emotional experience in planning certain exercises for patients in therapy that would counteract the effects of the original trauma they had suffered. The potential for progress in one's personal development as well as in Voice Therapy is not merely a function of identifying destructive thoughts, releasing the associated feelings, and achieving insight. "Until patients learn to take definitive actions that are in opposition to the prohibitions of the voice, they tend to repeat early patterns of maladaptive behavior and continue to live in a narrow range with significant limitations" (R. Firestone, 1988, p. 209). Therefore, the strongest challenge to the voice is to change those behaviors that are based on its dictates. These changes can be facilitated by formulating and carrying out corrective suggestions, the fourth and final step in Voice Therapy methodology.

Because corrective suggestions pose the most direct challenge to destructive behaviors, there is considerable resistance to putting them into actual practice. Although people may collaborate on an equal basis with a therapist in formulating the suggestion, they may later reverse their point of view in relation to the desire to change. At these times people can distort the situation in a paranoid way, mistakenly believing that the therapist has a stake in their changing, rather than facing their own ambivalence about altering their well-established self-limiting behaviors (R. Firestone, 1988).

When a corrective suggestion is instituted, anxiety is aroused because it involves taking risks and deliberately engaging in constructive behavioral changes that feel unfamiliar and uncomfortable. In a sense one is giving up one's crutches before one knows whether or not one can walk (R. Firestone, 1997a). Nevertheless, when people maintain the new behavior and resist reverting to acting out the old one, the voices driving the destructive behavior gradually fade and may eventually disappear.

"Corrective suggestions, if consistently followed, bring about changes in the emotional atmosphere and often lead to a corrective emotional experience" (R. Firestone, 1988, p. 209). For example, one man whose self-centeredness and air of superiority provoked anger in his friends made a concerted effort to control his belittling remarks and to take an interest in other people's views and opinions. Once he stopped manipulating his interpersonal environment in this negative way, he generated a new set of circumstances in his interactions. The congenial responses of his friends created an unfamiliar, although more positive, emotional climate.

Maintaining a Daily Journal

As an adjunct to Voice Therapy, some people have found it worthwhile to identify what they are telling themselves, in terms of the voice, by maintaining a daily journal, as described earlier in this chapter. The authors have developed a specific format for this type of journaling: On the left-hand side of a page, people record their destructive thoughts, again in the second-person format; and on the right-hand side of the page, they write a more congenial and realistic point of view in the first-person format. Individuals who are attempting to break an addictive pattern of behavior write down the thoughts that induce them to engage in the behavior as well as the voices that punish them for indulging (L. Firestone & Catlett, 2004). The process of recording in writing both aspects of the personality—the self and the antiself—facilitates an awareness of the events and interactions that trigger the self-attacking process and helps people separate their real point of view from those thoughts that are opposed to their self-interest and hostile toward.

EXPANDING THE CAPACITY FOR FEELING

There are a number of methods that can help people increase their capacity for feeling. In the authors' experience we have found that feeling release therapy and identifying voice attacks in Voice Therapy are valuable in this regard. In feeling release sessions people express emotions that are often primal in nature—that is, deep expressions of intense childhood trauma. They are able to trace the source of these primal feelings to events in childhood and to situations that they had found too threatening to fully experience at the time. In exploring their thoughts, feelings, and memories they gain a new perspective on their early childhood, their present-day behavior, and their way of living. They come to see how, on an unconscious level, they were avoiding experiences that might have reminded them of the fear, deprivation, and anxiety they had suffered as children (R. Firestone, 1985).

Learning to Accept All Feelings Uncritically

As a result of these types of deep feeling experiences, people can learn that all of their feelings, including irrational feelings, are acceptable. Distinguishing the primal elements of emotional reactions from present-day feelings enables people to respond more appropriately to events that arouse feelings of anger, hurt, sadness, or fear. This awareness helps defuse melodrama and overreactions, allowing time for reflection and for the consideration of the consequences of one's actions (R. Firestone & Catlett, 2009).

In applying this new knowledge and insight to everyday life, people can learn to enlarge their capacity for feeling. People who are close to their emotions, especially poignant feelings of sadness, often experience a sense of inner harmony (Oatley, 1996; Parrott & Harre, 1996). This deeper awareness of oneself—of one's sorrow, anger, fear, shame, envy, joy, happiness, exhilaration—allows a person to feel centered and tends to dispel self-critical thoughts, self-hating ruminations, and distortions of others. Remaining connected to their emotions enables people to feel more energetic and vital in their lives (R. Firestone et al., 2003).

Learning to Cope Effectively With Anger

Anger is a normal and inevitable reaction to frustration (Bandura, 1973; N. Miller & Dollard, 1941). It can be a source of energy and vitality when people understand its nature, accept it as an inherent part of their emotional makeup, and learn how to utilize it constructively. Like all feelings, anger must be allowed free reign in consciousness while actions must be subject to moral considerations. The choice to express one's anger outwardly involves reality issues (a consideration as to whether expressing one's anger would be in one's best interest) as well as moral concerns. Dealing with angry feelings is vital for mental health and facilitates the pursuit of goals and priorities (R. Firestone & Catlett, 2009).

On the other hand, the inability to express anger appropriately has obvious negative consequences; for example, when inappropriately acted out in interpersonal relationships, or at the extreme in antisocial, violent behavior (De Zulueta, 1993; Gilligan, 1996; Kecmanovic, 1996; Volavka, 2002; Waller, 2002). Therefore, it is important to identify both the primal elements in anger and the voices that are associated with it. A person can then have control over whether his or her anger will be expressed in adaptive or maladaptive ways.

Individuals who are afraid to acknowledge angry feelings may internalize them and turn these feelings against themselves, which can lead to self-destructive acts or at times suicide (Fonagy, 2004; Gilligan, 1996; McFarlane & van der Kolk, 1996). Others may express anger or hostility indirectly through passive-aggressive manipulations, physical symptoms, or psychosomatic illnesses, or they may try to disguise their aggressive feelings through compliance or with a phony persona.

For the most part, Allison, 31, had a calm, composed manner, rarely raising her voice. She disguised any negative feelings with a sweet, syrupy tone and a phony smile. Suppressing her true feelings was taking a toll; Allison was chronically exhausted and suffered from a mild depression. She entered therapy and in a feeling release session she explored powerful feelings of anger and rage repressed since childhood. The following is an excerpt from her journal:

> If I feel anger, I feel strong, competent, womanly, self-possessed. I know who I am and what I feel. I know my opinions and don't feel afraid to say them. I'm not afraid of anyone. I'm interested in other opinions, even if I don't agree with them. I am not threatened; the way I feel about myself as a person is not dependent upon how I interact with anyone else.
>
> However, if I don't feel my anger, then I feel a basic low grade self-attack. A slight down feeling that builds on itself. I become afraid of other people's reactions. If I don't catch on quickly, my strength fades away. I have learned that I have to feel the anger even if it is not rational. To not feel it is a slow suicide. Interestingly, when I do feel it, I love it. I like feeling strong. I like feeling powerful. I like feeling like me. At times I am still unaware of my anger. The voice attacks and self-critical thoughts start before I know that I had a flash of anger first.
>
> I'm surprised that feeling my anger makes me feel more like a woman, more attractive, more sexual. I grew up with the feeling that it is far more

acceptable for a man to be angry than a woman. My view has been that women are conniving, manipulative, and weak in their anger, more passive in it by resorting to tears and creating overwhelming guilt in the offending person or, on the other hand, becoming a shrew-like bitch. The male anger that I witnessed from my father was like a seething volcano that upon eruption was totally out of control and terrifying.

So throughout my childhood, and most of my adult life until recently, I have avoided being conscious of my anger. I learned early to suppress it and reached a point where I had absolutely no idea of when I was angry. The anger immediately metamorphosed into self-hate, self-attacks, and a willingness to totally sell my soul in order to avoid any kind of conflict. I developed a fake, phony smile in order to placate and essentially lost any sense of myself.

Recently, in recognizing and expressing anger when I feel it, I am realizing that there is another option in terms of verbalizing my anger that is effective and allows me to find my own strength as an independent person. It has a great effect on how I feel about myself as a woman. It allows me to feel equal to not only any other woman, but also to men. I like feeling equal to a man, and particularly am aware of that in a loving, sexual situation. I want to make love, I want to be loving, I want to share that experience on an equal basis. I didn't realize that learning about my anger would impact my feelings regarding sexuality, but I believe that they are strongly connected.

In therapy, Allison learned to accept her angry feelings uncritically. She recognized that in the past she had suppressed them and often projected them onto another person when they felt too threatening. In exploring the primal components of her anger, she began to express it appropriately, which changed her way of being and interacting with people in her interpersonal world. Perhaps most importantly, Allison realized, with some surprise, that in suppressing her anger she had also subdued other aspects of her personality, including her sexuality, self-confidence, and feelings of independence and equality.

CHALLENGING MANIFESTATIONS OF THE FANTASY BOND IN COUPLES

The single most important factor that contributes to the deterioration of love and friendship in a relationship is the individual defenses of the people involved and the formation of a fantasy bond. However, as described in Chapter 7, people who develop this type of destructive bond often deceive themselves and each other by imagining that they still love each other long after the feelings of love have diminished (R. Firestone et al., 2002). It is difficult for people to disrupt addictive attachments because they are largely unaware that they are living dishonestly, that they have little genuine personal contact with their partner, or that they are alienated both from themselves and from each other. In pointing out people's tendencies to ignore this painful reality, Laing (1985) described a couple he was consulting with:

> They are both engulfed by their own miserable mirage of intimacy. They are desperately estranged from each other yet they are too terrified to realize that they are simply separate. They could not come together because they could not bear to be apart. They had both become a part of the other. She had become his frustrating mother, who always kept him out, and he had become her impinging, penetrating, raping parents, always trying to get in. Both felt completely at home. Both loved their home, the typical beautiful home for a miserable mirage between two beautiful people who are ugly to each other. (p. 18)

The primary fantasy bond originally formed by the child is later extended to others in the form of an addictive attachment or an over-dependency on a person in one's adult life. This externalization of the fantasy bond is supported by agreed upon indications that one *belongs* to one's partner and by other symbols that reinforce a pretense of love. However, this illusion detracts from or may altogether extinguish the real behavioral operations of love—the companionship, affection, sexuality, and playfulness that characterizes the early phases of a relationship (R. Firestone, 1985, 1987a).

There are steps that people can take to break a fantasy bond and recapture some of the feelings that they experienced initially in the relationship. (1) First, they can become aware of any retreat from independence, and, secondly, they can explore their relationship for evidence of a fantasy bond. If they discover that they are behaving in certain ways that could not be considered loving, they can admit this truth to each other rather than attempting to cover it up. This exploration entails both partners examining and disclosing how they are honestly feeling in the relationship, as well as their level of satisfaction and happiness. This truthful appraisal is crucial in order to begin to untangle the destructive ties that have led to a diminished sense of self in each person. It is valuable for people to identify the defensive behaviors that they are using in an attempt to maintain an illusion of security and safety or to create emotional distance. These include responses such as possessiveness, role-playing, and offering false reassurances of love on the one hand, or withholding patterns, self-denial, and dishonest communications that interfere with genuine closeness and intimacy on the other hand.

(2) In this exploration, people often become aware that their own perceptions of the state of the relationship are not very reliable. When people are living within their defenses, in a mirage or illusion, they are usually unaware of the fact. Therefore, it is helpful to solicit feedback from a perceptive friend, because he or she usually has a more objective view of the relationship.

(3) People can admit that they have critical, hostile voices toward themselves and their partners. If the communication between the partners is open and respectful, they can reveal the content of these destructive thoughts to each other. Clearly, timing and sensitivity is crucial in this kind of conversation. Partners need to be open to hearing some of the negative ways the other has been thinking about him or her. They also need to reassure each other that the voices they are disclosing do not represent their real point of view, but rather that they reflect hostile attitudes incorporated from significant figures in their past.

The process of communicating with one's partner in this format is part of Voice Therapy methodology when applied to couples. In giving away one's voices, each person takes full responsibility for his or her destructive thoughts as well as for the behaviors he or she has acted out based on the voice. This is done without attributing blame to the other person, as people say; for example, "When you said that, I had a voice attack telling me you don't care about my feelings," as opposed to, "You're saying that just proves that you don't care about me!" In addition, both people make a concerted effort to remove the sarcastic or snide tone from the voice attacks on each other and to express them in a nondramatic style and with care for the other's feelings. Each strives to listen without reacting to the voice statements as personal criticisms. In the authors' experience we found that most people feel relieved rather than personally attacked to hear their partner's voices about them. They report that they feel better to hear the negative voices they have been sensing through their partner's overt behaviors brought into the open (R. Firestone & Catlett, 1999).

Listening to one's partner express his or her voice attacks requires assuming an open and minimally defended stance. The results are beneficial for both parties in that partners "develop the ability to listen to one another with understanding and compassion" (R. Firestone et al., 2002, p. 85). In instances where people do not yet feel comfortable revealing their destructive thoughts to a partner, they can talk with a trusted friend and reveal the voices that they have toward themselves and about the relationship.

(4) Partners can learn to face the emotional pain and sadness involved in attempting to restore intimacy to their relationship without retreating to a defended posture. They can learn to remain vulnerable rather than withdrawing and maintaining emotional distance. For example, one woman revealed to her husband that following the birth of their daughter she had lost her interest in sex. She was fearful that knowing the truth of how she felt her husband would reject her. She had been trying to cover up her lack of feeling by going through the motions of making love, which had only confused her husband. In therapy sessions, she examined the emotions underlying her lack of sexuality. She expressed anger and resentment and traced it to incidents that had traumatized her as a child. Her husband was sensitive and patient with her during this time and encouraged her to talk about her feelings while they were sexual. Gradually she regained her sexual desire, and she and her husband resumed the intimate and passionate sexual relationship they had previously shared.

Both partners can strive to openly express their tenderness and affection toward one another, especially in situations where sexuality has become less passionate and less central in the life of the couple. They can change negative stereotypic attitudes toward the opposite sex, challenge self-critical voices about their bodies and their sexuality, and develop more mature views of sex as a natural function that enhances one's sense of self and feelings of happiness (R. Firestone & Catlett, 1999).

(5) People in couples can give up the need to always be right. They can use the technique of *unilateral disarmament* to prevent mild disagreements or arguments from escalating to out-and-out hostility or verbal abuse. In many instances, it is relatively simple to interrupt the cycle of accusation and counteraccusation before one or both partners say or do something they later regret. The technique consists of one person dropping his or her stake in winning and then reaching out to the other. Expressing oneself verbally with statements like, "It doesn't really matter who's right or wrong, it's much more important for me to feel close to you right now," usually defuses the argument.

The expression of physical affection combined with statements of caring and understanding are disarming to the other person, who often feels touched by this gesture of peacemaking. As a result the hostility can dissipate. The technique of unilateral disarmament does not imply that one is surrendering one's point of view or necessarily deferring to the views and opinions of the other person. It merely indicates that the peacemaker places more value on being close than on winning his or her point (R. Firestone et al., 2002).

In numerous battles of the will that occur within couple relationships, the specific argument or *battle* can be won; but so often the *war* or the relationship is ultimately lost, and the individuals involved suffer accordingly. The technique of unilateral disarmament has the potential for averting this negative outcome and for helping partners create closer, more loving relationships.

(6) People can honestly expose their fears of being alone and separate, including fears of rejection, abandonment, and the ultimate loss of themselves or their partner. They can stop pretending that *belonging* to another person will protect them. In a couple's seminar, Tamsen addressed this issue.

> **Tamsen**: I think that one sure sign of a fantasy bond between two people is that it's unequal. Often, the woman seems to be depending on the man to be saved. And if the man shows any weaknesses, which of course every person has, then the woman hates him for it…or she has to make herself weaker than him. On the other hand, I've seen men who, after they become involved sexually with a woman, are very desperate to be with her all of the time. I think it must be because they are fearful of losing her. They focus on the woman constantly, and feel that they'll do anything to keep her. So the man has this illusion going on, too.
>
> **Julian**: What I've come to realize is that for me, the woman becomes the savior as soon as I form a relationship with her. Then I have to hang onto it because if I'm free of the woman or the relationship, then I'm back in that situation of feeling really alone and separate. If I hang onto the relationship, it may be a miserable state, but at least I'm not alone. So I'm this pathetic guy going along with anything to hold on.
>
> **Denise**: I've recently realized that my problem isn't my husband. We might fit into something together, but he's not my problem, my problem is myself. I don't want to be alone, but I'm afraid to relate closely, and that's my dilemma. So I live in this in-between state where I'm not alone, but I'm not close either.
>
> **Dr. Firestone**: I liked the way Denise described the dilemma that people get into. She said that people are uncomfortable giving and accepting genuine affection with another person but they're also uncomfortable being alone. So they form a fantasy bond or imaginary connection. It's kind

of a solution, but it becomes an addiction. Routines and habits give the illusion of security and safety, but you're really not close or relating. And that's really a rather terrible situation. People maintain a fantasy rather than the reality of the relationship, and that makes things worse. The more the discrepancy between what's really going on and the fantasy of what's going on, the more the relationship will suffer.

(7) People can move toward increased independence and show respect for one another's boundaries, goals, and priorities separate from their own self-interest. They can come to see that the wants, desires, and motives of their partner are as important as their own. As individuals evolve in their personal development, they come to realize, on a deep level, that in order to be close to another person, one has to be separate and autonomous.

(8) It is important to identify and make a concerted effort to break any patterns of dominance and submission and to strive to establish equality within one's relationships. Many individuals engage in actions that seem to reflect an unconscious belief that by subordinating themselves to a more dominant person and relinquishing their own point of view, they can somehow achieve security, safety, and immortality. Recognizing an imbalance in one's relationship is often the first step in disrupting patterns of authoritarianism and compliance that significantly diminish the independence and vitality of both partners. Breaking into this alliance often arouses existential anxiety in both people. This topic is discussed in greater depth in Chapter 12, "Learning to Love."

By becoming more open and nondefensive, individuals become less reactive and punitive when their partner expresses anger or reveals hostile voice attacks in relation to them. They are then able to reestablish channels for authentic communication that allow for greater intimacy. It is also worthwhile to increase one's interactions with other people, friends, and family members, who can provide a broader basis for reality-testing (R. Firestone et al., 2003).

The authors have developed a questionnaire to evaluate the quality of couple interactions that can be used by partners to explore and challenge elements of a fantasy bond in their relationship. The questionnaire assesses the behaviors and traits of each partner along six dimensions that characterize an ideal relationship as compared with those that characterize a fantasy bond. The six dimensions were derived from key defensive behaviors that men and women revealed in the course of discussing their difficulties in sustaining a close, intimate relationship (R. Firestone &

Exhibit 9.1

COUPLES INTERACTIONS CHART

Interactions in an Ideal Relationship	Interactions in a Relationship Characterized by a Fantasy Bond
Non-defensiveness and openness	Angry reactions to feedback; closed to new experiences
Honesty and integrity	Deception and duplicity
Respect for the other's boundaries, priorities, and goals, separate from oneself	Overstepping boundaries; other person seen only in relation to oneself
Physical affection and personal sexuality	Lack of affection; inadequate or impersonal, routine sexuality
Understanding—lack of distortion of the other person	Misunderstanding—distortion of the other person
Noncontrolling, nonmanipulative, and nonthreatening	Manipulations of dominance and submission

Catlett, 1999). These behaviors, which characterize how most people conduct themselves within a fantasy bond, include: defensiveness, dishonesty, duplicity, lack of respect for boundaries, superiority, contemptuousness, diminished affection and routine, impersonal sexual relating, lack of understanding and empathy, and manipulations of dominance and dependency. (See Exhibit 9.1, Couples Interactions Chart, and Exhibit 9.2, Behavioral Checklist for Couples.)

CHALLENGING MANIFESTATIONS OF THE FANTASY BOND IN FAMILY RELATIONSHIPS

In Chapter 7, which outlined manifestations of the fantasy bond within family constellations, various parental styles of relating were discussed. These included role-playing in place of genuine relating, communicating through double messages, transmitting fears to a child, and teaching children defensive methods for coping with anxiety and stress either overtly through instruction or lecturing or covertly through the process

Exhibit 9.2

BEHAVIORAL CHECKLIST FOR COUPLES

How would you describe yourself and your partner along these dimensions on a scale of 0 to 4?

0 = Not Usually, 1 = Infrequently, 2 = Some of the Time, 3 = Frequently, 4 = Most of the Time

SELF	**PARTNER**
Nondefensive and open	Nondefensive and open
0 1 2 3 4	0 1 2 3 4
Respect for the other's boundaries	Respect for the other's boundaries
0 1 2 3 4	0 1 2 3 4
Vulnerable	Vulnerable
0 1 2 3 4	0 1 2 3 4
Honest and nonduplicitous	Honest and nonduplicitous
0 1 2 3 4	0 1 2 3 4
Physically affectionate	Physically affectionate
0 1 2 3 4	0 1 2 3 4
Sexuality (satisfaction with sexual relationship)	Sexuality (satisfaction with sexual relationship)
0 1 2 3 4	0 1 2 3 4
Empathic and understanding	Empathic and understanding
0 1 2 3 4	0 1 2 3 4
Communication (sense of shared meaning, feel understood)	Communication (sense of shared meaning, feel understood)
0 1 2 3 4	0 1 2 3 4
Noncontrolling (nonmanipulative, nonthreatening)	Noncontrolling (nonmanipulative, nonthreatening)
0 1 2 3 4	0 1 2 3 4

How would you rate yourself along these dimensions?

Self-Confident
0 1 2 3 4

Sense of well-being
0 1 2 3 4

Optimistic
0 1 2 3 4

of imitation. In relation to the intergenerational transmission of parents' specific fears and idiosyncratic defenses, the authors believe that the majority of parents, unconsciously and inadvertently, teach their child to form a fantasy bond so that both parent and child can feel secure in an insecure and uncertain world (R. Firestone, 1990b). This illusory merger may be conceptualized as an invisible umbilical cord, a lifeline, a survival mechanism, and an imagined state of symbiosis that children use to partially gratify basic needs and that adults long for throughout their lives.

The draw to remain connected to someone else in one's imagination remains strong and exerts a compelling pull on each person. In relation to child-rearing, the failure to distinguish between a fantasy bond and a secure attachment between mother and infant has led to considerable confusion in the literature and in popular discourse (Parr, 1987) (Note 1). Several theorists have questioned the adaptive function of behaviors that reinforce the belief that a magical connection somehow exists in reality. For example, developmental psychologist Jerome Kagan (1984) expressed skepticism regarding the popularity of the term and the practice of bonding between mother and infant. He conjectured that powerful needs may be driving parents to form an imagined connection with the infant to replace the umbilical cord, the real physical connection, severed soon after birth:

> The sacredness of the parent-infant bond may be one of the last unsullied beliefs. The barrage of books and magazine articles on . . . the necessity of skin-to-skin bonding between mother and infant in the first postnatal hours is generated by strong emotion, suggesting that something more than scientific fact is monitoring the discussion. (p. 57)

Concurring with Kagan's statement, Robert Hoekelman (1983) asserted that "It will take the public a long time to appreciate that instant bonding is not necessarily essential to successful parenting" (p. xv). Macfarlane's (1977) research suggested that "for many women the development of maternal love is a fairly gradual affair" (p. 117).

When exposing destructive bonds within the family, we direct our efforts toward understanding the underlying fears and anxieties in each family member and toward identifying the specific behaviors of each individual that support the imagined fusion that provides a sense of safety, albeit false, in the face of such fears. Although we are aware that most adults are still imprisoned by the effects of their early programming, especially in relation to the tendency to unknowingly slip into a dependency bond with loved ones, we have found that people can transcend their upbringing, learn to exist as separate individuals, and relate with genuine love and affection to their mates and children (R. Firestone, 1990b).

Respecting the Child as a Separate Person

> Human minds reside quite separately from one another in single individuals. Minds can stimulate each other to produce a kind of joint creation, but each single mind must remain free to be stimulated and to develop its own ideas. (Harper, 1981, p. 6)

Children must be perceived as human beings with respect for their separate identities. Children do *not* belong to their parents or their families, they belong to themselves. Therefore, parents need to refrain from patronizing their children, categorizing them, defining them, or speaking for them. Speaking for a child is particularly dehumanizing because it makes the child feel unseen and generally misunderstood. Furthermore, many parents, based on their own experiences in childhood, incorrectly assume that they know what their child is feeling, and they relate to him or her on that basis. This type of misattunement invalidates the child's experience and tends to make him or her distrust his or her own perception of reality.

Parents who respect the individuality and independence of their children do not treat them as possessions or property. They do not attempt to live vicariously through their children or their accomplishments. They understand intuitively how to let a child be. This entails allowing the child to feel that he or she is a person in his or her own right, distinct from other people or family members. The child who is possessed by his or her parents will experience unnecessary guilt as he or she strives for autonomy and personal freedom. When this is the case, the child and/or parents tend to equate independence with defiance. When this happens, children who do emancipate themselves suffer from survivor guilt and tend to attack themselves for moving toward independence and/or surpassing one or both parents personally or vocationally (R. Firestone, 1987b).

It is crucial for parents to learn how to let go, that is, to allow their child the maximum freedom possible at each age level. In so doing parents are indicating that they believe in the child's inherent potential for making healthy choices and in his or her capacity to regulate his or her emotions (R. Firestone, 1990b). Bruno Bettelheim (1987), in his book *A Good Enough Parent,* called attention to an essential goal in child-rearing that would be facilitated by parents adopting a nonproprietary, nonintrusive attitude toward their children. "The goal in raising one's child is to enable him, first, to discover *who* he wants to be, and then to become a person who can be satisfied with himself and his way of life" (p. 47).

Unfortunately, many parents are unintentionally disrespectful of their children when they use them as part of their own defense against death anxiety. In using their children for the purposes of symbolic immortality, parents must necessarily shape the child into a replica of themselves so as to complete an unbroken chain, a continuity of likenesses from one generation to the next. Labeling, categorizing, and, in effect, assigning a specific identity to the child are ways of accomplishing this primarily unconscious goal.

In their ongoing discussions, many parents in the friendship circle realized that their negative styles of relating within their couple relationships extended to their children. They became increasingly aware of the times they overstepped their children's boundaries, intruded on their privacy, or spoke for them. In their talks, they revealed the ways in which they violated the rights of their children to choose their own careers, select their own friends, and develop as separate individuals with their own distinct identities. They recognized how they often projected negative feelings toward themselves onto their children without being aware of doing so.

> **Ruth** (mother of 9-year-old Nicole): The older Nicole got, the more critical I felt toward her because that's the way I was treated by my parents. I was the "bad kid" in my family, and I saw Nicole that way, but I knew it wasn't right. I was projecting my own feelings onto her, either worrying about her or being critical of her. Today things are so much better, and I'm happy, but it's terrible to think of what could have happened.
>
> **Dr. Firestone**: I wish every parent was committed to the freedom of their child and to the best situation and at the least would agree to explore the possibilities.
>
> **Tamsen**: If you approached the situation with the welfare of the child in mind, then everything that would be done would be sensitive to what makes that child the most themselves. Instead, I think that as parents, we're so compelled to do the thing that we were programmed to do and sometimes we don't even see the kid. All we see is ourselves as a little kid and we're

trying to give ourselves what we didn't get, and it's totally inappropriate to what they're experiencing.

Ian (father of 3-year-old Caitlin): I feel more focused on Caitlin when I feel distant from Valerie [wife] and I want to be seen as special by my daughter. I want some kind of special relationship. I want her to love me in some way, to make that connection, so I can feel safe to have at least one person who loves me. I have a fear that I haven't identified yet, but it's something—a fear of being completely alone [sad]. At least I have this one connection in the world. I mean, I'm really embarrassed to say this but when she looks at me as if she needs me, I feel O.K. in some way. I know it's a terrible burden for her. But there's something about having that special connection with one person in my life that's reassuring in relation to my being alone and in relation to death, too.

Dr. Firestone: Everyone wants to be special to their child, but when parents are hurt and damaged in their own upbringing, they direct a lot of emotional hunger toward the child, which is not helpful.

Judy (**to Ian**): You have to feel compassion for yourself in it, too. Your mother was so emotionally hungry toward you, Ian. She invested everything in you and that's a big burden for a child.

Ian: I'm so embarrassed that I'm looking for that connection from anybody.

Dr. Firestone: When you love your children, you're sensitively tuned to their needs, to their developmental level, and to their boundaries. You want them to do as much for themselves as possible for their age not to make them excessively dependent. Also you don't want to be unnecessarily restrictive and critical. You want to restrict them only in relation to protecting them from any dangers.

In talks like this discussion, parents learned about flaws in their patterns of child-rearing and tried to improve themselves. When they talked about their own painful childhood experiences as well as about their problems with their children, they found they were able to be more loving and respectful of their children.

Distinguishing Emotional Hunger From Love

Unresolved feelings of loss or trauma from childhood are often manifested in the form of emotional hunger. The degree of emotional hunger experienced by parents determines how driven they are to maintain a fantasy bond with their child. They often confuse their intense feelings of need and desperation for those of genuine love and affection for their children. Feelings of emotional hunger are sometimes experienced as deep internal sensations, ranging in intensity from a dull ache, to a sharp pain, to a generalized agonizing emotional state. Parents often seek physical contact with their child in an attempt to relieve this ache or longing. This type of physical affection, however, drains the emotional resources of the child rather than nourishing him or her, and represents a form of *taking from* rather than *giving to* the child (R. Firestone, 1990b).

To challenge this style of interacting with a child, one needs to differentiate between loving responses and those based on emotional hunger. Three factors are valuable in making this distinction: "(1) the internal feeling state of the parent, (2) the actual behavior of the parent in relating to the child, and (3) the observable effect of the parent's emotional state and behavior on the child's demeanor and behavior" (R. Firestone, 1990b, p. 52). Some parental behaviors are indicative of unfilled dependency needs from the past; these include living through the child, an anxious over-concern leading to over-protective responses, an exaggerated focus on the child's appearance, and an exclusion of the other parent.

Another behavior is *parentification,* a condition that often develops as insecurely attached children reach kindergarten age. Studies have shown that a number of five-year-old children who were categorized as having a disorganized attachment exhibited either benevolent, solicitous caregiving responses or aggressive, controlling caregiving behaviors toward their parents (Jacobvitz & Hazen, 1999). Parental behaviors based on emotional hunger are evident when parents who lack emotional intimacy in an adult relationship turn to their child to fulfill this need. The inappropriate focus creates an inordinate pressure on the child that can later contribute to sexual withholding in his or her adult relationships (R. Firestone et al., 2006).

Parents can learn to recognize the effects of their emotional hunger on the child, even though initially they may not be able to identify the underlying feelings in themselves. These effects include clinging behavior on the part of the child, a spaced-out, dazed facial expression and/or a pulling away from or indifference to a parent. Research has shown that these behaviors are the diagnostic signs of an anxious or an avoidant attachment pattern between parent and child. Indications the child has been a victim of emotional hunger are observable in toddlers who have excessive *stranger anxiety,* and in older children who tend to manifest passive-aggressive, withholding patterns and who report feeling suffocated, drained, or depleted. In contrast, "the loved child actually *looks* loved; he [or she] is lively and displays independence appropriate to his [or her] age level" (R. Firestone, 1990b, p. 52).

Advantages of an Extended Family

In attempting to offer a secure, nurturing environment for their children, parents could include other people who might be of potential value to their child, thereby creating an extended family arrangement. An extended family can be defined as consisting of one or more adults in addition to the child's biological parents, i.e., a relative, neighbor, or friend, who has an interest in the child and maintains consistent contact over a period of time (R. Firestone & Catlett, 1999).

From our experience with individuals and families over the past 35 years, the authors have found that children thrive in an atmosphere of sharing and congeniality where they are not solely dependent on one or two specific adults to gratify their needs (R. Firestone et al., 2003). An extended family relationship provides the child with a friend or ally in whom he or she can confide, an adult who is relatively unbiased with respect to the child's relationship with his or her parents and who is free of the proprietary interest that many parents take in their children. These types of relationships offer parents assistance in situations when their relationship with their child has become complicated by their emotional limitations. Seeking this type of involvement from relatives and close friends effectively breaks into the fantasy bond between a parent and child.

An extended family can serve all the functions of the traditional nuclear family, including affection, socialization, financial resources in a crisis, and emotional support and guidance. Neuropsychiatrist Bruce Perry (2006) has emphasized the importance of extended families in terms of creating a proper environment for optimal brain development in infants and young children.

> Of the 250,000 years or so that our species has been on the planet, we spent 245,000 years living in small transgenerational hunter-gatherer bands of 40–50 individuals . . . . For each child under the age of 6, there were four developmentally more mature persons who could protect, educate, enrich, and nurture the developing child—a ratio of 4:1. In contrast, our modern world is defining a caregiver-to-child ratio of 1:4 as a "best-practice" ratio for young children (1/16th the relational ratio the human brain is designed for) . . . . (pp. 44–45) Fragmented, mobile nuclear families separate children from extended family members. A host of factors combine to produce hundreds of thousands of children growing up in homes and communities that are impoverished in relationships. (pp. 45–46)

On a practical level, parents can begin to pursue an extended family arrangement by exchanging babysitting and other childcare functions with other parents. Attending a parent education class, a shared play group, or a parent support group could be a step in this direction. On an emotional level, parents can relinquish the myth of the perfect parent, which is an unrealistic expectation that puts pressure on them to fill designated conventional roles. As parents relinquish these roles, they are able to relate as real persons to their children. In a previous work (R. Firestone, 1990b), the first author explained why this is so important:

> When [parents] behave in a manner that is natural or personal and dispense with roles, they are experienced by their children as human and lovable. The child desperately needs to feel love for his parents, and if he is deprived of the opportunity, it causes him or her unbearable pain .... it is crucial that parents come to realize how important it is for their children to be allowed to love them. (p. 182)

CHALLENGING MANIFESTATIONS OF THE FANTASY BOND IN SOCIETY

> The loss of the self has increased the necessity to conform, for it results in a profound doubt of one's own identity.... He [modern man] has become free from the external bonds that would prevent him from doing and thinking as he sees fit. He would be free to act according to his own will, if he knew what he wanted, thought, and felt. But he does not know. (Fromm, 1941, pp. 280–281)

Moving Away From Conformity

To maintain freedom requires the personal integrity to represent oneself directly and honestly to others. This implies a certain level of self-knowledge and self-understanding. Learning to expand one's capacity for feeling in general is essential to this endeavor. It is important to express negative feelings, such as anger, straightforwardly and to refuse to be deceptive or duplicitous in one's communications as a way of disguising them. Knowledge and acceptance of oneself comes from developing a realistic self-concept and questioning the validity of one's self-critical thinking. It necessitates recognizing aspects of one's personality that are undesirable or hurtful, and then modifying them in a positive direction. In this regard the methods of Voice Therapy facilitate the process of identifying and modifying negative characteristics rather than attacking oneself for one's weaknesses or shortcomings. It serves no valid purpose to attack oneself, it is far more adaptive to change and move on with one's life.

Developing more positive attitudes toward oneself imbues one with a stronger sense of self and the moral courage to live according to one's principles (R. Firestone & Catlett, 2009). Taking an unconventional, dissenting position when necessary also frees one from the existential guilt that one experiences in submitting to negative social prohibitions, institutionalized measures, or restrictions that one disagrees with. Being an individualistic free-spirit, however, triggers anxiety states and leaves one feeling alone, isolated, and separate. As Abraham Maslow (1968) pointed out: "Each step forward is a step into the unfamiliar and is possibly dangerous.... It frequently means a parting and a separation, even a kind of death prior to rebirth, with consequent nostalgia, fear, loneliness[,] and mourning" (p. 204). Thus, becoming a freer person implies experiencing one's aloneness and separateness in the world, and therefore requires ego strength and courage.

Maintaining One's Independence and Equality

> In our effort to escape from aloneness and powerlessness, we are ready to get rid of our individual self either by submission to new forms of authority or by a compulsive conforming to accepted patterns. (Fromm, 1941, p. 156)

In *Escape from Freedom*, Erich Fromm (1941) described people's tendency to relinquish their independence and individuality to merge themselves with somebody or something outside themselves in order to acquire the strength and power that they lack as individual selves. In describing the *authoritarian personality* Fromm noted the parallels between religion and nationalism in relation to their restriction of personal freedom:

> The authoritarian character loves those conditions that limit human freedom, he loves being submitted to fate.... Fate may be rationalized philosophically as "natural law" or as "destiny of man," religiously as the "will of the Lord," ethically as "duty"—for the authoritarian character it is always a higher power outside of the individual, toward which the individual can do nothing but submit. (pp. 192–193)

The tendency to submit one's will to that of a higher power is not exclusively a trait of the authoritarian personality. Most people tend to reject a truly democratic process because in giving up their autonomy early in life to form a fantasy bond with their parents, they now find it difficult to live an independent existence according to their own values. As Fromm emphasized, they no longer know what they want. As a result, people who are passive and submissive are susceptible to the opinions of others and especially to the influence of charismatic, authoritarian leaders who promise them certainty and safety (R. Firestone & Catlett, 2009).

An individual needs courage to combat destructive societal influences such as prejudice and intolerance, and to resist the appeal of toxic, charismatic leaders. To uphold one's principles in the face of strong social pressures to conform to myriad overt and covert power plays on the part of these leaders, one needs determination and a personal code of morality. Rollo May's (1981) observations of societies around the world point up the importance of having integrity.

> A pressure toward conformism infuses every society. One function of any group or social system, as Hannah Arendt has pointed out, is to preserve homeostasis to keep people in their usual positions. The danger of freedom to the group lies exactly at that point: that the nonconformist will upset the homeostasis, will use his or her freedom to destroy the tried and true ways. (p. 191)

To counteract the tendency to rely excessively on others, especially on a power-struck leader, as a savior or *ultimate rescuer,* requires that one develop oneself personally in many of the areas discussed in this chapter. By breaking addictive patterns individuals would become more centered and aware of their wants, needs, and desires. By striving to overcome personality traits based on attitudes of dominance or submission, people would develop more independence and personal power. They would make a concerted effort to not be judgmental or parental, and to not regress to childlike modes of behavior, both of which lead to polarization and inequality in a relationship. By challenging victimized feelings and passive-aggressive tendencies, and learning to express anger more directly, people would come to accept responsibility for their own lives and problems rather than relying on others, including leaders, to solve them.

Furthermore, people can learn to discriminate between manifestations of personal power and power plays that are overtly or covertly negative. Being oneself, asserting one's beliefs, and directing one's own life are very different from controlling and manipulating others. Extending this concept to social processes, it is especially important to be able to identify direct and indirect, subtle forms of destructive power and control that exist within governments, corporations, and society as a whole.

In a previous work, the authors described three different aspects of power that individuals can learn to identify and become familiar with: (1) *Personal power* is based on strength, confidence, and competence that people gradually acquire in the course of their development: it represents a movement toward self-realization and transcendent goals in life, and its primary aim is mastery of self, not others; (2) *negative power*, based on passive-aggression, is manifested in behaviors indicating weakness, incompetence, and self-destructive tendencies that manipulate others in the interpersonal world by arousing their feelings of fear, guilt, and anger; and (3) *aggressive power*, characterized by disrespectful or hostile tendencies, is exercised through the use of force and/or coercion to control others. It can be manifested within a relationship or in a political or social movement. Totalitarian governments under the leadership of toxic individuals exemplify this type of destructive power.

Learning to identify individuals who seek out and obtain power through destructive means is an important step in maintaining one's independence and equality, and helps one resist becoming part of a compliant *followership* in relation to this type of leader. As we described in Chapter 5, in most cases the personality structure of these leaders reflects underlying attitudes of narcissism, vanity, and sociopathic tendencies (Kellerman 2004), as well as feelings of inferiority. In terms of the unequal parent-child polarity described earlier, they lean toward the parental side, acting superior and judgmental while denying their child-selves. They also attempt to compensate for feelings of helplessness and powerlessness in relation to death by achieving power over other people (Lipman-Blumen, 2005).

On a practical level people can educate themselves regarding historical trends and learn to discriminate between government policies that lead to authoritarian, restrictive practices and those that are more congruent with the consolidation of democratic principles and enhanced personal freedom for citizens. As McClelland (1975) reminds us, "Power must have a positive face too. After all, people cannot help influencing one another; organizations cannot function without some kind of authority relationships" (p. 257).

Developing the Capacity for Judicious Thinking

The state of being without a system of values is psychopathogenic, we are learning. The human being needs a framework of values, a philosophy of life…in about the same sense that he needs sunlight, calcium[,] or love. (Maslow, 1968, p. 206)

In relation to accurately appraising their government and other aspects of political life, it is crucial for individuals to develop a questioning attitude in relation to established opinions, rules, and standards. They should refrain from automatically believing what they read or hear in the media. At the same time, people need to be wary of developing across-the-board cynical attitudes toward authority and the so-called inevitability of warfare as a means of settling disputes between people and nations (R. Firestone, 1994b).

As noted earlier, the psychotherapy experience, in strengthening one's point of view and the subsequent insight into oneself, supports the development of one's capacity for creative and judicious thinking. In addition, achieving insight into the origins of the voice and altering destructive ways of living based on its prescriptions tend to strengthen the self-system, enabling people to think more rationally. They are better able to distinguish and react appropriately to mixed messages, to dispute stereotypic thinking, and to spot contradictions between a person's words and deeds. The dishonesty and duplicity manifested by defended individuals in their relationships and families are mirrored in many of society's value systems and social institutions (R. Firestone, 1985). Therefore, this type of constructive, critical thinking is essential if we are to move toward a more democratic society.

Developing one's internal system of values rather than automatically adopting externally determined values is vital to questioning and combating destructive social processes. In formulating one's ideals and values, it is worthwhile to identify specific developmental circumstances that are conducive to the optimal evolution of human beings as well as those forces that are detrimental to their mental health and emotional well-being. An awareness of these positive and negative factors is significant in helping people formulate their basic value system and can assist them in choosing how to conduct their personal lives as well.

As the participants in the longitudinal study explored these issues, they came to understand the effects that both positive and aversive behaviors had on their lives, and an implicit set of values gradually evolved. These ideals and values were based on sound mental health principles. For example, they discovered that being altruistic and generous helped them challenge negative attitudes toward themselves and enhanced their own sense of well-being (R. Firestone, et al., 2003). At each juncture in this evolution, these people challenged their most strongly held illusions and were willing to face the anxiety and pain that are an inevitable part of any movement toward independence, equality, and individualistic, creative, and rational modes of thinking and being.

CONCLUSION

Years of research and observational study of people's resistance to a better life have enabled the authors to understand the subtleties of defense formation and to develop methods to cope with these mechanisms. In this chapter we have described several major ways that people can discover and alter their defenses in everyday life that, while serving to minimize death anxiety, disturb their overall adjustment and limit personal satisfaction. These include: (1) coming to know oneself and one's foibles through self-analysis, a process that involves developing an awareness of one's destructive thoughts and fantasies, identifying deadening routines and addictions in one's life, and taking steps to change these practices; (2) entering into friendships and more extensive group processes where people challenge themselves to be honest in their personal communication of ideas and feelings; and (3) participating in a talk therapy that allows for the deep release of feelings and the development of insight into one's personality, and that helps one cope with one's projections and unconscious resistance.

Methods of coping with the self-parenting process have been outlined and corrective suggestions have been indicated, including identifying and breaking specific addictive behaviors and routines. This chapter has also presented a format in which voices are identified, their origin understood, and corrections to alter destructive behaviors are introduced. It is also important to maintain a journal or talk with a trusted friend about one's critical voices; ideally, these would be followed by an attempt at a realistic appraisal of the material that has been revealed.

In addition, specific techniques for challenging fantasy bonds have been delineated. Within the couple, these include recognizing aspects of merged identity, moving toward independence, noticing and challenging habitual abuses of one's feelings and personal boundaries, as well as using unilateral disarmament in disputes. Partners can give away their attacking voices and take back negative projections. In regard to childrearing, the authors have recommended: perceiving and treating one's child as a separate person, not taking a proprietary or possessive interest in one's children, appreciating their unique makeup and not coercing them to fit a particular mold, not living through their productions, and generally respecting their boundaries and individuality. A distinction has been made between emotional hunger and love: The former has a destructive effect that takes from rather than gives to the child, draining his or her resources and leading to an anxious, insecure attachment. On the other hand, love has a positive effect that leads to a secure attachment pattern. Lastly, in coping with fantasy bonds in relation to society, the authors have suggested challenging conformity and certain aspects of conventionality. They have emphasized the importance of people developing independence and equality as well as a unique system of values. In so doing one can have a stronger sense of self and the moral courage to resist capitulating to destructive societal influences.

NOTES

1. Re: confusion between a fantasy bond and a secure attachment, as well as the difference between parental love and emotional hunger, see video documentary *Hunger Versus Love* (Parr, 1987).

10 The Value of Psychotherapy

It is all right to say, with Adler, that mental illness is due to "problems in living"—but we must remember that life itself is the insurmountable problem.
—*Ernest Becker*, The Denial of Death *(1973/1997, p. 270)*

When I was a graduate student in clinical psychology working for my PhD, I invested my time and energy in my own personal psychoanalysis. It was not a requirement at the university I attended but I could not imagine becoming a psychotherapist without that experience as part of my training. The sessions opened up a new door to my self-understanding and insight. I was very excited before each session, arrived early to contemplate my state of mind before I was called in, and the sessions became the central issue in my life at the time. The experience was not always pleasant; many painful feelings surfaced and there was a great deal of anger in my transference feelings toward my analyst. One day after an angry session, I walked to my car and in getting in, I somehow managed to slam my head in the door as it closed. It hurt like hell but there I was sitting alone in my car laughing uproariously. It was clear to me that I had punished myself for the rage and guilt I felt in the session. At times I could not tell the difference between the analyst and my father (both doctors), but I gradually worked through my residual anger and in the process developed much knowledge and self-awareness. It was a difficult period, but I discovered so much and I was impressed with the realization that there was no other conceivable means to have digested what I had learned in those three years. As a result I approached my work as a psychotherapist with a deep respect and dedication to the process and a significant regard for my patients.

As I began to work in my chosen field, I recognized that there were other important rewards that I had not dreamed of as a student. Nowhere in my personal life were people as honest and feeling as my patients were in their sessions with me. I continued throughout my career as a psychotherapist to learn from each and every person who I worked with. I learned about myself and I increased my overall knowledge about life. There was a breadth and a depth of experience that I felt was unavailable in any other profession.

In emphasizing the importance of a psychotherapy experience for the mentally healthy individual as well as for those who are suffering, we are aware of some of the pitfalls. For one, talk therapy or depth therapy involves considerable time and effort and is expensive. Second, although the majority of practitioners of our profession are both competent and compassionate, some have not always lived up to these high standards. Nevertheless, the experience of getting to know oneself is so much worth the effort that financial sacrifices could be made and chances taken. Many people have progressed even in bad therapy, because they took their own lives seriously and were devoted to self-knowledge. There is no experience that is comparable in offering a person the opportunity to think, talk, and feel freely about his or her personal life.

Aside from the curative aspect for those with special problems, the process of psychotherapy offers the maximum potential for the individual to live an adventurous and creative life. Self-limiting psychological defenses can be effectively identified and challenged in a psychotherapy context. In sessions specific defenses against death anxiety can be recognized and the issue of mortality can be addressed directly. The associated pain and anguish about one's personal death and the death of one's loved ones can best be expressed in this format.

PRINCIPLES OF AN EFFECTIVE PSYCHOTHERAPY

The psychotherapeutic alliance is a unique human relationship, wherein a devoted and trained person attempts to render assistance to another person by both suspending and extending himself. Nowhere in life is a person listened to, felt, and experienced with such concentrated sharing and emphasis on every aspect of personal communication. As in any other human relationship, this interaction may be fulfilling or damaging to either individual. To the extent that a new fantasy bond or illusion of connection is formed (for example, doctor-patient, therapist-client, parent-child), the relationship will be detrimental; whereas in a situation that is characterized by equality, openness, and true compassion, there will be movement toward individuation in both parties. Our therapy helps a person to expose and challenge dependency bonds and destructive "voices," remnants of negative childhood experiences that seriously impair his or her sense of self, spirit, and individuality.... My theoretical approach to psychotherapy represents a broadly based, coherent system of concepts and hypotheses that integrate psychoanalytic and existential views. (R. Firestone, 1990d, p. 68)

Because my theoretical position implicitly challenges conventional views of the family, the principal opposition to my work has been expressed by individuals who adhere strictly to an idealized conception of the family. However, the accumulating evidence of the widespread incidence of emotional disturbance and child abuse in "normal" family constellations caused me to question the essential structure of the nuclear family. Despite my own personal biases and protective attitudes toward parents, I have been unable to resist the compelling nature of clinical material that links psychopathology and personal limitation to destructive family bonds. Similarly, my approach does not deny the importance of biochemical or constitutional factors in the etiology of neurosis, but in most cases, I have found patients' maladaptive attitudes and behavior to be directly related to, and over-determined by, environmental components. (p. 71)

A fundamental principle underlying Separation Theory and Voice Therapy reflects the first author's personal view of people as being innocent rather than inherently bad or corrupt. Human beings are not innately destructive or self-destructive; they become aggressive, violent, or self-destructive only in response to rejection, fear, and emotional pain.

The corollary to this basic assumption about human nature is my belief that no child is born bad, sinful, or evil. I have found that the defenses that the child forms are appropriate to actual situations that threaten his or her emerging self. As emphasized earlier, people come by their defenses and limitations honestly, and indeed many should be congratulated on surviving their early programming. My belief has always been that an individual's unnecessary torment, as contrasted with ontological suffering, had a definitive cause in his or her early relationships.

My basic philosophy stresses the primary value of the unique personality of the patient and his or her personal freedom and potential for self-realization. There is a focus on each person's sense of self in opposition to the invalidation of self caused by maintaining defenses. Helping preserve the experience and life of each person is given priority over supporting or maintaining the existence of any group or system, whether it be a couple, family, ethnic group, political group, nation, or religion. The emphasis on feeling and sustaining every aspect of one's experience is central. In particular feeling one's true sadness frees one to experience happiness and exhilaration (R. Firestone, 1997a).

It is important that people uncritically accept all of their thoughts and feelings, including anger, envy, and jealously; these are internal processes that hurt no one. Only actions, including verbal actions, should be subjected to moral as well as reality considerations. Religious beliefs and attitudes that equate thoughts and feelings with behaviors in terms of morality are psychologically damaging to people who, in trying to lead decent lives, struggle to suppress any thought or feeling they judge as unacceptable or bad (R. Firestone & Catlett, 2009; A. Miller, 1980/1984; Prescott, 1975).

Similarly, an acceptance of one's sexuality and sexual identity is vital. However, developing a mature attitude toward sexuality is made difficult in a society that promulgates distorted views of sex through its social mores, institutions, and media. Indeed, "the unnecessary and unnatural suppression and distortion of sexuality in Western society has led to an exaggerated, prurient interest in sexuality, perverse attitudes, and actions, and a general increase in aggressive acting out behavior" (R. Firestone et al., 2006, p. 3).

Another closely related basic assumption is that people need to develop their own autonomy, sense of self, and value system. When individuals formulate their own values and ethics from within, rather than being outer-directed, they can chart the course of their lives in a manner that is harmonious and well-integrated (R. Firestone et al., 2003).

My approach also emphasizes the pursuit of transcendent goals that go beyond the narrow confines of self and family. The search for meaning is seen as fundamental to living a fulfilling life. Like Viktor Frankl (1946/1959), who believed that pursuing happiness as an end in itself was doomed to failure, I feel that happiness is only achievable incidentally, as a by-product of seeking meaning in one's life, and through compassion, generous acts, and concern with the well-being of others. According to Frankl, meaning also implies that "man is responsible and must actualize the potential meaning of his life.... Being human always points, and is directed, to something, or someone, other than oneself—be it a meaning to fulfill or another human being to encounter" (p. 133). Frankl noted that one way "we can discover this meaning in life [is] creating a work or doing a deed" (p. 133). This focus on transcendent goals is not a moral issue; rather it represents a sound mental health principle. By involving themselves in goals that have a deeper meaning than immediate gratification, people increase their capacity for feeling worthwhile and expand their life space (R. Firestone, 1997a).

In contrast to many conceptual frameworks, my theoretical approach represents a powerful intrusion on self-limiting defenses and offers no solace in that it provides no *loopholes*. It offers no illusions, no means of escaping existential despair or the inevitable vicissitudes of life; however, it shows that people can choose to brave a new world in which honesty is paramount and adventure and awareness are truly valued.

Many of the principles described above reflect the personal qualities of the emotionally healthy, nondefended individual who necessarily lives with a heightened sense of vulnerability and sensitivity in relation to both interpersonal pain and existential realities. Ontological issues of being and nonbeing, separateness, aloneness, personal freedom, responsibility, and the search for meaning with which the undefended person contends are the same as those discussed by Irvin Yalom (1980) in *Existential Psychotherapy* and by other existential and humanistic theorists, including James Bugental (1976), Abraham Maslow (1968), Rollo May (1958), and Kirk Schneider (2004). In describing the therapeutic implications of each of these ultimate concerns, death, aloneness, freedom, responsibility, and meaninglessness, Yalom (1980) wrote:

> Death helps us understand anxiety, offers a dynamic structure upon which to base interpretation, and serves as a boundary experience that is capable of instigating a massive shift in perspective....*Freedom* helps us understand responsibility assumption, commitment to change, decision and action; *isolation* illuminates the role of relationship; whereas *meaninglessness* turns our attention to the principle of engagement. (p. 213)

In explaining how freedom and responsibility are inextricably connected, Yalom cited Sartre's conceptualization of freedom, the view that human beings are not only free, but they are also *doomed to freedom.* Yalom went on to assert that "Furthermore, freedom extends beyond being responsible for the world (that is, for imbuing the world with significance): *one is also entirely responsible for one's life, not only for one's actions but for one's failures*" (p. 220).

VOICE THERAPY

Voice Therapy was originally developed as a means to elicit and identify a person's negative thoughts and attitudes toward self, bringing them more into consciousness. As a psychotherapeutic methodology, Voice Therapy has thus far proven to be largely effective in gaining access to patients' core defenses and in facilitating changes in their maladaptive behaviors (R. Firestone, 1988). The procedures are relatively simple and easily applied; nonetheless the techniques deal with deep-seated character defenses and crucial psychological issues. Therefore, their application requires the skill of a professional who is sensitive to the guilt and anxiety involved in breaking away from habitual defenses and symbiotic relationships.

As is true in most depth psychotherapies, at the point where the patient becomes aware that present-day limitations are closely related to early experiences in the family, intense feelings of anger, grief, and outrage are aroused, and there is a strong tendency to turn this rage against the self. At this stage serious regression may occur, and there may be a corresponding breakdown in the therapeutic relationship. Therapists working with these specialized techniques should have a complete understanding of the underlying theory to effectively help patients through critical phases in their development (R. Firestone, 1990d).

Goals of Voice Therapy

Voice Therapy methodology exposes and elucidates the basic split in patients' thinking and feeling about themselves and their fundamental ambivalence about people and events. A major goal of Voice Therapy is to separate out elements of the antiself system, those aspects of personality that are antithetical toward the person, that affect him or her adversely, and that support the compulsion to repeat destructive patterns of the past. The therapist is also sensitive to and able to access elements of the self-system—the patients' unique points of identity—to help patients give value to themselves.

Another goal is to increase patients' awareness of the self-destructive internal dialogue and of the particular events, circumstances, and situations that are likely to activate their self-attacks. Through this process patients are learning a technique that they can use effectively after formal sessions are over. Indeed the method of identifying thoughts that go against one's best interests is *unusually* adaptive as an ongoing form of self-investigation that patients can utilize for continuous change and personal development.

In addition, because of its emphasis on taking action, Voice Therapy is practically oriented in that it directly challenges repetitive patterns of compulsive and self-defeating behaviors, allowing certain patients to develop and go beyond results they may have achieved in other therapies. Voice Therapy sessions provide an opportunity for patients to develop and practice countermeasures—ways of living and being—that they will continue to use in challenging their defenses (R. Firestone, 1988; R. Firestone et al., 2003).

In a previous work (R. Firestone, 1988), the first author delineated what I consider to be the ultimate goals of psychotherapy, which are to help individuals: (1) remain vulnerable and open to experience and feelings; (2) maintain the ability to respond appropriately to both positive and negative events in their lives; and (3) achieve a free and independent existence. These goals are concerned with the ongoing personal development of patients and are closely related to the model of mental health that I described in the same work: "We perceive the healthy, adjusted individual as moving *away* from defenses, support systems, and painkillers toward openness, feeling, and emotional responsiveness, while changing from an inward, self-parenting posture to an active pursuit of gratification in the external world" (p. 257).

Achieving these essential goals requires making incisive inroads into patients' character defenses, not merely symptom reduction or minor shifts in defense mechanisms or addictions (R. Firestone, 1990c) (Note 1).

Remaining Vulnerable and Open to Experience and Feelings

Many people conceptualize vulnerability as a negative trait or weakness and view invulnerability as a strength. In contrast, we conceptualize vulnerability in positive terms and perceive openness to the possibility of being emotionally hurt as a powerful position to take in life. Living a relatively undefended, vulnerable life implies self-acceptance, inner strength, and the capacity to deal with uncertainty (R. Firestone &

Catlett, 2009). As Lifton (2003) rightly observed: "To live with ambiguity is to accept vulnerability" (p. 198).

To achieve the goal of remaining open and undefended, patients should refrain from overreliance on substances that would alter their experience or suppress painful feelings. This implies taking actions that go beyond simply being receptive and open to feedback; it involves continually confronting addictive patterns, routines, and other self-protective behaviors that cut one off from truly experiencing one's life.

Maintaining an open, receptive stance entails the ability to uncritically accept all thoughts and feelings, including anger, as described in chapter 9. In Voice Therapy patients are encouraged to freely express their angry feelings when they arise. Therapist and patient then evaluate the meaning or the underlying cause, explore the primal components, and discuss ways of dealing with the anger in the current situation. This approach to anger offers patients relief and an understanding of their emotions, enabling them to act responsibly with regard to these feelings (R. Firestone & Catlett, 2009).

A related goal is learning to experience deep sadness without resorting to defensive maneuvers. As a clinician, I have found that many patients have an initial reluctance to experience or express these deep feelings. Prior to therapy, they tend to confuse sadness with depression, a state that generally involves self-castigation, attacks, and anger turned against the self (Note 2). Anticipating sad feelings appears to arouse primal fears and considerable tension, whereas the actual experience of this feeling frequently brings relief. After expressing emotional pain or deep sadness, people usually feel more unified or integrated and report a stronger sense of identity. When these painful feelings are accepted or allowed full expression, there is a corresponding reduction in compulsive reliving and in attempts to manipulate or control others in the interpersonal environment.

When individuals are open to their emotions and able to tolerate irrational, angry, competitive, or other so-called unacceptable feelings, they are not compelled to act these out on friends and family members. This manifestation of mental health has broad implications. For example, in cases of emotional and physical child abuse, the *inability* to accept feelings of anger, hostility, and resentment causes many parents to extend these very feelings to their children. When parents are able to recognize and accept the destructive feelings they have at times toward their children, tension is reduced and damaging responses are minimized. In general people who remain vulnerable and open to experiencing painful emotions tend to be more willing to take appropriate risks in life and are more humane toward others (R. Firestone, 1988).

When Voice Therapy techniques are used as an adjunct to a psychoanalytically oriented therapy, patients gradually become aware of their needs and desires within the transference relationship. They develop trust in the therapeutic setting and are able to risk asking directly for what they want. The inevitable limits to personal gratification inherent in the boundaries and discipline of psychotherapy necessarily lead to frustration of the patient's primitive wishes. Through this corrective emotional experience, patients learn on a deep level that they can survive without the gratification of their primal needs and come to terms with their anger at being frustrated.

This is the crux of the analytic therapeutic process, because in the course of facing their anger at the inevitable frustration, patients strengthen their independence and sense of self. This is a critical step in psychotherapy, which contributes to the development of a mature orientation to life. Patients recognize that as adults, they can afford to be vulnerable because they are no longer helpless and powerless as they were as children or completely dependent on their parents for survival (R. Firestone et al., 2003).

Maintaining the Ability to Respond Appropriately to Both Positive and Negative Events

Prior to therapy, many patients, especially those who were cut off from their feelings, had melodramatic overreactions to personal slights yet displayed a curious lack of feeling in response to real adversity. In Voice Therapy, patients are able to reconnect to long-suppressed feelings and explore the primal and realistic elements of the anger, sadness, and grief they are expressing during sessions. They become increasingly aware of specific events that trigger reactions that are too intense or inappropriate to their present-day lives. They gradually learn how to respond with appropriate feeling to both positive and negative experiences. Moreover, by fully experiencing their emotional reactions and then responding from an adult perspective, they are better able to cope with anxiety and stress and are far less susceptible to regressing and forming neurotic symptoms.

Learning to Live Without Illusions of Connection— Achieving a Free and Independent Existence

In Voice Therapy, individuals alter their self-concept in a positive direction and give up the previously held negative identity formed within the family system. In addition, they break with their idealization and protection of family members. When Voice Therapy techniques are utilized in the context of couples' therapy, partners move toward independence by challenging illusions of connection with one another. They learn to distinguish between the distortions and projections based on the voice, and a realistic perception of the partner's positive and negative traits. Both people learn to realistically assess their own assets and liabilities. (See Exhibit 9.1.) This process leads to an acceptance of ambivalent feelings toward oneself and one's partner and to a more stable and honest perspective rather than one based on illusion or fantasy. Subsequently they are encouraged to tolerate the anxiety of change rather than retreating from or otherwise altering the situation. They learn that by using self-discipline, they can gradually increase their tolerance for genuine intimacy rather than maintaining emotional distance or reverting to illusions of connection that promise safety and security (R. Firestone & Catlett, 1999).

Similarities and Differences Between Voice Therapy and Other Therapeutic Methods

Separation Theory integrates aspects of several diverse approaches including psychoanalytic, cognitive-behavioral, emotionally focused methodologies, and existential psychotherapies (R. Firestone, 1997a). The specialized techniques of Voice Therapy are similar in certain respects to Cognitive-Behavioral Therapy (Beck, Rush, Shaw, & Emery, 1979), Rational-Emotive Therapy (Ellis & Grieger, 1977), Dialectic Behavioral Therapy (DBT) (Linehan, 1993), and Gestalt Therapy; however, there are a number of significant differences.

Most cognitive-behavioral therapies are short-term or time-limited interventions and are largely concerned with patients' reactions to present-day events. For example, Beck (1976) believed that it was unnecessary to explore causes of patients' distorted thinking, and asserted that: "the therapist focuses more on *how* the patient misinterprets reality rather than on *why*" (p. 319). Our approach is at variance with Beck's in that we are concerned with the dynamic origins of the voice. In Voice Therapy patients automatically make connections between their current problems, destructive thinking processes, and early family experiences.

Our theoretical approach and methodology are more deeply rooted in the psychoanalytic approach than in cognitive-behavioral or Gestalt models. Our theoretical focus is on understanding the psychodynamics of the patient's disturbance in the present, and our methods are based on Separation Theory, a theory of personality that emphasizes a primary defensive process.

Both Beck and Ellis recommend pointing out the illogic of the patient's thinking, whereas in our approach, the therapist neither refutes the patient's logic nor focuses on it; rather patients make their own symbolic or direct memory connections to the sources of their disordered thinking. When utilizing Voice Therapy techniques, therapists do not take an educational, analytical approach, nor do they directly persuade their patients to think or behave rationally. As noted, the goal is to help individuals discover what they are telling themselves about significant situations in life and to assist them in moving away from destructive parental attitudes and prohibitions. Gestalt therapy is similar to Jungian psychotherapy in that its practitioners try to integrate negative elements—the *shadow self*—into the patient's personality, whereas Voice Therapy methods help the patient identify and separate these destructive elements.

In recent years cognitive-behavioral therapies have begun to focus more on feelings, at times employing exercises to elicit emotional responses. However, their focus is still primarily on correcting the patients' disordered thinking. In contrast, Voice Therapy techniques bring patients' strong emotions to the surface; in addition, our overall approach incorporates deep feeling release sessions that access patients' most intense and primitive feelings. This helps to free them from the constraining influences of destructive self-parenting (R. Firestone, 1988). Clinicians trained in Separation Theory and Voice Therapy methodology report that utilizing these techniques tends to create a sensitive and moving atmosphere in the session that enhances each patient's feeling of compassion for him or herself.

QUALITIES OF THE EFFECTIVE PSYCHOTHERAPIST

The cumulative effects of interpersonal relationships...typically in childhood—[have] made the patient "ill" and...another human relationship, with a professionally trained person and under particularly benign circumstances, can provide corrections in the patient's self-esteem and in the quality of his or her interpersonal relationships with significant others. (Hans Strupp, 1989, vol. 44, pp. 717–718)

The personality of the therapist largely determines the emotional quality of the interaction that takes place between patient and therapist. Research has shown that a number of specific personality characteristics of the therapist are correlated with the ability to form and sustain a constructive therapeutic alliance (Beutler & Clarkin, 1990; Stolorow, 1992; Wampold, 2001). These characteristics are common to therapists across a wide range of treatment modalities.

Although all forms of psychotherapy challenge defenses to varying degrees and in general have positive results (Seligman, 1995), there are certain elements that are crucial to effective psychotherapy and a successful outcome. First, the therapeutic process must support the truth and place it above any form of protecting false assumptions about the family, society, or human beings. Therefore, therapists must be open to the painful realities that patients reveal and must refuse to place social conformity over the interests of their individual patients (R. Firestone, 2002).

Ideally the therapist would have integrity and personal honesty and be uncompromising in his or her approach to defenses that limit and debilitate patients. As a catalyst and facilitator, he or she must also be sensitive to the wide range of addictive patterns that may be manifested by the patient and have the courage to help expose and interrupt these patterns.

Therapists must be exceedingly skillful in helping their patients reconnect to themselves and their lives. To move toward this goal, the therapist, like an artist, must be sensitive to the patient's real feelings, qualities, and priorities, and distinguish them from the overlay on the personality that prevents the patient from reaching his or her full potential. Effective therapists do not try to fit their patients into a particular theoretical framework or model. Instead, they are willing to experience the truths that their patients reveal over the course of treatment and to respond as patients' individual needs dictate (R. Firestone, 1997a). Otto Rank (1935, quoted in Kramer, 1996) asserted that:

No therapy can succeed unless it is flexible enough to allow for whatever approach seems to be necessary for different individuals.... After all, it is the client who counts and it is his psychology that we have to study and follow instead of creating therapeutic ideologies to suit certain individual therapists or special schools. (p. 262)

Rank further explained that although each patient obviously possesses a number of human elements common to all people, these human potentialities should only be used as hypotheses when getting to know a particular patient. According to Rank, effective therapists base their understanding of each patient on the contents of his or her unique productions (e.g., dreams, fantasies, narratives, and mode of relating to the therapist), rather than on a specific conceptual model of human behavior.

In my work as a psychotherapist, I view the psychotherapy experience as a personal adventure and important learning experience. When I open the door to the waiting room I am fascinated to know this new person who has come to me for help and I am excited to find out as much as possible about him or her. I want to learn a great deal in the first session because I will generally be involved with this person for a long time. The session is not only diagnostic—an attempt to determine the core problem and correct therapy application—but also personal. I want to know how I feel about this individual. I particularly want to test how he or she responds to feedback and interpretation in order to determine the prognosis. For this reason the initial sessions are very exciting and there are a number of personal exchanges back and forth. When the overall interaction has a positive valence, I accept the client or patient. I know that both of us are about to have a unique and powerful experience.

Good therapists are nonintrusive in their interpretations, never predetermining or setting personal agendas for patients, nor do they impose their values and biases on patients' development. Instead they attempt to gain greater access to the patient's point of view. They suspend judgment regarding patients' communications, while exploring with them the relationship between past experience and present disturbance. Although strong in their optimism and belief in the possibility of personal growth and change, they do not underestimate the strength of a person's defense system and are sensitive to the fear underlying resistance.

Effective therapists do not set themselves apart nor do they assume a parental, caretaking function. As much as possible they avoid establishing a doctor/patient bond. Instead they are open to investigating voices within themselves as part of the countertransference reaction and are aware of their own self-limiting behavior patterns. In this respect Voice Therapy tends to be a *great equalizer;* that is, the therapist is a real person in the therapeutic relationship, not a superior human being applying a predetermined technique.

In addition the effective therapist would be capable of relating to the patient in empathic exchanges in which the interpersonal contact resonates phenomenologically with the intrapersonal. The therapist responds by reaching into him or herself and reaching out to the patient. Simultaneously maintaining internal feelings for him or herself and external feelings toward the patient allows for real communication and rapport, *compresence*. Laing (1985) specified that this condition is an essential ingredient of a positive therapeutic encounter (R. Firestone & Catlett, 2009). The communication that takes place during these moments is largely nonverbal yet potentially curative. The combination of empathy, compassion, and derived insightfulness is effective in producing positive therapeutic movement.

The therapist can be conceptualized as a *transitional object* in that he or she provides a genuine relationship for the patient during the transition from depending on self-nurturing processes to seeking satisfaction in real relationships in the external world. In serving this function, therapists would remain human—that is, they would be interested and warm as well as direct and responsible. This would hold or sustain the patient as he or she moves away from fantasy gratification toward authentic relationships and the pursuit of personal and vocational goals.

The good therapist anticipates the termination phase by continually encouraging the independent development of healthy ego functioning. Excessive dependence on the therapist and attempts to seek fusion are discouraged; instead, transference reactions are interpreted and worked through with sensitivity and proper timing.

In summary, because there is a great deal of controversy in the field of psychology regarding the most effective methods of psychotherapy, the least the therapist can offer the patient is an honest interaction, marked by personal integrity, strength of character, and the moral courage to challenge the status quo. The therapeutic process offers the patient a renewed opportunity for personal development that transcends virtually any mode of experience. Fierman (1998) asserted that: "Effective psychotherapy frees the human spirit and results in a person who is creative, loving, independent and comfortably interdependent with others, spontaneous and more fully utilizing his innate talents and aptitudes, and willing to take risks in pursuing personal, gratifying, and socially-relevant interests" (para. 7). Therefore, this opportunity for growth must not be limited or interfered with by the therapist's defenses or tendencies to deny unpleasant truths that may be uncovered by the patient over the course of treatment (R. Firestone et al., 2003).

QUALITIES OF THE IDEAL PATIENT

The ideal patient or client is a person who enters therapy with a strong desire to expand his or her life or to overcome emotional distress; at the same time, he or she takes responsibility for his or her own well-being and personal growth. These patients refrain from idealizing or reifying the therapist; instead they avail themselves of the therapist's expertise to learn as much as they can about themselves. In addition they are able to utilize the therapist as a positive role model and gradually become skilled at challenging and overcoming destructive defenses and regressive trends in their own personality.

Ideal patients are relatively open and nondefensive and are therefore willing to seriously consider their therapist's interpretations rather than shut off communication through various behavioral resistances, such as "lateness to a session, leaving the session before the time is up, extended silences, and premature terminations" (Langs, 2004, p. 104). The ideal patient would not be deeply embedded in a debilitating fantasy bond and would be relatively emancipated from dependency ties with his or her family. Many patients who initially progress rapidly have sought professional help because the fantasy bond with their partner has been disrupted by an affair, separation, divorce, or death. In his book *Love and Death in Psychotherapy*, Robert Langs (2006) delineated a number of criteria for patients entering therapy:

> For their part, patients are required...to cooperate with and respond to the reasonable interventions of their therapists; to attend sessions regularly and pay the therapist's fee in timely fashion, to be honest and forthright and not conceal information and feelings from their therapists; to respect the valid ground rules and boundaries of their therapy as established by the therapist, and to explore any impulse to do otherwise; and to be prepared to end treatment when their emotional problems have been resolved. (p. 19)

Ideal patients tend to possess some degree of ego strength, resilience, and courage, which enables them to take the risks necessary to challenge the identity they formed in their family. It takes a good deal of courage to live without one's customary defenses and without the companionship of the destructive thought process. Ideally patients would have an adventurous spirit and be open to experimenting and taking chances, for people must take risks before they know for certain how they are going to feel after significant changes. They are entering a new emotional world and must be flexible enough to become accustomed to the vast difference between the new environmental conditions and the world they knew as children (R. Firestone et al., 2002).

LIMITATIONS POSED BY THERAPISTS' DEFENSES

> In general, therapists have tended to underestimate the extent to which the vicissitudes of their personal lives, and especially traumatic events, affect their work with, and loving or unloving attitudes towards, their patients.... This is another aspect of love in psychotherapy that needs further scrutiny. (Langs, 2006, p. 16)

Many therapeutic failures can be attributed to limitations imposed on the patient by the therapist's own defense system. Negative personality traits, such as narcissism, phoniness, and hostility are particularly detrimental or toxic to the patient (R. Firestone, 2002).The fact that therapists have defenses is understandable. Because they are the products of the same familial and societal processing that their patients were subjected to, they will unintentionally continue to process their patients unless they themselves are emancipated. For this reason it is necessary for therapists to be sensitive to the destructiveness of defenses and have compassion for themselves and others.

Therapists who tend to be intellectually defended and removed from their feelings often experience discomfort when clients express strong emotions. By their response or lack of response, they often unintentionally inhibit further expression of feelings, causing their patients to become increasingly alienated from, rather than closer to, themselves. Another factor limiting the effectiveness of psychotherapy is the fact that its practitioners often have a misunderstanding of core defensive processes. At the time of seeking therapy, most people are frequently in a state of anxiety or depression because their defenses are no longer working effectively. In a sense, their symptoms can be conceptualized as manifestations of potentially positive change, a possible movement toward emotional health rather than deterioration.

Conventional therapies that attempt to restore patients to their premorbid, anxiety-free state by strengthening their defenses inadvertently do patients a disservice. In trying to relieve their patients' pain and help them reestablish psychological equilibrium, proponents of these therapies are condemning their patients to a limited life experience. In this case, patients' defenses will continue to restrict them and interfere with their lives even though they may feel more comfortable.

According to Rollo May (1983):

> The kind of cure that consists of adjustment, becoming able to fit the culture, can be obtained by technical emphases in therapy....The patient accepts a confined world without conflict, for now his world is identical with the culture. And since anxiety comes only with freedom, the patient naturally gets over his anxiety; he is relieved from his symptoms because he surrenders the possibilities which caused his anxiety. (pp. 164–165)

Any attempt to support dishonest defenses or misperceptions that temporarily reduce a person's discomfort does a serious injustice to both the patient and the therapist in the long run. Adjustment or even *feeling good* may be inappropriate to circumstances that are intolerable and unacceptable. Indeed fitting into a pathogenic society may represent a form of psychopathology. Every therapist faces a dilemma in his or her practice: whether to serve the interests of society or those of his or her patient when they are in conflict. Just as the physician upholds the oath of Hippocrates, the therapist should be devoted to helping his or her client above all other considerations, both personal and social.

To varying degrees many psychotherapists are defended against death anxiety and unintentionally and unconsciously avoid topics that might trigger feelings of existential dread and anxiety in their patients or themselves. Langs (2004) observed that many therapists are reluctant to explore the depths of their patients' unconscious thoughts and feelings, noting that "the paradox for all forms of psychotherapy is that the conditions of treatment that are most ideally healing are the very conditions that evoke the most frightening forms of existential death anxieties in both parties to therapy" (p. 70).

However, according to Langs, most therapists fail to provide these ideal healing conditions for their patients: "Rather than confronting and processing their existential death anxieties towards personal insight and resolution, both patients and therapists prefer to deal with these issues through denial mechanisms" (p. 70). Langs (2006) went on to comment:

"It therefore takes a great deal of self-processing and years of doing therapy...for therapists to sufficiently master their existential and other forms of death anxiety so as to be truly loving of their patients" (p. 168).

A key issue in training successful therapists is the selection process. Candidates for training in psychotherapy or psychiatry are drawn primarily from the fields of clinical psychology and medicine. Those who come from the field of medicine are often dogmatic, parental, and pedantic in their approach to patients and act out the doctor/patient dichotomy; whereas those from clinical psychology, with its focus on research, are often too intellectual or analytical. As a result, many trainees and interns appear to lack sufficient empathy, concern, or intuitive understanding of people and human behavior. Although certain behaviors, attitudes, and personal qualities can be learned or developed by therapists during training or in supervision, basic elements of personality are often highly resistant to change. In fact, some research (Henry, Strupp, Butler, Schacht, & Binder, 1993; Siqueland et al., 2000) has shown that training and supervision may have negative effects on an intern's or a novice therapist's personality and basic attitudes (R. Firestone, 2002).

SELECTING A THERAPIST

In considering what criteria to use in selecting a therapist, it is worthwhile to note that there is an analogy between the qualities of an *ideal* parent and those of a therapist who would provide the essential elements for an effective psychotherapy. First, the ideal parent would be interested in and sensitive to the emergence of the child's unique qualities and behaviors. Similarly, the therapeutic process is one of inquiry in which effective therapists suspend judgment while listening with empathy and questioning themselves regarding the patient and the sources of his or her disturbance.

Second, the ideal parent would resist any regressive tendencies within him or herself that predispose indifference, hostility, or rejecting behaviors toward the child. In much the same manner the good therapist refrains from acting out elements of negative transference, attempts to maintain a neutral and empathic posture, and refuses to reject the patient for his or her communications no matter how distorted or negative they may be.

Third, good parents accept all of their children's feelings, thoughts, and opinions uncritically, while teaching them to control undesirable, aggressive, or provoking behaviors. By the same token effective therapists emphasize freedom of speech and emotional expression while helping patients confront and examine the consequences of their self-defeating or self-destructive behaviors.

Fourth, the concept of *attunement* in attachment theory and child development is analogous to the manner in which good therapists respond to their patients' verbal and nonverbal communications. Effective parents try to adjust their responses to their infant so that they are contingent on its nonverbal cues and gestures; they attempt not to intrude with responses that are based on their own agenda or on distortions or projections. Because attunement is never perfect (it is estimated that good parents are attuned to their infants only one-third of the time), parents also make a concerted effort to repair disruptions that invariably occur (D. Stern, 1985). Similarly, an effective therapeutic alliance is the outgrowth of a series of interactions in which the therapist attempts to remain sensitively attuned to the verbalizations and nonverbal cues of the patient. When the therapist senses a break in the attunement with the patient (e.g., committing a therapeutic error), he or she attempts to repair the disruption by admitting the error or miscommunication.

Parents who are still in touch with how they felt as a child are more capable of having an empathic understanding of their child (R. Firestone, 1990b). In seeking a therapist people should look for someone who strives to understand their feelings, narratives, fantasies, and unconscious processes, who sees and accepts them for who they really are, and who is intuitively able to resonate with his or her patients.

There are several questions that one can consider during the initial interview or first session with a psychotherapist before making a decision. These include: (1) Does the therapist seem like a real person or someone who is playing a role? (2) Is the therapist friendly and warm, yet sensitive to the boundaries inherent in the therapy setting? (3) Does the therapist seem to have an optimistic outlook on life? (4) Does the therapist have respect for you as a person or does he or she seem condescending? (5) Do you feel really listened to and understood? (6) Do you have the sense that this situation is going to be a safe place to explore your thoughts, feelings, and deepest concerns?

In describing personal qualities of therapists that would facilitate the development of an effective therapeutic alliance, Alice Miller (2005) provided several valuable guidelines for selecting a therapist:

> We need assistance from a therapist who can accept us for what we are, who can give us the protection, respect, sympathy, and understanding we need in order to realize how we have become what we are....

What we do *not* need is an educator, someone who "has plans" for us.... No, we need precisely the opposite: a *partial* companion, someone who can share with us the horror and indignation that is bound to arise when our emotions gradually reveal...how the little child suffered.... We need such a companion—what I have called an "enlightened witness.".... What I am describing here is entirely realistic. It is possible to find out one's own truth in the partial, *non-neutral* company of such a (therapeutic) companion. (pp. 22–23)

THE DILEMMA OF PSYCHOTHERAPY

Therapy is concerned with...helping the person experience his existence— and any cure of symptoms which will last must be a by-product of that. (Rollo May, 1983, p. 164)

It is obvious that a nondefended approach to life—the outcome of a successful psychotherapy—is not without psychological challenges. Therapeutic progress leads to the patient's increased ability to function and respond appropriately to his or her interpersonal world; but at the same time, it inevitably leads to a heightened sense of awareness and new levels of vulnerability (Note 3). Prior to therapy, people's defensive patterns served the function of numbing them to the pain inherent in everyday living. In therapy, as they abandon habitual defenses patients become more sensitive to reality and to a world that is abrasive and destructive to the undefended person. Furthermore, the conventions and mores of society are generally opposed to the state of openness brought about by the process of dismantling defenses.

As patients move away from imagined support systems, they experience their true state of aloneness and often feel considerable guilt and fear in relation to separating from illusions of connection with their partner and other family members. They tend to find themselves in a high-risk situation. Although more capable of sustaining genuinely close and intimate relationships, they may feel more hurt by interactions with loved ones whose defended behaviors previously went unnoticed.

There are many other painful issues that psychologically healthy individuals face in the course of everyday life. Their strength, independence, and self-confidence frequently arouse dependency feelings in others who turn to them for support and leadership. The increased responsibility and emotional load put more pressure on the individual at the same time that he or she is moving away from his or her own dependency relationships. In addition passive, dependent individuals tend to be paranoid toward a strong person, and these negative reactions are confusing and demoralizing. People who have progressed in therapy are also more, not less, sensitive to external issues, such as crime, poverty, economic recession, illness, and the threat of terrorism.

Furthermore most people are unaware of how much they are afraid of freely pursuing their goals, attaining personal power, and finding satisfaction in loving interactions. They tend to underestimate the pain and anxiety involved in establishing a new identity and developing long-lasting, close relationships without fantasy elements. Finally all people are confronted with an insurmountable problem in life—the fact that they are imprisoned in a body that will eventually deteriorate and die. Recovering aspects of their child-selves and emotional vitality makes them more poignantly aware of the inevitable loss of self and consciousness through death. Who wants to live with this new awareness, this heightened vulnerability to rejection, loss, and death? Therein lies the dilemma, for how can the therapist symbolically influence the patient to embrace life fully in the face of a predictable future with an ultimately negative outcome?

The essential dilemma of therapeutic improvement or so-called cure can be stated as follows: The patient who progresses in therapy faces an increased awareness of death and possibly intensified feelings of death anxiety. As one studies the situation, the alternatives are clear: Without challenging destructive aspects of ourselves, we will gradually submit to an alien, inimical point of view and shut down our authentic selves and unique outlooks; on the other hand, disrupting powerful, self-protective defenses intensifies our awareness of life's tragic dimensions and at times confronts us with feelings of helplessness and dread.

Patients' fears of change are related to each dimension of life described above: an increased potential for feeling both happiness and distress, the problematic nature of intimate relationships, the circumstances of a troubled world and destructive societal forces, and the fear of losing through death everything gained through expanding one's boundaries. Juxtaposed against this fear is the knowledge that only by abandoning defenses and fantasy bonds can one avoid inflicting incidental damage on other individuals. This becomes a moral issue.

Ideally an effective psychotherapy would enable the patient to discover an implicit ethical approach toward him or herself and other human beings. In recognizing and gradually giving up the authority of the voice as an anti-feeling, anti-life, regulatory mechanism, a person feels far less victimized or blaming and far more compassionate. One becomes an explorer, an investigator, as it were, uncritically accepting and examining one's most irrational thoughts and feelings, while viewing others and the world with a very real curiosity and concern. Because progress in psychotherapy brings us closer to the awareness of death, it can help us put it in its proper perspective and use it to develop meaningful goals in life (see chapter 12 in R. Firestone, 1988).

THE DEATH OF PSYCHOANALYSIS AND DEPTH PSYCHOTHERAPY (NOTE 4)

> Today it has become evident that American social conditions do not favor the acceptance of psychoanalytic ideas. (Gedo, 2000, p. 39) In North America the resistance to its message has penetrated the psychoanalytic community itself, so that depth psychology has been watered down and replaced by mythic variants.... This is, indeed, the twilight of our profession in the New World. (p. 52)

When one considers the paradoxical aspects of psychotherapy practice described above, it is easy to understand why many people reject or are resistant to psychoanalysis or other depth therapies as a means for relieving emotional distress or solving problems in living. Several factors have been proposed to explain the gradual demise of these forms of psychotherapy, including prolonged treatment time, monetary considerations, managed care, and increased medicalization of psychology. However, we believe that the demise of psychoanalysis and depth psychotherapy is closely related to an implicit cultural movement to squelch serious inquiry into family dynamics and interpersonal relationships, particularly the physical, sexual, and emotional abuse of children. Clearly, this is an extremely dangerous trend for society, for how can we hope to develop a better quality of family life if we do not honestly scrutinize the dynamics of present-day family interactions? We must also effectively account for the high rate of adolescent suicide, violence in our schools, the widespread use of drugs, and many other symptoms of emotional disturbance in our young people.

When the first author was a practicing psychotherapist (1957–1977), psychoanalysis and depth psychotherapy were flourishing and had a prominent place in the foreground of a cultural revolution. At that time, the majority of clinical psychologists considered it a virtual necessity to experience their own depth analysis to better understand the individuals they would be treating. There was a spirit of optimism and idealism that permeated the mental health profession and a deep investment in the psychological approach to emotional maladies.

It was an era when millions of young people were fighting for their ideals in a valiant attempt to find a better life. The youth movement was characterized by sentiments that opposed the way people were living meaningless lives; challenged the status quo materialism of the American scene; favored self-development, self-expression, and sexual freedom; exposed the weaknesses and hypocrisy in the traditional family; and placed a high value on individuality and human decency. As Jacoby (1983) noted: "There was an obvious affinity between the youthful rebellion and psychoanalysis" (p. 39).

The youth movement and its aspirations were thwarted by the fact that its positive thrust was accompanied by an extraordinary guilt and fear reaction that led to the ever-increasing utilization of drugs and alcohol. These young men and women simply could not cope with their personal demons, reflections of their childhood trauma. Their misguided attempt to quiet the emotional pain and anxiety of breaking symbolic dependency bonds and seeking autonomy weakened them and eventually led to the demise of their movement.

During this period of experimentation and upheaval, people were concerned with their personal psychological development more than ever before. The so-called antipsychiatry campaign reflected in the work of Laing (1960/1969) and Cooper (1970) and the influence of Eastern thought (Watts, 1961) generated a process of change that affected the culture at large. At this time, many psychologists were involved in sensitivity training groups, marathons, workshops, and encounter groups, procedures that broke out of the narrow confines of the psychotherapy office setting and extended into the business arena, education, and even international relations. People were challenging the status quo in every aspect of their psychological lives and were willing to look at painful issues.

In the course of these events many important but disturbing truths were being revealed. The hidden aspects of sexuality and family life were brought into sharp focus and people's most cherished defenses were threatening to be uncovered. Nothing was considered too sacred to be exposed to scrutiny. The pattern of honest exposure was reflected in the humor expressed during those times.

Although the truth may eventually promote healing, when first manifested it generally inspires terror. Something had to be done about the discomfort. This same story has echoed throughout time. There was the expected counterattack and it affected both the youth movement and the practice of psychotherapy.

What is of primary concern is the fact that the methodologies of free association, dream analysis, feeling release therapies, group encounters, and the like were valuable resources, windows into the unconscious mind and an illumination of previously unavailable psychological phenomena. Because these methods revealed deep-seated secrets of family dynamics, they were, by their essential nature, threatening to the status quo in the social milieu. The ensuing reaction of society was predictable and eventually this so-called menace was effectively extinguished.

The bulwarks of society, initially outraged by these new developments, gradually homogenized and integrated some of the ideology. This partial ingestion was more effective at undermining the progressive movement than a direct confrontation. At that time everyone spoke in psychological terms, the jargon of self-help and self-actualization ran rampant, and people mouthed the platitudes of the freedom movement until they became banal. Then, subtly at first, and later with increased momentum, there was an insidious conservative backlash that invalidated much of what had been learned. The subsequent decline of psychoanalysis and depth therapy over the following 35 years can be attributed in large part to this reactionary movement that sought, among other things, to deny the veracity of insights achieved by both patients and therapists in the treatment modality.

Like other attempts that have been made throughout history to suppress knowledge and insight, these efforts were on a par with book burning and other egregious forms of censorship. When this type of revelation is stifled, in spite of all of our amazing technological advances, we are thrown back into the Dark Ages. As family therapist Cloe Madanes (1999) rightly observed:

> The very existence of the therapist as a humanist, as a social activist, as a systemic thinker is under attack. We must challenge the institutions that oppress our field in order to preserve not only the right to freely practice therapy, but also the right of clients to freely choose therapy without medication and even the right to freedom of thought. (p. 57)

Malevolent societal forces have succeeded in almost completely suppressing important knowledge concerning the widespread incidence of emotional, physical, and sexual child abuse in so-called normal families and the ensuing long-term harmful effects. Currently, cultural attitudes of indifference and denial continue to exert a powerful influence on the field of psychotherapy and have, in large part, transformed it from a creative, compassionate enterprise to a weak and frightened community of mental health professionals irresponsibly dispensing drugs or other quick fixes that support the status quo.

THE FUTURE OF PSYCHOANALYSIS AND DEPTH THERAPY?

> The idea of the unconscious carries with it the implication that life is harder than we realize, because we act not only in accord with visible circumstances but against fears and angers we find so alarming that we refuse even to acknowledge them. And so psychoanalysis also admires the courage to look with unflinching curiosity at oneself, to attempt not to be a turtle with its head pulled in. (Luhrmann, 2000, p. 290)

Over the years, science has repeatedly threatened our most precious illusions and self-confidence. In *The Origin of Species* Darwin (1859/1909) indicated that we are simply products of evolution rather than beings created by God. Freud taught us that motives and choices in life, believed to be manifestations of free will, are largely governed by the unconscious. In previous investigations we have found that not only are people driven by unconscious forces, but also that they internalize an alien aspect of personality in the form of destructive voices that are basically suicidal in intent and diametrically opposed to their happiness and well-being. These scientific conclusions challenge our sense of omnipotence, our belief in a higher being, and our trust in our conscious thinking processes. They are blows to our egos and feelings of infallibility.

Nevertheless, we believe that the future of psychotherapy lies in facing the essential truths about human beings and their personal interactions in their families of origin. There is hope in identifying the internalized destructive aspects of the personality and in learning to reroute behavior in directions that are more productive. To revive the humane practice of depth psychotherapy, therapists must support research that emphasizes the importance of early psychosocial environmental influences on personality development. Clinicians must also challenge restrictive societal pressure, sacred illusions concerning family life, and their own psychological defenses in order to reestablish a legitimate practice of depth therapy that moves away from the medical model.

Hopefully, in the future, the field of psychology will become more cognizant of the true source of emotional pain and suffering and develop better techniques to cope with hostile elements in the personality. Ideally, by counteracting the dictates of inimical thought processes and disrupting illusions of connection, psychotherapy could offer people a unique opportunity to fulfill their human potential, thereby giving life its special meaning (R. Firestone, 1997a).

It is obvious that clinical work and psychotherapy that help people express their feelings and combat their voice attacks are time-consuming and require a good deal of emotional investment on the part of patients. Nevertheless, only in depth psychotherapy or in a comprehensive treatment program that utilizes experiential as well as cognitive-behavioral methodologies can these affects and destructive thought patterns be accessed and worked through.

In summary, these disciplines offer hope for a better understanding of psychological trauma and favor psychotherapeutic interventions that involve accessing patients' emotions associated with the trauma. As such, they could potentially have a positive effect on the future of psychoanalysis and depth therapy. Without this resurgence much meaning in life will be sacrificed, a uniquely valuable therapeutic tool will be lost, the future will be bleak for those individuals suffering from emotional distress, and a powerful methodology to help mankind move toward a truly compassionate and moral approach to life shall have been abandoned. From this perspective it is a moral imperative to revive the disciplined study and practice of psychotherapy and integrate the valuable data of human experience derived from this source. We must rise to the challenge despite the threat to our most precious illusions and defenses. The authors are convinced that the tens of thousands of individuals whose lives have benefited from depth psychotherapy share this concern.

NOTES

1. See Louis B. Fierman's (1998) essay about the clinical triad of *cure* in psychotherapy: relief of symptoms, optimum social adjustment, and enhanced creativity. Fierman underscores an important point when he elaborates on the meaning of *optimum social adjustment:*

> As with neurotic symptoms, social adjustment may be influenced by a wide variety of therapist interventions, including both directive and nondirective therapies. As

with neurotic symptoms, patients may improve their social adjustment in exchange for perceived approval, indulgences, and dependency gratification from their therapists. In addition, as with neurotic symptoms, relapse and recidivism are likely to occur unless the therapy successfully addresses and affects basic personality and character structure and releases human potential for integrated autonomous functioning. (para. 6)

2. Re: sadness and depression: In discriminating between *adaptive sorrow* and *defensive sorrow* (which includes anger turned against the self), Valliant (1997) delineated several components of adaptive sorrow including, "Compassion for self; Relief follows [the expression of sad feelings]; Good memories integrated with bad; Hopeful about the future; Feels close to others"; whereas aspects of defensive sorrow include, "Self-blame, self-pity, self-attack; Frustration [after expressing sorrow]—hopelessness; Bad memories predominate; Feels more distant" (p. 238).
3. In "Civilization and Its Discontents," S. Freud (1930/1961a) described the emotionally healthy or *cured* patient as one who is able to derive satisfaction from love and work. Rogers (1961) defined therapeutic improvement or progress as allowing the patient to experience him or herself as a more real person, a more unified person.
4. Portions of this section are adapted from "The Death of Psychoanalysis and Depth Therapy" (R. Firestone, 2002). © 2002 by the American Psychological Association. Adapted with permission.

11 Facing Death With Equanimity and Appropriate Feelings

Stripped of all their masquerades, the fears of men are quite identical; the fear of loneliness, rejection, inferiority, unmanageable anger, illness and death.
—Rabbi Joshua L. Liebman

Anxiety is the experience of the threat of imminent non-being.
—Rollo May, "Contributions of Existential Psychotherapy" (1958, p. 50)

As long as man is an ambiguous creature he can never banish anxiety; what he can do instead is to use anxiety as an eternal spring for growth into new dimensions of thought and trust.
—Ernest Becker, The Denial of Death (1973/1997, p. 92)

In concluding *The Denial of Death,* Ernest Becker (1973/1997) argued that it is impossible for people to find any viable solution to the problem of death or the anguish inherent in the human condition, neither through the heroic roles prescribed by their society nor through religion or psychotherapy (R. Firestone & Catlett, 2009). As described in the previous chapter, therapeutic progress does not lead to a state of prolonged happiness or the absence of problems or distress in life. Indeed, as noted in an earlier work, our clinical data "support the hypothesis that death anxiety increases as people relinquish defenses, refuse to conform to familial and societal standards, reach new levels of differentiation of the self, or expand their lives" (R. Firestone, 1994b, p. 237).

As McCarthy (1980) emphasized, "If the goal of the psychoanalytic work is the patient's freedom and autonomy, and the patient retains the unconscious fears that autonomy equals death or the loss of the self, then the positive outcome of the analysis may be as anxiety-provoking as the original inner conflicts" (p. 193). Expressing similar sentiments, Becker (1973/1997) cited Rank's assertion that psychology fails to offer a way out of the dilemma in which recovered patients find themselves:

> "Psychology as self-knowledge is self-deception," he [Rank] said, because it does not give men what they want, which is immortality. Nothing could be plainer. When the patient emerges from his protective cocoon he gives up the reflexive immortality ideology that he has lived under—both in its personal-parental form (living in the protective powers of the parents or their surrogates) and in its cultural *causa-sui* form (living by the opinions of others and in the symbolic role-dramatization of the society). What new immortality ideology can the self-knowledge of psychotherapy provide to replace this? (pp. 271–272)

In opening people up to genuine feeling about their lives, the therapeutic process gives them a sense of personal freedom that makes them even more aware of potential losses. In living a more satisfying, fulfilling life, it is logical that people would become acutely aware of and have anticipatory feelings about the inevitable loss of loved ones and of themselves through death.

In addition, we have observed that serious, long-term regression often follows an unusual success or achievement. This phenomenon was originally noted by S. Freud (1916/1957b) in his essay, "Those Wrecked by Success." After describing frustration and deprivation as casual factors in neuroses, Freud observed that neurotic illness sometimes followed positive circumstances:

> So much the more surprising, and indeed bewildering, must it appear when as a doctor one makes the discovery that people occasionally fall ill precisely when a deeply-rooted and long-cherished wish has come to fulfillment. It seems then as though they were not able to tolerate their happiness; for there can be no question that there is a causal connection between their success and their falling ill. (p. 316)

In a previous work (R. Firestone, 1990a), the first author described cases of regression precipitated by positive circumstances and explained that this seemingly paradoxical reaction is understandable when death anxiety is taken into account: "Any experience that reminds an individual that he possesses strength, independence, personal power, or acknowledged value as a person will make him acutely conscious of his life and its eventual loss" (p. 127). Similarly, Piven (2004a), commenting on Freud's essay, elaborated further:

> The clinical literature is replete with instances where individuation in adulthood continues to threaten death and annihilation. Experiencing one's own feelings and ideas, acting upon one's own desires against anonymous conformity, even sexual pleasure itself can threaten one with guilt, punishment, loss of love, even psychotic fragmentation, death, and extinguishment of the ego. (p. 174)

In each of the circumstances described above, people experience myriad frightening emotions. Is there a remedy for the dread, despair, and terror that tend to emerge when contemplating one's personal mortality? Are there ways to reduce the devastating impact of death anxiety or prevent some of the more damaging consequences of denial or other defense formations?

In this chapter, we attempt to provide some possible answers to these questions. We first describe numerous emotional responses that people have to death awareness, including a number of maladaptive reactions. Next, we describe methods that people in our longitudinal study have found useful in dealing with the disturbing feelings and thoughts that arise when contemplating the process of dying, the death of a loved one, and their own demise. We also delineate some of the changes that took place in people as a result of many years of sharing their feelings about existential issues.

EMOTIONAL RESPONSES TO DEATH AWARENESS

Terror and Fear

Death anxiety encompasses a wide range of disturbing emotions; prominent among these affects is a profound, almost paralyzing, fear or terror when an individual considers the cessation of all consciousness at the moment of death. Clinicians and researchers tend to divide the fear and terror surrounding death into its different aspects: they are personal reactions to (a) the process of aging, deterioration, and dying; (b) being on one's deathbed; and (c) the omnipresent prospect of death throughout life. In delineating the fears, worries, and concerns reported by individuals when contemplating their personal mortality, Yalom (1980) stated:

> One may … worry about the act of dying, fear of pain of dying, regret unfinished projects, mourn the end of personal experience, or consider death as rationally and dispassionately as the Epicureans who concluded simply that death holds no terror because "where I am, death is not; where death is, I am not. Therefore death is nothing to me" (Lucretius). (Note 1)
>
> Yet keep in mind that these responses are adult conscious reflections on the phenomenon of death; by no means are they identical to the primitive dread of death that resides in the unconscious—a dread that is part of the fabric of being, that is formed early in life at a time before the development of precise conceptual formulation, a dread that is chilling, uncanny, and inchoate, a dread that exists prior to and outside of language and image. [p. 45]

Similarly, in his descriptive account of the *mortal terror* experienced at these moments, Piven (2004a) wrote: "Despite the vast difference between adult and childish conceptions of mortality, death anxiety may often derive from infantile fear and trembling, which people attempt to surmount through repression and defenses which adjust them to a dangerous world" (p. 44). In general, reminders of death, illness, or loss of a loved one tend to arouse these feelings of unconscious primitive dread from the past. In coming face to face with death, most people experience powerful regressive tendencies, tend to turn against themselves, and distance themselves from their loved ones (R. Firestone et al., 2003).

Fears Related to the Dying Process

As has been documented in many books, including Jessica Mitford's (1963) *The American Way of Death,* most people understandably try to avoid thinking about the painful process of dying. With few exceptions, most individuals tend to experience conscious fear reactions when they witness a person deteriorating, gradually weakening, and struggling to breathe his or her last breath. The process of dying reminds us that we too are fallible and triggers fears that Metcalf and Huntington (1991) described in their book *Celebrations of Death.* They concluded that these fears contribute to an "endless shying away from confrontation with mortality [that] is undeniably a marked feature of American culture" (p. 201).

Refraining from telling terminal patients the truth about their condition is a manifestation of this fear and was a common medical practice until recently. Several years ago in one of our discussion groups, a nurse commented about doctors with whom she was working at that time:

> In the hospital where I worked the personnel were never allowed to talk about dying, and I was furious at that. The doctors knew that the patient was dying, the patients probably knew they were terminal, but no, everybody was pulling the wool over their eyes. The card at the foot of these patients' beds stated: "Do not discuss diagnosis. Patient does not know that he's terminal." Ostensibly this was done to protect the patients, but I know that on another level, it was also done for the doctor's comfort and the family's comfort.

Fears Related to Imagining Being on One's Deathbed

Needless to say, the fear and horror associated with the contemplation or imagination of being on one's deathbed can be torturous for a feeling person. Anticipatory fears relate primarily to the immediacy of the inevitable; other less important but painful problems involve: the anticipation of physical suffering, embarrassment at the possibility of losing control of physical functions, mortification at being totally dependent on others for care, and frustration at the lack of mobility. The image of being in such a condition intensifies one's dread about the dying process as well as one's fears in anticipating the end of one's life. These distressing emotions were succinctly portrayed by Tolstoy (1886/2004) in *The Death of Ivan Ilyich and Other Stories*.

In chapter 1, there is a description of a conversation that takes place at the funeral of Ivan Ilyich, a conventional Russian bureaucrat. Ivan's widow approaches a colleague of her husband, Pyotr Ivanovich, trying to solicit funds to supplement the income her husband bequeathed to her. As Pyotr listens to her graphic description of Ivan's deathbed suffering, he is at first struck by the horror of it all, but within moments employs an intellectual defense and is restored to his usual calm and objective demeanor.

> [Ivan's widow]: "The last few days his sufferings were awful."
> "Did he suffer very much?" asked Pyotr Ivanovich.
> "Oh, awfully!... For three days and nights in succession he screamed incessantly. It was insufferable. I can't understand how I bore it; one could hear it through three closed doors. Ah, what I suffered!"
> "And was he really conscious?" asked Pyotr Ivanovich.
> "Yes," she whispered, "up to the last minute. He said goodbye to us a quarter of an hour before his death, and asked Volodya [Ivan's young nephew] to be taken away too."

The thought of the sufferings of a man he had known so intimately, at first as a light-hearted boy, a schoolboy, then grown up...in spite of the unpleasant consciousness of his own and this woman's hypocrisy, suddenly horrified Pyotr Ivanovich.... "Three days and nights of awful suffering and death. Why, that might at once, any minute, come upon me too," he thought, and he felt for an instant terrified.

But immediately, he could not himself have said how, there came to his support the customary reflection that this had happened to Ivan Ilyich and not to him, and that to him this must not and could not happen; that in thinking thus he was giving way to depression, which was not the right thing to do....

And making these reflections, Pyotr Ivanovich felt reassured, and began with interest enquiring details about Ivan Ilyich's end, as though death were a mischance peculiar to Ivan Ilyich, but not at all incidental to himself. (pp. 84–85)

In her therapy session, a woman recalled being with her grandfather at the moment of his death, an event that effectively altered the course of her life. She was 18 at the time and was studying in her room when she heard her grandfather coughing for several minutes, then silence. She ran across the hall to her grandparents' room, where she found her grandfather slumped in an armchair next to his bed. She ordered her mother to call an ambulance and sent her grandmother downstairs to get whiskey, which she hoped might revive him, despite the fact that a nitro-glycerin tablet placed under his tongue appeared to have had no effect.

I was frightened and horrified, yet strangely calm. I knew I couldn't save him: he was on the verge of death. I felt completely helpless. On some level though, I felt reassured because at that time, I still believed in heaven and hell, and thought my grandfather was passing from this life into his new life. He raised his left hand and held it behind his ear as though he were listening to something (being hearing impaired, he often gestured in this way). Naïvely, I thought that he might be hearing the sound of angels singing or something like that. I bent down and looked into his eyes and saw stark terror reflected back, which I interpreted as his own startling recognition of empty space, nothingness, blankness. Suddenly I knew that what he had seen was reality, that in that last second, he understood the truth: there was nothing there, there was nothing after death. I felt his pulse, and could detect none.

I felt sad when my grandmother came into the room with the whiskey, and I didn't have the heart to tell her that it was too late. The remainder of that long night, amidst trying to comfort my grandmother and performing other tasks, I found myself humming a familiar hit tune of that era: "Enjoy yourself, it's later than you think." At first, I wondered where the phrase came from: later I was to recognize that it was the first inkling of an unconscious, then conscious determination to take my life seriously. My grandfather had been the only loving figure in my life for the past 10 years, and I knew he had really cared for me. His death, together with the recognition that there was no time to waste, turned out to have positive consequences. At 19, I was married and at 20, with no regrets, I left the restricted environment of my childhood for a new life.

Some people report experiencing sadness rather than fear or dread if they envision themselves on their deathbed, anticipating death in the immediate sense. For example, in a group discussion, Tamsen described feelings she went through while imagining the final moments of her life; these thoughts and feelings had arisen unbidden one night just as she was falling to sleep:

> Tamsen: I've hardly ever consciously thought about how I would feel if I were dying or if I were close to death, but the other night, I was lying in bed and I started thinking, "Someday I'm going to be lying here and I'm going to know that I'm just about to lose all consciousness." [tearful, sad]
>
> It was so painful to me to have that thought. I didn't imagine nothingness or blackness, but I did think, "This is the end of all of this; this is the end of my life as I know it." And I didn't believe that I would go on existing in any way, and it made me so sad to think of that.

Fears of Death Itself

The fear surrounding an awareness of death as the end of one's existence as one knows it has been articulated in many descriptive terms such as *dread, anxiety, angst, panic,* and *terror.* Fear of the unknown, the seeming randomness and impersonal manner with which death strikes, and the uncertainty regarding the time and place of our own disappearance from life torture us during those moments when we are unable to distract ourselves from everyday reminders of the temporal nature of our lives. The thought of never again seeing, hearing, tasting, smelling, or feeling any sensation of pain or pleasure, and never again being with our loved ones is almost unbearable, and at the same time beyond the realm of our imagination. We have never before experienced anything approaching nonexistence and cannot imagine it. Yet, like Tamsen in the example above, we can appreciate what we will lose.

Many people, religious and nonreligious alike, think of death as a punishment for misdeeds or for sins of commission or omission. According to Rank, people have the tendency to refuse life (to not live fully) in order to be spared the sentence or penalty of death (for simply being alive). The conceptualization of death as retribution also has its roots in childhood. Many unwanted children grow up feeling that they do not deserve to be alive and do not belong in the world. As adults, they may displace these feelings of unworthiness onto imagining some vague wrongdoing they believe they have committed for which they experience painful guilt feelings and seek the punishment of death for relief. This may have been the case in some instances of suicide by the *expendable child* as described by Sabbath (1969) and documented by Israel Orbach (1988) in *Children Who Don't Want to Live*.

Interestingly some research has shown that churchgoers, individuals who are extrinsically religious and who believe in a literal heaven, hell, and final judgment day, scored higher on certain measures of death anxiety than those who are nonbelievers and other individuals who, while intrinsically religious or spiritual, do not believe in literal afterlife scenarios. For example, Mikulincer and Florian (2008) reported findings from research indicating that "commitment to religious beliefs and practice protects people from intrapersonal worries concerning the consequences of death to the body and the self, but magnifies worries about the consequences of one's death for family and friends as well as the fear of punishment in the hereafter" (p. 45).

These research findings tend to make intuitive sense; many deeply religious individuals do, in fact, torture themselves with images of hell and purgatory. For example, a man whose parents strictly interpreted the Bible and held dogmatic beliefs about heaven and hell recalled coming across a copy of Dante's *Inferno*, the edition containing the engraved illustrations by Dore, in his father's library when he was eight years old. In browsing through the volume, he was horrified by pictures of tormented souls struggling to *survive* their eternal imprisonment in the many levels of hell. He remembered his body shaking uncontrollably as he turned the pages. Because he was not permitted in the library without his father's permission, he was unable to question his parents about the disturbing pictures. For several weeks afterward, he woke up terrified from nightmares reminiscent of the gruesome, gory images he had glimpsed in the book. As an adult in therapy, he realized that these visual images were still indelibly stamped in his mind. They were vivid representations of a more general fear of punishment that he often experienced, not only in relation to perceived or real misdeeds but also for any pleasurable experiences that he enjoyed.

Becker (1973/1997) offered a further explanation for the vague, unreasoning expectation of punishment that many individuals experience when they think of death. Becker argued that the focus of the fear and dread of death:

> is the result of *the judgment* on man: that if Adam eats of the fruit of the tree of knowledge God tells him "Thou shalt surely die." In other words, the final terror of self-consciousness is the knowledge of one's own death, which is the peculiar sentence on man alone in the animal kingdom. This is the meaning of the Garden of Eden myth and the rediscovery of modern psychology: that death is man's peculiar and greatest anxiety. (pp. 69–70)

Fear of Death as the Final Separation From Loved Ones

As noted in chapter 3, separation anxiety and the associated feelings of aloneness, isolation, and disconnection are closely related to death anxiety. Throughout the life span, each separation, with its leave-takings and farewells, is a painful reminder of the ultimate separation from our loved ones at death. Older children and adolescents are particularly susceptible to fears of losing, through death, loved ones on whom they are still dependent. They are also able to contemplate their own deaths and visualize how empty, forlorn, and frightened they will feel. These emotional reactions were expressed in a small group of teenagers:

> **Cassie** (13): I don't really feel that scared about me dying. I just feel scared about the people I love dying. Also people who are much older than me, because they'll die when I am still a teenager.
>
> **Rosa** (15): When you die, you never get to see your friends again.
>
> **Dr. Firestone**: Is that the thing that's scary about death? That you don't get to see the people you love? Is that the scary part?
>
> **Rosa**: That's what scares me.
>
> **Cassie**: That's what scares me, too. One time I dreamed that my friends were going to move, and I was sleeping, and then I woke up and there was nobody there, and I was scared.

Dr. Firestone: Mickey, what's the scary part about thinking you're going to die?

Mickey (**14**): The scariest part is that you lose all your friends and also that you can't do anything anymore.

Dr. Firestone: So it's two different things. One, you can't be with your friends any more. And the other thing is you can't do anything, right? If you're dead, you can't even move, right?

Rosa: I think that not being able to see your friends is the worse thing. But I kind of hope that when I die, people will remember me and that way I won't lose all my friends.

All people fear and mourn the loss of the people that they love and, in some cases, the emotion of sadness and loss seems to be more unbearable than imagining one's own death. Loss of a loved one arouses the most tangible experience of death awareness. Depression, a sense of hopelessness, and suicidal urges often follow closely upon the death of a loved one or mate. In a large study conducted by Luoma and Pearson (2002), "The most striking finding was the approximately 17-fold increase in the rate of suicide for the youngest widowed White men (aged 20–34 years) in comparison with their married counterparts" (p. 1520).

Anger and Rage

There is a sense of outrage related to the fact that one must die, an anger and fury that one will be deprived of everyone whom one has come to love and cherish and that ultimately one's own life will be snuffed out. To many people death seems like a cruel hoax: they feel cheated—robbed of their fundamental birthright and heritage—life should be permanent, not temporary. They feel divested of the symbolic, spiritual aspects of their being and are left to directly confront their basic animal nature and the fact that they are trapped in a body that will gradually deteriorate, decay, and finally stop supporting all vital life functions. In a discussion group, Alex expressed the anger and rage he felt after hearing the news of a close friend's death.

Alex: [angrily, in a loud voice] I felt like saying to the person on the phone: "What do you mean it's over? What do you mean I can't do anything about it? What do you mean, he's gone forever? What do you mean by that? What do you mean I can't bring him back? What do you mean it's over? It's final? [cries deeply]

That was the most torturous part of that feeling. I remember learning in biology about the brain needing oxygen, and then when it didn't have any oxygen it was dead. It was not a living organism any more. It was not working. I couldn't fathom that, my own brain stopping. How could I not have my thoughts? How could everything be taken from me that way? It doesn't make sense. I can't understand it. And it goes back to that blackness, nothing. Not even sensing darkness. It's just nothing! Not existing!

Some people, unlike Alex, imagine a continuity of life after death, although consciously they know that the ability to sense endless nothingness is dependent on being alive and aware. Nonetheless, many individuals dread the experience as if it were a possibility or a reality. They imagine existing in this tortured state throughout infinity, much as they torment themselves about other, more realistic eventualities surrounding the death experience. Others fear premature burial or anticipate experiencing the sensation of being burned during cremation. They project feelings and sensations that they are familiar with in their everyday lives into a horrendous situation in the future that is based on an unconscious illusion of continuing to exist in some form after death.

Shame and Guilt

In the literature, shame is seen as "the more painful and distressing emotion because…the entire self is viewed as deficient…[whereas] guilt does not affect one's core identity. Rather, guilt is primarily concerned with a specific behavior" (Tangney & Mashek, 2004, pp. 157–158). Both shame and guilt are often experienced by individuals when confronted with reminders of death. For example, many people feel shame about their bodies and guilt about the pleasure potentially available through bodily sensations and feelings. There is a sense of betrayal in knowing that one is trapped in a body that will eventually die (R. Firestone et al., 2006). As noted earlier, Terror Management researchers have found that shame and disgust about the body were triggered in many subjects during experiments in which death had been made salient (Goldenberg et al., 1999).

Reactions of shame and guilt also may be exacerbated by internalized shame resulting from early childhood trauma that is generalized to a pervasive hatred of oneself. Many parents experience unconscious guilt for bringing children into the world, where they will be confronted with uncertainty, anxiety, and the inevitability of dying. Paradoxically some of the damage that parents unintentionally inflict on their offspring stems from strong benevolent, protective feelings that they have toward them, based on these feelings of guilt. In trying to spare their children the trauma of separations and to help them avoid vulnerability to death anxiety, they often deceive their children and teach them attitudes and defenses that later limit their lives and fix them at a level of development below their potential (R. Firestone, 1990a). Children often feel anger toward their parents for putting them in this dilemma in the first place, and this anger may be projected onto other aspects of life.

One excruciating form of guilt referred to as *death guilt* or *survivor guilt* by Lifton (1968/1991) and Lifton and Olson (1976) has to do with "the survivor's sense of painful self-condemnation over having lived while others died" (Lifton & Olson, p. 3). Lifton and Olson investigated this form of guilt in the survivors of Hiroshima and the Holocaust. They asserted that when this guilt is suppressed, the result is a kind of "psychic numbing—a diminished capacity for feeling of all kinds—in the form of various manifestations of apathy, withdrawal, depression, and overall constriction in living" (p. 5) (Note 2).

Individuals who, in their movement toward increased individuation, pursue priorities, interests, and goals that are distinctly different from those of their parents often experience painful feelings of survivor guilt. On an unconscious level they sense that they have failed to fulfill an expected symbolic function in relation to their parents. In being different, these individuals have made it impossible for their parents to live on through them or through their progeny. Symbolically, they are breaking the continuity between the successive generations within their family unit, in effect, leaving their parents to die, bereft of this comforting illusion.

Many people experience existential guilt and regret from "unused life, for 'the unlived' in us" (Becker, 1973/1997, p. 180). According to Yalom (1980), the failure to acknowledge one's existential guilt leads to despair and alienation, such as was experienced by Joseph K. in Kafka's (1937/1977) novel *The Trial*. Leading a conventional, banal existence, yet stubbornly unaware of his acts of omission, Joseph K. is imprisoned (symbolically) within narrow boundaries defined by the neurotic guilt in relation to individuating and moving forward in life, and existential guilt in relation to regressing and giving up on life. Becker proposed that this particular sense of guilt results from recognizing that one is leading a life that "is so safe that it is not heroic at all. To lie to oneself about one's own potential development is another cause of guilt. It is one of the most insidious daily inner gnawings a person can experience" (p. 179).

There is another type of guilt experienced by the person who is resolute, that is, one who has reached a high level of individuation. Tillich (1952) described this form of guilt as follows:

> Nobody can give directions for the actions of the "resolute" individual—no God, no conventions, no laws of reason, no norms or principles. We must be ourselves, *we* must decide where to go. Our conscience is the call to ourselves.... Having the courage to be as ourselves we become guilty, and we are asked to take this existential guilt upon ourselves. (p. 146)

In his book *The Courage to Be*, Tillich also noted the relationship between individuation and ontological anxiety: "It has been observed that the anxiety of death increases with the increase of individualization" (p. 50).

Sense of the Absurdity and Meaninglessness of Life

Many people respond to the finiteness of human existence by looking at life as absurd and meaningless, and experience feelings of despair and hopelessness. When these feelings persist and become a part of an individual's overall state of mind, there can be an increased risk of suicide as the person can see no reason to go on living. However, Camus argued "that to give in to the absurd would be in fact to deny it. Meaning is found in living the absurd, not in refusing it" (cited in Tomer & Eliason, 2008, p. 15). Furthermore, "Camus (1965) states very clearly that the absence of meaning does not necessarily mean that life is not worth living.... Suicide is by no means a proper solution to ... existential absurdity" (Orbach, 2008, pp. 289–290) (Note 3). According to Kierkegaard (1849/1954), despair is inherent in the human condition and therefore is an appropriate response to existential reality. Based on Kierkegaard's conceptualizations, Becker (1971) called attention to two kinds of despair, *neurotic* and *real:*

> Neurotic despair would be a reaction against losing the protection of one's life style and all the identifications that go into it.... But when this neurotic despair is peeled away one comes face to face with real despair over man's fate. Very few ever get to see the bare reality of this kind of despair because they never remove the neurotic defense against it. We might say that the problem of authentic growth in a person's life is to get rid of neu-

rotic despair and then make a creative solution of his existence in greater freedom and full knowledge. (p. 206)

Some people are capable of transforming despair regarding the absurdity of life into a more constructive, yet still realistic, outlook, as was the case with Anne Frank (1993), who wrote:

It's really a wonder that I haven't dropped all my ideals because they seem so absurd and impossible to carry out. Yet, I keep them, because in spite of everything I still believe that people are really good at heart. I simply can't build up my hopes on a foundation consisting of confusion, misery and death. (p. 263)

On a lighter note, reflecting on the absurdity of life and death, when asked to describe his most promising *immortality project,* Woody Allen quipped: "I don't want to achieve immortality through my work; I want to achieve it through not dying."

Sadness

In contrast to the feelings of despair described above, there is a poignant sadness that often arises when one contemplates the potential loss of self and loved ones. Expressing deep feelings of sadness and sorrow regarding these existential realities appears to have an ameliorative, rather than a disturbing, effect on individuals who are open to the experience. The process of feeling one's sadness, sorrow, and grief helps dispel self-hating thoughts and other painful ruminations about death.

In a group discussion, Brant described feeling sad when he embraced a close friend who was ill. Previously he had felt hopeless and futile about his friend's plight, but feeling sad for a few moments had made him feel better:

Brant: I would like to figure out for myself why the road back from despair and futility feels so sad.
Dr. Firestone: That's the only way to get back. It's the only way back to yourself. There are thousands of ways to remove yourself to avoid pain, but the only way back is to feel the sadness about life and to mourn your own death in a sense, and the death of those you love. If you don't, you cut off from the people you love the most.

Brant: When I look around the room at people and I feel what I am feeling right now, I have such a simple realization of their value to me [sad, cries].

Kurt: I spend so much time and energy avoiding sadness and the only way of realigning myself is to feel sad. Nothing else does it. I just have to feel it.

Tamsen: I feel so much better than I did earlier in the day, when I felt miserable and depressed about Raymond's predicament. It seemed childish to me in some way—how I was feeling. I had thoughts like, "Nothing matters. What's the use?" I recognize those feelings as the way I felt in my childhood. Right this minute, I feel really, really sad, but it's worth it to live, in spite of life being so sad.

Dr. Firestone: Often you don't get a chance to deal with sadness and that's the problem. Something interferes with the true depth of sadness or else you'd be able to get out of it, and then get back to a regular mood. I remember that when my father died, sharing that pain at his funeral was a relief.

Tamsen: That's an important part of an Irish wake, that it is a place to really feel something.

Dr. Firestone: Yes, that's a part of it. There's a sense of permission to feel sad. In "normal" everyday life, though, there's a sense of non-permission typically against feeling deep sadness.

The concept of *anticipatory grief* described by Ivancovich and Wong (2008) is similar in some respects to the authors' emphasis on the importance of mourning one's future death in the present day. Theorists and researchers have shown that this form of anticipatory grief or *anticipatory mourning* often lends new meaning to one's life and enhances one's ability to deal with personal distress and existential concerns. As Ivancovich and Wong put it: "Anticipatory grief of our own death as well as the death of a loved one may trigger the quest for meaning and spirituality" (p. 209). The authors have found that when people are able to fully express their sadness and grief related to existential concerns, they tend to feel closer to themselves and their loved ones. This form of poignant sadness appears to be more fundamental than other emotional responses—anger, rage, or fear—to the realization of death. In "Awareness of Death: A Controllable Process or a Traumatic Experience?" Moor (2002) noted that "In the actualisation process the fact of one's mortality brings forth fear, anger, sense of guilt, sadness" (p. 108). "This is the most usual order of mourning stages" (p. 110).

Anguish and Guilt About Leaving Loved Ones Behind

One of the most agonizing emotions that we experience when thinking about the future is focused on our deep worry and concern about the economic and psychological welfare of the people we will be leaving behind. Because we have experienced these feelings in the past in relation to previous personal losses, we identify strongly with the waves of grief and sorrow that our loved ones will experience after we are gone. When our relationships have been close, loving, and fulfilling, merely envisioning how people will feel without us can be especially distressing and sorrowful. When children and adolescents are involved, there may be strong guilt feelings about abandoning them while they are still dependent.

The project of imagining the reactions of others to one's own death has recently become an important topic in psychotherapy and counseling. In "Regret Therapy," for example, there is a concerted effort to cope with what is termed *future-related regret*. As Mannarino, Eliason, and Rubin (2008) noted, "Regret related to the end of life takes on a particular poignancy" (p. 324). In one study of terminally ill individuals and their caregivers, Wright (2003) found that they "not only develop a complex relationship with the ideas of death and dying, but also often move to a position of *carpe diem*, of living their lives differently, in the present, and of confronting regrets that cause distress" (cited by Mannarino, et al., p. 327).

PERSONAL REACTIONS

Personally, I, the first author, have felt all of the emotions and conceptualizations concerning death mentioned above at various times in my life. I have been particularly troubled by the terror of the unknown, a feeling of being trapped (no way to escape death and dying, no place to go to get away), the realization of the fact that I will completely lose consciousness of my thoughts and feelings and lastly that I will be dead forever. These fears, at times unreasonable, even illogical, have plagued me when I least expected them. No attempt to be logical, to accept reassurance or rational awareness that death is nothing other than nonexistence, and therefore not painful or agonizing, has exempted me from the torment. I have felt the primitive dread of the child's reaction to death, screamed out in my sleep that I can't stand it, awoke thrashing around as though attempting to break loose, and then after becoming fully awake recovered my composure. In some way, I welcomed the release of these emotions in my nightmares and oddly enough felt more relaxed after these occasions. In my normal waking hours, I am not so afraid but feel a poignant sadness. I have never been able to believe in traditional religion or any afterlife scenario. I am horrified about the possibility of losing my loved ones and in turn feel pained by the fact of their losing me.

In one situation I actually thought that I was dying, and this experience led me to develop an important insight. I was in a hotel in Atlantic City and as I walked through a crowded casino I felt very strange. It was something like feeling dizzy and weak and I felt myself passing out in the crowd of people. As I fell to the ground I knew it was all over, I thought that the sensations that I was feeling were my last. But, in spite of my previous fears and sadness about death, I wasn't afraid. I was just matter-of-fact.

The incident reminded me of my original fear of storms at sea. In my imagination I pictured huge seas, the crashing sound of waves, and the howling of the immense winds and these images terrified me. I am an ocean-going sailor and have made more than 10 ocean crossings. To my surprise, like my death fears, when I found myself in severe storm situations, I was actually unafraid.

Neurotic Emotional Responses

Many people respond to the prospect of dying and death with maladaptive behaviors that interfere, to varying degrees, with their ability to cope with life. For example, attachment researchers have found that people who are anxiously attached to a romantic partner react to reminders of death by becoming preoccupied with the possibility of rejection and abandonment and so become more dependent and clingy in interacting with their partners; whereas avoidantly attached or dismissive individuals become more critical of their partners and create distance in the relationship (Florian & Mikulincer, 2004).

Other individuals adhere to superstitious beliefs in relation to death. In particular, after a period of exceptional happiness or good fortune, they torture themselves with negative predictions, such as "Now what will happen to spoil this?" or "This can't go on forever, you know," or "See how good this feels? Well, you'll probably get hit by a truck." They tend to obsessively use this kind of thinking, as well as a morbid preoccupation with disaster and death, to obliterate their good feelings. For some, the thought of death will come to mind as a reminder of their mortality. This phenomenon, which is a function of the voice process, maliciously undermines the person's sense of well-being.

Feelings of claustrophobia, fears of being confined or suffocating, are masked forms of neurotic death anxiety. People are symbolically locked in an impossible situation. Paranoid reactions are also closely related to the fact of an inescapable fate, which gives rise to a sense of persecution. More severe forms of emotional disturbance can be traced, at least partially, to the early death of a parent or to failures in repression, as was noted in chapter 3.

Maladaptive behaviors that serve to protect these individuals from such overwhelming emotions include OCD, hysteria, sadism, masochism, agoraphobia, panic disorder, and certain perversions and fetishes. As Becker (1973/1997) pointed out:

> In the history of fetishists we see again and again that they are subjected to early trauma about bodily decay and death. (p. 228) Perversion has been called a "private religion"—and that it really is, but it testifies to fear and trembling and not to faith. It is an idiosyncratic, symbolic protest of control and safety by those who can rely on nothing—neither their own powers nor the shared cultural map for interpersonal action. (p. 241)

COPING WITH EMOTIONS ASSOCIATED WITH DEATH AWARENESS

> [This] balance is not easily struck—the effort to find a way to feel real while at the same time not becoming overwhelmed by the existential pain of our awareness of death.... Within this challenge to live with eyes and heart wide open rests the ultimate goal: how to be fully human. (Siegel, 2003, p. x)

As indicated above, many painful emotions arise in relation to death awareness. Over the past 30 years in their discussion groups and seminars, the people referred to throughout this book have been talking about and expressing their feelings regarding existential concerns. As a result, their perspectives on life and death have shifted significantly. Initially some were reluctant to speak about the subject because they thought it might be depressing for other participants. Almost everyone considered talking about these issues to be socially unacceptable, but for the most part, they have overcome these taboos and now speak openly about death.

People came to recognize that their fears of death were not simply phobic reactions, morbid preoccupations, or neurotic anxieties; they were realistic fears. On a deep level, they understood the randomness and impersonal nature of death, and therefore realized that they could blame no one or no thing for the fact of death. They made a concerted effort to become aware of their death fears in order to avoid unconsciously punishing those who brought love to their life, who caused them to value their existence, and who made them feel more about the inevitable loss of themselves and others through death. In their friendships and intimate relationships, they became more vulnerable, more respectful of one another, less judgmental, and more compassionate overall. Within their families, they became more involved with their children and those of their close friends, and generally invested more meaning in their lives (R. Firestone et al., 2003).

Deep Feeling Release

In a sense, the most appropriate reaction to the profoundly disturbing emotions that are aroused by the awareness of death is a primal scream, a primitive, untamed expression of the rage, anguish, and sadness that accompanies the realization that our lives are temporary. Cross-cultural studies (Metcalf & Huntington, 1991) have shown that in numerous societies throughout the world loud crying, wailing, and moaning are an established part of the rituals surrounding death. "In many societies, crying at funerals is not merely tolerated, it is required by custom, and at predetermined moments the entire body of mourners will burst into loud and piercing cries" (p. 44). For example, anthropologist Radcliff-Brown noted that the ritual wailing and weeping of an Andamanese Islander "creates within the wailer the proper sentiment [of sadness]" (p. 46).

In our experience with deep feeling release therapy, we have found that participants felt better and more centered in themselves after freely expressing powerful emotions in these types of sessions. They found it helpful to let out that type of scream, to sob with full abandon, and then to describe their reactions to the session and the insights they may have gained from the deep expression of their feelings.

Many of the people who went through this type of therapy were able to access deep feeling within a few sessions, as described in chapter 8. Some individuals sobbed, while others moaned loudly or shouted angrily. These sounds were not forced, but seemed to emanate involuntarily from deep within the person (R. Firestone, 1985). Some people uttered high-pitched screams, loud cries for help, angry curses, and injunctions such as "Leave me alone!" "Get Away!" and in relation to fears of dying—"I don't want to die!"

For example, in an individual session, Fred, who witnessed the deaths of Laotian peasants during the U.S. bombing in the 1970s, expressed his outrage:

> Fred: [deep moans, followed by an agonized yell] "Why? Why! What are you doing? How could you do this to them? They're human beings. They're innocent. They didn't do anything! They did nothing to you. What's the matter with you? Are you crazy? You're brutalizing and murdering innocent people! Oh. . . . I can't stand it!!" [long pause]

In another case, Esther (68), diagnosed with cancer, was undergoing radiation and chemotherapy. She expressed deep anger regarding the heavy toll that the fear of her own death and the harrowing cancer treatments were taking on her energy and spirit.

> I don't want to die! I want to live! I'll do anything I can to survive! God-damn it! I'm going to survive this! I survived the atrocities in my family, so I can survive this! I've got so much to live for. I'm not going to give up now. I can't give up. [cries]

In a group session, Barbara (45) said: "Yesterday was my birthday, and for some reason I started feeling terrible. This morning I looked in the mirror and saw what looked like an old lady. I had voice attacks telling me I was old, unattractive, not sexy anymore, something like 'You're getting closer and closer to death." I was so angry, I felt like screaming:

> **Barbara**: I hate my body. I hate being in my body! How can I get away? I've got to escape! There has to be a way out. I just can't die! It's not fair! I don't want to get old! I don't want to die! I won't give up and just go off by myself and die! [sobs deeply]

Diane [later]: When Barbara was going through those feelings, I was thinking to myself: "I am going to die. I'm getting older and I'm going to die." I felt so sad for myself when you [Barbara] were protesting the fact that you had to die. Then the next thought that I had was that I love my life. I don't want to use that, the fact that I am going to die, the fact that I am getting older, to stop me from living my life now. I want to use the pain about knowing that I'm going to die someday to enhance my life now.

Dr. Firestone: And I think it works that way. When death issues come up, the appropriate way to deal with them is not to deny them, but to feel the sadness. That will automatically enhance what is meaningful to you, just as avoiding those feelings can take you away from life. If you avoid death you avoid life.

When people first experienced these strong emotions, they expressed relief to be in touch with themselves: "That felt so good, I can't believe it!" "I've been waiting a long time to get that out!" Prior to expressing these deep feelings, many individuals had been afraid of what might come out if they allowed themselves to feel on this level. Not only did they overcome some of the fear of letting go, but they found that nothing horrendous happened to them. Instead, the discovery fostered feelings of security and optimism.

On a personal level, in recalling my own experience with deep feeling release sessions, I remember the unusually calm state of my own mind; nothing was threatening or overwhelming. My experiences were real, events were spaced in a manner that was digestible, and each memory was distinct and particularly lucid. People who experienced this type of therapy reported feeling unusually close to themselves, and said that the events in their lives left a strong imprint. They felt sensitive and sentimental in the best sense, and their lives took on a certain poignancy. Working in deep feeling release sessions had positive consequences because it molded each person's character and in fact was one of the building blocks of the friendship circle.

The opportunity to observe and participate in this exploration of the depth of human emotion left me feeling at ease with the expression of people's most intimate and deep-seated feelings. For this reason, I think that each person in my field should be required to undergo deep feeling release therapy as a fundamental part of his or her training in order to learn about the true source of psychological pain. Each should be exposed to the vast world of human emotion that barely surfaces with traditional methods. It is the most powerful environmental condition I can imagine to help a young practitioner acquire the depth of feeling and empathy suitable to the respectful practice of psychotherapy with a fellow human being.

Sharing Feelings in Discussion Groups

Although despair is endemic to the human condition, we suggest that there are ways to reduce the anxiety and dread that emerge when one contemplates one's mortality. As noted, people "can share their feelings about death and dying with close friends and associates and thereby find essential meaning in their existence" (Morrant & Catlett, 2008, p. 368).

In their early discussions, the participants identified specific defenses they had developed in an effort to protect themselves against an acute awareness of death and the associated anguish. Later, they continued to talk about ways of living more fully in spite of their limitations in time (Note 4). This discussion begins with Kathy describing her fearlessness as a young person and some of the self-destructive behaviors she had engaged in at that time.

> **Kathy**: During my childhood, I never was afraid of dying. In fact, I was very proud of the fact that I wasn't afraid to die, and it was a great thing to think, "I'm not afraid to die at all." And then when I started to have more serious relationships, I didn't believe that anymore. I thought, "Maybe I am afraid to die."
>
> And as my relationships grew stronger, I became aware of thinking, "Well, I'm not afraid of anybody else dying, but I am afraid of myself dying." And then when my relationship with my husband grew even more intimate and when we had a baby, then I started to feel that I was afraid of other people dying as well as myself.
>
> **Gus**: When I was in my 30s, I did a lot of sky-diving. I remember jumping out of the plane and being absolutely unafraid. I wasn't worried about the possibility that the chute might not open, or falling to my death. I took a lot of other chances, too, trekking off to the jungle in places where I could have been easily killed.
>
> Today I feel like I'm getting closer to some feeling about death for the first time in my life. It may sound corny, but when I am in a more open state, and it's a nice day, and I'm listening to some music that I love, then suddenly I get a feeling that, "Gee, there will be a time that I'll never be able to hear that music any more, or that I'll never feel the sunshine the way that I felt it that day." And this is the first time in my life that I'm starting to feel that. And I know it's because I'm letting things matter more to me.

Amanda: It makes me wonder how much of what happens in everyday life is a huge distraction from these feelings because I thought that my life would be very soft and feeling if I stayed feeling the way I feel right now in this talk. Because I do feel such a preciousness about my life, such a joy with the children that I'm close to, and I feel like I would live a soft existence. I would speak in a kind way with people. I think that all the rest are distractions—the arguments, the petty issues—because I really don't have to feel anything about death when I'm in that state.

Paul: I remember when I was about 9 years old lying in bed, it seemed night after night, until I resolved things in my mind. I was just tormented by the thought of dying and being dead forever. I remember going through a logical process, because I knew in my belief system that there was the thought of an afterlife, and it was a question of dealing with death through a decision as to whether or not to believe in God.

Even as a child I knew that I had that choice, that if I chose to believe in God then I didn't have to worry about death so much. And I chose that. I remember specifically making the decision to relieve myself by believing in God and then I could relax. It fit very nicely into my whole family structure, it was everything that I was supposed to do anyway. The other choice was too hard to even consider, and so I made a decision to believe in God and then I could sleep.

Raymond: The most vivid memory that I have is when I was 5 years old, both of my grandparents died within a few weeks of each other, and I remember going to my grandfather's funeral, which was the second funeral and standing up in the church pew and listening to all the things that were said, seeing him laid out in the church. A feeling of overwhelming loneliness came over me that he was gone. He's no different from the animals that I had seen dying, there's no basic difference. I think that's sort of the feeling that I've had about death most of my life, it happens, we're here and then we're gone.

About a year ago, my mother was filling me in on the details of how they both died. My grandmother had sent my grandfather, over his objections, to the hospital and they carried him out of the house and he was angry at her. While he was in the hospital, she caught pneumonia and died so that he didn't see her again. [Raymond's eyes tear up] Every time I tell this story I can't help but cry. My mother said that when they told my grandfather that she was dead, he looked really sad and he said: "I didn't even get to say goodbye" and I didn't know why that was so touching to me, but that was the only real feeling about that whole incident. It was so covered up with the trappings of the funeral and religion and everything. But just the poignant thought of missed opportunities, of not having something when you can.

I knew I couldn't tell the story without feeling really emotional about him saying, "I didn't even say goodbye, I didn't even tell her goodbye." At least it underscores that this is all we've got, the feelings while we are alive and to cut off those feelings, to deny those, is to not even live, in some way.

Tamsen: I've talked about my feelings about other people dying in this discussion, but I feel like the most painful thing for me to feel, which I've felt just a few times in my life, is that I have a feeling of loving my life, of loving myself in it. And I feel like I can't stand that feeling because I feel like I would miss being myself so much. [crying] So then I start feeling critical toward myself and other people so I don't have that feeling any more.

Eva: I grew up in a society where life and death were totally unexplained. I was very confused. I was very cut off and even when I faced a lot of deaths of people that I knew in my very early childhood from the Holocaust and when I was a young teenager in the Independence War in Israel, I didn't have any feelings. I went through the motions, I went to a lot of funerals, but I didn't feel anything. The first time in my life that I felt something strong for my life was when I was seriously ill, and before my surgery was taking place, I felt something for myself, and there were a few thoughts: it was the first time that I was thinking that I was glad that I was born, and that I had a chance to experience life, and that I would like to continue to experience life. I didn't want to die. This is really the first time I had a grasp of feeling that I was glad that I was born. I never felt something like that before. I existed, I lived, there was a lot of agony, some joys. Just today, sitting here, I was thinking also that I was so robbed of reality, of life and the knowledge about death and what can happen.

[to Tamsen] I was very touched when you said that you would miss yourself, your life, the fullness of your life, the richness, the happiness. I feel sometimes like this. I can't believe that I feel like I would miss myself not being, not existing. And I also have a strong feeling, and this is almost hard to say, that it would be a loss for people who know me because I let them know me some. [sad]

In the years following the series of discussions described above, men and women continued to talk about ways of living more fully in spite of one's limitations in time. The process of uncovering and challenging defenses against death anxiety and facing the issue of death squarely appears to have had the effect of shifting people's perspective on the subject in significant ways. In a discussion that took place more recently, the participants described the changes that had occurred in their feeling reactions and philosophical approach to life and death (R. Firestone et al., 2003).

Tamsen: I feel like I've changed in relation to the subject about death. We made a film a number of years ago, and in it I had a lot of feelings about myself dying and imagining that. Then three years ago, right around the same time, two people that I knew died. I started to have the feelings I always had whenever I had any reminders of death, which were "This is too terrible. I cannot stand this. I cannot stand it. I hate that it's true. I just cannot stand it! This is absolutely unbearable." And then for some reason, I had the thought, "Whose reaction is this that I'm having?" It crossed my mind that maybe this wasn't even my reaction. Then I remembered that my parents were so absolutely freaked out by the idea of death and so intolerant of the subject, and I could sense it in them. But those were the same feelings I felt.

So then I thought, "Well, how do I really feel about death?" And I thought that I didn't feel like they did. Even if I still felt panic, it would be my own feeling. I had never thought about, "What do I really think about it." I had some other thoughts; one was concerning what someone said about "accepting death." The Buddhists and other people say, "Accept death." It's such a funny way to put it. It doesn't matter whether you accept it or not, it's there. It's not up to us to accept or not accept. It just is. No matter what my reaction is, it's just there.

Also I had this image. We get so worked up about what's going to happen after death, but whatever it was, was happening before too. So I imagined this long, long endless period of nonexistence with this little tiny bump in it, of life. I feel like this little time here is such an incredible gift. So I feel a poignant sadness about my life today that I haven't felt before.

Dr. Firestone: That's one of the positive aspects of facing the death issue. It gives a poignant sense of meaning to life and happiness, which enlarges the experience instead of detracting from it.

Tamsen: I thought about that idea of "triumphing over death" and to me that also seems absurd. Because I am so powerless, it's not even a joke. But I thought that I can triumph over my defenses about death. I can triumph over the ways that I've defended myself against facing it. So I feel like I've changed and developed.

Dr. Firestone: It feels like people have a split between an alliance with death or an alliance with life. And a lot of the voice attacks represent a drive towards death and destruction and a movement away from living, from experience. Or you can ally yourself with living and feeling and embracing life.

Paul: I don't feel the way I described feeling years ago, the terror of dying. That feeling is different now. I don't feel the terror, but I feel such sadness. I feel such an absolute sadness, when I let myself really feel this. That it's almost more than I can stand. But it's not the terror of the unknown. It's just the sadness of not having the things that mean so much to me, and that I love so much now.

Kathy: I like what Tamsen said. It seems that you've come to a level of feeling in your life where you don't feel panicked and you're more comfortable with the idea of death, although you still experience sad feelings. But for me, I feel like I go in and out of that. At times I feel like, "You don't live forever, so you've got to challenge yourself and your experience, everything." And that does give me inspiration and motivation to really live a full life. And then, at other times when I'm feeling the closest I could feel to somebody, it's harder to hang in there and stay close because it is terrifying to realize I'm not going to have that person forever.

Dr. Firestone: It's a choice. Face the realities and embrace life or turn your back on life and protect against death. So I think it's valuable to challenge it, and particularly to talk about it freely.

Kathy: But I have to say, it's definitely a feeling that I go in and out of.

Dr. Firestone: So it's an intermittent experience for you. You could choose reality and live life fully even though you know that you will die. And you can bear it and you can bear the thought of losing yourself and others too. A lot of people think they can't bear it, so they don't enter a relationship or commit to anything. They're afraid of losing it, so they don't have it. And that's choosing death over life. Whereas the opposite is to embrace life and take your chances. And you can bear the loss anyway.

It's better to live and face death then never to have lived. But that's not a decision that most people make. A person just drifts into a state of denial and wards off all kinds of emotions and pain in their lives at great expense. See it's never worth it to take the drug. It's never worth it to kill the pain. That's the key issue. You can bear the pain. And that makes you strong.

Dean: I feel that exact same way, on both sides of the fence at any given moment. Sometimes so woefully indifferent to the fact that I'm going to die and distant from myself and people. When I wake up from that state, it frightens me because what wakes me up is the awareness that I'm going to die. And when that occurs, it's like, "No, I'm not ready. I want to see that person one more time. I want to take one more boat ride. I want to do something. I'm not ready yet." But during those periods where I'm indifferent, it's really frightening to me, when I wake up out of it. And the thing is it's so tough because death is both concrete and an abstraction. It's so concrete because it's everywhere. You see it everywhere. People you know die. People on the news die. And yet my own death is such a speculation. Who knows what happens? So in that speculation I can think many things.

I found that my mother dying recently has just brought this subject to the surface much more for me. I have so many moments where I think, "What if this was my last moment?" But it doesn't feel morbid to me; it just crystallizes a moment. And because I fly so much, I have a lot of times when

I'll be getting on a plane and I'll look around and I'll think, "Well, what if these are the people I'm going to die with?" But it doesn't feel as morbid as that sounds.

Raymond: I think that Tamsen captured a lot of my feelings, particularly since I have had to face this issue more or less head on in the past year and a half since I was diagnosed with cancer. There's nothing that can be done about it except live what is left of my life. But I loved your description of the long line of nonexperiences and the little dot of life, an eye blink. Life is just an eye blink in that perspective. And you seize the blink or you seize the moment, which is to seize life itself. But it's just a moment. It's a precious gift, as you said. It's so momentary in the perspective of things.

Dr. Firestone: One other thing, reflecting on death leads to a sense of altruism. It really does. I see people living that way here in this group of friends particularly. And it extends beyond our group of friends too, to anybody who crosses our path who needs something or wants something. There's a sense of fulfillment in that that somehow is counter to the death process. A very fundamental part of being alive is being generous and altruistic. I think it's part of human nature.

Raymond: We're all in the same boat.

Judy: I had a dream last night that three of us were transported to someplace in the future, and nobody else was there. [sad] Next, we went back in time and then Steve came in and told us that the whole world was going to explode, and someone said, "Let's sit down and plan for it." I think what the dream meant for me was that recently I've started thinking not only about my own death, but I had an awareness that everybody I know is going to die. This is different from feeling about another person, or even about myself dying. It's a different level of feeling, realizing that every single person I knew was going to die. [cries]

At first I felt really embarrassed to have that feeling, yet I think it leaves me in a very open state where everything is vivid. Yesterday I had a sweet, poignant, sad feeling. It was one of those days where everything was precious to me, every person was precious to me. I think that's why I dreamed that last night.

Dr. Firestone: Every person you know and every person you don't know is going to die someday. When I went to China and saw the millions of people, I thought, "My God, they're all up against it in the same way we are." And it's precisely that thought that could save the world.

Recognizing that we're all in the same boat throughout the world, it's precisely that—it's the very thing that people are overlooking, that people are all in the same boat and we're all going to die and it's a tragedy and there would be so much compassion for each other in that, for people everywhere. Feeling that has a very positive effect, I believe, because it makes you really see people as precious and lets you have a tender feeling for their situation, a rather tragic situation that we all face. It's really a sad thought, but it could have a positive effect, thinking about people in that situation and from that perspective.

When people felt deeply in the group situation, each person's expression affected the others and pain and anguish permeated the atmosphere of the room. Participants were attentive, exhibited exceptional compassion, and waited patiently for each person to finish without interrupting. Afterward there were affectionate responses and verbal support. We noticed that group members naturally reacted with a sensitivity usually seen only in trained therapists. This genuine empathy alone brought out a deep sadness in virtually all of us who witnessed the phenomenon.

CONCLUSION

There are many different death concerns and related fears. The authors believe that talking about death anxiety with a friend is helpful. However there are not many opportunities for this form of communication because people are often intolerant of the subject matter. There is the possibility of attending seminars and workshops on the subject that are available at universities and institutes.

Furthermore, it is of great importance to find a healthy outlet for expressing the underlying emotions about death and dying. A person could release these deep feelings when alone and private, but it is even more valuable to express them in the presence of other sympathetic individuals.

Overall, the people in the friendship circle have developed in their personal lives and relationships by facing death with appropriate feelings. Talking and feeling about existential concerns allowed them to feel more tenderness toward one another, to become more respectful and more open to closeness and intimacy. The entire process, which has taken place over a period of many years, involved first challenging defenses that in turn aroused feelings about death (i.e., sadness, rage, and fear). Second, experiencing and expressing these emotions, especially sadness, appeared to have an ameliorating effect. The more people learned about themselves, the more death became an issue, and the more they had to learn to deal with these painful feelings.

Becker (1973/1997) suggested: "How does one transcend himself; how does he open himself to new possibility? By realizing the truth of his situation, by dispelling the lie of his character [defenses], by breaking his spirit out of its conditioned prison" (p. 86). Essentially, these people's efforts to confront their fears about death and dying have addressed this issue. As an outgrowth of their experiences and talking together on a regular basis, they have become increasingly involved in formulating their own personal principles for living, setting goals in accordance with these values and principles, composing their life stories, and searching for their own personal meaning in life.

NOTES

1. Lucretius proposed that people fear death because on some level they still believe they somehow will be conscious after death. However if a person would really face the fact that "there will be no other self to remain in life and lament to self that his own self has met death, and there to stand and grieve that his own self there lying is mangled or burnt," he or she would have no need to fear death (cited by Flew, 1964, p. 90).

2. William Styron's (1976) novel *Sophie's Choice* portrayed the consequences of this form of self-blame and the painful self-accusations associated with *survivor guilt*.

3. The diary of Ellen West, Binswanger's (1958) suicidal patient, exemplifies the bitter cynicism of people who view life as ludicrous and pointless: "The world [is] a caricature and my life a hell.... The torture of having each day to tilt anew against the windmill with a mass of absurd, base, contemptible thoughts, this torment spoils my life" (p. 257). Binswanger conjectured that his patient's long-standing anxiety, dread, and guilt prevented her from living an authentic life, which contributed to her eventual suicide. Commenting on the fate of Ellen West, Orbach (2008) noted that "lack of meaning does not cause suffering; rather, suffering is the cause of lack of meaning" (p. 312). In other words, it is not the meaninglessness and absurdity of life that drives an individual to take his or her own life; instead, it is unbearable mental pain resulting from childhood trauma that intensifies the fear of death in certain individuals, which in turn predisposes hopelessness and despair, and which at times results in suicidal behavior.

4. Portions of the two discussions in this section are taken from two videotaped group meetings (1989, 1999). Transcripts of portions of the two meetings were later published in *Creating a Life of Meaning and Compassion* (R. Firestone et al., 2003, pp. 200–207).

12 Learning to Love

If it is true, as I have tried to show, that love is the only sane and satisfactory answer to the problem of human existence, then any society which excludes, relatively, the development of love, must in the long run perish of its own contradiction with the basic necessities of human nature.... That this need has been obscured does not mean that it does not exist.

—*Erich Fromm,* The Art of Loving *(1956, p. 133)*

The great aim of every human being is to understand the meaning of total love.... The universe only makes sense when we have someone to share our feelings with.

—*Paul Coelho,* Eleven Minutes *(2004, p. 116)*

If death anxiety is the poison, then love is the antidote. Love and loving make life bearable in relation to the dreadful predicament faced by the human race. Romantic love, loving friendship, love of self, love of nature, and love of humankind—each contributes to making life worthwhile and precious. Unfortunately, most people suffer from painful events in childhood that blunt their capacity to experience loving feelings toward others and to accept love when it is directed toward them. When people love or are loved, it makes them acutely conscious of their existence; they experience a heightened awareness of themselves and an enhanced sense of being and becoming. Paradoxically these uniquely positive

285

feelings come with a price—that of an especially poignant appreciation of a life that one knows is terminal. Thus any movement in the direction of expanding the experience of love in one's life and increasing one's options is exhilarating as well as painful and anxiety-provoking.

The awareness of their personal mortality inspired the individuals in our study to take their lives more seriously. When faced with significant decisions, they chose the ones that would make the best life story (Note 1). These people recognized the importance of making a powerful commitment to life and love. They placed great value on their personal freedom. This emphasis on freedom and responsibility was also manifested in a strong desire not to become embedded in a symbiotic relationship, or what Erich Fromm (1956) has referred to as:

> An egotism *a deu;* they are two people who identify themselves with each other, and who solve the problem of separateness by enlarging the single individual into two. They have the experience of overcoming aloneness, yet, since they are separated from the rest of mankind, they remain separated from each other and alienated from themselves; their experience of union is an illusion. (p. 55)

As individuals expanded their awareness of aloneness, of life and death, and of the essential dilemma and mystery of existence, they came to express a deep and abiding respect for people's feelings and their well-being. These sentiments are translated into extraordinary acts of kindness, sensitivity, and compassion toward one another as well as toward anyone who crosses their path. These people have elevated the concept of love and loving to a high level that plays a central role in their everyday lives (R. Firestone & Catlett, 2009).

Because children are hurt to varying degrees in their upbringing and form psychological defenses that limit their ability to freely feel their emotions, they are negatively affected in their capacity to give or receive love. Debilitating attitudes of fear and distrust, combined with insecurity and self-hatred, make feeling genuine loving emotions difficult if not impossible. Faced with these deterrents to self-love and love for others, one must develop oneself psychologically to regain these feelings. People can learn to love and to be loved, but like any other skill, it must be approached with discipline, effort, and passion in order to be mastered.

I can relate this subject to my own personal experience in developing my capacity to become a loving person in the romantic sense. Before I met my current wife, Tamsen, I had several close long-term relationships with women. In each successive relationship, I learned more about my defenses and any resistance I had to being sensitive, affectionate, and tender. My choices were continually improving in that I chose women who were less defended and more open to being loving and responsive to me. All along I was searching for a reciprocal love relationship, marked by equality and respect as well as by warmth and sexuality.

When I was a teenager and I imagined a loving relationship, I pictured a woman at my side who was loving and whom I loved, but she was sort of an appendage to me, more like those stories of an explorer with a native girl from the islands. But as I developed, I came to desire a genuine sense of equality with a woman, an intelligent give-and-take exchange with shared responsibility and decision-making. In my adult choices I was learning and moving in this direction.

Another influence that contributed to my development came from my practice of psychotherapy. As I listened to women clients criticizing and attacking their partners, I registered that some of their specific attacks corresponded to my own faults. I did not want to be the kind of man that they were describing and made a concerted effort to change. There were many ways that I was being subtly macho, inconsiderate, self-centered, or indifferent. I could see how these traits were hurtful.

When I met Tamsen and fell in love with her, I wanted to be completely open and vulnerable. But I noticed that I had two major defenses that kept me safe and somewhat distant in a close relationship with a woman. The first was that I would tend to be critical of her in my mind in a way of creating a caricature of her based on any fault or negative quality she might have. Second, I would tend to be disrespectful by playing the role of helper. I vowed to do neither, kept my vow, and felt much more vulnerable in the new relationship. Because of these insights I have been more loving and consistent throughout our relationship and we have been exceptionally close.

In this chapter, we examine several fundamental principles involved in developing one's capacity to both give and receive love. First, we describe our definition of *love* and elucidate its behavioral operations and expressions in human relationships. Second, we delineate what love is not; and third, we discuss the defenses that people in the friendship circle dealt with and the personal qualities they attempted to develop or improve upon to expand their capacity to love and be loved. We discuss jealousy and competition and exclusive versus nonexclusive relationships, with a view toward developing genuinely loving relationships where each partner would encourage the other to live and flourish. We believe that intimate relationships tend to be the most meaningful and satisfying when they are not based on imposing limitation and restrictions on one another. We agree in substance with Coelho's (2004) assertion: *"I am convinced that no one loses anyone, because no one owns anyone. That is the true experience of freedom: having the most important thing in the world without owning it"* (p. 90).

After Tamsen and I fell in love, became serious, and contemplated marriage, the issue of our personal freedom and in particular our sexual freedom came up as it does with many other couples. At the time I was involved with other women, but felt totally satisfied emotionally and sexually in my relationship with Tamsen. For better or worse, I would have been glad to comply with her desire for us to have a closed marriage, if that would have been her decision. She felt frightened about the issue of sexual freedom, but after considerable thought, she expressed her viewpoint, "I can't imagine being restrictive in any way of the person I love. I love you the way you are, as a free spirit." I appreciated her feeling for me in this matter and she has never wavered.

On the other hand, I felt the same trepidation about her being with another man in any form of sexual relationship. I knew it would be very painful for me if the situation arose. Nevertheless, I came to the same conclusion that I could not imagine restricting the woman I loved in any manner. I would have to suffer the potential anguish and deal with it if and when it came to pass. I saw the wisdom of both of our decisions. We wanted to really know each other and make no concessions to our individuality. We wanted to be freely chosen; anything else would have been a sham. If we were to eliminate rivals on the basis of form and control, we would never know how our relationship actually stood. With our open approach, we could truly believe that we were significantly valued and preferred.

WHAT IS LOVE? SOME PHENOMENOLOGICAL DESCRIPTIONS

> Man loves life, and, loving life, hates death, and because of this he is great, he is glorious, he is beautiful, and his beauty is everlasting. He lives below the senseless stars and writes his meanings in them.... Thus it is impossible to scorn this creature. For out of his strong belief in life, this puny man made love. At his best, he *is* love. Without him there can be no love...no desire. (T. Wolfe, 1934, p. 411)

Philosophers, poets, novelists, and social scientists have tried to define the meaning of the word *love* and to describe the emotions associated with the experience of *falling in love*. As Reik (1941) rightly observed, "Love is one of the most overworked words in our vocabulary. There is hardly a field of human activity in which the word is not worked to death" (p. 9). The use of the word *love* has become banal; worse yet, it has been used in situations where an objective view would deny its validity. For this reason, it is wise not to trust or believe words like *love* when they don't coincide with appropriate actions and other behavioral expressions, as when people say, "I love you" when they are seeking reassurance rather than conveying affection.

In "The Future of an Illusion," S. Freud (1927/1961b) succinctly stated his position on the subject: "Simple human love is impossible," whereas Laing (1989) in a personal journal declared: "Let's take a few breaths of fresher air. Let's start with the belief, hope, wish, that mutual love is possible."

The philosopher Irving Singer (2001) asserted that "There is no single entity, no discernible sensation or emotion, that is love.... Love is a form of life" (pp. 84–85). In *The Four Loves*, C. S. Lewis (1960) describes Eros as a self-centered form of love or narcissism unless it is directed outward: "One of the first things Eros does is to obliterate the distinction between giving and receiving" (p. 96). And Daisaku Ikeda (Gage, 1976) in a conversation with Arnold Toynbee portrayed love as follows:

> Abstracted love without practical application can be meaningless. I believe that the Buddhist concept of compassion...defined as removing sorrow and bringing happiness to others...gives love substantial meaning.... *Yoraku*—the second component of compassion in the Buddhist sense—means the giving of pleasure.... It is the joy of living...the ecstasy of life. (pp. 357–358)

But what is love, really? What does it mean to love someone, or to be loved by someone? It is indeed a challenging undertaking to define love in behavioral terms. In attempting to answer these questions, Post, Underwood, Schloss, and Hurlbut (2002) wrote that love might be conceptualized as *affirmative affection*. "We remember loving persons who conveyed this affective affirmation through tone of voice, facial expression, a hand on the shoulder in time of grief, and a desire to be with us.... Love implies benevolence, care, compassion, and action" (p. 4).

Tamsen: There is a sentence in Dave Eggers's book *A Heartbreaking Work of Staggering Genius* that I always loved. The narrator's parents have died, and he is alone with his younger brother in their parents' house in the Midwest. Rather than describe funerals, closing down a house, and traveling across the country to a new life, Eggers says: "As I am looking at him, he wakes up. He gets up and comes to me as I am sitting in the chair and [this is the part I love] I take his hand and we go through the window and fly up and over the quickly sketched trees and then to California."

That's what happened to me with Bob: we took each other's hands and flew up and over the trees and the ocean and then to the sun. And we took all of our friends with us. And we were all often brave and courageous, and at those times we soared high above the rest of the world. At other times, when we were fearful and intimidated, we started to fall from the sky and plunge toward earth. But through it all, I must say that I have been happy because I have been able to do what I always wanted to do: I have been free to create a world that is different from the one I was born into.

In a previous work (R. Firestone et al., 2003), the authors wrote:

Love can be defined as feelings and behaviors that enhance the emotional well-being of oneself and the other. Loving operations can be characterized as affection, respect for each person's boundaries, generosity, tenderness, and a desire for close companionship in life. Loving someone in one's thoughts and feelings is a necessary but insufficient component in creating a loving relationship. Love must also be expressed through loving behavior to optimally affect one's partner, family member, or friend. (p. 22)

According to R. D. Laing (personal communication, 1985), love represents a confluence of internal feelings of affection and tenderness and the outward extension of these feelings toward the other, a simultaneous combination of the intrapersonal and the interpersonal.

Sexual love is vital to one's sense of fulfillment in an intimate relationship in which erotic feelings and sexual responses are simply an extension of affection and communication. The combination of sexuality and close personal communication represents an ideal in a couple's relationship. Genuine love also requires valuing the other person's goals in life separate from one's personal needs and interests, and respecting the autonomy of the other. (Firestone et al., 2003, p. 23)

Love is truth and never involves deception, because, as noted previously, misleading another person fractures his or her sense of reality and is therefore a serious human rights violation that adversely affects mental health (R. Firestone et al., 2006). When mature love exists between two people, its expression is one of the most rewarding aspects of life. Our thinking about the nature of love is congenial with the words written by Fromm (1956): "There is only one proof for the presence of love: the depth of the relationship, and the aliveness and strength in each person concerned; this is the fruit by which love is recognized" (p. 103).

WHAT LOVE IS NOT

> What matters is that we know what kind of union we are talking about when we speak of love. Do we refer to love as the mature answer to the problem of existence, or do we speak of those immature forms of love which may be called *symbiotic union....* I shall call love only the former. (Fromm, 1956, p. 18)

To better understand what genuine love is, it is worthwhile to describe what love is not. Love is not selfish, possessive, demanding, or a proprietary right over the other. Love is never submission or dominance, emotional coercion, or manipulation. Love is not the desperate attempt to deny aloneness or the search for security that many couples manifest in their desire for a fused identity. D. H. Lawrence (1920/1982) addressed this theme when questioning what he considered to be destructive patterns of traditional coupling in the early 20th century: "Why could they not remain individuals, limited by their own limits? Why this dreadful all-comprehensiveness, this hateful tyranny? Why not leave the other being free, why try to absorb, or melt, or merge? One might abandon oneself utterly to the *moments,* but not to any other being" (p. 391).

Love is not to be confused with a deep longing to find total confirmation of oneself in the other. As Becker (1973/1997) observed: "If you find the ideal love and try to make it the sole judge of good and bad in yourself, the measure of your strivings, you become simply the reflex of another person. You lose yourself in the other, just as obedient children lose themselves in the family" (p. 166). Love is not a word to be casually bandied about as couples often do when trying to maintain control over one another; for example, "If you really loved me, you'd do thus and so." Nor does love relate to an inner state of mind that has no recognizable outward manifestations, as for instance when a child is told that "Mommy [or daddy] really loves you, but just doesn't know how to show it" (R. Firestone et al., 2006). In his work, Fromm (1956) described neurotic patterns of love, while focusing attention on a major obstacle to learning how to love: "The basic condition for neurotic love lies in the fact that one or both of the 'lovers' have remained attached to the figure of a parent, and transfer the feelings, expectations[,] and fears one once had toward father or mother to the loved person in adult life" (p. 94).

EXPANDING ONE'S CAPACITY TO LOVE

There are few experiences in life that make people feel more alive, that are more critical to a life of meaning, than genuinely loving or caring for another person. The authors feel that to develop emotionally and spiritually, one needs to learn how to love; to continue to search for love throughout life; to remain open, vulnerable, and positive; and to not become self-protective, cynical, or despairing when love fails (R. Firestone et al., 2006). We feel a sense of kinship with R. D. Laing (1976), who asserted that "The main fact of life for me is love or its absence. Whether life is worth living depends for me on whether there is love in life. Without a sense of it, or even the memory…of it, I think I would lose heart completely" (p. vii).

Unfortunately, genuine love is hard to come by and even more difficult to tolerate. This is particularly true when accepting love, because the beloved often suffers a recurrence of painful feelings of sadness when he or she attempts to let love into his or her life. Both giving and receiving love—exchanging psycho-nutritional products—are inhibited by primal pain, anxieties, and deep sadness (R. Firestone & Catlett, 1999). In fact people must learn to deal with the underlying sadness in order to remain close in a couple relationship.

The fear of love and intimacy is not only related to interpersonal fears and distress; it is also based on existential fear. As discussed in chapter 7, sexual intimacy combined with loving feelings arouses death anxiety because it represents a powerful intrusion into the false sense of safety and security achieved by forming a fantasy bond. Moreover, experiencing this combination of love and sex reminds people of the fragility of the physical body and of life itself (R. Firestone et al., 2006). As noted, findings from Terror Management Theory (TMT) studies tend to confirm both our views and Becker's (1973/1997) hypotheses regarding the correlation between sexual conflicts and fears of death. Researchers Goldenberg et al. (1999) have concluded that "Sex is a ubiquitous human problem because the creaturely aspects of sex make apparent our animal nature, which reminds us of our vulnerability and mortality" (p. 1173). In developing the ability to love and be loved, one will inevitably confront these reminders of one's mortality during the closest, most tender moments with a significant other.

Qualities to Develop in Oneself in Relation to Loving and Accepting Love

> Is love an art? Then it requires knowledge and effort. Or is love a pleasant sensation, which to experience is a matter of chance, something one "falls into" if one is lucky? This little book *[The Art of Loving]* is based on the former premise, while undoubtedly the majority of people today believe in the latter. (Fromm, 1956, p. 1)

Loving would come naturally if a person had been treated sensitively with love, affection, and positive attunement early on. There are two essential preconditions for expanding the ability to love and be loved. The first involves committing oneself to breaking with self-nurturing, self-protective, and addictive defenses. This entails recognizing that there are internalized voices that are constantly coaching us not to take chances, not to invest in a relationship, and not to trust others. The second precondition is learning to value oneself, which is a difficult endeavor because the capacity to see oneself as worthwhile and one's life as having intrinsic value is often seriously damaged during the formative years. For this reason, freeing oneself of one's early programming, overcoming defenses, and counteracting voices is an ongoing venture (R. Firestone, 1997a).

Expanding one's capacity for love also includes cultivating and strengthening those unique traits and behaviors representative of one's self-interest and self-affirmation. An effective way to pursue this goal is to identify one's positive qualities as well as those behaviors that one wishes to further develop in order to become a more loving person. Regarding a partner or potential mate, it is important to select someone who has personal qualities that are desirable for an enduring relationship. These include an affectionate nature, a nondefensive attitude toward feedback, a stable, rational approach to life, a sense of humor, and an easygoing manner. (See Exhibit 9.1, Couples Interactions Chart.) Instead people often make these choices based on very different criteria: superficial appearance, initial sexual attraction, social status, and, more subtly, physical appearances and character traits that are similar to those of one's parents.

Nondefensiveness and Openness

Two basic qualities necessary for developing the ability to love are a lack of defensiveness and an openness to experience. To become non-defensive in one's closest relationship requires an objective, balanced view of oneself and one's partner. As noted earlier, this also entails learning how to be receptive to negative feedback or criticism instead of engaging in intimidating modes of expression that effectively silence the other person.

Openness includes a genuine interest in learning and growing beyond one's defense system and self-protective routines. People who are open to the ambiguities of life have a strong desire to expand their boundaries and broaden their range of experiences. They view life as an adventure and a unique opportunity to find personal meaning, rather than to follow prescriptions imposed on them from external sources. People who are open and forthright in expressing their feelings, thoughts, dreams, and aspirations have a positive effect on others.

Honesty and Integrity

People who are honest and reliable represent themselves accurately to others as well as to themselves. One characteristic of an honest person's value system is an intolerance of any discrepancy between his or her actions and words. To attain this level of integrity, people must come to know themselves and be willing to face parts of their personality that may be unpleasant or undesirable. In overcoming defenses and personal limitations, people with integrity gradually modify themselves instead of hating themselves for their weaknesses or shortcomings. They develop an acute awareness of any remnants of falseness or insincerity in themselves (R. Firestone & Catlett, 2009).

Respect for the Other's Boundaries, Goals, and Interests

In a truly loving relationship, each partner recognizes that the motives, desires, and aspirations of the other are as significant as his or her own. Ideally a loving person would not conceptualize his or her own freedom and the freedom of the other as conflicting goals. Loving implies an enjoyment of the other person's emergence as an individual and a sensitivity to his or her wants and motives. Each partner feels congenial toward the other's aspirations and tries not to interfere, intrude, or manipulate in order to dominate or control the relationship.

To be close to another person, one has to be separate and autonomous; the closest that one can feel to another person is to feel one's separateness. This awareness is an integral part of having sensitive, tender feelings toward one another. Only when people are possessed of self, that is, centered in themselves and truly individualistic, are they predisposed to sustain healthy relationships in which the personal freedom of both partners is accorded the highest priority.

People with a well-developed sense of identity have a greater potential for love and intimacy than those who rely on others for affirmation of self. These individuals have succeeded, to a large extent, in emancipating themselves emotionally from an immature relationship with their parents. As a result they tend to have their own value system and to set their own course in life. As Stuart Johnson (1987) observed in relation to several individuals who had achieved a high level of self-differentiation:

> Individuals at this level of development no longer conceive of the needs for independence and togetherness as conflicting forces, either intrapsychically or interpersonally. Intimacy at this level involves an intense appreciation for togetherness and existential separateness, rather than fusion and merger. This represents the highest levels of individuation and separation of human development, which few individuals attain. (personal communication, cited by Schnarch, 1991, p. 222)

Physical Affection and Sexuality

The genuinely loving individual is spontaneous in expressing physical affection and sexuality in his or her couple relationship. Demonstrations of tender feelings and emotional closeness are good prognostic indicators for a long-lasting relationship. In a loving relationship both partners view sexual relating as a fulfilling aspect of life, a gift, and a positive offering of pleasure. They have mature attitudes toward sexuality and experience it as an integral part of their lives. Feeling good about themselves as men and women and sharing positive feelings about their bodies and sexuality enhance each person's sense of self and feelings of happiness.

Empathy and Understanding

There is no real understanding without empathy. Understanding involves perceiving a partner's strengths and weaknesses without exaggerating his or her positive or negative traits and behaviors. People who have evolved in their ability to love tend to value the differences as well as the commonalities between themselves and their partner. When partners talk freely about their attitudes or values with feeling and respect for the other, each partner feels understood and validated. In an intimate relationship, both honestly reveal their opinions and disagreements, and this disclosure has the positive effect of making each feel seen and unique. Understanding is an outgrowth of empathy in which a person is able to experience how the other feels in a given situation.

To facilitate this level of understanding in a relationship, one would strive to maintain an ongoing dialogue. Any interaction can be analyzed in terms of whether it is conducive to the expression of personal feelings or whether it serves to cut off or obscure them. An open dialogue that is candid, forthright, and characterized by compassion draws both partners closer to themselves and each other. In a relationship typified by real companionship, any hostility or anger existing between partners would not be acted out, but would instead be discussed in the couple's ongoing verbal dialogue (R. Firestone & Catlett, 1999).

Nonthreatening and Nonmanipulative Behavior

In learning how to love, one must learn to directly express one's wants and desires rather than resort to indirect manipulations that provoke anger or guilt in one's partner. The tyranny of the weak through passivity, powerlessness, victimization, passive-aggression, and other forms of negative power is effective in keeping each other in line. Individuals can be nagged, badgered, or intimidated into the desired behavior, but these rewards are hollow and short-lived. People can successfully imprison one another, but in the process they damage themselves and each other. The manipulation of another person through provocations subverts any genuine feelings that may exist.

In contrast, partners who have developed the capacity to love are not manipulative or threatening and have a positive effect on one another. The absence of control, manipulation, or threat helps maintain the flow of good feelings, which in turn contributes to building trust and feelings of security in the relationship (R. Firestone et al., 2002).

Identifying and Countering Human Rights Violations in Couple Relationships

Individuals striving to increase their ability to sustain a loving, romantic relationship would refrain from establishing unnecessary restrictions, manipulations, and power plays as a part of their style of relating. They would avoid immature, childlike or parental responses, hostility, duplicity, and role-playing and would challenge and attempt to eliminate self-destructive attitudes and behaviors that trigger guilt and fear in a partner. Each of these behaviors can be viewed as directly or indirectly representing an imposition on the other.

These manipulations are generally effective within the couple because most adults have not succeeded in outgrowing or transcending the fear and pain of their childhoods. Residuals of the hurt child exist in every person; no one has completely left behind the primitive fear, longing for love, feelings of helplessness, and guilt experienced during the formative years (R. Firestone, 1990b). Children are conditioned to believe that they are selfish for expressing their wants and needs and therefore learn to be indirect and fundamentally dishonest about their desires. As adults they continue to act on these distortions of self and are often manipulative themselves as well as vulnerable to manipulation by others.

In interpersonal relationships, manipulations and power plays are manifested in: (a) bullying, domination, and the use of force by authoritarian parental figures; (b) threats, which are considered by researchers (Tedeschi & Felson, 1994) to be coercive actions involving possible reprisals, loss of economic security, or abandonment on the part of a partner or family member; and (c) maneuvers unconsciously used by self-denying or self-destructive individuals to gain leverage over a partner or another family member by arousing fear, guilt, and anger (R. Firestone & Catlett, 1999).

People in the friendship circle were deeply concerned about any disrespectful or manipulative patterns of interacting with their mates and children. As a result they tried to face these destructive behaviors honestly and to eliminate them. They attempted to work through problematic aspects of their relationships. In particular, they increased their awareness of the types of communications and actions that impinged on each other's rights and on their own freedom. By identifying the specific behaviors and manipulations they used to intimidate and restrict their mates, as well as those that conflicted with their own integrity, they were able to gain control over actions they disapproved of.

The following dialogue was excerpted from a discussion group that took place during the early days of the friendship circle. The topics talked about in this meeting are indicative of the wide range of ideas that people were interested in at the time. In particular they were concerned about how they sabotaged their independence in couple relationships and the negative effect this had on their loving feelings for their mates.

Janet: I was thinking about the history of my relationship with you, Raymond. I had just started to blossom in college. I was making friends and for the first time, I was moving toward people. I started to feel like a different person and to know myself in a new way. I wasn't quiet and withdrawn anymore; I was outspoken and opinionated. That's when I met you; we were part of the same crowd of intellectual students. And even after we first got married, we were always socializing with them; I remember all of the lively discussions on all kinds of topics. And I was as active a participant as everyone else. But I gradually began to deteriorate. I became dull and quiet, and lost my self-confidence. I began deferring to you. I gave up my interests, and just went along with whatever you were doing. I became like a child. I didn't even know what I wanted anymore. I stopped pursuing my life and I think I was miserable after that.

    Raymond (Janet's ex-husband): That is such an accurate description of what happened to our marriage. I fell in love with you because you were different from the other girls at college; you were smart and interesting. You acted equal to me in every way; intellectually, practically, emotionally. I was thrilled with you as a wife because you were such an equal partner. I really think that couples sell out to each other and give up the very things they want. They completely lose sight of their goals. They give up their personal freedom and strength in order to be taken care of.

    Dr Firestone: That's where so many relationships deteriorate. You know, it's the nature of a person to move toward assertion but at the same time there's a tendency to seek dependency. So there's a conflict in every person: on the one hand they want to be free, to have their own life, and on the other hand, there's a strong desire for emotional dependency. They want another person to define them, but at the same time, they resent the person for it.

    Kurt: Yeah, people reproduce a kind of parent-child interaction very quickly with their mates. Within practically no time at all, they feel that they belong to the other person and assume that the other person belongs to them.

    Janet: I was thinking about my tendency to ruin things with a man by becoming more dependent and worried about my actions. The relationship always starts out going well, with me feeling happy and free to be myself.

Then I start to feel like I'm going to get in trouble if I maintain my freedom. I start to feel guilty for making even the simple choices in life if they are independent; if I go for myself then I feel real guilt.

Dr. Firestone: In a close relationship, a person's movements toward or away from the other may not coincide with the partner's preferences at the time. Therefore, both people would have to be accepting of each other's independent needs for their relationship to work. The minute they stop accepting the comings and goings of the other, the minute they attempt to place restrictions on that, they tend to lose the vitality of the relationship.

There's no way to successfully imprison another person. If you control them, if you manipulate them, if you have power over them, you lose any sense of relatedness. In a good relationship, they would not take a proprietary interest in each other. There would be no desire to change the person; instead there would be a love of the nature of the person; who and what they were. The last thing you would want to do is hold each other back. If the couple interaction hurts the individuals involved, you can't, in a proper sense, call it a love relationship.

Gus: I notice that whenever I would get involved with a woman I would want to be sexual, which is normal, but after making love I would immediately form a crazy attachment. I was obligated to her and she was obligated to me. Going to bed would cement the relationship. It would set up a whole hierarchy of obligations. I was responsible for her and everything that went with it. Making love was like a marriage.

Kurt: I do the same thing. Once I get attached, everything that used to be a wanting to do something with my girlfriend turns into a "have to" and I feel the same way about her responsibility to me. I know it's in me. I feel very confused on this subject and it's a major part of my misery with women. That's the way I act all the time and I hate it. Funny thing is, I saw the same traits, exactly, in my father. I guess I never learned any other way.

Jean: I don't think that this applies to men only. I can say the same thing about my relationship with my husband. I liked him right away, from the very beginning. We were so compatible; I liked sharing so many things with him. And when we got married, I thought we'd just continue to share things in the same way. And then suddenly we were married and everything that I had been loving doing with him took on the connotation of a "should."

Kurt: You know, the idealized picture of marriage and families programmed in people's minds is bullshit. You're supposed to think like a couple, and a selfish connotation is placed on independent thought or action. Recently the whole movement toward togetherness and so-called family values has really messed things up even more. But when you get down to it, people are scared about their mate's choices and even their own right to make choices. They're afraid to stray beyond their usual confines. They prefer to feel victimized.

Raymond: I can see that my lack of freedom is self-imposed. This made me think about my childhood. It made me think that I was really trained not to be free. From the very beginning, my mother controlled my movements. First, she was just bigger, more powerful. Later she maneuvered me by making me feel guilty. I realize that my father didn't help the situation any. He thought I was a mama's boy and didn't like me very much. She had control over everything I did. I was very restricted and later I began to restrict myself.

Sharon: I can identify with what you are saying, Raymond. I can see that in a lot of ways I restrict myself. When you were describing your family situation, I thought that in my family, my parents made all of my decisions for me. Down to my mother picking out my clothes for me when I was in high school. There was no sense of me doing something for myself. I think that's why I feel guilty when I start to make choices that are my own. One feeling I know I grew up with was that anything I did that was separate from my parents was definitely interpreted as an act of aggression against them and against the family unit—even when, in my own mind, it had nothing to do with anybody but me.

Dr. Firestone: You know, that seems to be where that guilt feeling starts. It's because parents have a proprietary interest in their children. They treat them as objects or possessions in such a way that the children believe that they belong to their parents. From the very beginning, there is a sense of a merged identity.

Jean: I know I was supposed to reflect my parents' style. They didn't say it outright but I was supposed to have their point of view. My sister was much more rebellious and that upset them. And anytime that I would move away from them and would live a different life, they would reject me. But anytime I did anything that reminded them of their way, they would grab onto it and reward it. They would make a big deal out of it. And to this day, I feel they have no interest in seeing the person that I am.

Dr. Firestone: Getting back to couple relationships and marriage, people are so perverse because in attempting to nail down and secure a tie to another person, we lose the most important aspects of the relationship. We lose whatever is special and foolishly substitute form for substance.

Jean: You lose the ingredients that make it what it is. You destroy the ingredients, give up feelings, and you're left with empty actions. You're left with a hollow shell of yourself and you lose real contact with the other person.

Sharon: I'm afraid to assume that I can trust and depend on anyone. I never can trust that a person will continue to want me. My lack of trust starts to make me act desperate and aggressive: I have to make him want me. And that kills it. I'm beginning to drive my boyfriend crazy with my desperation and possessiveness. I hate it but I can't seem to stop it. And I don't want to ruin the relationship.

Dr. Firestone: Yes, people think that they will be left or abandoned if they don't manage to control or manipulate their mates. They assume that if they don't restrict their partners, they will be taken advantage of. They will be mistreated or rejected. They don't consider that if their partners were free, they might choose them. And the most meaningful choice is a free choice.

Janet: Why do people give a negative connotation to personal freedom when in fact it's such a positive characteristic?

Dr. Firestone: They assume that freedom predisposes anarchy or destructive behavior or a lack of human decency toward one another in close relationships.

Coping With Feelings of Competition and Jealousy

Competitive feelings are based on a natural desire for attention, affection, love, and sex. They reflect an honest striving for one's goals and are triggered when rivals are seeking the same goal or love object (R. Firestone & Catlett, 1999). Competitive feelings must be recognized and uncritically accepted as an intrinsic part of one's psychological makeup, just as anger is a natural response to frustration. Competitive feelings vary from irrational to reasonable. Competitiveness is appropriate when two people are pursuing the same goal because the outcome has actual consequences for both winner and loser. For example, when two individuals are applying for the same job or are pursuing the same love object, real issues are obviously involved, and winning becomes vitally important to both people. Competitive feelings intensify when one is losing in a competition and tend to diminish when one is winning. Whereas all competitive feelings are acceptable, actions based on these feelings are subject to moral considerations and to concerns about one's best interest.

Individuals who were deprived as children tend to have exaggerated feelings of competitiveness, whereas those who were raised in a nurturing environment generally feel comfortable with competition and rivalry. The major problem with competitive feelings lies in the fear and guilt that cause many people to deny or rationalize these feelings, to turn against themselves, and to retreat from pursuing their goals in rivalrous situations.

A certain degree of jealousy is a normal part of everyday life because people are naturally envious of those who achieve or have more than they do. However, feelings of jealousy often contain a primal element from childhood that must be distinguished from present-day realistic concerns. If one is able to deal with these powerful emotions at the primal level where they exist, one is better able to compete more honestly and is less hurtful in personal interactions. By acting out jealous impulses people go against their own best interests and in the process may destroy a potentially fulfilling relationship with someone they truly care about.

Jealous feelings become exaggerated when one retreats from one's natural competitiveness. When people are self-denying and withholding they are inclined toward morbid, jealous brooding over imagined or real losses rather than toward active competition. People who hold back loving feelings and sexuality from their loved ones feel at a disadvantage in competing with a rival and this also tends to intensify jealous reactions (R. Firestone et al., 2006).

Lastly, feelings of competition or even jealousy can sometimes serve a positive function in an intimate relationship. At times, the threat of losing a partner or of a partner's infidelity can provide an incentive for positive action, and the impetus to develop oneself, change negative characteristics, and become more appealing than a rival (Person, 1988).

As a result of sharing life at close quarters, competitive feelings naturally arose among the individuals in the friendship circle. They attempted to act on their belief in a principle of respect for each other's freedom and independence, although this sometimes conflicted with their fears of competition, jealousy, or potential loss. They learned to identify and challenge their primal reactions and to thereby behave with more integrity when faced with competitive situations. They have found that rivalry—even sexual rivalry and its compounding problems—is not as devastating as they had initially imagined. Difficult as it may be to believe, many of these men and women have maintained friendly relationships with their rivals.

Personal Freedom and Responsibility in Interpersonal Relationships—Open Versus Closed Relationships

> Love lets the other be, but with affection and concern. (Laing 1967, p. 58)
> Perhaps men and women were born to love one another, simply and genuinely, rather than to this travesty that we call love.... We have to realize that we are as deeply afraid to live and to love as we are to die. (p. 76)

In the friendship circle, where people were exposed to direct competition for love, sex, and acknowledgment, the general respect for personal freedom was accompanied by sensitivity to how people are hurt.

All of the issues that arose were dealt with in a supportive atmosphere of understanding and concern. There were few if any secrets; everything was talked about openly. This unusual combination of truthfulness and sensitivity to each other's areas of vulnerability has allowed this group of friends to survive where so many other attempts to create a positive way of life have failed.

Sexuality in the friendship circle was not significantly different from that of the culture at large; some couples were monogamous while others were not. The only difference was that these people were honest about their choices and behavior. Although it was painful to discuss competitiveness and sexual rivalry openly, people preferred this approach to the deception they observed everywhere around them. Without deception there was virtually no so-called cheating . Sexual relationships were handled forthrightly with kindness and respect for each other's feelings.

In the early days of the friendship circle during group discussions, people spoke about every sort of feeling: anger, fear, competitive aspects of life, and sexuality. In this open forum it was inevitable that they would speak about their sexual attractions toward one another. People felt good to express these feelings and were especially gratified to be acknowledged as men and women in regard to their sexual nature. Talking about this previously unacceptable topic was freeing and people felt energized from the open exchanges.

On a feeling level this subject presented no problem for the participants. But the question of how to deal with these feelings on an action level posed a more serious challenge. The original couples were confused and pained as they contemplated the issues involved. Everyone worried about where this was headed.

None of us wished to disrespect the boundaries or freedom of our mates but where were we to draw the line in relation to sexuality? Would we disapprove of our mates going out to lunch or dinner with a person of the opposite sex? Would we impose limits on their flirting, accepting a casual kiss or hug, holding hands, minor sexual contact, or sexual intercourse? It was difficult to find a logical limit or point of demarcation. For the most part we were comfortable up to when our mates' relationships with others might become romantic or sexual.

Janet: It's my body, and my sexuality can't belong to someone else. I believe that if you restrict your mate's sexual freedom, it's not any different than other restrictions that are disrespectful. Why would sexual freedom be different than any other kind of freedom?

> **Esther**: Yes, where can you draw the line? Can your mate have a professional association with a person of the opposite sex? Are the two allowed to become friends? Are they allowed to feel affection for each other? Can they embrace or kiss? Or maybe it's sexual intercourse that's the unforgivable act. What right do we have to limit or control our loved ones in any way?
>
> **Gus**: I never thought about it that way.
>
> **Deborah** (Gus's wife): I feel really strongly about this. I see sex simply as another form of communication between two people. So placing limits on another person's sexual freedom would be no different than restricting their freedom of speech. It's inconceivable to me.

In bringing up the subject Janet was not personally defending an extramarital relationship or intended sexual involvement; she was struggling to achieve autonomy in her personal life. Janet was typical of the women in the group who were more active than the men in supporting every form of freedom. Perhaps this was because their gender had been denied equal status and independence in society and they were therefore more sensitive to issues of suppression. These women were lively and determined and their strength and personal power stood out. The strong character of these women had a positive effect on the men in the friendship circle.

Currently, in this group of friends, each couple has independently determined whether their marriage will be open or closed. Most importantly, they have lived by their decisions. Whatever their patterns of sexuality, men and women value the open communication about their sexual feelings. They appreciate being free of old attitudes that supported being inhibited and secretive, guilty, and inward about sexuality or of the traditional practice of being dishonest in the name of discretion. In our book *Fear of Intimacy* (R. Firestone & Catlett, 1999), we discussed open versus closed marriages:

> The issue of open versus closed sexual relationships for couples is quite complicated, no matter which policy is chosen. Generally speaking, it is unwise to be restrictive in a close personal relationship because this tends to foster resentment in one's partner. Yet most people are unable to cope with a partner's sexual freedom without suffering considerable pain. This creates a serious dilemma for most couples. The significant factor is that the partners first agree on a basic policy that is respectful of each other's feelings and desires, and then stand by their principles. The agreed-on principles should not be violated, or at least the partners should discuss changing the boundaries prior to making any alterations....

Deep and intimate relationships tend to be the most fulfilling when they are not restrictive. Marriages and other close personal associations that are based on respect for each other's independence and freedom are continually evolving rather than static. The *ideal* relationship would be open rather than an exclusive or closed system.

One negative effect of a closed attitude about outside sexual relationships is that in the process of relegating one's own sexuality to another...a person often becomes less sexually appealing.... As a result of this type of exclusivity, people often report a decline in their sexual desire and a deterioration in their overall sexuality with one another. In truth, this happens to many couples.

To further complicate matters, many people agree to the principle of fidelity, but later violate the agreement. This deception or violation of trust can have a more damaging effect on the relationship than the sexual infidelity itself. In this sense affairs cannot be considered to be morally wrong if the partners are open and honest and if the affair does not cause either party undue distress. On the other hand, an affair can be considered morally wrong when secrecy and deception are involved because the personal integrity of the individual partners is even more important than the sexual issues.

In our society, monogamous relationships are perceived to offer more security, certainty, and possibility of long-lasting love than nonexclusive relationships or open marriages. Many men and women are possessive and controlling of their mates in an attempt to compensate for feelings of inadequacy and fears of being in a competitive situation.... Most people in contemporary society are well aware that sexuality is pervasive in a variety of situations and cannot be excluded without blocking other aspects of one's life experience. (pp. 88–89)

In considering the restrictions imposed by an exclusive relationship, one finds that the manipulation and control people exercise extend well beyond the sexual arena. These maneuvers extend to many other facets of life together. To substitute obligation for free choice is to give up a vital function that is uniquely human. The best situation for individuals in a couple's relationship is to sustain their freedom of choice and not limit or place demands on each other through unnecessary rules and restrictions. However, there are many important factors to consider. Although placing limitations on one another generally has a negative prognosis for the relationship, this sacrifice may be worth it in some cases. For example, if a person perceives that an outside sexual affair would cause his or her mate excessive pain because of his or her exceptional vulnerability, it might be more appropriate and effective to remain exclusive. "Although restrictive attitudes in marriage violate the policy of supporting the freedom and independence of one's partner...this departure from the principle may still be workable. The concession or compromise is more likely to work when other strong positives are operant in the relationship and all other freedoms are respected" (Firestone & Catlett, 1999, pp. 89–90).

Several years ago, Dean, 47, business executive and father of two grown children, recorded his feelings about this subject:

> The free-flowing openness that exists among my friends has allowed me to develop close relationships with many women. These relationships, although not specifically sexual, are very fulfilling to me. I have learned that the expectation (and demand) that one person can, or should, fill your every need is a weight that few relationships can bear. Personal freedom, especially sexual freedom, is a constantly evolving, extremely important issue, with each person in the group of friends left to resolve it in their own way. The balance between freedom and focus, of exploring versus retreating, is complicated and so individual. There is no *one size fits all* solution.
>
> Currently I am only sexually involved with Cheryl, and I really enjoy her companionship, but I feel so lucky to be able to know and openly appreciate so many women. It is impossible to imagine this circle of friends developing over the years without this belief in personal freedom, best exemplified by my friends Bob and Tamsen, individually and in the example of their relationship. When I think of them in this regard, I am reminded of something that James Baldwin wrote: "Very few people believe in love and even fewer people believe in freedom. And the world works on the passion and efforts of those few remarkable people who believe in both."

CONCLUSION

Learning to love is a lifelong endeavor; therefore people should not criticize themselves as they strive to further develop their capacity for giving and receiving love. First, individuals who have the goal of becoming a more loving person need to accept and feel for themselves, that is, to value themselves and their experiences. Secondly, they need to increase their tolerance of having loving responses directed toward them instead of warding off a partner's love and affection. Thirdly, they need to trust that they can have their needs met by another person. This involves taking a chance on asking for what they want and need.

People who have been hurt in their earliest relationships find it difficult to trust that they can have their wants and needs met by other people. It is natural for people to try to protect themselves if they have been hurt in the past. However, the defenses that they erected as a protection have become the major barriers to letting love into their lives.

People can overcome basic limitations in their love lives even though there are powerful resistances, but they must have the courage and persistence to break with core defenses. In order to be free themselves, they must cope with painful emotions and sometimes revive traumatic memories from the past. They must also learn how to sweat through the anxiety that is inherent in combining genuine love and physical intimacy. In doing so, they come to realize, on a deep emotional level, that they can gradually increase their tolerance for love and being loved without being overwhelmed by primitive fears and existential anxieties.

We have expanded our definition of love to include a love of nature, beauty, and aesthetics, and a feeling of awe when regarding the wonders of the world and the miracle and mystery of life. Schneider (2007) described awe as "the cultivation of the basic human capacity for the thrill and anxiety of living or, more formally, the cultivation of the capacity for humility and boldness, reverence and wonder before creation" (p. 372). Like love, "awe mitigates against alienation" (p. 373). We appreciate the value of seeking beauty in life. The places where we have traveled, the backdrop of our lives, our personal interactions, and adventures all involve an aesthetic appreciation and love of natural wonders. We have learned that the circumstances that we create around us and the tasteful quality of our surroundings have a profound effect upon our feelings. We recognize that the manner in which we create our interpersonal and physical environment is an outward expression that reflects a basic positive attitude toward ourselves. In achieving practical success, we have collected beautiful things and enjoy their aesthetic qualities but are not materialistic or overly acquisitive.

In placing a high value on friendship and loving life, we have endeavored to form a lifestyle that has a balance between work and play. We have a serious work ethic but take our travels and vacationing equally seriously. There is also a balance between living life earnestly with depth of feeling and enjoying laughter and lightness. In dealing with important life and death issues, we have come to appreciate the value of love and loving in all of its aspects.

A poem about love:
LETTER

Because I am shy of death
and scared to admit she's dying,
I do not write *I miss you.*
    -afraid of the implications:
    The *I* turning to *I'll* to *I will.*
No *See you soon,*
can't wait. My well wishes
come out loaded or flat.
    Not wanting to hurt her,
    Not wanting her to hurt.
I write *I love you* above my name,
It gives me away.
I cross out the *I*, and then the *you.*
    Love unmoored meaning nothing
    A nothing to outlast us all.
                —Lena Firestone

NOTES

1. In his theory of eternal recurrence, Nietzsche ("The Birth of Tragedy," 1871/1956; and *Thus Spake Zarathustra*, 1885/2005) stressed the importance of seeking a meaningful existence in the form of a significant life project. His metaphoric concept indicated that a person has to make his or her life add up to something this time around, since it will be forever repeated.

13   Dimensions of a Meaningful Life

In the depth of winter, I finally learned that there was within me an invincible summer.

—*Albert Camus*

To achieve an authentic existence, one *must* make a passionate commitment to realize the possibilities and the potentials. One must also make choices and act on them. In other words, in order to create meaning in life by means of constructing an authentic existence, individuals have to recognize that they are free to make choices, decisions, and to act on them.

—*Israel Orbach, "Existentialism and Suicide" (2008, p. 284)*

The pursuit of a life of meaning, while not a solution to the death problem, is a valuable by-product of facing the anxiety, despair, and dread surrounding the existential dilemma. Existentialists have long asserted that meaning and meaninglessness are fundamental elements of the human condition that exert a powerful influence on people's thoughts, feelings, and actions. According to Wong (1998):

> The loss of traditions and traditional values has made the individual's quest for meaning far more difficult than it was in the past. In the postmodern society of disintegration and diminished expectations, nihilism and despair have replaced purpose and hope.... At certain points in life, everyone has

questioned what sustains their being and what makes life worth living.... Yet, mainstream psychology has been equivocal and hesitant in responding to the crisis of meaning. (p. 396)

However, in the field of clinical psychology, theorists Battista and Almond (1973), Frankl (1946/1959, 1967), Maslow (1968, 1971), Wong (2008), Yalom (1980), and others have written a great deal about the concept and have described potentially measurable variables associated with the search for meaning. For example, in summarizing Camus's position, cited above, Yalom wrote: "Camus started from a position of nihilism...and soon generated...a system of personal meaning—a system that encompasses several clear values and guidelines for conduct: courage, prideful rebellion, fraternal solidarity, love, secular saintliness" (p. 428).

In addition to assuming a certain attitude or stance toward existential issues of aloneness, meaninglessness, freedom, responsibility, and death, one must take concerted action in order to achieve a meaningful life interpersonally, vocationally, and socially in his or her world. Dedication and commitment are necessary. As Yalom (1980) emphasized: "Many have noted the rich connotations of the word 'will.' It conveys determination and commitment—'*I will do it!*'...The will is concerned with *projects*.... Effective psychotherapy must focus on patients' *project relationships* as well as on their *object relationships*" (p. 291).

In a relatively new discipline focused on delineating the parameters of personal meaning and a meaningful life, Wong (2008) and others have described a number of activities related to this type of commitment. These include formulating one's own system of values, conceptualizing, and then pursuing a life project or a major long-term goal or goals based on this value system, and composing a coherent narrative of one's life or life review. These activities tend to facilitate the establishment of what is meaningful for each individual and point toward the specific life goals that express or fulfill his or her unique personality and values. As Dobson and Wong (2008) emphasized: "To live authentically means to be truthful to one's core values and beliefs; it means to value what really matters and become what one is meant to be" (p. 179).

In pursuing a meaningful life, people in the friendship circle formulated goals and carried out many of the suggestions mentioned above. They conceptualized a *good life* not as a specific outcome, but rather as an ongoing psychological journey. Their purpose never was to arrive at a particular plateau in their personal development; rather it was to embark on a lifetime venture that challenged defenses and addictive, routine habit patterns. This process has enabled these individuals to feel increasingly alive, to remove obstacles to truthful communication and love, and to accomplish much in the real world.

In observing and documenting their efforts in this endeavor, the authors have gathered considerable information regarding both the type and quality of experience that is conducive to one's well-being, to a pursuit of transcendent goals, and to meaningful living. We found that living a better life involved a complex process of acculturation. In attempting to live without their customary defenses, these people have evolved toward a warmer, more growth-enhancing way of living and have gradually adapted to the vast difference between the new environment and the world they had known as children (R. Firestone, 1985).

Their positive growth and development were not achieved without substantial growing pains. In their discussions, men and women confronted their own personal demons and struggled with those of their friends. In their commitment to change, they had to suffer through states of anxiety and take the risks necessary for self-actualization. In the name of truth, they had to relinquish some of their most precious illusions. In striving to lead a more fulfilling life with a minimum of defenses and a close involvement with other persons, they felt an increased sense of vulnerability. In embracing life, they had a great deal to lose; they had to accept the painful fact of their mortality and this held a special poignancy (R. Firestone & Catlett, 2009).

WHAT CONSTITUTES A MEANINGFUL LIFE?

There is no particular formula for what constitutes a meaningful life for a given individual, nor should there be (R. Firestone et al., 2003). However, it is possible to ground one's goals for a better life in sound mental health principles that include an understanding of what it truly means to be a human being (P. Cohen & Cohen, 2001). The vision of a meaningful life, as described in this chapter, is the result of observing and working with individuals in the friendship circle as they have transformed their lives in ways that allowed them to more fully develop their human potential.

The essential qualities crucial to this development include: the ability to love and to feel compassion for self and others, the capacity for abstract reasoning and creativity, the ability to experience deep emotion, the desire for social affiliation, the ability to set goals and develop strategies to accomplish them, an awareness of existential concerns, the potential to experience the sacredness and mystery of life, and the search for meaning. Recent findings from neuroscience, anthropology, and evolutionary psychology suggest the existence of another fundamental human capacity, the ability to make moral judgments (R. Firestone & Catlett, 2009). For example, in *Moral Minds,* M. D. Hauser (2006) proposed that infants are born with the potentiality to form moral concepts, just as they are born with the potentiality to learn language.

As emphasized earlier, human beings have demonstrated their potential for aggression, greed, and territoriality throughout history, phenomena that led Sigmund Freud to postulate the death instinct as an explanatory principle. Theorists have tended to deemphasize the other qualities noted above that are uniquely and essentially human. The fundamental problem is that these singular human attributes are programmed out of the child to varying degrees, while frustration-derived aggression is cultured in. Because of their personal limitations and anxieties, most parents transform an extraordinary creature into an ordinary one. "They offer the gift of life and then unknowingly take it back. In attempting to socialize their children, they unwittingly deprive them of their humanity. Despite their best intentions, parents stamp out the very qualities that distinguish them from animals" (R. Firestone, 1990b, p. 318). As we have seen, challenging parental prohibitions through Voice Therapy is conducive to maintaining freedom of action in relation to self and others, and reawakens the desire to search for knowledge and meaning in life (R. Firestone, 1997a).

When we refer to *life-affirming* human potentialities in this chapter, we mean those capacities and personal qualities that enhance life for oneself and others, both qualitatively and materially. These qualities cannot be simplified or measured in quantitative terms alone. The process of developing these attributes is unique to each person's ability and circumstance. It involves having a desire for self-knowledge and self-understanding as well as a vision of one's future. If a meaningful life is fundamentally one in which we fully develop our human potentialities, describing what they are is central to our understanding of how to proceed.

Love, Compassion, and Empathy

As noted in the previous chapter, the most important life-affirming human quality may well be the ability to love—to feel compassion and empathy for, and express kindness, generosity, and tenderness toward, other people. In his writings, theologian Karl Rahner (cited by Halling,

1998) proposed that the love of another is the deepest act of which humans are capable. Empathy and compassion are based on the ability to understand another person's perspective—that is, to understand how we would feel if we were that person in any given situation.

Empathy originates in an ability to reflect on one's thoughts, feelings, and intentions and to find common ground in the experiences of others. The ability for self-reflection—that is, being able to examine one's own feelings and having an intuition regarding other people's intentions—is an ability that children develop at an early age (R. Firestone et al., 2003). Researchers Decety and Jackson (2006) have delineated three primary components of empathy, including "(a) an affective response to another person, which often, but not always, entails sharing that person's emotional state; (b) a cognitive capacity to take the perspective of the other person; and (c) emotional regulation.... Self-regulatory processes are at play to prevent confusion between self- and other feelings" (p. 54).

In expressing compassion, an individual would be warm, affectionate, and sensitive, particularly toward those people who are the closest. In addition, there would be a deep concern with the suffering of all people and an attempt made to alter their unfavorable circumstances. In his chapter "The Positive Psychology of Suffering and Tragic Optimism," Paul Wong (2007) proposed:

> Self-transcendence is demonstrated whenever we embrace suffering for the benefit of others.... On a more practical level stepping outside oneself to help others has been demonstrated to have an ameliorative effect. In the psychiatric rehabilitation field, for instance, it has become quite common for mental health consumers to become service providers. (pp. 245–246)

A person behaving in a compassionate manner looks for no reward beyond the gratification inherent in the act itself. Expressing love or kindness toward others is selfish in the best sense. When we take other people seriously, offer affection, and show concern for their needs separate from our own, we tend to have more positive self-regard.

Abstract Reasoning, Creativity, and the Ability to Experience Deep Emotion

Human beings have the unique capacity for abstract thought. However, because many people are damaged in their emotional development, their capacity to function creatively and intellectually is diminished and they have to deal with life in a shallow, concrete, or rigid manner. Therefore a basic aspect of an emotionally fulfilling life is using one's mental capacities to the fullest, in a way that supports rather than denies or degrades life.

Although many people believe that the capacity for thought is our most distinguishing feature, it is actually the interaction between thoughts and feelings that separates us from other animals. By utilizing the ability to access the moral emotions of compassion and empathy, people can choose to use their intelligence in an ethical manner. Examples of people utilizing their intelligence in combination with these moral emotions can be seen in the progress which has been made in procuring civil rights for members of minority groups; in the increase in respect for differences in gender, religious background, ethnicity, and sexual orientation; and in the rising emphasis on helping those in need. Humans have a remarkable ability to feel deeply, to reflect on their feelings, and to use both thought and feeling to create a full, alive, and meaningful life (R. Firestone & Catlett, 2009).

However, a convergence of findings from attachment research, neuroscience, and psychoanalysis has shown the negative impact that early aversive childhood experiences have on the child's developing mind and on his or her evolving ability to feel compassion and empathy, emotions that are necessary for moral development (Cozolino, 2002, 2006; Fonagy, 2001; Schore, 1994, 2003; Siegel, 1999, 2006). Other theorists, including Bohart and Greenberg (1997) and Decety and Moriguchi (2007), have described specific neurological pathways associated with emotional disorders that reflect deficits in empathy.

Social Affiliation

Human beings have a far greater capacity than any other animal for social affiliation—the ability to share thoughts, feelings, and experiences with others, as well as to nurture, support, and enjoy the companionship of their fellow beings. Developing this characteristic is vital to the achievement of a better life because individuals live, survive, learn, and grow only through interactions with others. Although it is of course possible to enjoy solitude and to use it creatively, it is the rare human being who lives in total isolation, and the even more unusual person who is able to do so successfully.

Becker (1971) largely agreed with developmental psychologists in observing that "The child begins to establish himself as an object of others before he becomes an executive subject" (p. 22). "Consciousness, then, is fundamentally a social experience: the infant must take the position of another object in order to gain a perception of the full dimensions of himself and his world. The child assumes the attitude of the succoring adult, and must then respond to meet that attitude" (p. 24). Social affiliation is generally crucial for one's personal development, even beyond the formative years. As Thorson and Laughlin (2008) noted when describing the loneliness suffered by many elderly people: "It is in isolation that we find the dark night of the human soul" (p. 276).

Because defenses so often impair one's ability to relate to others, it is particularly constructive to learn how to develop friendships. It is also valuable to create and sustain meaningful relationships with one's mate and children, and to have friendships with members of both genders. Living in harmony with family and friends in an atmosphere of congeniality is the professed goal of most people.

Imagination, Goal-Setting, and Planning for the Future

The ability to imagine, to conceptualize something new, and to plan for the future are uniquely human traits. Out of the potential for inventiveness and imagination come achievement, innovative and aesthetic pursuits, and material success. Becoming able to conceptualize the possibility of change is vital to both personal satisfaction and social progress (Maddi, 1998). Unfortunately, the ability to dream or picture the future can be damaged in the developing child by inadequate or destructive parenting (Brazelton & Greenspan, 2000).

Closely related to imagination is the capability to set goals and develop strategies to attain them. A critical aspect of a meaningful life involves envisioning goals that express one's unique identity and interests, as noted above, and then taking the actions necessary to realize these goals in the real world. Actively striving and competing for one's objectives rather than seeking satisfaction in fantasy alone is crucial to a fulfilling life. It is possible to reach one's full potential only when one's inner dreams and desires result in real accomplishments in the external world. It is also clear that success and achievement will have little personal value to an individual who has not developed his or her other human potentialities—that is, the capacity for feeling, loving, and social affiliation (R. Firestone et al., 2003).

An Awareness of Existential Realities

Our ability to imagine has not only afforded us remarkable accomplishments, but also burdened us with the horror of being able to conceptualize our own death. As emphasized throughout this work, the defended individual, faced with the fact of personal mortality, will tend to progressively retreat from living in a futile attempt to take control over death and to avoid the anxiety of the ultimate separation from oneself and loved ones. On the other hand, facing issues of mortality can imbue life with a special meaning in relation to its finality. Imagining the end of life in an undefended state of mind can heighten the awareness of the preciousness of each moment, increasing the likelihood of people investing more of themselves in their relationships. It can spur them to greater creativity and make them more compassionate toward other people who share their fate.

Spirituality and Mystery

All people possess the ability to have spiritual experiences that transcend the satisfaction of material needs and to sense mysteries that elude human understanding. At many points on the journey through life, people encounter events that bring out a deep appreciation of nature and the unknown, and generate spiritual experiences that evoke deep emotional responses. Tomer and Eliason (2008) have portrayed such events as "peak experiences" that are associated with "feelings of wonder, surprise, awe, and so on" (p. 9) and that pose questions about existence that are unanswerable by Aristotelian logic. William James (1902/2004) argued that "these peak experiences should not be conceptualized, however, as including only 'mystical states of consciousness,' either of Eastern or Western tradition" (cited in Tomer & Eliason, 2008, p. 10). Indeed, many people of no particular religious persuasion have reported having experiences that inspire awe and that at times have been life-transforming (R. May, 1983). It is when this search for meaning and spiritual awareness takes people to the edge of human understanding, where they accept the ultimate mystery of their lives and the limitations of science and rationality, that they know at the most profound level what it means to be fully human.

In a chapter titled "Courage and Transcendence," Paul Tillich (1952) articulated his view of the transcendent experience and posed the question as to "whether and how mysticism can be the source of the courage to be" (p. 154). "Theism in all its forms is transcended in the experience we have called absolute faith" (p. 179). "Only if the God of theism is transcended can the anxiety of doubt and meaninglessness be taken into the courage to be" (p. 180). Tillich went on to differentiate his use of the term *absolute faith* from other more religious forms of faith. According to Tillich, absolute faith does not lead to:

> Something separated and definite, an event which could be isolated and described. It is always a movement in, with, and under other states of the mind. It is the situation on the boundary of man's possibilities. It *is* this boundary. Therefore it is both the courage of despair and the courage in and above every courage. It is not a place where one can live, it is without the safety of words and concepts, it is without a name, a church, a cult, a theology. But it is moving in the depth of all of them. It is the power of being, in which they participate and of which they are fragmentary expressions.... *The courage to be is rooted in the God who appears when God has disappeared in the anxiety of doubt.* (pp. 182–183)

As individuals learn to accept the uncertainty and ambiguity of life, they may come to believe that there are no absolute truths to be discovered. They may determine that wherever there is an absence of fact, they have the right to choose and embrace their own beliefs regarding the origins and nature of life. Without knowledge, there is room for faith, and faith can take many forms. Some embrace traditional beliefs while other individuals tend to seek the "god" within themselves and develop their own belief system rather than accepting more formal religious teachings (R. Firestone et al., 2003).

The Search for Meaning

Viktor Frankl (1946/1959) has asserted that human beings are meaning-seeking creatures.

> Ultimately, man should not ask what the meaning of his life is, but rather he must recognize that it is *he* who is asked. In a word, each man is questioned by life; and he can only answer to life by *answering for* his own life; to life he can only respond by being responsible. (p. 131)

Wong (1998) and Orbach (2008) have elucidated Frankl's three types of values by which individuals can discover meaning: the creative, experiential, and attitudinal.

> Creative values are based on what an individual contributes to the world in terms of personal achievement and deeds. Experiential values refer to what the person receives from the world by means of experiencing or encountering

someone or something. Attitude values can lead to meaning by taking a stand toward unavoidable suffering or unchangeable situations. (Orbach, p. 286)

In his model of Existential Analysis, Langle (2007) further expanded Frankl's Logotherapy to encompass discrete actions and activities:

> Life's transitory nature puts the question of the meaning of our existence before us: I am here for what purpose? Three things are needed: a field of activity, a structural context and a value to be realized in the future. We can ask ourselves practical questions, such as: Is there a place where I feel needed, where I can be productive? Do I see and experience myself in a larger context that provides structure and orientation to my life; where I want integration? Is there anything that should still be realized in my life?... The sum of these experiences adds up to the meaning of life and leads to a sense of fulfillment. (p. 53)

We agree with Frankl's (1946/1959) assertion that "success, like happiness, cannot be pursued; it must ensue, and it only does so as the unintended side-effect of one's personal dedication to a cause greater than oneself or as the by-product of one's surrender to a person other than oneself" (p. 17). In a previous work (R. Firestone, 1988), the first author, stated:

> We must conclude that there is no hidden significance to life that may be discovered; rather it is only each individual's investment of himself, his feelings, his creativity, his interests, and his personal choice of people and activities, that is special. Indeed, we imbue experience with meaning through our own spirit rather than the opposite, and our priorities express our true identity. (p. 272)

There are numerous ways that people find meaning in life: through their personal relationships, work, creativity, dedication to a humanitarian cause, or love. When individuals are involved in transcendent goals, they gain a sense of purpose and of valuing themselves that cannot be achieved by any other means (R. Firestone, 1997a) (Notes 1, 2).

LIVING A MEANINGFUL LIFE

> The roots of social order are in our heads, where we possess the instinctive capacities for creating not a perfectly harmonious and virtuous society, but a better one than we have at present. (Ridley, 1996, p. 264)

Each dimension of a meaningful life challenges people's resistance to making changes or progressing in their lives. Individuals tend to have resistance to planning corrective experiences and following through with behaviors that increase self-esteem. They may also be reluctant to conceptualize definitive goals and take specific actions to move in a direction that brings out their positive attributes and traits. Similarly, they may find it difficult to conceptualize their own ideals and values or to conduct their lives according to these principles. Nevertheless, the following concepts are considered by the authors to be the essential building blocks for a meaningful life.

Formulating One's Own Values and Ethical Principles

Of course, philosophical systems of morality are complex enterprises, conjoining a number of quite different tasks…. All of them involve a theory about what is best and worst in human nature, an account of how to bypass or transform the worst so as to allow the best to flourish. (Rorty, 1993, p. 29)

As a result of our attempts to live a more alive, thoughtful, and meaningful life, an implicit value system has evolved based on psychological principles and an elucidation of behaviors that have a positive rather than a negative effect on an individual's sense of well-being. These behaviors counter self-critical attitudes, increase self-esteem, and tend to improve overall adjustment. The values described below were derived from a sensitive understanding of human nature and an awareness of psychological defenses that limit an individual's psychological development (R. Firestone & Catlett, 2009).

Personal Integrity

Integrity has been defined as "a quality or state of being complete or undivided" (Woolf, 1981, p. 595). When people are true to themselves and their ideals, they experience a feeling of being unified and whole. Being in touch with oneself on an emotional level is fundamental to this sense of being integrated. An individual who possesses integrity tends to be at ease with him or herself, whether alone or in the company of others. According to Boss (2004), integrity is a unifying principle, a basic disposition that overrides other virtues: "Without integrity, we are not truly virtuous because there is still disharmony within ourselves" (p. 411). Babbitt (1996) emphasized the fact that emotional emancipation from one's family-of-origin is a prerequisite for developing a high level of integrity: "A notion of being 'true to oneself' cannot by itself explain intuitions about personal integrity for people who are not individuated as people at all" (p. 114).

As noted above, moral courage is necessary in order to maintain one's personal integrity, particularly in adverse circumstances. Ellyn Bader (personal communication, 1999) has observed that in a personal relationship, one must be brave enough to thoroughly know oneself, including one's deepest self-doubts and inner demons, and courageous enough to directly communicate these feelings. Peterson and Seligman (2004) have categorized integrity as a virtue that is secondary to courage, noting that courage is dependent on "emotional strengths that involve the exercise of will to accomplish goals in the face of opposition, external or internal" (p. 29).

Honesty

Honesty is closely related to the concept of integrity and to communications that are direct and truthful. Bonhoeffer (1949/1955) asserted that "'Telling the truth'. . . is not solely a matter of moral character; it is also a matter of correct appreciation of real situations and of serious reflection upon them. . . . Telling the truth is, therefore, something which must be learnt" (p. 359). The kind of honesty described here is more personal than intellectual, more psychological than philosophical, and more heartfelt than thought out, and applies most directly to being nondeceptive and nonduplicitous in one's communications.

Generosity

Altruism and generosity are actions through which compassion and empathy are expressed. Generosity is a sensitive, feeling response to another person's wants and needs. Generous actions provide others with what is necessary in an understanding and timely manner. However, offering help in a way that causes another to feel small or indebted cannot be thought of as authentic generosity.

It is also generous to accept love rather than deflect it. The authors have formulated three steps involved in an appropriate response to a generous act. The first is being open to accepting help and permitting someone else to meet one's needs; the second involves expressing genuine appreciation verbally; and the third entails finding ways to respond or give back with thoughtful or loving actions. In this regard, it is not necessary to respond in kind but rather in a manner that reflects one's own nature and capabilities and the specific needs or concerns of the recipient. Involving oneself in each step of this cyclical process of giving and receiving counteracts critical voices about oneself.

Research has shown that altruism can also have a beneficial effect on an individual's physical health. For example, one study by Brown, Nesse, Vinokur, and Smith (2003) showed that people who provided emotional support to their spouses lived longer than those who received emotional support. True generosity not only involves looking after one's loved ones and their priorities but also extends to others in the larger society.

Independence

Independence can be considered an ideal or value because it is an energy source, offering vitality to, rather than draining energy from, others and the society at large. Overly dependent individuals place a burden and responsibility on other people, particularly their partners and families. Independent, autonomous individuals are neither submissive nor defiant in relation to external influences. As a result, they gradually evolve and formulate their own value systems, conceptualizing their own goals and priorities in life. The autonomous individual accepts responsibility for his or her own life and problems rather than prevailing upon others. Those who take power over their own lives, and develop their own values and ideals, generally have a positive effect on their interpersonal world.

Tolerance and Inclusiveness

Being tolerant implies open-mindedness, understanding, benevolence, and goodwill toward one's fellows. Tolerance begins with an accepting attitude toward oneself and extends outward. It also implies being free enough from vanity and illusions of invulnerability to be able to make mistakes without self-recrimination or destructive self-attacks.

People who are accepting of themselves tend to be more accepting of others. They are more inclusive and are more likely to be free of prejudice, biases, and sexual stereotyping. They take a strong position against sexist, racist, and fanatic religious attitudes, which lead to discrimination and cause emotional and physical suffering to large numbers of innocent people. Parents with prejudicial attitudes tend to encourage the same in their children toward other families, groups, and cultures who approach life differently. These distinctions support core beliefs that individuals who do not look *like we do,* who do not act *like we do,* are inferior, worthless, immoral, or even dangerous. The result of this early programming and its extension into society has a drastic negative effect on relationships and sets groups of people against one another.

Tolerance and inclusiveness are values of paramount importance in that the future of our civilization may well depend on our developing a nonprejudicial, nonbiased view of people who have different beliefs, customs, and ethnic backgrounds. For much the same reason, exclusiveness is a dangerous posture to adopt, especially in our modern world. As Henry Miller (1947) observed: "Wherever there is the jealous urge to exclude there is the menace of extinction. I see no nation on earth at present which has an all-inclusive view of things" (p. xxii). Similarly, the philosopher Peter Singer (2004) has pointed out that: "We need to ask whether it will, in the long run, be better if we continue to live in the imagined communities we know as nation-states, or if we begin to consider ourselves as members of an imagined community of the world" (p. 171).

Building a peaceful world would require a rejection of illusions of belonging to the best family, living in the greatest nation, or believing in the single true religion. It would also require rejecting all aspects of our superiority or omniscience. In his writing, Lifton (2003) has called attention to Albert Camus's assertion that "to live and to die as humans we need 'to refuse to be a god,' which means embracing 'thought which recognizes limits'" (p. 199). "Without the need for invulnerability, everyone would have much less to be afraid of" (p. 191).

It is difficult to convey a feeling for what is involved in the evolution of values and ideals as part of one's pursuit of a meaningful existence without describing how ordinary people live it on an everyday basis. For example, Dean, 56, whose journal excerpt appeared in chapter 12, portrayed his personal journey toward this goal as follows:

> Dean: Reflecting on my life since I took that "road less traveled" so long ago, I clearly found what I was looking for, and more. But I wonder what difference did it actually make? How would I be different if I had made other choices? A quick snap shot: I am 56 years old, in good health, emotionally and physically. Divorced but living with a woman whose companionship I have enjoyed for over 10 years. I have two grown children who I am close to and am now a grandfather. I have been relatively successful in business and am comfortable financially.

I am actively involved in a nonprofit organization that promotes psychological principles, produces educational materials for mental health professionals, and conducts public forums on violence and suicide prevention in our local community. I am a participant in ongoing discussion groups that develop and exchange philosophical and psychological ideas and personal feelings. I have written songs that surprise me with their feeling and insight and that seem to touch my friends deeply. I have traveled extensively and seen many beautiful and interesting places. For such a solitary child, I have many friends and am a valued member of my friendship circle. I have personal relationships with many men, women, and children. By any measure, one would say I am living a meaningful life.

The above is surely true, but the real story mostly lies below the surface "facts." Each of the glibly stated details was achieved in increments over the years with many disappointments and disillusionments along the way; every hard fought victory to escape the pull of the past was accompanied by unexpected, painful retreats. Whatever would have become of me, it is clear that without the support, the honesty and the inspiration of my friends, I would not be the person I am today.

I have come a long way from the depressed, confused young man who first met my friends so long ago. Though older in years, I am much younger in many ways than that callow youth. More hopeful, more open, less fearful. Still plagued by the demons, but learning to see myself and others with compassion and humor. Though far along this road, I am still excited and curious about what lies ahead. I am not religious, but my experiences here have made me more spiritual, more humbled by the mystery of existence. There is a Spanish saying that "the Road to Paradise is Paradise." Facing alone, and together, the joys and sorrows of everyday life, the jokes and romance, the frustrations, fears, and sadness, the unknown that waits around the next bend, facing it all with humor, honesty, compassion, kindness, and courage is, to me, the ideal—an authentic and fulfilling way of being and living.

Formulating and Taking Action to Achieve Meaningful Goals in Life

According to Maslow (1954), people have a built-in hierarchy of motives. They are motivated by physiological "needs for food, etc.; ... by needs for safety, protection, and care; by needs for gregariousness and for affection-and-love relations; by needs for respect...; and by a need for self-actualization or self-fulfillment of the idiosyncratic and species-wide potentialities of the individual person" (p. 2). Maslow also listed as "higher-level" the need for knowledge and understanding as well as "impulses to beauty, symmetry, and possibly to simplicity, completion, and order, which we may call aesthetic needs" (p. 2).

As Yalom (1980) has emphasized: "Self-actualized individuals, according to Maslow, dedicate themselves to self-transcendent goals. They may work on large-scale global issues—such as poverty, bigotry, or ecology—or, on a smaller scale, on the growth of others with whom they live" (p. 440). Orbach (2008) has made a distinction between lower-order meaning and higher-order meaning in differentiating everyday needs from transcendent goals. He cited Baumeister's (1991) argument that "desperate people do not ponder the meaning of life [high-order meaning] but search for needs fulfillment (low-order meaning)" (Orbach, p. 297). Interestingly, Baumeister also claimed that "people are capable of living happily without any coherent/explicit life philosophy.... This is because people can have meaning in their lives, even if they are incapable of articulating it" (Orbach, p. 296).

Setting Goals and Moving Toward Achievement

Many people in the friendship group have found it beneficial to identify short-term as well as long-term goals related to their personal development. They specified the undesirable traits they wished to change as well as the positive traits they wished to further develop. They also found it valuable to define career or vocational goals and goals for an intimate relationship and family life. This helped them prioritize everyday activities so as to move toward these goals. It was also helpful for individuals to identify the critical voices that emerged as they moved toward their goals and broke withholding patterns and other defenses that interfered with their progress (Note 3).

According to Emmons (1997), "On the one hand, goal commitment and positive expectations of anticipated outcomes can facilitate goal pursuit. On the other hand, high levels of threat appraisal and inter-goal conflict can interfere with goal pursuit and strengthen negative affect following failure to attain the goal" (cited by Mikulincer & Florian, 2008, p. 55).

As the people in the friendship group identified and began to pursue their goals, they discussed the resistance they encountered to achieving them. Some had difficulty conceptualizing their goals because they had been hurt early in life in their basic feeling about themselves and had turned against their own wants and desires—a fundamental part of their identity as human beings. Others seemed resistant to taking the practical steps necessary to achieve a stated goal. This was because, as noted earlier, many individuals who have suffered rejection and deprivation come to rely excessively on fantasy to gratify their wants and needs rather than seeking satisfaction in goal-directed behavior. Still others were exercising what existential psychologists (Rank, Nietzsche, Yalom) refer to as *negative will* or *counter-will* in relation to fulfilling their aspirations or accomplishing their personal life goals. For example, in a lecture "Neurosis as a Failure in Creativity," Rank (1935, quoted in Kramer, 1996) asserted:

> Instead of affirming or asserting his will, the neurotic has to find an excuse to prove to himself as well as to others his inability or incapability. *Instead of saying, "I don't want to do that," he says, "I cannot do it, because I am afraid or feel guilty."* This formulation contains the whole problem of neurosis in a nutshell. (p. 254) To the neurotic, the attainment of any definite goal means the end, in the sense of death. (p. 256)

Later in the same lecture, Rank further elucidated his concept of *negative will*, which the present author sees as similar in some respects to the antiself system. Rank suggested a solution to this impasse, that is, the patient needs to become creative in imagining life projects and in taking action toward fulfilling them:

> The neurotic type starts by saying no to life itself, and furthermore he manifests his rebellion against it by further noes, that is by setting his negative will against the laws of nature, or practically against his own *being....*
> And no relief...can be achieved...without therapeutically changing this fundamental attitude of a type who tries constantly to dominate nature within himself instead of without. In using creative imagination—instead of negative will—in order to change the world according to his own ideals, lies the essential difference between success and failure. (Kramer, 1996, p. 258)

The Therapeutic Value of Friendship

Developing a congenial, harmonious friendship with another person or persons represents a meaningful goal for most people. As the author noted in a previous work, "Neurosis originates through a social process and can potentially be altered in a social milieu" (R. Firestone, 1985, p. 31).

People in the longitudinal study identified their need for social affiliation and friendship as major goals in their lives and as crucial to their personal development. Through their shared endeavors, they have created a way of living that counters neurotic tendencies to relive the past. In the process, they found that it was virtually a necessity to share their struggle with friends who were supportive of their individuality and personal freedom. The friendships they have sustained over three decades have been a major factor in their achieving a more life-affirming existence.

Friendship, in contrast to a fantasy bond, is characterized by a lack of exclusiveness or possessiveness. Because friendships are based on free choice, they provide companionship without obligation. Friendship inevitably brings out aspects of an individual's personality that he or she may not have been aware of. It increases self-awareness and self-knowledge and encourages an individual to emerge from an inward, defended posture, enhancing one's feeling of self-worth and self-esteem. Social scientist Block (1980) emphasized that: "The experience of friendship...is not a mere luxury. For optimal functioning, it is an imperative" (p. 211).

In a previous work (R. Firestone & Catlett, 1989), the authors described friendship as "A dynamic, honest communication with feelings of respect and compassion between people" (p. 225). What makes friendship special and therapeutic is principally the sense of equality, common interests, and open communication. There are few subjects that are taboo with friends in their talking with each other. Friends tend to relate as independent individuals, with considerable give and take in terms of gratifying each other's needs. They refrain from playing roles or trying to apply conventional rules or impositions. As a result, people feel left alone to pursue their own priorities. A genuine friendship involves closeness without a false illusion of safety or security and thus enables an individual to experience the truth of his or her separate existence (R. Firestone, 1985).

It is of particular value for a person to have a close friendship with a member of each sex. The mutual sharing of ideas and feelings with both a man and a woman leads to an unusual perspective that one cannot achieve from just one or the other relationship.

The people in the longitudinal study found meaning and derived self-esteem from their ability to positively affect the lives of their friends as well as the lives of their mates and children. In furthering the personal development of the individual, these friends have helped one another expand their boundaries and achieve success in many areas. The process of sharing adventure, travel, and work has been essential to people's sustaining their long-term friendships. They have challenged and inspired one another to be bolder in conceiving and realizing adventuresome projects. Because they have been willing to face their pain and to talk honestly with others about their feelings, these people have built enduring friendships. The essential feature of their friendships is not simply the fact that they spend time together, but that they do so in a truthful, sensitive, and undefended manner (R. Firestone et al., 2003).

The following are excerpts from an interview about friendship. These descriptions best portray the therapeutic value of this type of camaraderie.

Kathy (26): When I met my friends for the first time, I was struck by the sweetness, the warmth, the inviting feelings. It seemed like everyone was mixed together. There were harmonious exchanges between children and adults, and adults and adults. One of the most touching moments that I remember was one day we all were together and one of the children had been feeling bad. He talked about what had happened between his mother and him. He was able to express his feelings and was listened to and seen. It really gave me a sense that there was definitely individuation and free speech amongst these friends, and that each person was listened to and seen, which is what I had wanted my whole life.

Colin (16): The way my friends treat each other is much sweeter and much friendlier than other people I've met. They really think about other people's feelings and they're very sensitive and caring of other people. I think that because of growing up this way, I've tried to do the same type of thing. I remember once when I was about 3 years old, being carried around on somebody's shoulders and looking around the room. It was a very sad moment, I could see different people's faces, some were sad and some were crying. It made a big impression on me. It made me realize how much people feel for each other, seeing how sweet people were to each other.

Joan (40): One turning point in my life was when I became friends with Tamsen. She's simply a very kind and intelligent person, very straightforward, very strong, a good friend, and a very fun person to be around. It became a deep friendship where we could really talk about very personal things. The friendship allowed me to see the kind of woman I could become, because I'd never known a woman who could be strong and attractive to men and humorous and honest.

Lynn (23): I was raised to know that communicating is talking, listening, being open to what you hear, and knowing that you're being heard. One thing that helped my friends and me in growing up was learning how to communicate better with each other. When we were about 13, we started having talks with my older brother Steve. I felt really close to everyone who went to those talks. I feel that it helped me learn how to express myself better and to communicate my feelings to my friends and other people.

Tamsen (51): I think a meaningful life is one that offers people a chance to really be themselves, to find out who they are and what they like to do.

It's also a life where they can come to know who somebody else is. For two people to really make contact with each other is an incredible experience. I believe in people being friends and sharing life. I think that in that, they become even more aware of themselves, become more themselves.

Amanda (56): Having a close relationship with many people has challenged my defenses because we talk openly and honestly with each other. Within this kind of friendship, there's a level of understanding yourself, of understanding the things that kill your spirit that you weren't even aware of. I had no idea of the ways that I defended myself, the ways I guarded against my life, the ways I protected myself, that limited my life and my spirit. I never had any friends; I didn't know it really mattered. I know it may sound naïve, but friendship, true friendship is so therapeutic. I mean, you can experience yourself in a new way. You can have a life.

The Importance of Sexuality

Healthy sexuality, which is a natural extension of affectionate, friendly feelings, is a simple and pleasurable combination of attitudes and actions that involves giving and receiving for both parties. If uncorrupted by negative social prohibitions, ignorance, stereotypic thinking, childhood trauma, or sexual abuse, people would not be limited in their capacity to enjoy this natural function (R. Firestone et al., 2006).

Issues of sexuality were a primary concern for the group of friends and every aspect of sexual life has at one time or another been the subject of group discussions. These people place a significant value on their sexuality, and view sexual expression as a positive offering. There is a clean-minded attitude toward the body and sexuality; tough or crude attitudes toward sex typically manifested in dirty jokes or other sneering comments on the subject are infrequent.

Within the larger society, people rarely receive real or accurate feedback about their sexuality. As a result, they are open to all sorts of misconceptions about themselves in relation to their sexuality. By contrast, the individuals in the friendship circle have had the benefit of exploring this subject matter in depth. They found that if sex is uncomplicated and easy, it contributes much to their general sense of well-being. Conversely, they learned that when sex is complicated by underlying issues, it can have a negative effect on their overall functioning.

People came to understand that although they feel especially gratified when sex is combined with love, they often experience a good deal of internal resistance to the combination. Although a relationship that is both sexually satisfying and emotionally close is highly desirable, it is difficult to attain, because intimate sexual relating is a significant intrusion into psychological defenses. These people discovered that trusting another person and allowing themselves to be vulnerable on an intimate level often aroused considerable sadness. Many reported that they were saddened or cried during a particularly close sexual experience. They felt deeply moved to be gratified by another person, yet were painfully aware of how much they stood to lose.

As men and women became more cognizant of these issues, they expanded their boundaries and experienced more satisfaction in life. They gradually changed many of the ways they had limited or controlled expressions of affection and sexuality in their intimate relationships. In essence, they came to perceive sexual intimacy as "a way of being together," as Sam Keen (1997) described it, that is, "not having (mutual possession) or doing (exercising skills) but being present and vulnerable in the fullness of [one's] being" (p. 207).

People can learn to tolerate the anxiety evoked by the combination of love and sexuality and sustain a real closeness with their partner. In strengthening their own point of view in relation to their sexuality, they can develop more fulfilling sexual relationships than they previously thought possible (R. Firestone et al., 2006).

Transcendent Goals

Akin to how Maslow (1954) delineated his hierarchy of human needs, the authors have differentiated three levels of goals and priorities that individuals attempt to fulfill: the first is the need for food and shelter; the second is the motivation to find love and sexual fulfillment and a satisfying family life; and the third is the pursuit of transcendent goals. With respect to the third level, most people have an intuitive sense that there is something more to life. That is, there is a core need to work toward self-actualization and to formulate, live by, and guide life according to one's principles. In fact, the search for meaning and purpose in life is as fundamental to human beings as is their drive for self-preservation. When an individual's defenses preclude this pursuit, he or she often suffers from a form of emotional poverty, feels empty, without a center, and exists in a state of despair (Kierkegaard, 1849/1954).

In seeking personal meaning, individuals tend to go beyond their basic needs and wants and engage in activities and causes that they regard as having a greater significance for themselves, society, and the future. According to Rollo May (1983), the pursuit of a transcendent goal requires the ability to use one's imagination to move beyond the immediate concrete situation. It implies a sense of caring or, more accurately, "the capacity to stand outside and look at oneself and the situation and to assess and guide oneself by an infinite variety of possibilities" (p. 147).

People in the friendship circle have found meaning in expressing their altruism through acts of kindness to individuals both within and outside of their immediate families and group of friends. In addition, they have provided financial support and helped to produce documentary films for both the psychology profession and the general public. When participating in the films as subjects, they revealed the process of self-inquiry described in this book and contributed stories of their personal development.

> **Tamsen**: I really think that each of my friends was concerned about the quality of their life. I think that they were dissatisfied with following the path that everybody told them they should follow. Everybody told them that if they got married and bought a house, and had kids and lived in suburbia and their kids grew up and went to college that this was going to bring them happiness. I think that they questioned that. They didn't think that that was the answer. They didn't think that that's where happiness or meaning was. I think that each person wanted something more, something beyond that, I believe they wanted to have a meaningful life.
>
> **Dr. Firestone**: There are many different approaches to a meaningful existence. For myself, I have found profound meaning in my work as a psychotherapist, my work in the friendship circle, my development of psychological theory, my art, my romantic love life, my children and family, and my friendships; but at times when I am not communicating my ideas in books, articles, and films, I feel that something very important is missing.

Recently, one of our friends, Kyle, 62, listed several changes he has made over the years in relation to modifying fundamental attitudes about people and his philosophy of life. As a result of pursuing both personal and transcendent goals developed in the context of talking with his friends, he observed the following changes in himself:

> (1) Acquiring an appreciation for sharing and generosity—a major switch from being selfishly protective financially (almost to the point of paranoia) to enjoying sharing and being generous with my money.
>
> (2) Slowly dropping depression and wasting time moping and seeing the bleaker side of things, and changing my sense of humor from caustic

and cutting, often abrasive and sarcastic, to a more normal appreciation for the funny things in life.

(3) Learning to enjoy travel and adventure—the sense of motion, energy, and discovery, an appreciation of nature. Feeling a new spirit of wanting others to see and enjoy these things too, and to have a good time.

(4) Offering what I can to make life better for the people around me. I particularly like driving and taking people to places I think they will appreciate, and I support their individual undertakings whether they be in art, science, or exploring new places.

Composing a Life Story or Narrative

In the process of trying to develop oneself personally and to identify guiding principles to live by, it is valuable to have a perspective on one's life, which can be facilitated by writing a life history. As Paul Wong (2008) has observed: "Story-telling is essential to develop self-identity and holistic self-understanding. All the studies of attribution processes, defense mechanisms, and belief systems only reveal some aspects of us. Only the creative process of story-telling is capable of revealing the whole, full-bodied person actively engaged in the dynamic business of living" (p. 76).

Attachment researchers Mary Main and Judith Solomon (1986) and neuropsychiatrist Dan Siegel (1999) have also emphasized the value of constructing a coherent narrative of one's life and particularly one's attachment history. Writing such a narrative often elicits deep feeling and helps resolve some of the early trauma and loss from childhood. Siegel (2001) noted: "Coherent narratives can be seen to reflect the ability of the 'interpreting' left hemisphere [of the brain] to utilize the autobiographical, mentalizing, and primary emotional processes of the right hemisphere in the production of 'coherent' autonoesis, or self-knowledge" (p. 89).

Wong (2008) includes a variety of creative efforts in his description of life narratives that when composed can give direction and meaning to one's life: "Story-telling encompasses a wide range of narrative devices and processes, such as letter-writing, journaling, life review and reminiscence, and myth making. It involves the ability to weave a story by connecting different fragments, filling in the gaps, and reconciling the contradictions" (p. 76) (Note 4).

In the process of composing his life history, Dean was able to connect relevant events from childhood to his adult experiences in a way that helped him make sense of his past and gave meaning to the present. Following are several excerpts from a more extensive personal history:

> My first memories are shadowy: me as a toddler playing with my mother on a kitchen floor, piles of un-ironed laundry nearby; me riding a little red pedal-car on an oil-stained driveway. Gradually experiences fill in the gaps. I remember thinking that she was beautiful and wanting to please her (before I learned that it was impossible). I would find trinkets around the house and present them to her as if they were fine gifts. I wanted to be with her all the time. I didn't seem to notice her rages or at least I can't remember them clearly until I was around four or five.
>
> As I got older her anger became more evident. Memories of her sudden rages, the flying glass, the slammed doors and drunken curses still visit my dreams. Like a shell-shocked veteran diving for the bushes at the sound of a backfire, a sudden angry shout or slammed door can send me diving for the protection I only found by shutting everything and everyone out. It seemed she directed most of her anger at my father and my sister. "I will break your neck" was her war cry as she chased her around the house.
>
> Over the years, I have enjoyed wonderful moments of intimacy, sexual fulfillment and companionship. At the same time, my relationships were limited and hurt by either my defenses or those of my partner in developing a closeness and independence. Afraid to be like my father, I have a tendency to shut down at the first sign of conflict. Like my father, I will sacrifice myself to appease a troubled woman and then resent and silently punish her for it. Again, without the support and insight of compassionate friends, I can't imagine not being dragged under by the undertow of my earliest examples and training. I have become more able to recognize these damaging patterns and, though far from healed, I have become a much better friend to the women in my life.

SPIRITUALITY AND THE MYSTERY OF LIFE

A crucial element in pursuing a meaningful life involves developing our sense of the sacred, expanding the spiritual dimensions of our experience, and exploring the mysteries of existence (R. Firestone et al., 2003). Harvard scientist E. O. Wilson (Petzinger, 2000) emphasized that "the predisposition to religious belief is the most complex and powerful force in the human mind, and in all probability an ineradicable part of human nature" (p. R16). Yet presently, more than at any time in history, science has made a serious intrusion on religious belief systems. Wilson stated that, "The more we understand from science about the way the world really works, all the way from subatomic particles up to the mind and on to the cosmos, the more difficult it is to base spirituality on our ancient mythologies" (p. R16). Nonetheless, in spite of recognizing the impact on belief systems caused by scientific advances and the realization that we are not fully conscious of our motivations, one cannot rule out faith, because so much is still unknown.

In *Creating a Life of Meaning and Compassion,* the authors (R. Firestone et al., 2003) explained that:

> Aristotelian logic and modern science not only fail to explain existence, they preclude its possibility. All that we know in the scientific sense points to the fact that something cannot come from nothing; even if one postulates a God, one is burdened by the question of where could that essence have come from. Faced with this preposterous logical contradiction, we are left with a hypothetical problem that goes beyond human intelligence and intellect. . . . We are forced to accept the blow to our vanity and face the painful truth of our intellectual limitations, but there is a consolation. We are left with the fact of mystery, free to contemplate the awesome spectacle of existence of all varieties. . . . There is more to life than we usually consider. There is still magic in the world. (p. 380)

We agree with Wilson (Petzinger, 2000) when he emphasizes that "whatever we feel in our hearts, we need to believe that there is some ultimate measure of sacredness, whether you perceive it as secular in origin through the organic evolution of humanity, or whether you conceive of it as God directed" (p. R16). He has suggested that we must be "proactive in seeking it and defining it instead of reactive in the traditional manner of taking the sacred texts and beliefs handed down to us and trying to adapt them to an evolving culture" (p. R16).

The concept of spirituality usually refers to various belief systems about life after death, nirvana, religious faith, relegation to heaven or hell, reincarnation, and such. In an extended context it refers to a deep concern about matters of morality, how to live one's life and find meaning, and about one's essential connection to oneself, others, one's natural surroundings, and the universe at large.

Most individuals in the friendship circle do not participate in organized religious practices as such; few attend church or involve themselves in other types of formal worship. They personally hold a wide range of beliefs about creation and the existence or concept of God or a Superior Being. Some believe in prayer while others are agnostics or outright atheists. In spite of their lack of organized religion, it would be a gross misconception to consider these people lacking in a sense of spirituality. Their mode of existence has a deep spiritual quality, a regard for the sacredness of life and humanity that pervades every aspect of their being. This spiritual quest is not an isolated phenomenon, practiced on designated occasions, but instead is lived out every hour of every day. Their life together and its extension to the larger world around them reflect their existential awareness of aloneness, of life and death, and the essential dilemma and mystery of existence. They are actively concerned with moral principles and human rights issues that transcend conventional morality. In their interactions, they exhibit a deep and abiding respect for people's feelings, their well-being, and personal freedom (R. Firestone & Catlett, 2009).

DISCOVERIES AND INSIGHTS

> There is nothing in man or nature which would prevent us from taking some control of our destiny and making the world a saner place for our children. (Becker, 1975, p. xviii)

Over the many years spent and sharing every aspect of life at close quarters, our friends have been challenged in their search for a meaningful existence by the concepts that have emerged out of their personal struggles. They learned to trust the open forum and expression of ideas above individual definitions and categorization of ourselves. In the democratic process, all points of view are acceptable, all feelings and all forms of emotional expression are valued. People have been able to gain perspective in this unique atmosphere and to evaluate their lives.

The authors have offered other people this same opportunity by sharing what we have learned in our books, articles, films, and presentations. This is our legacy. Some of our ideas are described in the following paragraphs:

1. Regarding the individual, we learned that:

People can change any behavior, even the most difficult. It is a question of motivation and overcoming resistance, but it also takes courage because modifying defenses cannot be accomplished without considerable pain and anxiety.

People are driven by unconscious and even self-destructive motives. They have an alien part of their personality that is opposed to their best interest and that predisposes self-destructive behaviors. Identifying this process can help to bring these unconsciously motivated behaviors under control and can allow a person to expand his or her life.

Addictions and routines are deadly and take a huge toll on people's lives.

Personal vanity and superiority are not only destructive and unpleasant to others, but they have a negative effect on the perpetrator as well. They limit and put great pressure on the vain individual to maintain his or her image. In addition, although people vary and have different skills and capabilities, no one is essentially more important or valuable than another—each individual has equal value as a person.

People are not born bad. The destructive patterns of behavior they engage in are the result of early childhood neglect, abuse, and/or trauma.

A coherent story is valuable for a person's mental health because it helps the individual make sense of his or her past. This process makes the individual aware of his or her ongoing existence and inspires him or her to make what remains of life the best story possible. In this regard we emphasize the significance of making life a real adventure, developing one's personal values, challenging routines and trying new things, and the central importance of self-knowledge.

2. Regarding feelings, we learned that:

All feelings and thoughts are acceptable and must be experienced uncritically, whereas actions must be limited and subject to moral and realistic considerations. It is particularly important to recognize angry and competitive feelings and to not prejudge them or make them fit a rational form of thinking and feeling, even though they must be regulated in relation to action. People who can feel their anger but who can control and master its expression are generally more powerful in their lives.

When intense emotions are experienced in daily life, they usually relate to primal feelings from the past. Therefore, it is adaptive to look for the real source of these exaggerated feelings rather than accept them at face value. Only significant life and death issues warrant intense emotional reactions, and these events occur only rarely.

3. Regarding interpersonal and social relationships, we learned that:

Kindness and generosity are sound mental health principles in that they challenge the voice process.

It is important to live with integrity, to make one's actions coincide with one's words and goals. When there is discrepancy between words and actions, it is more adaptive to trust behaviors, body language, and expressive features over the spoken word. In the family, this type of duplicity has an especially negative effect on the mental health of the children.

There is no room for prejudice, status, or the superiority of one group over another. Parental and judgmental behaviors that manifest these attitudes are destructive to people's well-being.

It is valuable to develop an implicit morality that is sensitive to what hurts people and to apply this when relating to one's mates, family members, and friends.

It is inadvisable to think in terms of ideologies and absolutism. It is advisable to be forthright in communicating ideas, while at the same time admitting fallibility.

Nothing is more destructive in a personal relationship than to be dishonest and mislead the other. Confusing a person's sense of reality is harmful to his or her sense of well-being. When one member of a couple is unfaithful, the deception involved is often more traumatic than the infidelity.

Many people profess an overall love of humanity while they treat the people in their personal lives poorly. Love is not an abstraction. "Love begins at home."

The pursuit of personal power is an admirable undertaking. It involves control of one's own life, goal-directedness, independence, and freedom. Manipulative power plays, such as the use of negative power, or attempts to control through weakness, are harmful and destructive to both the recipient and the perpetrator. Surplus power over others in the form of utilizing force, bullying, coercion, and domineering behaviors are obviously destructive.

Men and women have more commonalities than differences. Stereotypic thinking and prejudices must be challenged and reformulated. Equality is a necessary component in successful relationships that maintain intimacy.

Friendship cannot exist in a vacuum. Therefore, there is value in working together on mutual projects, sharing endeavors with other people to achieve common goals. In our experience, this combined effort has led to intellectual stimulation, travel, exploration, and overall financial success.

Ultimately, ensuring the rights of any individual takes precedence over perpetuating the existence of any social unit. It is important to be aware of the dangers of blind conformity and group identification.
4. Regarding methods for change, we learned that:

Developing the capacity to offer and accept direct feed back in a non-defensive manner allows people to process valuable information. They are free to agree or disagree but realize that it is advisable to explore ideas about oneself even when the ideas are jarring at first.

It is important to give away one's voices, to say the negative thoughts and self-attacks to a trusted friend in order to evaluate them objectively. In isolation these self-critical attacks flourish and feed on themselves. It is also valuable to challenge cynical distrustful attitudes toward other people in the same manner. Negative attitudes, both toward self and others, foster a sense of alienation.

The key to changing is understanding resistance. Once an individual gets beyond the resistance, he or she is able to form spontaneous conclusions and insights and to make progress. Therefore, in any therapy process, it is important to understand and to focus on resistance.

5. Regarding children and child-rearing, we learned that:

The myth of motherly love and the idealization of family life in general must be challenged in order to be able to improve these relationships and institutions. Mothers are, to varying degrees, as capable of offering a secure attachment to their child as are fathers and other family members. If family matters are sacrosanct and beyond analysis, if objective evaluation is inhibited, then there is little possibility for progress or improvement in patterns of child-rearing.

In the first few years of the developing person's life, especially the preverbal years, trauma can have a particularly destructive impact. Therefore, child-rearing practices must be taken seriously, especially in these first years of life. In fact, it is advisable to consider the family dynamics even before the child is born. Damage that is done during a child's preverbal stage is difficult to change because the reactions to trauma are hard-wired in the young brain that is still developing.

In terms of child-rearing practices, one should not treat children as younger than they are. Children must be allowed to do as much for themselves as they are able to.

When parents regard their children as extensions of themselves, they often project their own negative traits onto them. In a sense, they use their children as waste receptacles for their projections. Even when these attitudes are not acted out by parents, children sense them through behavioral cues that most parents are largely unaware of.

Discipline, which entails guidance, should not be confused with punishment that is characterized by meanness or cruelty. It is important to be firm but compassionate in socializing our children.

Children's independence must not be misinterpreted as defiance. A major defense against death anxiety is to use one's children as an immortality project by trying to live on through them. For this defense to work, parents have to force their children into a certain mold to ensure a kind of sameness with them (the parents). Therefore, a concerted effort must be made to not create a carbon copy of oneself, but instead, to permit one's children to freely develop their own interests, goals, and priorities in life.

6. Regarding existential issues, we learned that:

It is better to face the truth, however ugly or painful, than to resort to defense formation. The irony of the neuroses, character disorders, or psychoses is that the individual's psychological defenses, in most cases, are the disease.

All people are faced with the same existential dilemma. We are all separate and alone, cursed with the consciousness of our own eventual demise, and must overcome the same obstacles to maintaining our independence, our spirit, and our integrity. By acknowledging death as a reality instead of resorting to defensive denial, we can best meet the challenge and embrace life more fully. People everywhere confront the same essential problems and struggle for survival. Therefore, we are all brothers and sisters, and there is no room for indifference to suffering, starvation, poverty, prejudice, rampant nationalism, ethnic strife, or warfare.

CONCLUSION

The authors share the belief of many philosophers that the pursuit of a meaningful life requires some consideration and conscious reflection about existential issues. However, we do not agree with other thinkers who believe that this requires a prescribed adherence to a code derived from divine status—or from human beings accorded near-divine status. To the contrary, we recognize that to pursue a more meaningful existence, one must seek to develop one's own potentialities and values in a unique manner. Our approach is centered on supporting the people we care about—family, friends, clients, and acquaintances—as they strive to fulfill their own vision of a better life in spite of their limitation in time (R. Firestone et al., 2003).

> For the people in the friendship circle, achieving a more meaningful life involved years of struggle and a strong commitment to coping with their

own personal defenses. We do not wish to imply that people must follow a particular pathway in an attempt to achieve the "good life" nor do we believe that people must necessarily find their way in a social context as described here. We merely hope that in facing their own pain and the issue of personal mortality, readers might be inspired to take their own lives seriously and pursue their own form of self-realization.

Part of the good life involves a concern for other people, starting with your own family, giving value and respect to other human beings, serving others, wanting to better the world you live in, to help, to heal, to share, making your life the best story possible. (Documentary film *Friendship: A Life of Meaning and Compassion,* Parr, 2002)

NOTES

1. Most existentialists and humanists make a distinction between self-actualization and self-transcending goals, such as altruism, dedication to a cause, and creativity. Yalom (1980) stressed the point that we would be well-advised "not to settle for a nonself-transcendent purpose in life.... Buber... notes that, though human beings should begin with themselves (by searching their own hearts, integrating themselves, and finding their particular meaning), they should not end with themselves" (p. 439).
2. Mikulincer and Florian (2008) have noted that "the subjective construal of one's own mortality and the meanings people attach to death are an inherent part of the meanings they attach to their own life and a reflection of the motives, goals, concerns and values that guide their behaviors in everyday life encounters" (p. 54). See their discussion of Emmons's (1992, 1997) review of the research on personal strivings commitment to personal goals (pp. 54–57), as well as Emmons's Striving Assessment Scale (Emmons, 1992). Roy Baumeister (1991) has contended that personal meaning in one's life is achieved through the fulfillment of four important human needs: the need for (1) Purpose, (2) Values, (3) Efficiency, and (4) Self-Worth. In this sense, according to Baumeister, "The search for meaning is evolutionarily adaptive" (cited by Orbach, 2008).
3. A potentially helpful exercise for overcoming resistance to taking action in relation to one's goals consists of listing one's wants, interests, and goals on the left-hand side of a page. In the middle column, one lists any destructive voices that might prevent one from pursuing these wants and goals. On the right-hand side of the page, one writes down a realistic point of view about one's wants and goals. (See R. Firestone et al., 2002, Figure 6.4 "Going after What You Want.")
4. In her work narrative researcher Janette McDonald (2007) has focused attention on the transformational value of story-telling as part of the grieving and meaning-making processes following the death of a loved one. She noted that "The telling of a story that surrounds the death of a loved one holds the potential for significant personal transformation because in telling it one reflects on and views the experience from a different emotional place each time it is retold" (p. 276).

My Life and Legacy

ROBERT W. FIRESTONE

MY LIFE

I was born in Brooklyn, New York, September 8, 1930. My father was a medical doctor and my mother, a dress designer. I had one sister, two years younger. We lived in a two-story brick house in a row of similar homes, but a stairway led from the street down to our basement and the entrance to my father's office. As a young baby, I was seriously ill and was later told that I had come close to death. My parents had been anxious and worried, and I learned, as an adult, that my illness had not only been painful but embarrassing to my father. I always felt that I was a disappointment to him, never the son that he wanted. Perhaps that explains why he was hypercritical toward me. I accompanied him on his rounds to visit patients in their homes, and I loved the car rides; but he was awkward with me and would launch into a critical commentary. To tell the truth, I never knew exactly what he meant by these attacks; they didn't make any sense to me, but they hurt.

My parents considered us to be the ideal family, and their friends constantly reiterated this point. My mother and father were affectionate and kind to each other, they cuddled in bed and never fought. I was ashamed to be unhappy in such a wonderful family, and in general I hid my feelings. I played by myself, made up games, and read a great deal.

341

When I was about six or so, I joined a bunch of other kids on my street and we spent our waking hours in sports activities of every sort and hung out together. We only came home for dinner or bedtime; otherwise, we rarely saw our parents. With these friends we formed our own separate world and I was kind of the ringleader. We were mischievous but never got into any real trouble.

I was basically a shy child, unhappy and confused. I was put ahead one grade, and so I was always the smallest kid in my class and hated school from kindergarten to my PhD. I felt socially retarded because I was younger than my classmates, rarely said anything, and felt unpopular. One teacher sent a note home indicating that she suspected that I was deaf. My father was angry that anyone would think that, as a doctor, he wouldn't have known if I had had a hearing loss. The truth was I just didn't like the bossy and unpleasant woman and refused to answer her.

I am Jewish and my family went to a Reformed temple. They were not very religious. At the temple there was a great deal of talk about the Holocaust. Refugees told terrible tales of persecution that frightened me. Some said that the same thing could happen in America. I pictured storm troopers knocking on our door and taking our family away.

I can't remember too much about my childhood. It seems so hazy and remote from my present life. There were some humiliating moments: the time I couldn't get up the courage to ask permission to leave the classroom and defecated in my pants; the time a dog tried to mount me as I walked down the street, and him growling in my ear while kids were pointing and laughing, and there was the taunting of a bully. But overall those occasions were rare. There were also good times, like the holidays when there would be lots of friendly people around having fun. But mostly I remember a lonely feeling, a somber mood and sadness. I had many fears. I was particularly afraid of heights, especially after falling from the roof of my garage and hitting my head on the concrete. I recall thinking a lot about death and feeling scared about my future. I wondered how I would get along in life.

In my early teens, during World War II, my father enlisted in the Navy and became an officer. He was stationed in Miami, and our family moved from our home in Brooklyn into a hotel in Miami Beach. I felt displaced and missed my friends; they were my entire life at the time. Everything got worse when we moved away from the beach to the city of Miami. There I ran into prejudice and became enormously self-conscious about being Jewish. I felt lost. At the same time I was developing as a sexual person and felt awkward meeting girls. I was extremely guilty about my sexuality, my feelings, and desires.

When my father was shipped overseas to Okinawa, our family moved back to Brooklyn. In high school, things slowly began to change for the better. I grew rapidly and became tall, realized that I was intelligent, and was aware that girls liked me and were attracted to me. I was still shy but I found that if I could get them alone, everything went well. I was also learning something even more fundamental. Before this time, I felt different and abnormal, like I just didn't fit in. Now I no longer wished to fit in; I liked being different and unconventional. I began to like myself.

There were other lessons that I incorporated during those teen years. I knew life wasn't necessarily happy; there were the very real existential issues of loneliness, aloneness, and personal pain. I was determined to formulate and maintain my own values in a seemingly meaningless world. In addition, I knew that I would invest all of myself in the pursuit of my goals, win or lose. Within these principles, I would live with absolute honesty and integrity; I would at least have a sense of harmony within myself and would be able to look in the mirror without flinching.

I entered Syracuse University as a pre-med student. During the first year I met a pretty blond coed at a dance. I liked her, and we started dating. She was more sexually advanced than I was, and we spent our dates on a blanket in the park. During the Christmas break she went home to her wealthy family in Scarsdale, and when she told them about our relationship, they insisted that she break up with me. I was everything that they hated: poor, Jewish, and without a promising future. She ended the relationship and I was miserable all through the following semester.

That summer, I had planned to travel to California with a close friend. Just before we left, his mother feigned a heart attack, and he did not come. So I set out for the West Coast on my own, which turned out to be a blessing in disguise. I learned that I could be alone and felt self-confident and freewheeling. I hitched rides with some real characters along the way, met many interesting people, mostly women, and experienced the beautiful, ever-changing landscape of the United States.

When I returned to Syracuse, I decided to become a clinical psychologist instead of a medical doctor. I found psychology courses to be the most exciting curriculum and was fascinated by the field. I was so moved by a movie called *The Snake Pit*, about a devoted psychiatrist helping a mentally ill woman, that I was inspired to change my career. I had always been drawn toward helping people who were distressed. When I was a very young child, I assisted a handicapped girl in my neighborhood. My family commented on my tendency to feel for or help those who were limited, hurt, discriminated against, or regarded as underdogs. My adolescent fantasy was to become a doctor in the slums and offer my services to the poor.

During the spring semester of my second year I met my future wife, Louise, and we fell in love. She was pretty, smart, and adventurous. We decided to migrate to California in the fall; I would be going to Berkeley to finish my Bachelor's Degree and she would be doing her student teaching.

Our driving trip across country was anything but relaxing for me. I was uncomfortable because I hadn't told my parents that I was taking a girl with me. I was guilty about having premarital sex. I felt anxious during the trip and even more so when we arrived in Berkeley. I was not only on my own but I felt responsible for Louise as well. At times, I experienced anxiety states and full-blown panic attacks. Those painful moments were the low point of my life.

In spite of my anguish, I completed my Bachelor's Degree in psychology. Soon after arriving in California, Louise and I moved in together and in the spring after my graduation, we were married. I was 20 years old, ready for graduate school, but about to be drafted into the army. Fortunately, President Eisenhower had just authorized a bill exempting certain college students from the draft.

Next were my years in graduate school. Louise and I were very poor. My father had told me that anyone who got married should support themselves. So I worked at odd jobs: a carpenter's helper building houses, a machinist in a furniture factory, an assembly line worker in a leather goods plant, and an attendant and part-time research assistant working for a veterinarian on a cancer project. Finally, I got a job in my field, working for a well-known but controversial psychiatrist, John Rosen. His work was unique because he applied direct analytic techniques to schizophrenic patients, a therapeutic undertaking many considered to be futile.

When I was employed in this experimental program, Louise and I lived with the same disturbed, psychotic patients whom I also worked with on a daily basis. This experience provided me with an unusual opportunity to understand the dynamics of severe mental illness. It was a time of important insights. I immediately felt comfortable with the patients; I liked them and found that I understood them. I was learning new things from them every day and developing my own ideas. I had never before been involved in a creative endeavor of this magnitude. My brain was racing from one idea to the next and pieces of the puzzle kept coming into perspective. One insight led to another and another as I developed my theory and understanding of the fantasy bond. There is a state of enchantment and rapture that accompanies the thrill of discovery. It was a painful and frantic time, but also exciting and joyful. It was painful experiencing and empathizing with the torment of the patients and frantic in the sense that so much was happening to me intellectually and emotionally in such a short time. The year and a half working with Dr. Rosen served as both an internship and an opportunity to develop and write a dissertation on schizophrenia for my doctorate.

After graduating with a PhD in clinical psychology, we moved to Los Angeles, I started my private practice as a psychotherapist, and Louise and I had our first child. The next years were spent building my practice and emerging from our many years of financial hardship, buying our first home, and raising our three children. Professionally I was working long hours, elaborating, adapting, and applying my original theory on schizophrenia to a broader spectrum of patients' problems.

For approximately 20 years I was involved in private practice. My schedule was full. I started working with clients early in the morning and usually finished with a group session at about 8:30 in the evening. I felt happy with my patients' progress in therapy and was continually expanding my theoretical concepts. However, I had not contributed to the scientific literature beyond my original dissertation. Financially, I was moderately successful. My friends and I bought a small boat, and our families vacationed together. In the late 1960s, Louise and I took our first trip to Europe. I was leading a more or less conventional life both personally and professionally.

Then in the 1970s my life changed completely. Over the years my family and I had been growing closer with my friends and their families. We spoke about our personal lives and often discussed philosophical ideas. When I told them about my group therapy sessions with clients, it sparked a desire in them for the same open forum. We decided to try communicating our deepest feelings on a regular basis. We all pledged to be completely responsible for ourselves and our own therapy. There was no formal leadership, although there were many psychologists in the group. Gradually people turned to me for guidance, but I continued to function as both participant and observer. This group of highly intelligent individuals became the nucleus of a larger movement that led to the formation of a unique lifestyle.

During this time, there were three pivotal developments in my life. First, I met Marty. We became close friends and had a common interest in psychology and business. My friends and I became involved with his importing business, and it was the first of many joint entrepreneurial ventures. More importantly, Marty and I both had the desire for and vision of a better way of living. We wanted to live and share life more closely with other congenial people, but in the early 1970s, it was only a dream.

The second development was a sad one. My relationship with Louise had been slowly deteriorating. We still cared about each other and enjoyed our sexual relationship, but we were no longer two people who shared intimacy and romance. It was like we were traveling together in a car, but we were each looking out of different windows and never sharing the same view. I was troubled about how to save the vitality of our relationship. Our love of 20-some years was dying and I wanted more.

The third development was that a couple who were close friends of mine were breaking up, and the man wanted to live on a small sailboat. I suggested that if we all chipped in, we could buy a large vessel that he could live on and we could sail locally. Everyone liked the idea and we pooled whatever money we had and bought an unfinished, 80-foot wooden schooner, the *Vltava*, and began to work on it and sail it.

About this time, I met Tamsen, the woman who would eventually become my second wife. She was a natural beauty, highly intelligent, gifted and intuitive in relation to people, and she had a great sense of humor. Everyone loved her; she lit up their lives. She was excited about our growing circle of friends and threw herself into the boat-refurbishing project. Our courtship consisted of working long hours together on the boat, frequenting hardware stores and lumberyards. We were friends for more than two years before we became lovers. When I fell in love with Tamsen, I realized that I had always been looking for a special woman, but after I met her my search was over. I was overjoyed and this extraordinary woman became the catalyst for the new lifestyle that was forming in and around us.

The friendship circle was expanding rapidly. Everyone was sharing the many aspects of their lives: the group talks, sailing and working on the *Vltava*, and even some fledgling business ventures. As an adjunct to my office therapy, I conducted several marathon weekends away from the city for some of my patients. These settings allowed for free expression of feelings and the challenging of defenses. Once again, my friends, upon hearing about this, wanted to try it themselves. We arranged to meet at Lake Arrowhead for a weekend encounter. This experience brought us closer to ourselves and to each other. We felt free and were in high spirits. Someone said, "Wow, this is wonderful, I never felt so good in my life. I wish the weekend would never end." Then another person said, "Why don't we live like this in our everyday lives?" These comments were emotionally stirring and motivating. The result is that my family, friends, associates, and I have been living a life based on that type of experience for the past 30 years.

In the late 1970s, my friends approached me and asked me to devote myself full time to this group of people and to the formation and ongoing development of the emerging new lifestyle. I would have to abandon my successful practice of psychotherapy, live much less extravagantly, and take a chance that this new way of living would endure. But none of these was the most serious consideration for me in relation to the decision. My biggest concern was that I would be turned to as a therapist. I valued my relationship in the group and did not want to do therapy as such; nor did I want to accept responsibility for my friends' psychological well-being in any way. Most importantly, I did not want to be limited in my own participation. They assured me that their intentions had always been to look after themselves, but I still had some doubts. There were a number of factors that convinced me to accept their offer. I felt close and loving feelings toward these people and thought it was a great environment for my children. I loved the project and recognized that it would offer a rare opportunity to develop my ideas. This was an environment in which a group of people lived and worked together in close proximity, where they could talk regularly and honestly reveal their innermost secrets and deepest emotions. In essence, it was a unique psychological laboratory where I could learn so much. Although there was much turmoil at first and a painful process of acculturation for the group as a whole, I have never regretted my decision.

One issue that soon arose was that there was a widespread use of drugs in our neighborhood and a few of the teenagers within our group were part of that culture. Some of their friends had overdosed and we knew we had to do something about the situation. I suggested that we start a discussion group for them that they could use to work out their conflicts, and that we also involve them in the *Vltava* project. They embraced both ideas. In their talks they learned about their relationships and their emotions, and drugs were no longer an issue. It was a sad and painful time for all of us because the young people talked openly about how we, as parents, had hurt them and let them down.

The teenagers became a vital part of the crew of the *Vltava*. For a couple of years, all of us, adults and teenagers, spent our spare time building and sailing the schooner. Then in 1974, we sailed to Mexico, and while anchored in Cabo San Lucas, someone suggested sailing to the Mediterranean. Then someone else said, "Why stop at the Med? When you're half-way around the world, why not go all of the way?" And so it was decided that we would attempt a circumnavigation.

A year later we said goodbye to families and friends and set sail on a voyage around the world. Over the next 18 months, we shared glorious and sometimes agonizing experiences at sea, and visited many interesting and exotic countries. The teenage crew was aboard the vessel the entire trip, and the other adults and I joined them whenever we could get away from work. In Jamaica, as the time for some of us to return home approached, we thought that because sailing together was bringing us so much joy, it would be great to work together. So while the *Vltava* was making her way around the world, we started three small businesses—a jewelry importing business, an interior design company, and a computer sales organization—and moved them into a suite of offices. Beginning with only a minimum amount of investment capital, these business ventures succeeded beyond our dreams, and eventually there were new and even more profitable enterprises. Every person benefited from the new wealth and, even more significantly, we are still working together three decades later. The teenagers, now men and women with their own children, have also remained close friends.

Over the next 25 years, many new and interesting people either joined or were born into the friendship circle. In spite of the growing numbers, the talks and open forum continued and these people were able to retain their honesty. Ideas were discussed freely, and powerful emotional expressions were not only tolerated, but also welcomed. We all learned a great deal from the experience and we developed in our personal and professional lives. We focused our energy and concerns on our children; we were aware of the attitudes and behaviors that had hurt us when we were growing up and did not want to repeat the damage. Without realizing it, a new implicit morality was evolving in the group based on what we were learning from the talks. Indeed, the entire friendship circle benefited from these insights, and without predetermining or planning it, a new society had eventuated.

As I had hoped, I was one of the beneficiaries of the group experience. I expanded my knowledge in the field and, in addition, I developed as a theorist, author, and contributor to the professional literature. Before my involvement, I had never had the confidence to share my ideas in print. Since then, I have written journal articles, contributed chapters to edited books, authored 12 books in my field, and made a number of documentary films to elucidate my ideas.

In 1978, I divorced Louise, although we remained friends until her death. Later that same year, I married Tamsen and we have been very happy. Each of us has grown in a union free of conventional boundaries, marked by mutual respect, love, and support for each other's individuality and freedom. In summary, I have sailed the world over, spearheaded several large, successful business ventures, and my personal life has flourished with family and friends. I have lived a free and adventurous existence, traveled extensively, enjoyed my sexuality, and have always appreciated and loved my work. My days have been enriched by the closeness and camaraderie I have found with a number of male friends, as well as by the long-term meaningful relationships I have with several significant women. It has been most rewarding to raise my children, my grandchildren, and the children of my friends. I feel they were fortunate to be born into this extended family atmosphere. This way of living has not only added positive dimensions to all of our lives and made child care functions much easier and more comfortable, but has also provided an opportunity for my grown children to share my life and maintain warm personal contact. My life is an ever-changing landscape, unpredictable, and full of people. I am never bored.

It is impossible to do justice to the many complexities of my existence in the new environment, but I want to pay tribute to the friendship circle because many of the ideas in this book were either formulated or elaborated upon in conjunction with these intelligent and courageous individuals. My relationship to the group and our experiences together could be considered a love story, not the narrow definition of what one usually thinks of as romantic or sexual love, although certainly not exclusive of that connotation, and not the spiritual meaning of the word, although when love is omnipresent it reaches a level of spirituality. I am talking about a love of people who are special to me, of marvelous places, of my natural surroundings, in particular the sea, of sharing projects, both material and ideological, with others in close personal interaction, a love of feeling and adventure, and ultimately a love of life itself.

MY LEGACY

At the present time, I am 78 years old. I am not dying in the immediate sense of illness or incapacitation, but can begin to imagine what I believe will be my legacy. Early in my life, I decided that I wanted to do something of importance, make a contribution to humankind, and be of significant value to others. The major thrust of my life in this regard has been my involvement in the field of psychology. For 50 years I have been absorbed in developing my understanding of resistance in psychotherapy, and people's resistance to a better life in general. I have studied this subject in various populations ranging from extreme psychotics, to neurotic patients in psychotherapy, to a normal population of comparatively high-functioning individuals. The theory and methodology that have emerged from this work are at the core of my legacy. My contribution to my field involves many different aspects.

I have developed my own theoretical approach, Separation Theory, which integrates psychoanalytic and existential concepts in psychology in a manner that lends itself to an effective approach to psychotherapy. In the process, my associates and I have contributed to the knowledge of how social structures and culture are formed out of the combining of individual psychological defenses against death anxiety. I have described how the denial of death and various defenses against death anxiety lead to limitation in life. In the course of our investigations we have identified core psychological defenses that adversely affect personal relationships, society, and issues of morality in everyday life.

I have introduced and explained the importance of the fantasy bond as a unifying psychological concept that explains how human beings seek comfort and security in fantasies of fusion that insulate them from emotional pain, in particular from their tragic awareness of death's inevitability. Any eventuality that threatens the fantasy bond arouses aggression. This explains how people are polarized by their secular customs, belief systems, and religions against other people with dissimilar ways of living and viewing the world. It is a core issue in prejudice, genocide, ethnic strife, and religious wars and therefore relevant in understanding and changing the destructive orientation of humankind. Hopefully, insight into the dynamics of the fantasy bond could lead to a worldview that encourages people to value life and humanistic ideals for all human beings. I believe that it is our personal responsibility to assure that all people on the planet share the necessities of a good life, including food, shelter, and the absence of abject poverty.

I have elaborated on how the fantasy bond essentially involves a self-parenting process that leads to a pseudo-independent posture toward life, insulates one from others, and hurts one's personal relationships. We nurture and punish ourselves and our children throughout our lifetime in a manner similar to the way we were treated in our developmental years. For this reason, we spend the majority of our lives reliving rather than living, thereby restricting our vitality and creative potential.

I have introduced the concept of the Voice, a system of destructive thoughts and attitudes that supports the fantasy bond and makes up the antiself system, an alien aspect of the personality. I have explained how negative attitudes are incorporated at times of stress, which has an overall destructive effect on the life of the individual. My associates and I have developed therapeutic techniques that expose this destructive thought process, allow for the release of the associated feelings, identify the source of self-attacks, and suggest a more adequate means of coping with life.

My work, under the auspices of the Glendon Association, a not-for-profit organization that disseminates psychological information, has been made available to the profession at large. Glendon has held workshops, offered lectures, and presented numerous documentary films at universities, hospitals, and clinics all over the world. My wife Tamsen has developed PsychAlive, www.psychalive.org, a Web site which makes these ideas more available to the general public. In the future, I plan to broaden the scope of her work utilizing the Internet to reach out to more people. My ultimate hope is that my ideas will benefit people both in and out of the psychology profession.

Eventually, as already noted, my intellectual theory and understanding were applied to a group of more than 100 men, women, and children in their routine living. For 30 years, we have lived and worked together to form a better way of life, through our shared vision. Each of us has invested our knowledge, our intelligence, our skills and talents, our stories, and our deepest feelings in this pursuit. In the words of Dr. Stuart Boyd (1982):

> [In this group] everyone is committed, to the best of personal ability, to the principle of open and honest communication of feeling, attitude, and belief. The commitment to truth is not to philosophical-epistemological truth but to the truth of feeling. And here lies the extraordinary power of this entire complex interweaving of work, play, and social relationships. The overall effect of this continuing, though varying, commitment is one of heightened

trust, intimacy, and happiness, which in turn leads to remarkable vigor and enthusiasm and cooperation and enjoyment in all they undertake, be it sailing, big business, baseball, folk dancing, travel, or entertainment. It seems to me that they have achieved the power of a group of high intelligence, high courage, high trust, without losing individuality. This is not the awesome efficiency of a Sparta; it is Athenian, democratic, touched with laughter and light and strength.

The Friendship Circle does not, and never would, presumably, cover all levels of society, has no pretensions to control or power within the body politic, is a limited and self-limiting set of friends. Yet there is within the community, to me, that sense of the centrality of the web of relationship, *but* without losing, in fact asserting, the primacy of the individual, which makes what has evolved so paradoxical yet so engaging.

To whatever extent I have contributed to this amazing group phenomenon, I feel that the lives of every individual reflect my personal legacy. I am proud to be associated with furthering the fulfillment and realization of their personal destiny. My legacy extends to my effect on my patients as well as my friends. They have had a profound influence on my life and I on theirs. I sincerely hope that they retain the feeling of love and respect I have had for them and continue to give themselves value.

In conclusion, my most important legacy relates to my nurturance and influence on the people closest to me with whom I share the deepest feelings of love. When I die, I will leave 12 children and at least as many grandchildren. I feel that I know them well and have so much love for each of them. I feel that they know me, too. I am proud that they are all decent people with positive values. We have always been a close and loving family, sharing life daily and maintaining personal contact.

There are many significant men and women in my life with whom I have loved, fought, and cried. We have had a powerful impact on one another and in the end have absorbed some of each other's best qualities. Each individual has brought something unique and precious that has been incorporated into our culture. I know that the way in which I lead my life and express my ideas has been a force for good. My friends have incorporated my zest for life, my humor, my personal freedom, my love of adventure, and my love of nature and aesthetics. More importantly, they have emulated my love of people, my generosity, my openness and vulnerability to painful issues, and my burning desire to search for the truth.

Lastly, I imagine leaving behind my wife, Tamsen. I could never bear the extreme pain of losing her and I know what a horror she would experience losing me. She would never again find things so funny. I fear for the loss she will experience, along with the loss for my children and for my special friends. For all the people I have touched in my life, I would like to believe that I have left an indelible imprint that has helped to make them better people.

References

Alexander, F. (1946). *Psychoanalytic therapy: Principles and application.* New York: Ronald Press.

Alexander, I. E., & Adlerstein, A. M. (1965). Affective responses to the concept of death in a population of children and early adolescents. In R. Fulton (Ed.), *Death and identity* (pp. 111–123). New York: John Wiley. (Original work published 1958)

Anthony, S. (1973). *The discovery of death in childhood and after.* Harmondsworth, UK: Penguin Education. (Original work published 1971)

Arieti, S. (1974). *Interpretation of schizophrenia* (2nd ed.). New York: Basic Books.

Armstrong, K. (2006). *The great transformation: The beginning of our religious traditions.* New York: Anchor Books.

Arndt, J., Greenberg, J., Pyszczynski, T., & Solomon, S. (1997). Subliminal exposure to death-related stimuli increases defense of the cultural worldview. *Psychological Science, 8,* 379–385.

Babbitt, S. E. (1996). *Impossible dreams: Rationality, integrity, and moral imagination.* New York: HarperCollins.

Bach, G. R., & Deutsch, R. M. (1979). *Stop! You're driving me crazy.* New York: Berkley.

Bader, E., & Pearson, P. T. (1988). *In search of the mythical mate: A developmental approach to diagnosis and treatment in couples therapy.* New York: Brunner/Mazel.

Bakan, D. (1968). *Disease, pain, & sacrifice: Toward a psychology of suffering.* Boston: Beacon Press.

Balint, M. (1985). *Primary love and psycho-analytic technique.* London: Maresfield Library. (Original work published 1952)

Bandura, A. (1973). *Aggression: A social learning analysis.* Englewood Cliffs, NJ: Prentice Hall.

Barnia, G. (1996). *The index of leading spiritual indicators.* Dallas, TX: Word Publishing.

Bassett, J. F. (2007). Psychological defenses against death anxiety: Integrating Terror Management Theory and Firestone's Separation Theory. *Death Studies, 31,* 727–750.

Bateson, G. (1972). *Steps to an ecology of mind.* New York: Ballantine.

Battegay, R. (1991). *The hunger diseases.* Toronto: Hogrefe & Huber.

Battista, J., & Almond, R. (1973). The development of meaning in life. *Psychiatry, 36,* 409–427.

Baumeister, R. (1991). *Meanings of life.* New York: Guilford.

Beck, A. T. (1976). *Cognitive therapy and the emotional disorders.* New York: New American Library.

Beck, A. T., Rush, A. J., Shaw, B. F., & Emery, G. (1979). *Cognitive therapy of depression*. New York: Guilford Press.

Beck, A. T., Sethi, B. B., & Tuthill, R. W. (1963). Childhood bereavement and adult depression. *Archives of General Psychiatry, 9*, 295–302.

Beck, R. (2004). The function of religious belief: Defensive versus existential religion. *Journal of Psychology and Christianity, 23*, 208–218.

Becker, E. (1964). *The revolution in psychiatry: The new understanding of man*. New York: Free Press.

Becker, E. (1971). *The birth and death of meaning: A perspective in psychiatry and anthropology* (2nd ed.). New York: Free Press.

Becker, E. (1975). *Escape from evil*. New York: Free Press.

Becker, E. (1997). *The denial of death*. New York: Free Press. (Original work published 1973)

Berke, J. H. (1988). *The tyranny of malice: Exploring the dark side of character and culture*. New York: Summit Books.

Berne, E. (1961). *Transactional analysis in psychotherapy*. New York: Grove.

Betchen, S. J. (2005). *Intrusive partners, elusive mates: The pursuer-distancer dynamic in couples*. New York: Routledge.

Bettelheim, B. (1979a). Individual and mass behavior in extreme situations. In *Surviving and other essays* (pp. 48–83). New York: Knopf. (Original work published 1943)

Bettelheim, B. (1979b). Remarks on the psychological appeal of totalitarianism. In *Surviving and other essays* (pp. 317–332). New York: Alfred A. Knopf. (Original work published 1952)

Bettelheim, B. (1985). Punishment versus discipline. *Atlantic Monthly, 256*, 51–59.

Bettelheim, B. (1987). *A good enough parent*. New York: Knopf.

Beutler, L. E., & Clarkin, J. F. (1990). *Systematic treatment selection: Toward targeted therapeutic interventions*. New York: Brunner/Mazel.

Binswanger, L. (1958). The case of Ellen West: An anthropological-clinical study (W. M. Mendel & J. Lyon, Trans.). In R. May, E. Angel, & H. F. Ellenberger (Eds.), *Existence: A new dimension in psychiatry and psychology* (pp. 237–364). New York: Simon & Schuster.

Blatt, S. J., McDonald, C., Sugarman, A., & Wilber, C. (1984). Psychodynamic theories of opiate addiction: New directions for research. *Clinical Psychology Review, 4*, 159–189.

Bloch, D. (1978). *"So the witch won't eat me": Fantasy and the child's fear of infanticide*. New York: Grove.

Block, J. D. (1980). *Friendship*. New York: Macmillan.

Bohart, A. C., & Greenberg, L. S. (Eds.). (1997). *Empathy reconsidered: New directions in psychotherapy*. Washington, DC: American Psychological Association.

Bonhoeffer, D. (1955). *Ethics* (N. H. Smith, Trans.). New York: Simon & Schuster. (Original work published 1949)

Boss, J. A. (2004). *Ethics for life: A text with readings* (3rd ed.). New York: McGraw-Hill.

Bowen, M. (1978). *Family therapy in clinical practice*. New York: Jason Aronson.

Bowlby, J. (1980). *Attachment and loss: Vol. III. Loss: Sadness and depression*. New York: Basic Books.

Bowlby, J. (1988). *A secure base: Parent-child attachment and healthy human development*. New York: Basic Books.

Boyd, S. (1982). *Analysis of the friendship circle.* Unpublished manuscript.

Brazelton, T. B., & Greenspan, S. I. (2000). *The irreducible needs of children: What every child must have to grow, learn, and flourish.* Cambridge, MA: Perseus.

Brooks, D. (2002, June). The culture of martyrdom [Electronic version]. *The Atlantic Online.* Retrieved 10/9/08 from http://www.theatlantic.com/doc/print/200206/brooks

Brown, S. L., Nesse, R. M., Vinokur, A. D., & Smith, D. M. (2003). Providing social support may be more beneficial than receiving it: Results from a prospective study of mortality. *Psychological Science, 14,* 320–327.

Bugental, J. F. T. (1976). *The search for existential identity.* San Francisco: Jossey-Bass.

Bukay, D. (2006). The religious foundations of suicide bombings: Islamist ideology [Electronic version]. *The Middle East Quarterly, 13.* Retrieved 10/9/08 from http://www.meforum.org/artucke/1003

Castaneda, C. (1974). *Tales of power.* New York: Simon & Schuster.

Cavaiola, A. A., & Lavender, N. J. (2000). *Toxic coworkers: How to deal with dysfunctional people on the job.* Oakland, CA: New Harbinger Publications.

Choron, J. (1964). *Death and modern man.* New York: Collier Books.

Clark, T. W. (2002). Spirituality without faith [Electronic version]. *The Humanist, 62,* 30–35.

Coelho, P. (1998). *Veronika decides to die* (M. J. Costa, Trans.). New York: HarperCollins.

Coelho, P. (2004). *Eleven minutes* (M. J. Costa, Trans.). New York: HarperCollins.

Cohen, A. B., Pierce, J. D., Jr., Chambers, J., Meade, R., Gorvine, B. J., & Koenig, H. G. (2005). Intrinsic and extrinsic religiosity, belief in the afterlife, death anxiety, and life satisfaction in young Catholics and Protestants. *Journal of Research in Personality, 39,* 307–324.

Cohen, F., Ogilvie, D. M., Solomon, S., Greenberg, J., & Pyszczynski, T. (2005). American roulette: The effect of reminders of death on support for George W. Bush in the 2004 presidential election. *Analyses of Social Issues and Public Policy, 5,* 177–187.

Cohen, F., Solomon, S., Maxfield, M., Pyszczynski, T., & Greenberg, J. (2004). Fatal attraction: The effects of mortality salience on evaluations of charismatic, task-oriented, and relationship-oriented leaders. *Psychological Science, 15,* 846–851.

Cohen, P., & Cohen, J. (2001). Life values and mental health in adolescence. In P. Schmuck & K. M. Sheldon (Eds.), *Life goals and well-being: Toward a positive psychology of human striving* (pp. 167–181). Kirkland, WA: Hogrefe & Huber.

Comte-Sponville, A. (2006). *The little book of atheist spirituality* (N. Huston, Trans.). New York: Viking.

Cooper, D. (1970). *The death of the family.* New York: Vintage Books.

Cozolino, L. J. (2002). *The neuroscience of psychotherapy: Building and rebuilding the human brain.* New York: W. W. Norton.

Cozolino, L. (2006). *The neuroscience of human relationships: Attachment and the developing social brain.* New York: W. W. Norton.

Dalai Lama. (1999). *Ethics for the new millennium.* New York: Riverhead Books.

Dalai Lama. (2000). *Transforming the mind: Teachings on generating compassion.* London: Thorsons.

Darwin, C. (1909). *The origin of species.* Danbury, CT: Grolier. (Original work published 1859)

de Beauvoir, S. (1976). Epilogue to *A very easy death.* In E. S. Shneidman (Ed.), *Death: Current perspectives* (pp. 523–526). Palo Alto, CA: Mayfield Publishing. (Original work published 1966)

Decety, J., & Jackson, P. L. (2006). A social-neuroscience perspective on empathy. *Current Directions in Psychological Science, 15,* 54–58.

Decety, J., & Moriguchi, Y. (2007). The empathic brain and its dysfunction in psychiatric populations: Implications for intervention across different clinical conditions. *BioPsychoSocial Medicine,* 1:22. Retrieved 1/25/08 from http://www.bpsmedicine .com/content/1/1/22

De Zulueta, F. (1993). *From pain to violence: The traumatic roots of destructiveness.* London: Whurr Publishers.

Didion, J. (2005). *The year of magical thinking.* New York: Vintage Books.

Diekstra, R. (1996). The epidemiology of suicide and parasuicide. *Archives of Suicide Research, 2,* 1–29.

Dobson, W. L., & Wong, P. T. P. (2008). Women living with HIV: The role of meaning and spirituality. In A. Tomer, G. T. Eliason, & P. T. P. Wong (Eds.), *Existential and spiritual issues in death attitudes* (pp. 173–207). New York: Lawrence Erlbaum.

Dugan, M. N. (1977). Fear of death: The effect of parental behavior and personality upon the behavior and personality of their children. *Dissertation Abstracts International, 38*(3), 1318-A.

Durkheim, E. (1951). *Suicide: A study in sociology* (J. A. Spaulding & G. Simpson, Trans.). New York: Free Press. (Original work published 1897)

Elgee, N. J. (2004). Laughing at death. In J. S. Piven (Ed.), *The psychology of death in fantasy and history* (pp. 291–310). Westport, CT: Praeger.

Ellis, A., & Grieger, R. (1977). *Handbook of rational-emotive therapy.* New York: Springer.

Ellis, A., & Harper, R. A. (1975). *A new guide to rational living.* North Hollywood, CA: Wilshire Book Co.

Fairbairn, W. R. D. (1952). *Psychoanalytic studies of the personality.* London: Routledge & Kegan Paul.

Farberow, N. L. (1980). Introduction. In N. L. Farberow (Ed.), *The many faces of suicide: Indirect self-destructive behavior* (pp. 1–12). New York: McGraw-Hill.

Feldman, M., & Hersen, M. (1967). Attitudes toward death in nightmare subjects. *Journal of Abnormal Psychology, 72,* 421–425.

Felitti, V. J., Anda, R. F., Nordenberg, D., Williamson, D. F., Spitz, A. M., Edwards, V., et al. (1998). Relationship of childhood abuse and household dysfunction to many of the leading causes of death in adults: The Adverse Childhood Experiences (ACE) study. *American Journal of Preventive Medicine, 14,* 245–258.

Ferenczi, S. (1955). Confusion of tongues between adults and the child. In M. Balint (Ed.), *Final contributions to the problems & methods of psycho-analysis* (E. Mosbacher & others, Trans., pp. 156–167). New York: Basic Books. (Original work published 1933)

Fierman, L. B. (Ed.). (1965). *Effective psychotherapy: The contribution of Hellmuth Kaiser.* New York: Free Press.

Fierman, L. B. (1998). You'd be paranoid too if everyone were against you [Electronic version]. *Psychnews International, 3*(3). Retrieved 3/22/07 from http://userpage.fu-berlin.de/expert/psychnews/3_3pn3_3d.htm

Firestone, L. (1987). *Intimations of mortality: Young children's concepts and feelings about death and their parents' beliefs and explanations.* Unpublished manuscript.

Firestone, L. (1991). The Firestone Voice Scale for Self-Destructive Behavior: Investigating the scale's validity and reliability (Doctoral dissertation, California

School of Professional Psychology, 1991). *Dissertation Abstracts International, 52,* 3338B.

Firestone, L. (2006). Suicide and the inner voice. In T. E. Ellis (Ed.), *Cognition and suicide: Theory, research, and therapy* (pp. 119–147). Washington, DC: American Psychological Association.

Firestone, L., & Catlett, J. (2004). Voice therapy interventions with addicted clients. *Counselor: The Magazine for Addiction Professionals, 5*(5), 49–69.

Firestone, R. W. (1957). *A concept of the schizophrenic process.* Unpublished doctoral dissertation, University of Denver.

Firestone, R. W. (1984). A concept of the primary fantasy bond: A developmental perspective. *Psychotherapy, 21,* 218–225.

Firestone, R. W. (1985). *The fantasy bond: Structure of psychological defenses.* Santa Barbara, CA: Glendon Association.

Firestone, R. W. (1986). The "inner voice" and suicide. *Psychotherapy, 23,* 439–447.

Firestone, R. W. (1987a). Destructive effects of the fantasy bond in couple and family relationships. *Psychotherapy, 24,* 233–239.

Firestone, R. W. (1987b). The "voice": The dual nature of guilt reactions. *American Journal of Psychoanalysis, 47,* 210–229.

Firestone, R. W. (1988). *Voice therapy: A psychotherapeutic approach to self-destructive behavior.* Santa Barbara, CA: Glendon Association.

Firestone, R. W. (1990a). The bipolar causality of regression. *American Journal of Psychoanalysis, 50,* 121–135.

Firestone, R. W. (1990b). *Compassionate child-rearing: An in-depth approach to optimal parenting.* Santa Barbara, CA: Glendon Association.

Firestone, R. W. (1990c). Prescription for psychotherapy. *Psychotherapy, 27,* 627–635.

Firestone, R. W. (1990d). Voice therapy. In J. Zeig & W. Munion (Eds.), *What is psychotherapy? Contemporary perspectives* (pp. 68–74). San Francisco: Jossey-Bass.

Firestone, R. W. (1990e). Voices during sex: Application of voice therapy to sexuality. *Journal of Sex & Marital Therapy, 16,* 258–274.

Firestone, R. W. (1993). The psychodynamics of fantasy, addiction, and addictive attachments. *American Journal of Psychoanalysis, 53,* 335–352.

Firestone, R. W. (1994a). A new perspective on the Oedipal complex: A voice therapy session. *Psychotherapy, 31,* 342–351.

Firestone, R. W. (1994b). Psychological defenses against death anxiety. In R. A. Neimeyer (Ed.), *Death anxiety handbook: Research, instrumentation, and application* (pp. 217–241). Washington, DC: Taylor & Francis.

Firestone, R. W. (1996). The origins of ethnic strife. *Mind and Human Interaction, 7,* 167–180.

Firestone, R. W. (1997a). *Combating destructive thought processes: Voice therapy and separation theory.* Thousand Oaks, CA: Sage.

Firestone, R. W. (1997b). *Suicide and the inner voice: Risk assessment, treatment, and case management.* Thousand Oaks, CA: Sage.

Firestone, R. W. (2000). Microsuicide and the elderly: A basic defense against death anxiety. In A. Tomer (Ed.), *Death attitudes and the older adult: Theories, concepts, and applications* (pp. 65–84). Philadelphia: Brunner-Routledge.

Firestone, R. W. (2002). The death of psychoanalysis and depth therapy. *Psychotherapy: Theory/Research/Practice/Training, 39,* 223–232.

Firestone, R. W., & Catlett, J. (1989). *Psychological defenses in everyday life.* Santa Barbara, CA: Glendon Association.

Firestone, R. W., & Catlett, J. (1999). *Fear of intimacy.* Washington, DC: American Psychological Association.

Firestone, R. W., & Catlett, J. (2009). *Ethics in interpersonal relationships.* London: Karnac.

Firestone, R. W., & Firestone, L. (1998). Voices in suicide: The relationship between self-destructive thought processes, maladaptive behavior, and self-destructive manifestations. *Death Studies, 22,* 411–443.

Firestone, R. W., & Firestone, L. (2006). *Firestone Assessment of Self-Destructive Thoughts (FAST) manual.* Lutz, FL: Psychological Assessment Resources.

Firestone, R. W., & Firestone, L. (2008a). *Firestone Assessment of Violent Thoughts (FAVT) manual.* Lutz, FL: Psychological Assessment Resources.

Firestone, R. W., & Firestone, L. (2008b). *Firestone Assessment of Violent Thoughts— Adolescent (FAVT-A) manual.* Lutz, FL: Psychological Assessment Resources.

Firestone, R. W., Firestone, L., & Catlett, J. (2002). *Conquer your critical inner voice: A revolutionary program to counter negative thoughts and live free from imagined limitations.* Oakland, CA: New Harbinger Publications.

Firestone, R. W., Firestone, L. A., & Catlett, J. (2003). *Creating a life of meaning and compassion: The wisdom of psychotherapy.* Washington, DC: American Psychological Association.

Firestone, R. W., Firestone, L. A., & Catlett, J. (2006). *Sex and love in intimate relationships.* Washington, DC: American Psychological Association.

Firestone, R. W., & Seiden, R. H. (1987). Microsuicide and suicidal threats of everyday life. *Psychotherapy, 24,* 31–39.

FirstLink. (2008). *Elderly suicide.* Retrieved 10/19/08 from http://www.myfirstlink.org/html/elderly_suicide.html

Fitzgerald, F. S. (1960). *Six tales of the Jazz Age.* New York: Scribner. (Original work published 1920)

Flew, A. (Ed.). (1964). *Body, mind, and death.* New York: Macmillan.

Florian, V., & Mikulincer, M. (2004). A multifaceted perspective on the existential meanings, manifestations, and consequences of the fear of personal death. In J. Greenberg, S. L. Koole, & T. Pyszczynski (Eds.), *Handbook of experimental existential psychology* (pp. 54–70). New York: Guilford.

Fonagy, P. (2001). *Attachment theory and psychoanalysis.* New York: Other Press.

Fonagy, P. (2004). The developmental roots of violence in the failure of mentalization. In F. Pfafflin & G. Adshead (Eds.), *A matter of security: The application of attachment theory to forensic psychiatry and psychotherapy* (pp. 13–56). London: Jessica Kingsley.

Fournier, R. R., Motto, J., Osgood, N., & Fitzpatrick, T. (1991). Rational suicide in later life. In D. Lester (Ed.), *Proceedings, 24th Annual Meeting, American Association of Suicidology, Boston, Massachusetts, April 17–21, 1991* (pp. 7–8). Denver, CO: American Association of Suicidology.

Frank, A. (1993). *The diary of a young girl.* New York: Bantam Books.

Frankl, V. E. (1959). *Man's search for meaning* (Rev. ed.). New York: Washington Square Press. (Original work published 1946)

Frankl, V. E. (1967). *Psychotherapy and existentialism: Selected papers on logotherapy.* New York: Simon & Schuster.

Freud, A. (1966). *The ego and the mechanisms of defense* (Rev. ed.). Madison, CT: International Universities Press.

Freud, S. (1957a). Mourning and melancholia. In J. Strachey (Ed. and Trans.), *The standard edition of the complete psychological works of Sigmund Freud* (Vol. 14, pp. 243–258). London: Hogarth. (Original work published 1917)

Freud, S. (1957b). Some character-types met with in psychoanalytic work. In J. Strachey (Ed. and Trans.), *The standard edition of the complete psychological works of Sigmund Freud* (Vol. 14, pp. 311–333). London: Hogarth. (Original work published 1916)

Freud, S. (1961a). Civilization and its discontents. In J. Strachey (Ed. and Trans.), *The standard edition of the complete psychological works of Sigmund Freud* (Vol. 21, pp. 64–145). London: Hogarth. (Original work published 1930)

Freud, S. (1961b). The future of an illusion. In J. Strachey (Ed. and Trans.), *The standard edition of the complete psychological works of Sigmund Freud* (Vol. 21, pp. 5–63). London: Hogarth. (Original work published 1927)

Freud, S. (1962). Further remarks on the neuro-psychoses of defence. In J. Strachey (Ed. and Trans.), *The standard edition of the complete psychological works of Sigmund Freud* (Vol. 3, pp. 159–221). London: Hogarth. (Original work published 1896)

Frey, R. J. (2003). Depersonalization disorder. *Gale Encyclopedia of Mental Disorders* [Electronic version]. Retrieved 10/3/08 from http://findarticles.com/p/articles

Friedman, M., & Rholes, W. S. (2007). Successfully challenging fundamentalist beliefs results in increased death awareness. *Journal of Experimental Social Psychology, 43,* 422–438.

Fromm, E. (1941). *Escape from freedom.* New York: Avon Books.

Fromm, E. (1956). *The art of loving.* New York: Harper.

Furer, P., & Walker, J. R. (2008). Death anxiety: A cognitive-behavioral approach. *Journal of Cognitive Psychotherapy, 16,* 167–182.

Gage, R. L. (Ed.). (1976). *Choose life: A dialogue: Arnold Toynbee and Daisaku Ikeda.* Oxford, UK: Oxford University Press.

Gedo, J. E. (2000). A time of discontent: Contemporary psychoanalysis in America. In S. de Schill, *Crucial choices—crucial changes: The resurrection of psychotherapy* (pp. 39–54). Amherst, NY: Prometheus Books.

Gilligan, J. (1996). *Violence: Our deadly epidemic and its causes.* New York: G. P. Putnam's Sons.

Goldenberg, J. L., Cox, C. R., Pyszczynski, T., Greenberg, J., & Solomon, S. (2002). Understanding human ambivalence about sex: The effects of stripping sex of meaning [Electronic version]. *Journal of Sex Research, 39,* 310–320.

Goldenberg, J. L., Pyszczynski, T., McCoy, S. K., Greenberg, J., & Solomon, S. (1999). Death, sex, love, and neuroticism: Why is sex such a problem? *Journal of Personality and Social Psychology, 77,* 1173–1187.

Gove, W. R., & Hughes, M. (1980). Reexamining the ecological fallacy: A study in which aggregate data are critical in investigating the pathological effects of living alone. *Social Forces, 58,* 1157–1177.

Greenberg, J., Pyszczynski, T., Solomon, S., Simon, L., & Breus, M. (1994). Role of consciousness and accessibility of death-related thoughts in mortality salience effects. *Journal of Personality and Social Psychology, 67,* 627–637.

Grollman, E. A. (1990). *Talking about death: A dialogue between parent and child* (3rd ed.). Boston: Beacon Press.

Guntrip, H. (1969). *Schizoid phenomena: Object relations and the self.* New York: International Universities Press.

Halling, S. (1998, November 19). *Meaning beyond "heroic" illusions? Transcendence in everyday life.* Paper presented at Seattle University under the sponsorship of the Ernest Becker Foundation and the Piggott-McCone Endowed Chair.

Haney, C., & Zimbardo, P. (1998). The past and future of U.S. prison policy: Twenty-five years after the Stanford Prison Experiment. *American Psychologist, 53,* 709–727.

Harper, R. A. (1981). Limitations of marriage and family therapy. *Rational Living, 16*(2), 3–6.

Hart, J., & Goldenberg, J. L. (2008). A terror management perspective on spirituality and the problem of the body. In A. Tomer, G. T. Eliason, & P. T. P. Wong (Eds.), *Existential and spiritual issues in death attitudes* (pp. 91–113). New York: Lawrence Erlbaum.

Hasin, D. S., Keyes, K. M., Hatzenbuehler, M. L., Aharonovich, E. A., & Alderson, D. (2007). Alcohol consumption and posttraumatic stress after exposure to terrorism: Effects of proximity, loss, and psychiatric history. *American Journal of Public Health, 97,* 2268–2275.

Hauser, M. D. (2006). *Moral minds: How nature designed our universal sense of right and wrong.* New York: HarperCollins.

Hazan, C., & Shaver, P. R. (1987). Romantic love conceptualized as an attachment process. *Journal of Personality and Social Psychology, 52,* 511–524.

Heckler, R. A. (1994). *Waking up, alive: The descent, the suicide attempt, and the return to life.* New York: Ballantine.

Hellinger, B. (with G. Weber & H. Beaumont). (1998). *Love's hidden symmetry: What makes love work in relationships.* Phoenix, AZ: Zeig, Tucker.

Henry, W. P., Strupp, H. H., Butler, S. F., Schacht, T. E., & Binder, J. L. (1993). Effects of training in time-limited dynamic psychotherapy: Changes in therapist behavior. *Journal of Consulting and Clinical Psychology, 61,* 434–440.

Hilgard, J. R., Newman, M. F., & Fisk, F. (1960). Strength of adult ego following childhood bereavement. *American Journal of Orthopsychiatry, 30,* 788–798.

Hoekelman, R. A. (1983). Introduction. In V. J. Sasserath (Ed.), *Minimizing high-risk parenting: A review of what is known and consideration of appropriate preventive information* (pp. xiii–xvi). Skillman, NJ: Johnson & Johnson Baby Products.

Hoffer, E. (2006). *The passionate state of mind and other aphorisms.* Titusville, NJ: Hopewell Publications. (Original work published 1955)

Hoffman, S. I., & Strauss, S. (1985). The development of children's concepts of death. *Death Studies, 9,* 469–482.

Hughes, T., & McCullough, F. (Eds.). (1982). *The journals of Sylvia Plath.* NewYork: Ballantine Books.

Irvine, L. (1999). *Codependent forevermore.* Chicago: University of Chicago Press.

Ivancovich, D. A., & Wong, P. T. P. (2008). The role of existential and spiritual coping in anticipatory grief. In A. Tomer, G. T. Eliason, & P. T. P. Wong (Eds.), *Existential and spiritual issues in death attitudes* (pp. 209–233). New York: Lawrence Erlbaum.

Jacobvitz, D., & Hazen, N. (1999). Developmental pathways from infant disorganization to childhood peer relationships. In J. Solomon & C. George (Eds.), *Attachment disorganization* (pp. 127–159). New York: Guilford Press.

Jacoby, R. (1983). *The repression of psychoanalysis: Otto Fenichel and the political Freudians.* Chicago: University of Chicago Press.

James, W. (2004). *The varieties of religious experience.* New York: Touchstone. (Original work published 1902)

Janov, A. (1970). *The primal scream: Primal therapy: The cure for neurosis.* New York: Putnam.

Jung, C. (1957). *The undiscovered self* (R. F. C. Hull, Trans.). New York: New American Library.

Kafka, F. (1977). *The trial* (W. & E. Muir, Trans.). Franklin Center, PA: Franklin Library. (Original work published 1937)

Kagan, J. (1984). *The nature of the child.* New York: Basic Books.

Kaplan, L. J. (1978). *Oneness and separateness: From infant to individual.* New York: Simon & Schuster.

Karon, B. P., & VandenBos, G. R. (1981). *Psychotherapy of schizophrenia: The treatment of choice.* Lanham, MD: Rowman & Littlefield.

Karpel, M. (1976). Individuation: From fusion to dialogue. *Family Process, 15,* 65–82.

Kastenbaum, R. (1974, Summer). Childhood: The kingdom where creatures die. *Journal of Clinical Child Psychology,* pp. 11–14.

Kastenbaum, R. (2000). *The psychology of death* (3rd ed.). New York: Springer.

Kastenbaum, R. (2004). *Death, society, and human experience* (8th ed.). Boston: Allyn and Bacon.

Kastenbaum, R., & Aisenberg, I. (1972). *The psychology of death.* New York: Springer.

Katz, D., & Katz, R. (1936). *Conversations with children* (H. S. Jackson, Trans.). London: Kegan Paul, Trench & Trubner.

Kecmanovic, D. (1996). *The mass psychology of ethnonationalism.* New York: Plenum Press.

Keen, S. (1997). *To love and be loved.* New York: Bantam Books.

Kellerman, B. (2004). *Bad leadership: What it is, how it happens, why it matters.* Boston: Harvard Business School Press.

Kempe, R. S., & Kempe, C. H. (1978). *Child abuse.* Cambridge, MA: Harvard University Press.

Keys, A., Brozek, J., Henschel, A., Mickelsen, O., & Taylor, H. L. (1950). *The biology of human starvation* (Vol. 2). Minneapolis: University of Minnesota Press.

Kierkegaard, S. (1954). *The sickness unto death* (W. Lowrie, Trans.). New York: Anchor. (Original work published 1849)

Kipnis, L. (2003). *Against love: A polemic.* New York: Pantheon Books.

Koocher, D. (1973). Childhood, death, and cognitive development. *Developmental Psychology, 9,* 369–375.

Kosloff, S., Solomon, S., Greenberg, J., Cohen, F., Gershuny, B., Routledge, C., et al. (2006). Fatal distraction: The impact of mortality salience on dissociative responses to 9/11 and subsequent anxiety sensitivity. *Basic and Applied Social Psychology, 28,* 349–356.

Kramer, R. (Ed.). (1996). *Otto Rank: A psychology of difference: The American lectures.* Princeton, NJ: Princeton University Press.

Kyle, R. (1993). *The religious fringe.* Downers Grove, IL: InterVarsity Press.

Laing, R. D. (1961). *Self and others.* Harmondsworth, UK: Penguin Books.

Laing, R. D. (1967). *The politics of experience.* New York: Ballantine Books.

Laing, R. D. (1969). *The divided self.* London: Penguin Books. (Original work published 1960)

Laing, R. D. (1972). *The politics of the family and other essays.* New York: Vintage Books. (Original work published 1969)

Laing, R. D. (1976). *The facts of life: An essay in feelings, facts, and fantasy.* New York: Pantheon.

Laing, R. D. (1985). Foreword. In R. W. Firestone, *The fantasy bond: Structure of psychological defense* (pp. 17–20). Santa Barbara, CA: Glendon Association.

Laing, R. D. (1989). *The challenge of love.* Unpublished manuscript.

Langle, A. (2007). The search for meaning in life and the existential fundamental motivations. In P. T. P. Wong, L. C. J. Wong, M. J. McDonald, & D. W. Klaassen (Eds.), *The positive psychology of meaning and spirituality* (pp. 45–56). Abbotsford, BC, Canada: INPM Press.

Langner, T. S. (2002). *Choices for living: Coping with fear of dying.* New York: Kluwer Academic.

Langs, R. (2004). *Fundamentals of adaptive psychotherapy and counseling.* New York: Palgrave Macmillan.

Langs, R. (2006). *Love and death in psychotherapy.* New York: Palgrave Macmillan.

Lasch, C. (1984). *The minimal self: Psychic survival in troubled times.* New York: W. W. Norton.

Lawrence, D. H. (1982). *Women in love.* London: Penguin. (Original work published 1920)

Lazarus, H., & Kostan, J. (1969). Psychogenic hyperventilation and death anxiety. *Psychosomatics, 10,* 14–22.

Lester, D. (1968). The fear of death of those who have nightmares. *Journal of Psychology, 69,* 245–247.

Lester, D., & Tartaro, C. (2002). Suicide on death row. *Journal of Forensic Sciences, 47,* 1108–1111.

Lewis, C. S. (1960). *The four loves.* New York: Harcourt Brace.

Lieberman, A. F., Compton, N. C., Van Horn, P., & Ippen, C. G. (2003). *Losing a parent to death in the early years: Guidelines for the treatment of traumatic bereavement in infancy and early childhood.* Washington, DC: Zero to Three Press.

Liechty, D. (2004). The idol and the idolizers: Ernest Becker's theory of expanded transference as a tool for historical criticism and interpretation with an addendum on transference and terrorism. In J. S. Piven (Ed.), *The psychology of death in fantasy and history* (pp. 163–175). Westport, CT: Praeger.

Lifton, R. J. (1979). *The broken connection: On death and the continuity of life.* New York: Simon & Schuster.

Lifton, R. J. (1991). *Death in life: Survivors of Hiroshima.* Chapel Hill, NC: University of North Carolina Press. (Original work published 1968)

Lifton, R. J. (2003). *Superpower syndrome: America's apocalyptic confrontation with the world.* New York: Thunder's Mouth Press.

Lifton, R. J., & Olson, E. (1976). The human meaning of total disaster: The Buffalo Creek Experience. *Psychiatry, 39,* 1–18.

Linehan, M. M. (1993). *Cognitive-behavioral treatment of borderline personality disorder.* New York: Guilford Press.

Lipman-Blumen, J. (2005). *The allure of toxic leaders: Why we follow destructive bosses and corrupt politicians—and how we can survive them.* New York: Oxford University Press.

Loy, D. (1992). Avoiding the void: The lack of self in psychotherapy and Buddhism. *Journal of Transpersonal Psychology, 24,* 151–179.

Luhrmann, T. M. (2000). *Of two minds: The growing disorder in American psychiatry.* New York: Alfred A. Knopf.

Luoma, J. B., & Pearson, J. L. (2002). Suicide and marital status in the United States, 1991–1996: Is widowhood a risk factor? *American Journal of Public Health, 92,* 1518–1522.

Macfarlane, A. (1977). *The psychology of childbirth.* Cambridge, MA: Harvard University Press.

Mack, K. Y. (2001). Childhood family disruptions and adult well-being: The differential effects of divorce and parental death. *Death Studies, 25,* 419–443.

Madanes, C. (1999, July/August). Rebels with a cause: Honoring the subversive power of psychotherapy. *Family Therapy Networker,* 44–49, 57.

Maddi, S. R. (1998). Creating meaning through making decisions. In P. T. P. Wong & P. S. Fry (Eds.), *The human quest for meaning: A handbook of psychological research and clinical applications* (pp. 3–26). Mahwah, NJ: Lawrence Erlbaum.

Mahler, M. S., Pine, F., & Bergman, A. (1975). *The psychological birth of the human infant: Symbiosis and individuation.* New York: Basic Books.

Main, M., & Solomon, J. (1986). Discovery of an insecure-disorganized/disoriented attachment pattern. In T. B. Brazelton & M. W. Yogman (Eds.), *Affective development in infancy* (pp. 95–124). Norwood, NJ: Ablex.

Mannarino, M. B., Eliason, G. T., & Rubin, J. (2008). Regret therapy: Coping with death and end of life issues. In A. Tomer, G. T. Eliason, & P. T. P. Wong (Eds.), *Existential and spiritual issues in death attitudes* (pp. 317–343). New York: Lawrence Erlbaum.

Maris, R. W. (1995). Suicide prevention in adults (age 30–65). In M. M. Silverman & R. W. Maris (Eds.), *Suicide prevention: Toward the year 2000* (pp. 171–179). New York: Guilford Press.

Maslow, A. H. (1954). *Motivation and personality.* New York: Harper & Brothers.

Maslow, A. H. (1968). *Toward a psychology of being* (2nd ed.). New York: Van Nostrand Reinhold.

Maslow, A. H. (1971). *The farther reaches of human nature.* Harmondsworth, UK: Penguin.

Maugham, W. S. (1963). *The razor's edge.* London: Penguin Books. (Original work published 1944)

May, R. (1958). Contributions of existential psychotherapy. In R. May, E. Angel, & H. F. Ellenberger (Eds.), *Existence: A new dimension in psychiatry and psychology* (pp. 37–91). New York: Basic Books.

May, R. (1981). *Freedom and destiny.* New York: Dell.

May, R. (1983). *The discovery of being: Writings in existential psychology.* New York: W. W. Norton.

McCarthy, J. B. (1980). *Death anxiety: The loss of the self.* New York: Gardner.

McClelland, D. C. (1975). *Power: The inner experience.* New York: John Wiley.

McCoy, S. K., Pyszczynski, T., Solomon, S., & Greenberg, J. (2000). Transcending the self: A terror management perspective. In A. Tomer (Ed.), *Death attitudes and the older adult: Theories, concepts, and applications* (pp. 37–63). Philadelphia, PA: Brunner-Routledge.

McDonald, J. E. (2007). A death is worth a thousand tellings: Transformation through storytelling. In P. T. P. Wong, L. C. J. Wong, M. J. McDonald, & D. W. Klaassen (Eds.), *The positive psychology of meaning & spirituality* (pp. 276–292). Abbotsford, BC, Canada: INPM Press.

McFarlane, A., & van der Kolk, B. A. (1996). Trauma and its challenge to society. In B. A. van der Kolk, A. C. McFarlane, & L. Weisaeth (Eds.), *Traumatic stress: The effects of overwhelming experience on mind, body, and society* (pp. 24–46). New York: Guilford Press.

McIntosh, J. L., & Hubbard, R. W. (1988). Indirect self-destructive behavior among the elderly: A review with case examples. *Journal of Gerontological Social Work, 13,* 37–48.

McNally, R. J. (1993). Self-representation in post-traumatic stress disorder: A cognitive perspective. In Z. V. Segal & S. J. Blatt (Eds.), *The self in emotional distress: Cognitive and psychodynamic perspectives* (pp. 71–99). New York: Guilford Press.

Mead, M. (1960). "One vote for this age of anxiety." In C. A. Glasrud (Ed.), *The age of anxiety* (pp. 174–177). Boston: Houghton Mifflin. (Original work published 1956)

Meerloo, J. A. M. (1968). Hidden suicide. In H. L. P. Resnick (Ed.), *Suicidal behaviors: Diagnosis and management* (pp. 82–89). Boston: Little, Brown.

Menninger, K. (1938). *Man against himself.* New York: Harcourt, Brace & World.

Metcalf, P., & Huntington, R. (1991). *Celebrations of death: The anthropology of mortuary ritual* (2nd ed.). Cambridge, UK: Cambridge University Press.

Meyer, J. E. (1975). *Death and neurosis* (M. Nunberg, Trans.). New York: International Universities Press.

Mikulincer, M., & Florian, V. (1998). The relationship between adult attachment styles and emotional and cognitive reactions to stressful events. In J. A. Simpson & W. S. Rholes (Eds.), *Attachment theory and close relationships* (pp. 143–165). New York: Guilford Press.

Mikulincer, M., & Florian, V. (2000). Exploring individual differences in reactions to mortality salience: Does attachment style regulate terror management mechanisms? *Journal of Personality and Social Psychology, 79,* 260–273.

Mikulincer, M., & Florian, V. (2008). The complex and multifaceted nature of the fear of personal death: The multidimensional model of Victor Florian. In A. Tomer, G. T. Eliason, & P. T. P. Wong (Eds.), *Existential and spiritual issues in death attitudes* (pp. 39–64). New York: Lawrence Erlbaum.

Mikulincer, M., Florian, V., & Hirschberger, G. (2004). The terror of death and the quest for love: An existential perspective on close relationships. In J. Greenberg, S. L. Koole, & T. Pyszczynski (Eds.), *Handbook of experimental existential psychology* (pp. 287–304). New York: Guilford Press.

Mikulincer, M., Florian, V., & Tolmacz, R. (1990). Attachment styles and fear of personal death: A case study of affect regulation. *Journal of Personality and Social Psychology, 58,* 273–280.

Mikulincer, M., & Orbach, I. (1995). Attachment styles and repressive defensiveness: The accessibility and architecture of affective memories. *Journal of Personality and Social Psychology, 68,* 917–925.

Milgram, S. (1974). *Obedience to authority: An experimental view.* New York: Harper & Row.

Miller, A. (1984). *For your own good: Hidden cruelty in child-rearing and the roots of violence* (H. Hannum & H. Hannum, Trans.) (2nd ed.). New York: Farrar, Straus, & Giroux. (Original work published 1980)

Miller, A. (2005). *The body never lies: The lingering effects of cruel parenting.* New York: W. W. Norton.

Miller, H. (1947). *Remember to remember.* New York: New Directions.

Miller, N. E., & Dollard, J. (1941). *Social learning and imitation.* New Haven, CT: Yale University Press.

Minois, G. (1999). *History of suicide: Voluntary death in Western culture* (L. G. Cochrane, Trans.). Baltimore, MD: Johns Hopkins University Press. (Original work published 1995)

Mitford, J. (1963). *The American way of death.* New York: Simon & Schuster.

Moncayo, R. (1998). Psychoanalysis and postmodern spirituality. *Journal for the Psychoanalysis of Culture and Society, 3,* 123–130.

Monsour, K. J. (1960). Asthma and the fear of death. *Psychoanalytic Quarterly, 29,* 56–71.

Moor, A. (2002). Awareness of death: A controllable process or a traumatic experience? *Folklore, 22,* 92–114.

Moore, C. C., & Williamson, J. B. (2003). The universal fear of death and the cultural response. In C. D. Bryant (Ed.), *Handbook of death and dying* (pp. 3–13). Thousand Oaks, CA: Sage Publications.

Morrant, C. (2003). Review of *Creating a Life of Meaning and Compassion.* Unpublished manuscript.

Morrant, C., & Catlett, J. (2008). Separation theory and voice therapy: Philosophical underpinnings and applications to death anxiety across the life span. In A. Tomer, G. T. Eliason, & P. T. P. Wong (Eds.), *Existential and spiritual issues in death attitudes* (pp. 345–373). New York: Lawrence Erlbaum.

Nagy, M. H. (1959). The child's view of death. In H. Feifel (Ed.), *The meaning of death* (pp. 79–98). New York: McGraw-Hill. (Original work published 1948)

Neimeyer, R. A. (2008). Introduction. In A. Tomer, G. T. Eliason, & P. T. P. Wong (Eds.), *Existential and spiritual issues in death attitudes* (pp. 1–3). New York: Lawrence Erlbaum.

Nelson, F. L., & Farberow, N. L. (1982). The development of an indirect self-destructive behaviour scale for use with chronically ill medical patients. *International Journal of Social Psychiatry, 28,* 5–14.

Nietzsche, F. (1956). The birth of tragedy. In *The birth of tragedy and the genealogy of morals* (F. Golffing, Trans.). New York: Doubleday. (Original work published 1871)

Nietzsche, F. (1966). *Beyond good and evil: Prelude to a philosophy of the future* (W. Kaufmann, Trans.). New York: Random House. (Original work published 1886)

Nietzsche, F. (2005). *Thus spake Zarathustra* (G. Parkes, Trans.). Oxford, UK: Oxford University Press. (Original work published 1885)

Noyes, R., Jr., Stuart, S., Longley, S. L., Langbehn, D. R., & Happel, R. L. (2002). Hypochondriasis and fear of death. *Journal of Nervous & Mental Disease, 190,* 503–509.

Oaklander, V. (1978). *Windows to our children: A gestalt therapy approach to children and adolescents.* Gouldsboro, ME: Gestalt Journal Press.

Oaklander, V. (2006). *Hidden treasure: A map to the child's inner self.* London: Karnac.

Oatley, K. (1996). Emotions: Communications to the self and others. In R. Harre & W. G. Parrott (Eds.), *The emotions: Social, cultural and biological dimensions* (pp. 312–316). London: Sage Publications.

Orbach, I. (1988). *Children who don't want to live: Understanding and treating the suicidal child.* San Francisco: Jossey-Bass.

Orbach, I. (2008). Existentialism and suicide. In A. Tomer, G. T. Eliason, & P. T. P. Wong (Eds.), *Existential and spiritual issues in death attitudes* (pp. 281–316). New York: Lawrence Erlbaum.

Pagels, E. (1988). *Adam, Eve, and the serpent.* New York: Random House.

Pagels, E. (2003). *Beyond belief: The secret gospel of Thomas.* New York: Vintage Books.

Parr, G. (Producer and director). (1985). *The inner voice in suicide* [Video]. Santa Barbara, CA: Glendon Association.

Parr, G. (Producer and director). (1987). *Hunger versus love* [Video]. Santa Barbara, CA: Glendon Association.

Parr, G. (Producer and director). (1991a). *Defenses against death anxiety* [Video]. Santa Barbara, CA: Glendon Association.

Parr, G. (Producer and director). (1991b). *Life, death, and denial* [Video]. Santa Barbara, CA: Glendon Association.

Parr, G. (Producer and director). (2002). *Friendship: A life of meaning and compassion* [Video]. Santa Barbara, CA: Glendon Association.

Parrott, W. G., & Harre, R. (1996). Overview. In R. Harre & W. G. Parrott (Eds.), *The emotions: Social, cultural and biological dimensions* (pp. 1–20). London: Sage Publications.

Pausch, R. (2008). *The last lecture.* New York: Hyperion.

Paykel, E. S. (1974). Recent life-events and clinical depression. In E. K. Gunderson & R. H. Rahe (Eds.), *Life stress and illness* (pp. 134–163). Springfield, IL: Charles C. Thomas.

Perry, B. D. (2006). Applying principles of neurodevelopment to clinical work with maltreated and traumatized children: The neurosequential model of therapeutics. In N. B. Webb (Ed.), *Working with traumatized youth in child welfare* (pp. 27–52). New York: Guilford Press.

Person, E. S. (1988). *Dreams of love and fateful encounters: The power of romantic passion.* New York: Penguin Books.

Peterson, C., & Seligman, M. E. P. (2004). *Character strengths and virtues: A handbook and classification.* Washington, DC: American Psychological Association and New York: Oxford University Press.

Petzinger, T., Jr. (2000, January 1). Talking about tomorrow: Edward O. Wilson. *Wall Street Journal,* pp. R16, R18.

Piaget, J. (1959). *The language and thought of the child* (3rd ed.) (M. Gabain, Trans.). London: Routledge & Kegan Paul.

Piven, J. S. (2002). Transference as religious solution to the terror of death. In D. Liechty (Ed.), *Death and denial: Interdisciplinary perspective on the legacy of Ernest Becker* (pp. 237–246). Westport, CT: Praeger.

Piven, J. S. (2004a). *Death and delusion: A Freudian analysis of mortal terror.* Greenwich, CT: Information Age Publishing.

Piven, J. S. (2004b). Death, neurosis, and normalcy: On the ubiquity of personal and social delusions. In J. S. Piven (Ed.), *The psychology of death in fantasy and history* (pp. 245–266). Westport, CT: Praeger.

Post, J. M. (2004). *Leaders and their followers in a dangerous world: The psychology of political behavior.* Ithaca, NY: Cornell University Press.

Post, S. G., Underwood, L. G., Schloss, J. P., & Hurlbut, W. B. (2002). General introduction. In S. G. Post, L. G. Underwood, J. P. Schloss, & W. B. Hurlbut (Eds.), *Altruism and altruistic love: Science, philosophy, and religion in dialogue* (pp. 3–12). New York: Oxford University Press.

Prescott, J. W. (1975). Body pleasure and the origins of violence. *Bulletin of The Atomic Scientists, 10–20.* Retrieved February 27, 2004, from http://www.violence.de/prescott/bulletin/article.html

Pyszczynski, T., Greenberg, J., & Solomon, S. (1999). A dual-process model of defense against conscious and unconscious death-related thoughts: An extension of terror management theory. *Psychological Review, 106,* 835–845.

Pyszczynski, T., Solomon, S., & Greenberg, J. (2003). *In the wake of 9/11: The psychology of terror.* Washington, DC: American Psychological Association.

Rado, S. (1942). Pathodynamics and treatment of traumatic war neurosis (traumatophobia). *Psychosomatic Medicine, 4,* 362–368.

Radzinsky, E. (1996). *Stalin* (H. T. Willetts, Trans.). New York: Random House.

Randall, E. (2001). Existential therapy of panic disorder: A single system study. *Clinical Social Work Journal, 29,* 259–267.

Rank, O. (1941). *Beyond psychology.* New York: Dover.

Rank, O. (1968). *Modern education: A critique of its fundamental ideas.* New York: Agathon Press.

Rank, O. (1972). *Will therapy and truth and reality* (J. Taft, Trans.). New York: Alfred A. Knopf. (Original work published 1936)

Raveis, V. H., Siegel, K., & Karus, D. (1999). Children's psychological distress following the death of a parent. *Journal of Youth and Adolescence, 28,* 165–180.

Reik, T. (1941). *Of love and lust: On the psychoanalysis of romantic and sexual emotions.* New York: Farrar-Straus-Giroux.

ReligiousTolerance.org. (2008). New Age spirituality. Retrieved 5/3/08 from http://www.religioustolerance.org/newage.htm

Rheingold, J. C. (1964). *The fear of being a woman: A theory of maternal destructiveness.* New York: Grune & Stratton.

Rheingold, J. C. (1967). *The mother, anxiety, and death: The catastrophic death complex.* Boston: Little, Brown.

Richman, J. (1993). *Preventing elderly suicide: Overcoming personal despair, professional neglect, and social bias.* New York: Springer.

Ridley, M. (1996). *The origins of virtue: Human instincts and the evolution of cooperation.* New York: Penguin.

Robbins, P. R. (1998). *Adolescent suicide.* Jefferson, NC: McFarland.

Rochlin, G. (1967). How younger children view death and themselves. In E. A. Grollman (Ed.), *Explaining death to children* (pp. 51–85). Boston: Beacon Press.

Rodin, G., & Zimmerman, C. (2008). Psychoanalytic reflections on mortality: A reconsideration. *Journal of the American Academy of Psychoanalysis and Dynamic Psychiatry, 36,* 181–196.

Rogers, C. R. (1961). *On becoming a person: A therapist's view of psychotherapy.* Boston: Houghton Mifflin.

Roizen, J. (1997). Epidemiological issues in alcohol-related violence. In M. Galanter (Eds.), *Recent developments in alcoholism, Vol. 13* (pp. 7–40). New York: Plenum Press.

Rorty, A. O. (1993). What it takes to be good. In G. G. Noam & T. E. Wren (Eds.), *The moral self* (pp. 28–55). Cambridge, MA: MIT Press.

Sabbath, J. C. (1969). The suicidal adolescent: The expendable child. *Journal of the American Academy of Child Psychiatry, 8,* 272–289.

Sager, C. J., Kaplan, H. S., Gundlach, R. H., Kremer, M., Lenz, R., & Royce, J. R. (1971). The marriage contract. *Family Process, 8,* 311–326.

Saler, L., & Skolnick, N. (1992). Childhood parental death and depression in adulthood: Roles of surviving parent and family environment. *American Journal of Orthopsychiatry, 62,* 504–516.

Sandbek, T. J. (1993). *The deadly diet: Recovering from anorexia & bulimia* (2nd ed.). Oakland, CA: New Harbinger.

Schiff, M., Zweig, H. H., Benbenishty, R., & Hasin, D. S. (2007). Exposure to terrorism and Israeli youths' cigarette, alcohol, and cannabis use. *American Journal of Public Health, 97,*1852–1858.

Schnarch, D. M. (1991). *Constructing the sexual crucible: An integration of sexual and marital therapy.* New York: Norton.

Schneider, K. J. (2004). *Rediscovery of awe: Splendor, mystery, and the fluid center of life.* St. Paul, MN: Paragon House.

Schneider, K. J. (2007). The fluid centre: An awe-based challenge to culture. In P. T. P. Wong, L. C. J. Wong, M. J. McDonald, & D. W. Klaassen (Eds.), *The positive psychology of meaning & spirituality* (pp. 372–378). Abbotsford, BC, Canada: INPM Press.

Schore, A. N. (1994). *Affect regulation and the origin of the self: The neurobiology of emotional development.* Hillsdale, NJ: Lawrence Erlbaum.

Schore, A. N. (2003). *Affect regulation and the repair of the self.* New York: W. W. Norton.

Searles, H. F. (1961). Schizophrenia and the inevitability of death. *Psychiatric Quarterly, 35,* 631–665.

Searles, H. F. (1979). *Countertransference and related subjects: Selected papers.* Madison, CT: International Universities Press.

Seiden, R. H. (1984). Death in the West: A regional analysis of the youthful suicide rate. *Western Journal of Medicine, 25,* 1–8.

Seligman, M. E. P. (1995). The effectiveness of psychotherapy: The *Consumer Reports* study. *American Psychologist, 50,* 965–974.

Shaw, J. A. (2005, Fall). The cloak of invisibility over the New Orleans experience: Contributions to denial. *Out of Our Minds,* Issue No. 6, p. 5. Florida Psychoanalytic Institute.

Shneidman, E. S. (1966). Orientations toward death: A vital aspect of the study of lives. *International Journal of Psychiatry, 2,* 167–200.

Shneidman, E. S. (1996). *The suicidal mind.* New York: Oxford University Press.

Shneidman, E. S. (1999). Suicide. In A. A. Leenaars (Ed.), *Lives and deaths: Selections from the works of Edwin S. Shneidman* (pp. 176–197). (Original work published 1973)

Siegel, D. J. (1999). *The developing mind: Toward a neurobiology of interpersonal experience.* New York: Guilford Press.

Siegel, D. J. (2001). Toward an interpersonal neurobiology of the development mind: Attachment relationships, "mindsight," and neural integration. *Infant Mental Health Journal, 22,* 67–94.

Siegel, D. J. (2003). Foreword. In Firestone, et al., 2003, *Creating a life of meaning and compassion: The wisdom of psychotherapy* (pp. ix–x). Washington, DC: American Psychological Association.

Siegel, D. J. (2006). An interpersonal neurobiology approach to psychotherapy: Awareness, mirror neurons, and neural plasticity in the development of well-being. *Psychiatric Annals, 36,* 248–256.

Silverman, L. H., Lachmann, F. M., & Milich, R. H. (1982). *The search for oneness.* New York: International Universities Press.

Simon, L., Greenberg, J., Arndt, J., Pyszczynski, T., Clement, R., & Solomon, S. (1997). Perceived consensus, uniqueness, and terror management: Compensatory responses to threats to inclusion and distinctiveness following mortality salience. *Personality and Social Psychology Bulletin, 23,* 1055–1065.

Simon, N. M., Zalta, A. K., Otto, M. W., Ostacher, M. J., Fischmann, D., Chow, C. W., et al. (2007). The association of comorbid anxiety disorders with suicide attempts and suicidal ideation in outpatients with bipolar disorder. *Journal of Psychiatric Research, 41*, 255–264.

Singer, I. (2001). *Sex: A philosophical primer.* Lanham, MD: Rowman & Littlefield.

Singer, P. (1993). *Practical ethics* (2nd ed.). New York: Cambridge University Press.

Singer, P. (2004). *One world: The ethics of globalization* (2nd ed.). New Haven, CT: Yale University Press.

Siqueland, L., Crits-Christoph, P., Barber, J. P., Butler, S. F., Thase, M., Najavits, L., et al. (2000). The role of therapist characteristics in training: Effects in cognitive, supportive-expressive, and drug counseling therapies for cocaine dependence. *Journal of Psychotherapy Practice and Research, 9*, 123–130.

Solomon, S., Greenberg, J., & Pyszczynski, T. (2004). The cultural animal: Twenty years of terror management theory and research. In J. Greenberg, S. L. Koole, & T. Pyszczynski (Eds.), *Handbook of experimental existential psychology* (pp. 13–34). New York: Guilford Press.

Speece, M. W., & Brent, S. B. (1984). Children's understanding of death: A review of three components of a death concept. *Child Development, 55*, 1671–1686.

Stern, D. N. (1985). *The interpersonal world of the infant: A view from psychoanalysis and developmental psychology.* New York: Basic Books.

Stern, M. M. (1968). Fear of death and neurosis. *Journal of the American Psychoanalytic Association, 16*, 3–31.

Stolorow, R. D. (1992). Closing the gap between theory and practice with better psycho-analytic theory. *Psychotherapy, 29*, 159–166.

Stolorow, R. D. (2007). *Trauma and human existence.* New York: Analytic Press.

Strachan, E., Schimel, J., Arndt, J., Williams, T., Solomon, S., Pyszczynski, T., et al. (2007). Terror mismanagement: Evidence that morality salience exacerbates phobic and com-pulsive behaviors. *Personality and Social Psychology Bulletin, 33*, 1137–1151.

Strupp, H. H. (1989). Psychotherapy: Can the practitioner learn from the researcher? *American Psychologist, 44*, 717–724.

Styron, W. (1976). *Sophie's choice.* New York: Random House.

Suler, J. (2004). The online disinhibition effect. *CyberPsychology and Behavior, 7*, 321–326.

Suzuki, D. T., Fromm, E., & DeMartino, R. (1960). *Zen Buddhism & psychoanalysis.* New York: Harper & Brothers.

Tangney, J. P., & Mashek, D. J. (2004). In search of the moral person: Do you have to feel really bad to be good? In J. Greenberg, S. L. Koole, & T.Pyszczynski (Eds.), *Hand-book of experimental existential psychology* (pp. 156–166). New York: Guilford.

Tedeschi, J. T., & Felson, R. B. (1994). *Violence, aggression, and coercive actions.* Washington, DC: American Psychological Association.

Thompson, M. P., Kaslow, N. J., Price, A. W., Williams, K., & Kingree, J. B. (1998). Role of secondary stressors in the parental death-child distress relation. *Journal of Abnor-mal Child Psychology, 26*, 357–366.

Thorson, J. A., & Laughlin, A. M. (2008). The dark night of the soul. In A. Tomer, G. T. Eliason, & P. T. P. Wong (Eds.), *Existential and spiritual issues in death attitudes* (pp. 257–278). New York: Lawrence Erlbaum.

Tillich, P. (1952). *The courage to be.* New Haven, CT: Yale University Press.

Tolstoy, L. (2004). *The death of Ivan Ilyich and other stories*. Hertfordshire, UK: Words worth Editions Ltd. (Original work published 1886)

Tomer, A., & Eliason, G. (1996). Toward a comprehensive model of death anxiety. *Death Studies, 20*, 343–365.

Tomer, A., & Eliason, G. T. (2008). Existentialism and death attitudes. In A. Tomer, G. T. Eliason, & P. T. P. Wong (Eds.), *Existential and spiritual issues in death attitudes* (pp. 7–37). New York: Lawrence Erlbaum.

Trueman, D. (1984). Depersonalization in a nonclinical population. *Journal of Psychology, 116*, 107–112.

U.S. Department of Justice, Employee Assistance Program (EAP). (2007). *Youth depression and suicide*. Retrieved 10/19/08 from http://usdoj.gov/jmd/ps/youth-dep-suicide.htm

Utech, M. R. (1994). *Violence, abuse and neglect: The American home*. Lanham, MD: AltaMira Press.

Valliant, L. M. (1997). *Changing character: Short-term anxiety-regulating psychotherapy for restructuring defenses, affects, and attachment*. New York: Basic Books.

Vergote, A. (1988). *Guilt and desire: Religious attitudes and their pathological derivatives* (M. H. Wood, Trans.). New Haven: Yale University Press. (Original work published 1978)

Violence Prevention Coalition of Greater Los Angeles. (1991). Alcohol and violence: How alcohol abuse is linked to violence. *Injury Prevention Network Newsletter, 8*(2), 1–2.

Vlahov, D., Galea, S., Ahern, J., Resnick, H., & Kilpatrick, D. (2004). Sustained increased consumption of cigarettes, alcohol, and marijuana among Manhattan residents after September 11, 2001. *American Journal of Public Health, 94*, 253–254.

Volavka, J. (2002). *Neurobiology of violence* (2nd ed.). Washington, DC: American Psychiatric Publishing.

Waller, J. (2002). *Becoming evil: How ordinary people commit genocide and mass killing*. New York: Oxford University Press.

Wampold, B. E. (2001). *The great psychotherapy debate: Models, methods, and findings*. Mahwah, NJ: Lawrence Erlbaum.

Wass, H., Dinklage, R., Gordon, S., Russo, G., Sparks, C., & Tatum, J. (1983). Young children's death concepts revisited. *Death Education, 7*, 385–394.

Watts, A. (1961). *Psychotherapy East and West*. New York: Vintage.

Wexler, J., & Steidl, J. (1978). Marriage and the capacity to be alone. *Psychiatry, 41*, 72–82.

Whang, L. S., Lee, S., & Chang, G. (2003). Internet over-users' psychological profiles: A behavior sampling analysis on internet addition. *CyberPsychology and Behavior, 6*, 143–150.

Willi, J. (1982). *Couples in collusion: The unconscious dimension in partner relationships* (W. Inayat-Khan & M. Tchorek, Trans.). Claremont, CA: Hunter House. (Original work published 1975)

Willi, J. (1999). *Ecological psychotherapy: Developing by shaping the personal niche*. Seattle, WA: Hogrefe & Huber.

Williams, T. (1954). *Cat on a hot tin roof*. New York: Penguin.

Wilson, E. O. (1998, April). The biological basis of morality [Electronic version]. *Atlantic Monthly, 281*(4), p. 53.

Wilson-Starks, K. Y. (2003). *Toxic leadership*. Retrieved 10/27/07 from www.transleadership.com

Winnicott, D. W. (1958). *Collected papers: Through pediatrics to psycho-analysis*. London: Tavistock Publications.

Winnicott, D. W. (1965). Ego distortion in terms of true and false self. In D. W. Winnicott, *The maturational processes and the facilitating environment: Studies in the theory of emotional development* (pp. 140–152). Madison, CT: International Universities Press. (Original work published 1960)

Wolfe, B. (2008). *Existential issues in anxiety disorders and their treatment.* Retrieved 9/21/08 from http://www.barrywolfe.com/articles/anxiety_disorders.php

Wolfe, T. (1934). *You can't go home again.* New York: Harper & Row.

Wong, P. T. P. (1998). Meaning-centered counseling. In P. T. P. Wong & P. S. Fry (Eds.), *The human quest for meaning: A handbook of psychological research and clinical applications* (pp. 395–435). Mahwah, NJ: Lawrence Erlbaum.

Wong, P. T. P. (2007). The positive psychology of suffering and tragic optimism. In P. T. P. Wong, L. C. J. Wong, M. J. McDonald, & D. W. Klaassen (Eds.), *The positive psychology of meaning and spirituality* (pp. 238–259). Abbotsford, BC, Canada: INPM Press.

Wong, P. T. P. (2008). Meaning management theory and death acceptance. In A. Tomer, G. T. Eliason, & P. T. P. Wong (Eds.), *Existential and spiritual issues in death attitudes* (pp. 65–87). New York: Lawrence Erlbaum.

Woolf, H. B. (Ed.). (1981). *Webster's New Collegiate Dictionary.* Springfield, MA: G. & C. Merriam.

Wright, K. (2003). Relationships with death: The terminally ill talk about dying. *Journal of Marital and Family Therapy, 29,* 439–454.

Yaacovi, E. (2003). *A terror management perspective of parenting strivings and representations.* Unpublished doctoral dissertation, Bar-Ilan University, Ramat Gan, Israel.

Yalom, I. D. (1980). *Existential psychotherapy.* New York: Basic Books.

Yalom, I. D. (2008). *Staring at the sun: Overcoming the terror of death.* San Francisco: Jossey-Bass.

Zilboorg, G. (1943). Fear of death. *Psychoanalytic Quarterly, 12,* 465–475.

Zimbardo, P. G., & White, G. (1972). *Stanford Prison Experiment slide-tape show.* Stanford, CA: Stanford University.

Index

Life
  good, 310
  lack of direction in, 69–70
  meaningful, 318–319
  meaninglessness in, 267–268
  unlived, 185, 266
Life-affirming death awareness, 6
"Life Fear and Death Fear" (Rank), 26
Life story. *See* Narratives
Lifestyles
  inward, 123–126
  isolation, 64–66
  microsuicidal, 117
  open versus defended, 8–10
  outward versus inward, 60
Lifton, Robert, 89, 90, 91, 156, 234
  view on survivor guilt, 266
  view on tolerance and inclusiveness,
    322
Lipman-Blumen, J., 79, 97, 98
Listening to partner, 174, 207
Literal immortality, 84
  afterlife, 85–86
  Eastern belief systems, 86–87
  enlightenment, 87
  magical thinking, power of, 85
  nondenominational spirituality, 86
  reincarnation, 85
  religious dogma and rituals, 84–85
  sexuality, 88–89
  Western religious belief systems,
    85–86
*Losing a Parent to Death in the Early
  Years* (Lieberman et al.), 46
Love, 285, 312–313
  as affirmative affection, 289
  children, 286
  competition and jealousy, coping with,
    301–302
  death anxiety, comparison, 285
  and death anxiety, comparison of,
    285–287
  definitions of, 288–291
  distinguishing from, emotional hunger,
    216–217
  expanding one's capacity to, 292–293
  fantasy of, 157
  human right violations, identifying,
    297–301
  importance of, 286
  neurotic, 292

qualities to develop in oneself, 293–297;
  see also Qualities of love
sexual freedom, 288
sexual intimacy, 292–293
story about, 286–287
what love is not, 291–292
Love and Death in Psychotherapy
  (Langs), 241
Loy, David, 27
Luoma, J. B., 264

M
Macfarlane, A., 213
Madanes, Cloe, 250
Magical thinking, 94–96, 163–164.
  See also Fantasy bond
Mahler, Margaret, 32
Main, Mary, 331
Maladaptive behaviors, 126–128, 272
Man against Himself (Menninger), 108
Mannarino, M. B., 270
The Many Faces of Suicide (Farberow),
  108
Maris, R. W., 129
Marriages, 144
  open versus closed, 304–305
  partner's expectations, 149–150
  security, 153
Marx, Karl, 102
Maslow, Abraham, 220, 231
  view on meaningful goals in life,
    323–324
  view on self-actualization and
    individuation, 78
Masturbation, 64
Maternal love, 213
Maternal rejection, 41
Maugham, W. Somerset, 95
May, Rollo, 221, 231, 243, 329–330
McCarthy, James B., 256
McClelland, D. C., 222
McIntosh, J. L., 129
Meaning
  and meaninglessness, 308
  search for, 317–318
Meaningful goals in life, achieving, 323
  composing a life story or narrative,
    331–332
  importance of sexuality, 328–329
  setting goals and moving toward
    achievement, 324–325